THINKING ABOUT GLOBAL GOVERNANCE

One of the more prolific and influential analysts of multilateral approaches to global problem-solving over the last three decades is Thomas G. Weiss. *Thinking about Global Governance: Why People and Ideas Matter* assembles key scholarly and policy writing.

This collection organizes his most recent work addressing the core issues of the United Nations, global governance, and humanitarian action. The essays are placed in historical and intellectual context in a substantial new introduction, which contains a healthy dose of the idealism and ethical orientation that invariably characterize his best work.

This volume gives the reader a comprehensive understanding of these key topics for a globalizing world and is an invaluable resource for students and scholars alike.

Thomas G. Weiss is Presidential Professor of Political Science at The City University of New York's Graduate Center and Director of the Ralph Bunche Institute for International Studies. He was President of the International Studies Association (2009–10) and Chair of the Academic Council on the UN System (2006–9). He was editor of *Global Governance*, Research Director of the International Commission on Intervention and State Sovereignty, Research Professor at Brown University's Watson Institute for International Studies, Executive Director of the Academic Council on the UN System and of the International Peace Academy, a member of the UN secretariat, and a consultant to several public and private agencies. He has authored or edited some 40 books and 160 articles and book chapters about multilateral approaches to international peace and security, humanitarian action, and sustainable development. His latest authored and co-authored volumes are *What's Wrong with the United Nations and How to Fix It* (Polity, 2009); *UN Ideas That Changed the World* (Indiana University Press, 2009); *Global Governance and the UN: An Unfinished Journey* (Indiana University Press, 2010); and *Humanitarianism Contested: Where Angels Fear to Tread* (Routledge, 2011).

THINKING ABOUT GLOBAL GOVERNANCE

Why people and ideas matter

Thomas G. Weiss

Routledge
Taylor & Francis Group

LONDON AND NEW YORK

First published 2011 by Routledge
2 Park Square, Milton Park, Abingdon, Oxon OX14 4RN

Simultaneously published in the USA and Canada
by Routledge
711 Third Avenue, New York, NY 10017

Routledge is an imprint of the Taylor & Francis Group, an informa business

British Library Cataloguing in Publication Data
A catalogue record for this book is available from the British Library

Library of Congress Cataloging in Publication Data
Weiss, Thomas George.
    Thinking about global governance: why people and ideas matter/
Thomas G. Weiss.
    p. cm.
    Includes bibliographical references and index.
    1. United Nations—Reform. 2. United Nations. Security Council.
    3. International organization. 4. Humanitarian intervention. I. Title.
    JZ4984.5.W455 2011
    341.23—dc22
    2011004291

ISBN: 978–0–415–78192–3 (hbk)
ISBN: 978–0–415–78193–0 (pbk)
ISBN: 978–0–203–80705–7 (ebk)

Typeset in Bembo and Stone Sans
by Florence Production Ltd, Stoodleigh, Devon, UK

Printed and bound in Great Britain by the MPG Books Group

CONTENTS

ABBREVIATIONS

ACUNS	Academic Council on the United Nations System
CHR	Commission on Human Rights
CONGO	Conference of Non-Governmental Organizations in Consultative Status with ECOSOC
DHA	Department of Humanitarian Affairs
DPA	Department of Political Affairs
DPKO	Department of Peacekeeping Operations
DRC	Democratic Republic of the Congo
ECOSOC	Economic and Social Council
ECOWAS	Economic Community of West African States
EU	European Union
FAO	Food and Agriculture Organization
G-7/G-8	Group of Seven/Group of Eight
G-20	Group of 20
G-77	Group of 77
HLP	High-level Panel on Threats, Challenges and Change
IASC	Inter-Agency Standing Committee
ICISS	International Commission on Intervention and State Sovereignty
ICRC	International Committee of the Red Cross
IDP	internally displaced person
ILO	International Labour Organization
IMF	International Monetary Fund
ISA	International Studies Association
ITU	International Telecommunications Union
MDG	Millennium Development Goal
MSC	Military Staff Committee
NAM	Non-Aligned Movement

NATO	North Atlantic Treaty Organization
NGO	nongovernmental organization
NIEO	New International Economic Order
OAU	Organization of African Unity
OCHA	Office for the Coordination of Humanitarian Affairs
ODA	official development assistance
OECD	Organisation for Economic Co-operation and Development
OHCHR	Office of the High Commissioner for Human Rights
OPEC	Organization of the Petroleum Exporting Countries
OSCE	Organization on Security and Co-operation in Europe
P-5	permanent five members of the Security Council
UK	United Kingdom of Great Britain and Northern Ireland
UNCTAD	United Nations Conference on Trade and Development
UNDP	United Nations Development Programme
UNEP	United Nations Environment Programme
UNESCO	United Nations Educational, Scientific and Cultural Organization
UNHCR	United Nations High Commissioner for Refugees
UNICEF	United Nations Children's Fund
UNIFEM	United Nations Development Fund for Women
UNU	United Nations University
US	United States of America
WFP	World Food Programme
WHO	World Health Organization
WMD	weapon of mass destruction
WTO	World Trade Organization

ACKNOWLEDGMENTS

The author and publishers would like to thank the following for granting permission to reproduce material in this work:

1 Reinvigorating the international civil service
Thomas G. Weiss, 2010
From Global Governance: A Review of Multilateralism and International Organizations 16, no. 1 (2010): 39–57. Copyright © 2010 by Lynne Rienner Publishers, Inc., reproduced with permission by the publisher.

2 How UN ideas change the world
Thomas G. Weiss, 2010
Review of International Studies 36, no. 1, Special Issue (2010): 3–23; also in Nicholas Rengger, ed., *Ethical Evaluations and Global Orders* (Cambridge: Cambridge University Press, 2010). Reproduced with permission by the puslisher.

3 What happened to the idea of world government?
Thomas G. Weiss, 2009
International Studies Quarterly 53, no. 2 (2009): 253–71. ©Wiley Blackwell, reproduced with permission by the publisher.

4 Moving beyond North-South theater
Thomas G. Weiss, 2009
Third World Quarterly 30, no. 2 (2009): 271–84. © Taylor & Francis Ltd, www. informaworld.com, reproduced with permission by the publisher.

5 World politics: continuity and change since 1945
Thomas G. Weiss and Sam Daws, 2007
In *The Oxford Handbook on the United Nations*, ed. Thomas G. Weiss and Sam Daws (Oxford: Oxford University Press, 2007), 3–18 only (19–38 unnecessary). Author's own material, reproduced with permission by the publisher.

6   An unchanged Security Council: the sky ain't falling
    Thomas G. Weiss, 2005
    The final, definitive version of this paper has been published in *Security Dialogue* 36, no. 3 (2005): 367–9. By SAGE Publications Ltd. SAGE Publications, Inc., All rights reserved. ©

7   The "third" United Nations
    Thomas G. Weiss, Tatiana Carayannis and Richard Jolly, 2009
    Global Governance: A Review of Multilateralism and International Organizations 15, no. 1 (2009): 123–42. Copyright © 2009 by Lynne Rienner Publishers, Inc. Reproduced with permission by the publisher.

8   Framing global governance, five gaps
    Ramesh Thakur and Thomas G. Weiss, 2009
    In Giuliana Ziccardi Capaldo, ed., *The Global Community: Yearbook of International Law and Jurisprudence 2008*, vol. I (Oxford: Oxford University Press, 2009), 77–98. Author's own material, reproduced with permission by the publisher.

9   Governance, good governance, and global governance: conceptual and actual challenges
    Thomas G. Weiss, 2000
    Third World Quarterly 21, no. 5 (2000): 795–814. © Taylor & Francis Ltd, www.informaworld.com, reproduced with permission by the publisher.

10 Pluralising global governance: analytical approaches and dimensions
    Leon Gordenker and Thomas G. Weiss, 1995
    Third World Quarterly 16, no. 3 (1995): 357–87. © Taylor & Francis Ltd, www.informaworld.com, reproduced with permission by the publisher.

11 Political innovations and the responsibility to protect
    Thomas G Weiss, 2010
    Copyright 2010 by Georgetown University Press. Thomas G. Weiss, "Reinserting 'Never' into 'Never Again': Political Innovations and the Responsibility to Protect," in *Driven from Home: Protecting the Rights of Forced Migrants*, ed. David Hollenbach (Washington, DC: Georgetown University Press, 2010), 207–27. Reproduced with permission by the publisher.

12 The fog of humanitarianism: collective action problems and learning-challenged organizations
    Thomas G. Weiss and Peter J. Hoffman, 2007
    Journal of Intervention and State-Building 1, no. 1 (2007): 47–65. © Taylor & Francis Ltd, reproduced with permission by the publisher.

13 The humanitarian impulse
    Thomas G. Weiss, 2004
    In *The UN Security Council: From the Cold War to the 21st Century*, ed. David M. Malone (New York: International Peace Academy, 2004), 37–54. Copyright

© 2004 by the International Peace Academy, Inc. Reproduced with permission by the publisher.

14 The sunset of humanitarian intervention? The responsibility to protect in a unipolar era
Thomas G. Weiss, 2004
The final, definitive version of this paper has been published in *Security Dialogue* 35, no. 2 (2004): 135–53. By SAGE Publications Ltd. SAGE Publications, Inc., All rights reserved. ©

15 The politics of humanitarian ideas
Thomas G. Weiss, 2000
The final, definitive version of this paper has been published in *Security Dialogue* 31, no. 1 (2000): 11–23. By SAGE Publications Ltd. SAGE Publications, Inc., All rights reserved. ©

16 Principles, politics, and humanitarian action
Thomas G. Weiss, 1999
Ethics & International Affairs XIII (1999): 1–22. ©Wiley Blackwell, reproduced with permission by the publisher.

17 A research note about military-civilian humanitarianism: more questions than answers
Thomas G. Weiss, 1997
Disasters 21, no. 2 (1997): 95–117. ©Wiley Blackwell, reproduced with permission by the publisher.

FOREWORD

When the United Nations was created 65 years ago, it was against the backdrop of unimaginable human suffering and a catastrophic breakdown of basic values. Ever since then, the UN has stood for the protection of individuals and the promotion of a value-based framework for dealing with the major challenges of our times. As simple and powerful as this mission may seem, its implications are not yet accepted by everyone alike. Aside from political opposition to multilateralism, a fear of the abstract and a lack of understanding continue to feed skepticism of the UN around the world. For many years, Thomas G. Weiss has dedicated himself to overcoming this fear and building such understanding. As he rightly points out, this is a Sisyphean task, but one which he has taken on with admirable diligence and dedication.

However similar Thomas G. Weiss may have felt to King Sisyphus, this remarkable collection of essays clearly reflects a very different fortune. While it too is the product of continuous efforts, the work put into it has been far from futile. On the contrary, the papers included in this book have not only shaped the academic and policy debate on many critical issues, they have also addressed particularly difficult questions such as the desirability of a world government, the permanence of the North-South divide, or the legitimacy of using military means to achieve humanitarian ends. Assembled in their present form, they take the reader on a highly insightful intellectual journey through the evolution of the United Nations, the growing prominence of non-state actors, and the ascent of humanitarian action.

Thomas G. Weiss has seen the UN from within. There he was confronted with many, if not most, of its strengths and weaknesses. As an academic he has dug deeper and thought further about them, and this collection reflects the full depth and breadth of this exercise. It stands as an impressive testimony to the idealism and scholarship of its author and is an indispensable guide for anyone thinking about global governance.

Kofi A. Annan

PREFACE

My aversion to "collected works" goes back to my first trip to the former Soviet Union in the late 1960s, when I found pamphlets of Lenin's speeches in taxis and volumes of works by him and other acceptable Communist Party writers in hotels. Were such collections really of any use unless one was totally bereft of reading matter? I remembered a friend who once recounted that everyone in his über-literate family was obliged to read whatever was available, including the back of cereal boxes at breakfast.

Despite my discomfort about collected works—and the unease with the fact that I was long enough in the tooth to be writing a first draft of an intellectual auto-biography—Craig Fowlie was persuasive when he proposed this book. In February 2010 as I was stepping down as president at the annual meeting of the International Studies Association in New Orleans, he caught me in a vulnerable moment and approached me about compiling a retrospective of my writings over the last 35 years. He explained that useful teaching and research functions could be served by pulling together such essays; and moreover, a key challenge would be to re-examine and provide a structure for the various international relations puzzles that I have been struggling to assemble over that period of time. Craig was uncommonly kind in his evaluation—and flattery works. I am grateful to him and Routledge for the opportunity to put this volume together, and also to Nicola Parkin who oversaw its production. Most importantly, I wish to compliment the sharp eye and mind of Martin J. Burke and Danielle Zach, advanced graduate students at The CUNY Graduate Center who shepherded the quality-control process for this book; I am profoundly grateful.

Deciding what to include and exclude was anything except obvious. "Dilettante" would perhaps be a way to describe an intellectual itinerary that has included long-standing interests in international peace and security, political economy, behavior and misbehavior by international organizations, humanitarian action, and most recently intellectual history. "Eclectic" would be a kinder description.

That said, what unites my work over the years might appear to some as a curious conviction—namely, community interests are almost invariably shortchanged. Within the United States, the country's interests are customarily sacrificed on the altar of individualism. Internationally, and now globally, the welfare of the commons is typically and tragically trampled by great powers as well as by tin-pot dictators and megalomaniacs. I have steadfastly argued that multilateral cooperation is a way to attenuate not only American exceptionalism and big-power arrogance but also common thugs.

My analyses of contemporary world politics might very well "depress Dr. Pangloss," the character in Voltaire's *Candide* who proclaimed that all is for the best in this best of all possible worlds. In fact, the gaps are enormous between what is on the books—spelled out in the UN Charter, international treaties, as well as public statements by politicians and diplomats—and what transpires. Ours cannot possibly be the best of all possible worlds. I remain persuaded that good people and good ideas can make a difference to the quality of human life and international society. Hence, *mea culpa* for the prescriptive and passionate elements in some of what follows.

A career in any business, let alone the academy, involves heavy debts accumulated in both deliberate and unintended encounters with too many smart people to mention, but a few nonetheless stand out. I want to register their names at the outset.

However, I begin with an aside. I have no talent as a natural scientist. However, I might be in any future life as I prefer their normal collaborative operating style to the more solitary routine of social scientists. Over the years, I have actively sought and benefited enormously from collaboration on scholarly as well as policy books and articles. As such, pride of authorship always gave way to harvesting new insights, getting the analysis right, and stretching the envelope covering important issues. In the pages that follow, mainly single-authored articles are interspersed with co-authored ones.

While some of the following individuals appear in chapter by-lines, others do not. But here I would like to register my intellectual debt to all of those whose work and influence undergird mine. While they receive no royalties, they are entitled to a drink or two.

Let me list them in relationship to the three main parts of this book. The list is longest concerning the first two parts—on the United Nations system and then the closely related one on non-state actors and global governance. Concerning subjects that have motivated me since graduate school, I begin with my dear friend and mentor, Leon Gordenker, whose own scholarship and unpretentious demeanor have always provided a beacon; as I pulled together these essays and reflected on them, I became even more fully aware of the extent to which I am indebted to him. From those first years in graduate school at Princeton University, I also would like to acknowledge efforts by Richard H. Ullman, Edward L. Morse, and Richard Falk who helped recycle a Harvard jock into an acceptable scholar. Over the years, my remedial education has continued through collaboration with S. Neil MacFarlane,

Ramesh Thakur, and Sam Daws. Meanwhile, David Forsythe and Roger Coate taught me much in writing our UN textbook; Craig Murphy invariably helped with insights on a variety of projects, personal and professional; and Rorden Wilkinson has been a stimulating younger partner in editing the Routledge Global Institutions Series. Finally, I note with gratitude my collaboration between 1999 and 2010 with Richard Jolly and Louis Emmerij, as well as Tatiana Carayannis, in orchestrating the United Nations Intellectual History Project, a long-overdue effort to document the world organization's ideational contribution to economic and social development.

The third part of the book deals with my preoccupation over the last 20 years, namely the humanitarian struggle to protect and help people caught in the blast of armed violence. Let me begin with Larry Minear, with whom I actively collaborated over ten years on the Humanitarianism & War Project. Lessons-learned versus lessons-spurned was the theme song of our efforts from 1990 to 1998. This focus continued with a younger comrade-in-arms, Don Hubert, who was an essential part of my team at the Research Directorate for the International Commission on Intervention and State Sovereignty (ICISS) that produced *The Responsibility to Protect* (R2P) and an accompanying research volume. Similarly, I acknowledge another younger analyst, Peter Hoffman, who went from my classroom to ICISS before collaborating on the theory of new wars and new humanitarianisms. Finally, Michael Barnett and I have been working over the last several years, first on an edited book and more recently an authored one that seek to re-examine humanitarian shibboleths and rethink standard operating procedures and principles.

The book begins with some overly generous words from Kofi Annan, for which I am truly grateful. I have had the distinct privilege of knowing him in a variety of capacities—as a senior UN official, secretary-general, Nobel laureate, head of a foundation, and most importantly as a human being. The planet is better off for his unstinting efforts as I am personally for my encounters with him.

All of this cooperation has taught me much, including the importance of good working environments. These have included collegial situations and supervisors in the 1970s and 1980s in the UN system itself (the late Oscar Schachter at UNITAR and Jack Stone and Jan Pronk at UNCTAD), and in the late 1980s and 1990s at the International Peace Academy and Brown University's Watson Institute (especially its then president Vartan Gregorian). The most congenial and rewarding of my "homes" has, since 1998, been the Ralph Bunche Institute for International Studies at The City University of New York's Graduate Center. William Kelly hired me when he was provost and has consistently and enthusiastically supported my professional activities as well as tolerated my sense of humor since as president.

Finally, the person with the greatest impact on my life is my wife. Living with her since long before the first essay in this volume appeared has been not only enriching and fulfilling but also really fun. I therefore dedicate *Thinking about Global Governance: Why People and Ideas Matter* to Priscilla Read.

TGW

New York City, April 2011

INTRODUCTION

The warm feeling induced by the request from a serious publisher to make a selection from my previous work lasted only a few moments. It chilled when I began to look over the titles and tried to recall the arguments in the 175 or so articles and book chapters written since 1973. I was flattered to join an impressive group of other colleagues in a book series of previously published essays, but what to make of three and a half decades of work? I asked myself whether I would sheepishly end up referring to Ralph Waldo Emerson's essay on "Self Reliance" and his justification that a "foolish consistency is the hobgoblin of little minds."

It turned out that the essays included here are not so inchoate as to tempt me to revise them. Apart from this introduction, all of the chapters appear essentially as originally published. I have not tried to eliminate overlap or repetition from one essay to another—to do so would have left puzzling gaps in logic and narratives. So each essay still stands on its own and can be read without reference to others. I have, however, eliminated typos and inaccuracies and made them all conform to a common style of the new empire (that is, United States). I have never been sure what had the longer odds, world peace or similar spelling and punctuation on both sides of the Atlantic.

Because pressing human problems have preoccupied me, the shelf-life of my writing often is shorter than that of more theoretically inclined colleagues. Hence, I have privileged essays published since the late 1990s. In a few cases older ones that were ahead of the curve and widely cited are included. Fortunately, my writing generally shows continuity except for an early (1975) and never revisited Prince Kropotkin phase of philosophical anarchism[1]—although some students at the London School of Economics recently asked me to return to what apparently is now fashionable in critical IR circles!

While I considered rewriting to reflect how my thinking has evolved, it seemed fitting to leave the originals intact, only eliminating material that was superfluous.

It is comforting to recall a riposte by the twentieth century's greatest economist, John Maynard Keynes. When he was criticized during the Great Depression for having changed his views on monetary policy, he explained: "When the facts change, I change my mind. What do you do, sir?"[2] If Lord Keynes can do so, certainly lesser mortals can as well.

The following pages are part autobiography, part intellectual history, and part reflection on how my research interests and writing have developed over the years. I have organized the material into three parts and initially explain why I view them as representative and significant. For the sake of clarity, the endnotes to this introduction refer to my 40 authored or edited books that contain more data, illustrations, and in-depth arguments on the same topics for those readers who are looking for more.

The first six essays deal with both the evolving nature of the United Nations and the ever-changing world in which it was born in 1945 and has continued to operate since. Many pundits see the world organization as a pale, stodgy, and unchanging imitation of what the original signatories of the Charter aspired to establish. Most observers view the United Nations as a rigid bureaucracy without sparkle, wit, or creativity. The general public—especially in the United States, where it is endlessly stimulated by the mass media—see a traveling circus, a talk shop, and paper-pushers. On and off there are tales of corruption. There are elements of truth in such stereotypes, but they project an unjust view of international secretariats and their contributions.

The first group of essays surveys both the role of individuals and ideas in a complex mosaic of operations. While many pundits lament the absence of reform, in fact the UN system has evolved so much that its founders might well not recognize today what they created in 1945. From the outset of my career as both a UN official and as an analyst, I have wanted to amplify the "voices"[3] of many individuals who have worked in and around what my colleagues and I in the UN Intellectual History Project call "the three United Nations" (that of governments, of international civil servants, and of civil society and experts). What has been the result? It is hard to formulate a better answer than the one from the second secretary-general, Dag Hammarskjöld: "The UN was not created to take mankind to heaven, but to save humanity from hell."

The four longish essays that comprise the second part of the book deal with non-state actors and global governance. One of the main reasons for the growing interest in global governance derives from the expansion both in numbers and importance of non-state actors, including civil society and for-profit corporations. This growth has been facilitated by the so-called third wave of democratization,[4] which involves institutional networks congruent enough to facilitate greater transnational and trans-governmental interactions.[5] The establishment of the Global Compact at the Millennium Summit of 2000 was a barometer indicating that intergovernmental organizations like the UN no longer by themselves occupy center stage for students of international organization. The private sector—both the for-profit and not-for-profit species—was recognized as a necessary partner for the world organization. The United Nations itself accepted that state-centric structures—not only governments but also their creations in the form of intergovernmental organizations—no longer enjoy a monopoly over collective efforts to improve international society and world order. They share the crowded governance stage with many other crucial actors.

The final part contains seven essays that relate to humanitarian action under duress (that is, assisting and protecting civilians caught in the throes of war) in the post–Cold War era. The ten years before and certainly the decade after September 11, 2001,[6] merit James Rosenau's label of a "turbulent world."[7] Humanitarian action has provided the fulcrum for my analytical energies since the late 1980s. Many of my fellow bleeding-heart colleagues balked at what I insisted on calling "military humanitarianism,"[8] or at least "humanitarian politics."[9] The essays focus on the behavior and misbehavior of aid agencies, the use of military force to protect human beings, and the emerging yet contested norm of "the responsibility to protect," now commonly abbreviated as R2P. My point of departure—political, legal, and moral—is clear: a well-grounded interpretation of sovereignty does not preclude intervention in the face of mass atrocities. And my solution is likewise apparent: using outside military forces is desirable and worthwhile in halting such suffering. Military deployments in the face of conscience-shocking disasters have sometimes made matters worse, but they have also saved lives and improved world order. The fact that humanitarian intervention is selectively applied clearly remains a problem; we must squirm when looking at carnage and displacement in Darfur, northern Uganda, and the Democratic Republic of the Congo (DRC). Political will remains, as always, in short supply, which provides a *sotto voce* in the articles throughout the book. Libya in early 2011 is encouraging.

I would now like to examine in more detail the context animating my thinking for each essay. In the process, I hope it becomes clear why they appear in these pages.

The United Nations, *Plus ça change* . . .

Speaking in 1960 Charles de Gaulle called the United Nations *le machin*, thereby conveying his disdain for multilateral cooperation in comparison with the real red meat of international affairs, namely vital interests and realpolitik. He conveniently ignored that the formal birth of "the thing" was not the signing of the UN Charter in June 1945, but rather the adoption of the Declaration by the United Nations in Washington, DC, in January 1942. The 26 countries that defeated fascism and, by the way, saved France, anticipated the establishment of a world organization as an extension of their war-time commitments. The national delegates in San Francisco were not pie-in-the-sky idealists. They did not view the moving parts of the UN system as liberal playthings to be tossed aside when the going got tough but rather as essential for postwar order and prosperity.[10]

By questioning the world organization's relevance and by calling for its demolition, numerous other politicians and pundits have made careers; mine has concentrated on the Sisyphean task of building understanding of the United Nations—hence, this book's cover. And a portion of my professional energies have gone into strengthening the International Studies Association (ISA, for which I served as president, 2009–10) and the Academic Council on the United Nations System (ACUNS, for which I served as chair, 2006–9). I had the opportunity to work for the United Nations (1975–85) and have examined the world organization from a particular angle, namely the desperate need for a third generation of intergovernmental organizations to move beyond the "anarchy" that Hedley Bull[11] and most students of international relations take as a point of departure.

In fact, Rube Goldberg could not have come up with a better design for futile complexity than the current array of UN organizations. With a separate budget, governing board, organizational culture, and independent executive head, each focuses on a substantive area and more often than not is located in a different city or different continent from relevant partners. In 1969, Sir Robert Jackson was asked to examine the development system and began the *Capacity Study* by comparing the UN to "some prehistoric monster."[12] Jackson's lumbering dinosaur is now more than 40 years older and no better adapted to the twenty-first century's climate.

Mark Malloch Brown, who was British minister charged with UN matters and before that deputy-secretary-general and administrator of the UN Development Programme (UNDP), quips that the world organization is the only one on earth where over coffee or around water coolers reform is a more popular topic than sex.[13] Continual talk of drastic overhaul became feverish before the 2005 World Summit, but like earlier attempts this latest endeavor led to no transformation. The UN continues to limp along much as it has since its creation. Nonetheless, I have not abandoned hope that the world organization can be made to work better. A collaborative textbook was written with that conviction and is now in its sixth edition, *The United Nations and Changing World Politics*,[14] and a toolkit comes with my latest single-authored book, *What's Wrong with the United Nations and How to Fix It*.[15]

The first essay in the book, a 2010 piece from the journal *Global Governance* titled "Reinvigorating the international civil service," is based on the John Holmes Memorial Lecture that I delivered after stepping down as ACUNS chair. This very topic of international secretariats was the subject of my 1974 doctoral dissertation whose last paragraph in part reads: "[W]hile 'world interest' is a lofty and idealistic concept, it is significant that one group of individuals, the international civil service, is theoretically committed to the concept's realization. . . . Thus, it is necessary to investigate how one can maximize the contribution of—or minimize the detraction from—human administrative structures at the global level."[16] Based on first-hand experience during ten years as a UN staff member in Geneva, as well as my analytical musings before and after, my firm conclusion holds that the margin for maneuver by international civil servants is greater than most people believe. Creative leaders at all levels provide evidence of constructivism in action. State interests of course circumscribe what is possible, but definitions of those interests are neither etched in stone nor imposed exogenously. At the United Nations, as everywhere else, people matter in determining outcomes.

The second article, "How UN ideas change the world," is based on a lecture that I had prepared for the annual meeting of the British International Studies Association in 2009, which appeared in print the following year.[17] This essay from the *Review of International Studies* represents lessons from the United Nations Intellectual History Project that I had the pleasure of directing with Richard Jolly and Louis Emmerij for over a decade with substantial support from seven foundations and eight like-minded governments. This independent research endeavor resulted in our capstone book, *UN Ideas That Changed the World*, which builds on the 16 volumes produced by the project.[18] This article explores the proposition that international organizations live or die, thrive or shrivel up, because of the quality and relevance of the policy ideas that they put forward and sustain. It is essential to examine the good, the bad, and the ugly—which this essay does by assessing the nature of ideas, albeit recognizing that most (especially those of the world body) have multiple origins and various carriers, and by evaluating their impact and the UN's value-added.

The next contribution appeared in 2009 in *International Studies Quarterly*, "What happened to the idea of world government?" Some colleagues undoubtedly thought that, unlike former US president William J. Clinton, there had been lingering effects of my having inhaled as well as smoked, but this critical self-reflection is based on my presidential address at the 50th Annual Meeting of the International Studies Association in New York. After years of identifying gigantic problems and then proposing what was realistic—namely, tinkering with the existing system—I went back to explore why so many global citizens of the 1930s and 1940s were able to think more boldly about supranational authority. Intriguingly, even in the land of black helicopters, they were not a fringe group. Their numbers included not only a scientific luminary such as Albert Einstein but also such visible entertainers as Ronald Reagan, E.B. White, and Oscar Hammerstein. Future US senators Alan Cranston and Harris Wofford sought to spread the message of world federalism among university students. Other prominent individuals associated with the world government idea included at one time or another Kurt Vonnegut, Walter Cronkite, H.G. Wells, Leonard Woolf, Peter Ustinov, future Supreme Court justices William Douglas and Owen Roberts, and future senators Estes Kefauver and vice-president Hubert Humphrey. Not only did *Reader's Digest* feature articles, but also as late as 1949 a "sense of Congress" resolution supported turning the UN into a world federation and was sponsored by 111 representatives, including two future presidents, John F. Kennedy and Gerald Ford, as well as the likes of Mike Mansfield, Henry Cabot Lodge, Christian Herter, "Scoop" Jackson, and Jacob Javits. And the list goes on.

Yet, why has no student of mine ever even looked into the theoretical possibilities of a world state? Why is the topic not mentioned in polite company, with anyone who broaches it treated as either naïve or in favor of a global Leviathan?

Answers are found here (including the most obvious, the Cold War), but one of them is the fault of the author and his colleagues: a lack of imagination from knowledgeable observers who care about international cooperation. Because the Concert of Europe flopped, because Tsar Alexander's Hague conferences failed to end war, because the Kellogg–Briand Pact was never a serious proposition, and because Immanuel Kant's and Woodrow Wilson's collective security visions were incorporated in the moribund League of Nations and were still-born in the United Nations, we no longer see our scholarly role as including thinking about drastically different world futures.

Next is a provocative, at least for some friends from the global South, 2009 article titled "Moving beyond North-South theater" from *Third World Quarterly*. My ten years in active UN service were in what at the time was the most pro–Third World of UN bodies—the UN Conference on Trade and Development (UNCTAD). That experience led me to write on North-South negotiations and the dynamics of multilateral negotiations.[19] While I value the agenda-setting contribution in the 1950s and 1960s of both the Non-Aligned Movement (NAM) and the Group of 77 (G-77) developing countries, this article points to the dysfunctional roles that the aging troupes of actors from the North and the South currently play in what Conor Cruise O'Brien once described as the "sacred drama" of the United Nations.[20] My interest in these matters first found its way into an article in 1976 in *World Politics* on the World Food Conference. It was one of the earliest efforts to identify the peculiar dynamics of multilateral development diplomacy—including regional caucuses and group negotiations, the advocacy of NGOs, the contributions by international civil servants, the stage of global ad hoc conferences—and developed into a book on that conference.[21] The predictable antics between the industrialized North and the global South continue to impede any sensible regrouping of voices, which should change from issue to issue. The former senior Canadian diplomat and UNICEF official Stephen Lewis has lamented, "Alas, man and woman cannot live by rhetoric alone"[22]—unless, of course, one is employed as a diplomat in UN missions in New York or Nairobi, Geneva or Bangkok.

Dramatic and largely symbolic and theatrical confrontations, rather than a search for meaningful partners, is the usual way to proceed in international forums. With a push toward consensus as the operating principle—the preferred route for UN negotiations—lowest common denominators offer one way for 192 states (the current UN membership) to agree on a resolution, work program, or budget. Another allows each country to interpret a vague text in the way that it sees fit or to participate or ignore programs that it dislikes. Neither is the best collective way to solve global problems. This essay provides some encouraging examples (including the agreements on land mines, the International Criminal Court, and gender) of changed stances within the supposedly iron-clad country categories. The North-South divide holds back the generation of norms and policies to ensure human security, or even survival, in a globalizing world. Moreover, developing countries, including those now in the Group of 20 (G-20), abandon solidarity when they claim that it is in their perceived interests to do so. Issues-based and interest-based rather than ideology-based negotiations are required.

Virtually all discussions of politics revolve around judgments about continuity and change, the theme for the next article that I wrote with Sam Daws, "World politics: continuity and change since 1945." This is the substantive part of the introduction to the 40 chapters of the 2007 authoritative publication, *The Oxford Handbook on the United Nations*.[23] The flavor of this essay provides the subtitle for the first part of the current volume, "*Plus ça change*." Scholars and practitioners correctly point to the most fundamental continuity in the UN, or the more things change, the more they remain the same: to wit, the fundamental units of the international system and of the UN—sovereign states—are here to stay. At the same time, today's world politics differ fundamentally from those of 1945. Such new threats as pandemics, climate change, terrorism, and proliferation of weapons of mass destruction (WMDs) have emerged or evolved; new non-state actors have appeared and older ones have been transformed; new norms and conventions have proliferated; and new intergovernmental and nongovernmental organizations populate the landscape. Change can be measured quantitatively or qualitatively, and Kalevi Holsti's *Taming the Sovereigns* probes the ways of calculating it: "These include change as novelty or replacement, change as addition or subtraction, increased complexity, transformation, reversion, and obsolescence."[24] On any scale, these kinds of changes suggest a radically altered if not transformed international system, but we still have institutions with more in common to the world of 1945 than the one in which we live.

No institution reflects the political order at the conclusion of World War II—rather than today's—more than the principal UN organ charged with the maintenance of international peace and security, which explains the inclusion of a short op-ed from *Security Dialogue* in 2005, "An unchanged Security Council: the sky ain't falling." In view of the constraints of space here, I include this truncated version of a 2003 article in the *Washington Quarterly*, "The illusion of UN Security Council reform," written during preparations for the 60th anniversary of the United Nations in 2005.[25] It spells out the critical need for altering the membership in and standard operating procedures of the Security Council as well as the even more dramatic reasons why no reform would take place. The five permanent members (P-5) of the Security Council must agree to widen membership in the powerful club and give up their vetoes—the equivalent of asking turkeys to vote in favor of Thanksgiving or Christmas dinner. Moreover, every possible solution creates more problems than it solves. I declined a request from the journal's editor to update it in 2010. The 2003 article remains an accurate reflection of contemporary reality and will remain so for the foreseeable future.

Space did not permit including a substantial body of work that began with "Moscow's UN policy," written in 1990 by Meryl A. Kessler and me that appeared in *Foreign Policy*.[26] For students born after the fall of the Berlin Wall in November 1989 and even for some of us longer in the tooth, it is often hard to recall the extent to which the Cold War paralyzed the Security Council. Over a number of years,

I explored the repercussions from *glasnost* and *perestroika* in Moscow when Mikhail Gorbachev came to power in 1985, including the return of the United Nations to the center of the conflict-management business. While now part of the operating assumptions of world politics, the dramatic shifts in attitude in both Moscow and Washington were once "news" because they permitted a vast and rapid expansion of UN activities, especially peace operations. After having been missing in action, the world organization even deployed to regions that had been flash-points of superpower rivalry. If the UN could be helpful in the "backyards" of the two superpowers, was the sky not the limit?

Such euphoria did not last long, even if the world body was again more central to world politics. I persuaded Jim Blight, my trusting co-editor of a book of case studies on two Third World regions, to accept what turned out to be an unfortunate title, *The Suffering Grass: Superpowers and Regional Conflict in Southern Africa and the Caribbean*.[27] Apparently librarians order books with their main titles as a guide. And while this one referred to a widely known (at least in UN circles) Swahili proverb about the results of elephants fighting or making love—an apt metaphor, we thought, for the possible outcome of Soviet-American rapprochement in the Third World—the cute packaging meant that book sales were limited mainly to agricultural colleges.

Why have the nuts-and-bolts of international administration and negotiations interested me since graduate school? The straightforward answer could be captured by lengthening the title of John Ruggie's edited volume from the early 1990s— "multilateralism matters, and it should matter more."[28] While my computer's spell-check still does not like the word, "multilateralism" now is popping up in the media and blogs and not just in international relations scholarship. The use of the term is not just a fad but a reflection of contemporary world politics. Charles Krauthammer's so-called unilateral moment lasted two decades,[29] but the "multilateral moment" should now last longer, and with luck permanently.

Non-state actors and global governance

The importance of people, specifically intellectual and operational leaders in the international civil service, was a thread running through several essays in the first part. Less visible perhaps was the second element of this book's subtitle. The importance of ideas emerges here and is especially prominent in the third part of the volume.

The discipline of international relations—and within it the subfield of international organization, which is where I situate myself—until recently has had a poor analytical grasp of the impact of what, rather routinely, are now labeled "ideational factors." While I have never fancied myself a theorist, I discovered at the beginning of the 1990s that, like Molière's Monsieur Jourdain, I had been speaking "constructivist" prose for some time. Ideas, norms, and principles matter; but in international politics, power matters more because institutionalization is so weak.

At the same time, Thucydides in his Melian dialogue did not get it totally right. Of course, the strong do what they will and the weak what they must. Yet ideas shape both what the strong and the weak think is possible, or are willing to tolerate without resisting. The essays here trace an intellectual journey over three and a half decades. My conscientious objection to the Vietnam War made me sensitive to the post–World War II aversion to (or even revulsion against) idealism in international relations. Not to put too fine a point on it, I recognized why E.H. Carr, Reinhold Niebuhr, and Hans Morgenthau had adopted realism, and Kenneth Waltz had adapted it.[30] But the primacy of that school of thought had gone far too far—in the academy and especially in Washington, DC.

Over the course of my professional career, mainstream thinking about international cooperation has shifted decidedly away from beefing up the United Nations and other intergovernmental organizations and toward what many of us now call "global governance." My friend Ramesh Thakur and I struggled to understand the origins and itinerary of this idea.[31] While many urged us to go back to the Garden of Eden, or at least to 1945, we trace the term to a shotgun wedding between academic theory and practical policy in the 1990s. James Rosenau and Ernst Czempiel published their theoretical *Governance without Government* in 1992,[32] when Sweden launched the policy-oriented Commission on Global Governance under the chairmanship of Sonny Ramphal and Ingmar Carlsson. The 1995 publication of its report, *Our Global Neighbourhood*,[33] coincided with the first issue of the journal *Global Governance: A Review of Multilateralism and International Organization*. Now, a veritable cottage industry continually produces analyses of the topic.

"Governance" includes both informal and formal values, norms, practices, and institutions. It is most useful to think of "global governance" at any moment as the capacity of the international system to provide government-like services in the absence of a world government. Global governance encompasses an extremely wide variety of cooperative problem-solving arrangements that may be visible but informal (e.g., practices or guidelines) or result from temporary units (e.g., coalitions of the willing). Such arrangements may also be more formal, taking the shape of hard rules (laws and treaties) as well as constituted institutions with administrative structures and established practices to manage collective affairs by a variety of actors, including state authorities, intergovernmental organizations, nongovernmental organizations, private sector entities, and other civil society actors.

At the national level, we have governance *plus* government. Despite well-known weaknesses, lapses, and incapacities, governmental institutions in most parts of the world routinely and predictably exert authority and control, complemented by softer forms of social order and capital. For the globe, we have governance *minus* government and thus only the feeblest of imitations—institutions that routinely help ensure postal delivery and airline safety, to be sure, but that routinely can do little to address such life-threatening problems as climate change and ethnic cleansing.

The "field"—if that is the term—of global governance emerged for two concrete reasons and one more subjective reason. First, beginning in the 1970s, interdependence and rapid technological advances fostered wider and wider recognition that a growing number of problems defy solutions by a single state or even by a coalition of the willing. Other examples surround us, but the development of a consciousness about the human environment, which was made visible especially at the 1972 and 1992 UN conferences in Stockholm and Rio de Janeiro, is an especially pertinent illustration of how we are all in the same listing boat in increasingly choppy waters.

Second, the growing interest in global governance reflected the need to get an analytical handle on the sheer expansion in numbers and importance of non-state actors. The 250 or so intergovernmental organizations like the UN are no longer the sole preoccupation of students of international organization. These institutions share the crowded governance stage not only with nearly 200 governments but also with both civil society and for-profit corporations: including some 7,500 international NGOs and 10,000 single-state NGOs with significant international activities as well as some 75,000 transnational corporations and their 750,000 foreign affiliates.[34] This panoply of institutions may not yet represent a "post-Westphalian" world, but this reality clearly is inadequately reflected in state-centric analytical perspectives.

The combination of intensifying interdependence, technological advances, and a proliferation of actors results in, to borrow an image from James Rosenau, a "crazy quilt" of authority,[35] with a patchwork of institutional elements that varies by sector and over time. Other images from non-scholars might be even more apt, including Gertrude Stein's characterization of Oakland—"there's no there, there"—or perhaps better still the Cheshire cat in *Alice in Wonderland*, a grinning head floating without a body or substance.

A third but less obvious reason for the emergence of the notion of global governance bears repeating here, namely the lack of big thinking from us international relations specialists. When interdependence was less and actors were fewer and states could solve or attenuate most problems, the idea of a world government was in the scholarly mainstream. Paradoxically, now when states cannot address a growing number of threats, world government is unimaginable.

That said, the exploration of the roles of non-state actors explains why many analysts of international affairs are in business these days. I have devoted much analytical effort not just to the United Nations and other intergovernmental actors but also to nongovernmental ones as well. The essays in the second part of the book probe this topic.

The first is an essay in *Global Governance*, "The 'third' United Nations," which I wrote in 2009 with Tatiana Carayannis and Richard Jolly. Perhaps most people think of the world organization as unitary; but the real one consists of three linked components. Inis Claude's classic textbook long ago distinguished the arena for state decision-making, the "first UN" of member states, from the "second UN" of staff members and secretariat heads who are paid from assessed and voluntary budgets.[36] The "third UN" is comprised of actors that are closely associated with the world organization but not formally part of it. This "outside-insider" UN includes NGOs, academics, consultants, experts, independent commissions, and other groups of individuals. Their networks often help to shifts ideas, policies, priorities, and practices that are initially resisted by governments and international secretariats. This broader embrace of what constitutes the world body is not only accurate but also crucial to understanding the itinerary of ideas in the international public policy arena. It is noteworthy that the for-profit sector has essentially been missing in action in relationship to the UN's past policy debates and operations. A foundation for a "fourth UN" has been laid with the Global Compact and other longer-standing ones such as employers at the International Labour Organization; and business will certainly be a more substantial part of a future intellectual and operational history of international organization.

The second essay grows from my fruitful collaboration with Ramesh Thakur mentioned above. "Framing global governance, five gaps," appeared in the *2008 Oxford Yearbook of International Law and Jurisprudence*. Both of us normally write quickly, but we struggled mightily for over half a decade to complete a book for which this article provides an overview. Because "global governance" means so many things to so many analysts, our principal battle was to find an organizing device to make this amorphous subject manageable and meaningful. That theoretical framework consists of the five gaps that the United Nations and other actors attempt to fill for global governance—in knowledge, norms, policies, institutions, and compliance. According to our book's subtitle, this is an "unfinished" and never-ending journey.

The subsequent essay, "Governance, good governance, and global governance: conceptual and actual challenges," is my earlier effort in a 2000 issue of *Third World Quarterly* to disentangle this topic. It adds an extensive discussion of the differences between the way this notion operates domestically and internationally. I mention my intellectual struggle with some trepidation and embarrassment because as an editor (2000–5) of the journal *Global Governance* presumably I should have been able to speak more easily and authoritatively about this mushy subject. Perhaps any analyst with an insight is the equivalent of one-eyed royalty in the kingdom of the blind? Expertise and insights are relative notions when we all grope to understand highly complex and continually changing phenomena.

The next contribution reflects work with Leon Gordenker, "Pluralising global governance: analytical approaches and dimensions." This 1995 introduction as guest editors to a special issue of *Third World Quarterly* provides our theoretical framing of a research undertaking that sought to conceptualize and contextualize the advocacy and operational links between NGOs and the United Nations. While UN Charter Article 71 was ahead of its time and made some room for NGOs from the outset of the world organization, the nature of that ever-changing relationship was for decades a minor concern for both analysts and international officials. "Until recently, the notion that the chief executive of the United Nations would have taken this issue seriously might have caused astonishment," wrote then secretary-general Boutros Boutros-Ghali in the foreword when the special issue was republished in book form. "The United Nations was considered to be a forum for sovereign states alone. Within the space of a few short years, however, this attitude has changed. Non-governmental organizations are now considered full participants in international life."[37] This book was one of the first to grapple with a topic that many have compared to herding cats—and it is still cited and in print.

A related analytical perspective is how the United Nations dealt with another type of body, namely what Chapter VIII of the UN Charter refers to as "regional arrangements" but most observers call "regional organizations," including such alliances as the North Atlantic Treaty Organization (NATO). Although not included in this collection, it is worth mentioning my learning-intensive effort to understand the theory and the practice of regional organizations with S. Neil MacFarlane that was published in 1992 in *Security Studies*.[38] This is relevant because I later edited a volume comparing subcontracting by the United Nations to both NGOs for development and humanitarian projects and to regional organizations for the provision of troops.[39] While a catchy formulation, I later understood more clearly that "subcontracting" accurately describes the relationship between the United Nations and NGOs because the UN channels resources from governments to NGOs to provide services and therefore has a certain authority over them. At the same time, subcontracting is hardly accurate to describe the relationship between the United Nations and regional organizations or various coalitions of the willing because certainly no principal-agent relationship exists between the world organization and troop contributors; the United Nations ends up begging them to do what it cannot.

Why have non-state actors interested me? The answer is found in the omnipresence of the almost fatuous moniker "international community." This term is not only an ideological mask for the politics and power lurking beneath the surface in international organization but also an intellectual shorthand that permits obfuscating which actors actually exacerbate or mitigate efforts to solve global problems.

Public international lawyers at least rely consistently on the UN Charter for their definition. Over time other observers and many social scientists have also included intergovernmental organizations in their definitions of international community because these organizations have been created by the "peace-loving [sic] states." Still other commentators have added to the definition any group, organization, or even individuals who are interested in a particular problem; and the membership changes over time and by issue-area.

A minimal requirement for any community consists of an agreed definition of who is included and a modicum of shared values. Clearly UN member states provide a clear definition by lawyers for membership but fall short on the shared values; and the motley assortment of actors in other definitions means that there is no agreed membership criteria, let alone clarity about values. A 2002 magazine cover of *Foreign Policy* says it all. A well-dressed man (undoubtedly a diplomat) stands on the prow of a rowboat and peers through a monocular (or a pirate's telescope) at a totally foggy horizon. The caption reads, "Where Is the International Community?" The main feature continues inside under the overall heading, "What Is the International Community?" The nine short commentaries share virtually no common ground, which leads the magazine's editors to quip: "This feel-good phrase evokes a benevolent, omniscient entity that makes decisions and takes action for the benefit of all countries and peoples. But involving the international community is a lot easier than defining it."[40]

Someday we might have an international community in more than name. At this time, it is fantasy. My efforts to identify the specific attributes and contributions of various actors in contemporary global governance permit us to better hold appropriate feet to the fire. Expressions like "the international community failed in Rwanda" or "the international community succeeded in establishing an International Criminal Court" are meaningless.

Humanitarian action in a turbulent world

An idea that I have investigated and then championed since the waning of East–West tensions concerns the feasibility and desirability of using outside military forces—approved or actually deployed by the United Nations—to protect human beings caught in the cross-hairs of armed conflicts. This idea remains controversial because of the sacrosanct character of state sovereignty, which supposedly prevents outsiders from interfering with the murderous behavior of local thugs unless they politely consent. Outside interference in domestic affairs, even if conscience-shocking behavior violates such agreed international legal standards as the 1948 Genocide Convention, is taboo.

Much of my analytical energy over the last quarter-century has confronted head-on the backward-looking notion of unreconstructed state sovereignty. After the 1991 deployment of armed force in northern Iraq to help the Kurds and then in 1992 to help halt the calamity in Somalia, the foundations of the Westphalian legal and normative framework were clearly shifting. While it is not included here because its contents now seem banal, one of the earliest investigations of the topic was written in 1992 by Jarat Chopra and me and appeared in *Ethics & International Affairs*; and the main title still guides my work, "Sovereignty Is No Longer Sacrosanct."[41] Libya is the most recent illustration.

My normative point of departure has always been that a proper interpretation of sovereignty does not preclude outside intervention when crimes against humanity are committed. And my solution is as well—outside military forces are desirable and worthwhile to halt such abuse. International deployments have saved lives and, often if not always, improved world order. Selective or half-hearted military deployments clearly can create difficulties—we have only to point to Darfur, northern Uganda, and the DRC to recall this ugly reality. To reinforce what I said above, political will remains, as always, in short supply.

The passion and commitment that began with an analysis of Operation Lifeline Sudan in 1989[42] is captured in my 2007 book, *Humanitarian Intervention: Ideas in Action*.[43] It is hard for anyone to substantiate the "creation" of an idea,[44] but I believe that I was working well before others on contemporary humanitarian intervention.

Of course the term has been used since the nineteenth century to describe imperial military efforts that were anything except humanitarian, but after the end of the Cold War, my concerns were to find a "peace dividend" in the form of using military forces to come to the rescue of civilians.[45]

While many critics have come down hard on me and others for either consciously or inadvertently contributing to "new imperialism" or to "new militarism,"[46] I remain proud of efforts to move from a "Westphalian" to a "post-Westphalian" order. In its most extreme form, the former argues that human suffering within country borders, no matter how ugly and grotesque, should not be an international concern unless it threatens the maintenance of peace and security between states. The move toward the latter—after centuries ending impunity and removing the license for state authorities to commit mass murder—is a step forward for the human species. In the twentieth century alone, wars, pogroms, genocides, and mass murder killed some 217 million people.[47] And this ghastly figure does not include many others who lived diminished lives as refugees, internally displaced persons (IDPs), detainees, widows or widowers, orphans, and paupers.

Usually I quickly reassure those uneasy about the onset of the post-Westphalian order that the sky over international society really is not falling. The new normative and political bar is set very low. After all, we are speaking of halting mass atrocities. As agreed triggers for international opprobrium and perhaps action, the 2005 World Summit identified "only" genocide, war crimes, ethnic cleansing, and crimes against humanity. This decision starts with the morally, legally, and politically obvious cases. We are not talking about dampening the 75 smoldering and potentially deadly conflicts that the International Crisis Group typically monitors. We are not trying to establish peace on earth nor to rid the planet of all human rights abuses. Surely it is not quixotic to say no more Holocausts, Cambodias, and Rwandas—and, occasionally, to mean it.

With the possible exception of the prevention of genocide after World War II, no idea has moved faster in the international normative arena than the responsibility to protect, the title of the 2001 report from the International Commission on Intervention and State Sovereignty (ICISS).[48] In the interests of full disclosure, I had the privilege of serving as its research director[49] and direct the Ralph Bunche Institute that houses the Global Centre for the Responsibility to Protect.

This section begins with my most recent effort to summarize the topic's status even if the politics of the General Assembly evolve almost daily. "Political innovations and the responsibility to protect" appeared in the 2010 edited volume, *Driven From Home: Protecting the Rights of Forced Migrants*. Like other essays in this part, it contains a strong dose of ethics—appropriate in a volume edited by a Jesuit priest who directs a human rights center. Its main purpose is to explore political innovations that could make "never again" an actuality instead of an aspiration. I was tempted to write a brief paragraph recommending the mother of all international political innovations, namely that states comply with and implement the international agreements that they have signed and even ratified. As Gary Bass puts it in his history of early efforts to halt mass atrocities, "We are all atrocitarians now—but so far only in words, and not yet in deeds."[50] My menu to advance the implementation of R2P has something for everyone: for analysts, conceptual clarity; for civil society, a long-term strategy; for UN reformers, a consolidated relief agency; for the military, more robust and numerous forces in Europe; and for weak fragile countries, enhanced state capacities.

The tortuous wars of the last 15 years—especially in Afghanistan and Iraq, which morphed into disingenuous and *ex post facto*, albeit humanitarian, justifications after the links to WMDs and Al Qaeda evaporated—defy easy categories. These armed conflicts do not really merit the adjective of "new" wars,[51] but the combination and intensity of lethal factors could be considered unusual. Moreover, they are especially problematic for both aid workers and soldiers whose efforts are no longer automatically on the side of the angels. In part, the unusual character of contemporary civil wars is suggested by the growing fatalities for both aid personnel and journalists working in war zones. I wrote the next article, "The fog of humanitarianism: collective action problems and learning-challenged organizations," with Peter J. Hoffman for the first issue of the *Journal of Intervention and State-Building* in 2007.[52] Among other things, we called for the aid industry to develop a humanitarian equivalent of military science; civilians were irritated.

My 20-year struggle continues in order to understand how public and private humanitarian organizations deal with new wars and new humanitarianisms,[53] and especially with the problem of internally displaced persons.[54] Michael J. Barnett and I collaborated on an unusual volume published in 2008 on the social science of humanitarian action titled *Humanitarianism in Question: Politics, Power, Ethics*; and this experiment continued in *Humanitarianism Contested*, published in 2011, with the apt sub-title, *Where Angels Fear to Tread*.[55]

In light of the dramatically changing contexts for coming to the rescue in war zones, the next three essays attempt to explain why governments and humanitarians do not react similarly in all emergencies. The first article is "The humanitarian impulse," which appeared in 2004 in a volume edited by David Malone, *The UN Security Council: From the Cold War to the 21st Century*. Politics and national interest calculations explain why we sometimes respond and sometimes do not. I prefer the word "impulse" although the "imperative" has characterized virtually all humanitarian discourse in the field. The latter entails an obligation to treat victims similarly and react to all crises consistently—in effect, to deny the relevance of politics, which consists of drawing lines and weighing options and available resources. How could I not share the lofty objective of a visceral, standard response? Yet humanitarian action is desirable, not obligatory. The humanitarian impulse is permissive; the humanitarian imperative is peremptory.

My 2004 contribution to *Security Dialogue*—titled "The sunset of humanitarian intervention? The responsibility to protect in a unipolar era"—adds another explanation for the inadequacy and inconsistency in military intervention for human protection purposes: in major crises little is possible unless Washington participates. The fact that the United States already was "distracted" in Iraq and Afghanistan—and remains so as I write—led me to argue that the threat was not too much military humanitarianism (the purported worry of many countries in the global South) but rather too little. Until the imposition of a no-fly zone in Libya, the heady days of the 1990s seemed like ancient history. That the presumed unipolar moment is over reinforces the obvious need for European militaries to pull more military weight, and for Western donors to better equip and train regional groups in Africa, Asia, the Middle East, and Latin America for more effective military operations for human protection purposes. There is, of course, no evidence that the citizens of wealthy Western countries are willing to finance such an expansion.

The 2000 essay in *Security Dialogue*, "The politics of humanitarian ideas," explores the ideational framework for coming to the rescue. While aid agencies struggle to make the case that humanitarian action should remain "pure" (that is, disinterested and apolitical), it rarely if ever has been. Humanitarians themselves care deeply about outcomes and lobby for resources and respect for international law. What could be more political? Moreover, some humanitarian interventions are more effective and timely than others because of political interests, which is also why some crises gain media and geopolitical attention. Indeed, if significant national interests are involved, states that send militaries and finance humanitarian assistance are far more likely to stay the course. Sometimes it is necessary to state the obvious.

The question arose during the tumultuous 1990s as to whether aid agencies, especially the humanitarian industry's gold standard of the International Committee of the Red Cross (ICRC), could maintain impartiality and neutrality in the face of UN Chapter VII military action. My answer was and remains "no." Should we not tackle contemporary conflicts by distinguishing between suffering by civilians and abuse by belligerents? Should we not distinguish between victims and perpetrators? My answer was and remains "yes." Military humanitarianism requires taking sides and clearly delineating thugs and victims. Humanitarians are necessarily political whereas the ICRC claims to be "apolitical." That conclusion led me to write what may be my most cited article, an essay in *Ethics & International Affairs* in 1999, that remained a decade after appearing among that journal's top-ten downloaded publications. "Principles, politics, and humanitarian action" juxtaposes a framework of "classicists" versus "solidarists." The former eschew public confrontations, avoid taking sides, deliver aid proportionally and without discrimination, and pursue consent as the sine qua non of engagement. The latter are not timid about advocating controversial public policies, taking sides with selected victims, skewing the balance of resource allocations, and overriding sovereignty as and when necessary. Ideal types are, of course, rare; and in-between "minimalists" and "maximalists" on a spectrum of political involvement and respect for traditional principles are many aid officials. This essay is part of an effort to redefine the concept of humanitarian action away from the neutral and pacifist versions that provided sensible guidance during the Cold War. The new version comprises the politicized and sometimes militarized humanitarianism that protects and assists individuals without the consent of the political authorities in the territory in which abuses are commonplace. Again, Libya provides a recent illustration.

My research and writing about robust humanitarian action have focused on the myriad of field problems encountered by aid agencies and militaries. Beginning with the humanitarian aftermath of the first Gulf War, followed by fumbling UN efforts in the Balkans along with NATO, I have endeavored to understand the dynamics of "military-civilian interactions." Having written and updated a book by that title,[56] I include here an older 1997 essay in *Disasters* that attempts to spell out the rudimentary framework for identifying costs and benefits, "A research note about military-civilian humanitarianism: more questions than answers." It suggests how to compare the actual human, economic, and political costs and benefits of military-civilian interactions. My argument points to the factors to be assessed even if plenty of questions remain. My primary aim is to help to illustrate the host of potential benefits in order occasionally to have something other than what I have called "collective spinelessness"[57] in halting mass atrocities.

Why have the details of humanitarian action preoccupied me? First, as part of my irredeemable idealism and guarded optimism—some would claim pig-headedness—I am not willing to admit that human beings cannot improve the ways that they organize themselves to protect and provide succor to war victims.[58] I continue to be appalled by the gaggle of nongovernmental organizations that flocks to every emergency, and I am even angrier that the so-called UN system of humanitarian agencies has more in common with feudalism than contemporary management practice. In this respect, I can refer readers to an article not included here but whose title says a lot, "Humanitarian Shell Games," which examines the counterfactual and sad story of the consolidation that almost took place during former UN secretary-general Kofi Annan's 1997 reform effort. Instead of a centralized and consolidated agency, the UN's main players—UNICEF, the World Food Programme, and the UNDP—all became Chicken Little's and saw the sky falling if their own claim to humanitarian turf were consolidated in the Office of the UN High Commissioner for Refugees. Instead of that centralization, member states in their wisdom hatched a bureaucratic mouse in the form of the Office for the Coordination of Humanitarian Affairs, a toothless and budget-less replacement for an equally weak predecessor, the Department of Humanitarian Affairs. Eyes glaze over at the usual solution, a call for enhanced "coordination," or a low-key and meaningless excuse for both individual UN organizations and NGOs to go their separate fund-raising ways.

Second, in the face of human calamities and the ugly term "ethnic cleansing," I continue to find that the moral imperatives and political realities of redefining sovereignty provide insights about the more general evolution of the interstate system. The definition of sovereignty is increasingly contingent rather than absolute. This development adds momentum to long-standing efforts in public international law to codify the willingness of states to consent to giving up elements of their sovereignty to secure predictability and stability. Sovereignty is no longer unfettered because it now includes a modicum of respect for human rights as an essential part of its definition. The responsibility for human rights in the first instance lies with the state. If a state, however, is unwilling or unable to honor its responsibility, or itself becomes the perpetrator of atrocities, then sovereignty disappears temporarily and the residual responsibility to protect the victims of mass atrocity crimes shifts upwards to the international community of states, ideally acting through the Security Council.

In short, domestic affairs ain't what they used to be. I am not as disheartened as many humanitarians with a new double standard of international society's fitful, inconsistent, and uneven use of military force to "save strangers."[59] Why? The answer is because we formerly had a single standard, namely doing nothing everywhere.

Concluding thoughts

We are not yet at a Copernican moment for state sovereignty because the lack of any overarching international authority still summarizes the essence of international relations. Like Copernicus, however, we could look at the same sun and planets that others have seen but reframe the relations among them. My CUNY Graduate Center colleague, the American historian David Nasaw, reminded me that the 13 original states during the American Revolution were operating under the Articles of Confederation but sought a "more perfect union" in 1787 at the constitutional gathering in Philadelphia. People across the planet and the weak confederation of 192 UN member states require a "Philadelphia moment."

The world has changed dramatically over the lifetime of this baby-boomer and even since the first of these essays appeared. I take some solace from the fact that the multilateralism that so-called realists once cavalierly dismissed as so much clutter is now the professional preoccupation of many scholars, policy analysts, and practitioners. One need not be enthralled—although I remain guardedly sanguine—about the changes in Washington's approach to rejoining the planet under Barack Obama's administration. At least we are entitled to a sigh of relief that the "my-way-or-the-highway" George W. Bush administration is over. Matters that were largely seen as peripheral—including consulting allies and respecting international legal obligations—are again central to American foreign policy and hence to the world's future.

Having become more of a historian in recent years leads me to conclude with a personal note. Looking through the articles reprinted here helps shed light on what explorations of the past can contribute to understandings of the present. At the end of the day and at the end of these essays, I am persuaded that we students of international relations face a moral imperative to understand world politics better. While better knowledge and greater comprehension do not guarantee sensible policies and institutions, they are necessary first steps in the unending quest for human betterment. These essays, I hope, represent a modest personal contribution to that end, and I wish younger readers well in their own explorations.

Notes

1 Thomas G. Weiss, "The Tradition of Philosophical Anarchism and Future Directions in World Policy," *Journal of Peace Research* XI, no. 1 (1975): 1–17.
2 Quoted in Alfred L. Malabre, *Lost Prophets: An Insider's History of the Modern Economists* (Cambridge, Mass.: Harvard Business School Press, 1994), 220.
3 Thomas G. Weiss, Tatiana Carayannis, Louis Emmerij, and Richard Jolly, *UN Voices: The Struggle for Development and Social Justice* (Bloomington: Indiana University Press, 2005).
4 Samuel P. Huntington, *The Third Wave: Democratization in the Late Twentieth Century* (Norman, Okla.: University of Oklahoma Press, 1991).
5 See Anne-Marie Slaughter, "America's Edge: Power in the Networked Century," *Foreign Affairs* 88, no. 1 (2009): 94–113, which updates and expands *A New World Order* (Princeton, NJ: Princeton University Press, 2004).
6 See Thomas G. Weiss, Margaret E. Crahan, and John Goering, eds., *Wars on Terrorism and Iraq: Human Rights, Unilateralism, and U.S. Foreign Policy* (London: Routledge, 2004); and Jane Boulden and Thomas G. Weiss, eds., *Terrorism and the UN: Before and After September 11* (Bloomington: Indiana University Press, 2004).
7 James N. Rosenau, *Turbulence in World Politics* (Princeton, NJ: Princeton University Press, 1990).
8 Thomas G. Weiss and Kurt M. Campbell, "Military Humanitarianism," *Survival* 33, no. 5 (1991): 451–65.
9 Larry Minear and Thomas G. Weiss, *Humanitarian Politics* (New York: Foreign Policy Association, 1995), Headline Series No. 304.
10 See Dan Pletsch, *America, Hitler and the UN* (London: Tauris, 2010).
11 Hedley Bull, *The Anarchical Society: A Study of Order in World Politics* (New York: Columbia University Press, 1977).
12 United Nations, *A Capacity Study of the United Nations Development System* (Geneva: United Nations, 1969), volume I, iii.
13 Mark Malloch Brown, "Can the UN Be Reformed?" *Global Governance* 14, no. 1 (2008): 1–12.
14 Thomas G. Weiss, David P. Forsythe, Roger A. Coate, and Kelly-Kate Pease, *The United Nations and Changing World Politics*, 6th ed. (Boulder, Colo.: Westview, 2010, 1st ed. 1994).
15 Thomas G. Weiss, *What's Wrong with the United Nations and How to Fix It* (Cambridge: Polity Press, 2009).
16 Thomas G. Weiss, *International Bureaucracy: An Analysis of the Operation of Functional and Global International Secretariats* (Lexington, Mass.: D.C. Heath, 1975), xix. See also David Pitt and Thomas G. Weiss, eds., *The Nature of United Nations Bureaucracies* (London: Croom Helm, 1986).
17 Due to my father's death, I was unable to deliver the lecture at BISA.
18 Richard Jolly, Louis Emmerij, and Thomas G. Weiss, *UN Ideas That Changed the World* (Bloomington: Indiana University Press, 2009). An earlier effort was Louis Emmerij, Richard Jolly, and Thomas G. Weiss, *Ahead of the Curve? UN Ideas and Global Challenges* (Bloomington: Indiana University Press, 2001). For the other titles produced by this project, see www.unhistory.org.
19 See Thomas G. Weiss and Anthony Jennings, eds., *More for the Least? Prospects for Poorest Countries in the Eighties* (Lexington, Mass.: D.C. Heath, 1983) and *The Challenge of Development in the Eighties: Our Response* (Oxford: Pergamon, 1982); and Thomas G. Weiss, *Multilateral Development Diplomacy in UNCTAD: The Lessons of Group Negotiations, 1964–1984* (London: Macmillan, 1986).
20 Conor Cruise O'Brien, *United Nations: Sacred Drama* (London: Hutchinson & Company, 1968).
21 See Thomas G. Weiss and Robert S. Jordan, "Bureaucratic Politics and the World Food Conference: A Research Note on the International Policy Process," *World Politics* XXVIII,

no. 4 (1976): 422–39; and *The World Food Conference and Global Problem Solving* (New York: Praeger, 1976).

22 Stephen Lewis, *Race against Time* (Toronto: Anansi Press, 2005), 145.

23 Thomas G. Weiss and Sam Daws, eds., *The Oxford Handbook on the United Nations* (Oxford: Oxford University Press, 2007).

24 Kalevi J. Holsti, *Taming the Sovereigns: Institutional Change in International Politics* (Cambridge: Cambridge University Press, 2004), 12–13.

25 Thomas G. Weiss, "The Illusion of UN Security Council Reform," *The Washington Quarterly* 26, no. 4 (2003): 147–61.

26 Thomas G. Weiss and Meryl A. Kessler, "Moscow's U.N. Policy," *Foreign Policy* 79 (Summer 1990): 94–112.

27 Thomas G. Weiss and James G. Blight, eds., *The Suffering Grass: Superpowers and Regional Conflict in Southern Africa and the Caribbean* (Boulder, Colo.: Lynne Rienner, 1992). More accurately titled edited volumes from that same period that also had better sales include Thomas G. Weiss, ed., *Collective Security in a Changing World* (Boulder, Colo.: Lynne Rienner, 1993); Thomas G. Weiss, ed., *The United Nations and Civil Wars* (Boulder, Colo.: Lynne Rienner, 1995); and Thomas G. Weiss and Meryl A. Kessler, eds., *Third World Security in the Post-Cold War Era* (Boulder, Colo.: Lynne Rienner, 1991).

28 John Gerard Ruggie, ed., *Multilateralism Matters: The Theory and Praxis of an Institutional Form* (New York: Columbia University Press, 1993).

29 Charles Krauthammer, "The Unipolar Moment," *Foreign Affairs* 70, no. 1 (1990–91): 23–33.

30 Like all graduate students, I read Edward Hallett Carr, *The Twenty Years' Crisis, 1919–1939* (New York: Harper Torchbooks, 1964); Hans J. Morgenthau, *Politics Among Nations: The Struggle for Power and Peace* (New York: Knopf, 1948); Rienhold Niebuhr, *The Irony of American History* (New York: Scribner, 1952); and Kenneth N. Waltz, *Man, the State, and War* (New York: Columbia University Press, 1954).

31 Thomas G. Weiss and Ramesh Thakur, *Global Governance and the UN: An Unfinished Journey* (Bloomington: Indiana University Press, 2010). Another collaboration was Jane Boulden, Ramesh Thakur, and Thomas G. Weiss, eds., *The United Nations and Nuclear Orders* (Tokyo: UN University Press, 2009).

32 James N. Rosenau and Ernst-Otto Czempiel, eds., *Governance Without Government: Order and Change in World Politics* (Cambridge: Cambridge University Press, 1992).

33 Commission on Global Governance, *Our Global Neighbourhood* (Oxford: Oxford University Press, 1995).

34 These numbers are based on Peter Willetts, "Transnational Actors and International Organizations in Global Politics," in *The Globalization of World Politics*, 4th ed., ed. J. Baylis, S. Smith, and P. Owens (Oxford: Oxford University Press, 2008), 330–47.

35 James N. Rosenau, "Toward an Ontology for Global Governance," in *Approaches to Global Governance Theory*, ed. Martin Hewson and Timothy J. Sinclair (Albany: State University of New York Press, 1999), 293.

36 Inis L. Claude, Jr., *Swords Into Plowshares: The Problems and Prospects of International Organization* (New York: Random House, 1956), and "Peace and Security: Prospective Roles for the Two United Nations," *Global Governance* 2, no. 3 (1996): 289–98.

37 Boutros Boutros-Ghali, "Foreword," in *NGOs, the UN, and Global Governance*, ed. Thomas G. Weiss and Leon Gordenker (Boulder, Colo.: Lynne Rienner, 1996), 7.

38 S. Neil MacFarlane and Thomas G. Weiss, "Regional Organizations and Regional Security," *Security Studies* 2, no. 1 (1992): 6–37.

39 Thomas G. Weiss, ed., *Beyond UN Subcontracting: Task-Sharing with Regional Security Arrangements and Service-Providing NGOs* (London: Macmillan, 1998). This is also a major theme in Joseph S. Lepgold and Thomas G. Weiss, eds., *Collective Conflict Management and Changing World Politics* (Albany: State University of New York Press, 1998).

40 "What Is the International Community?" *Foreign Policy* 132 (September/October 2002): 28–47. See also, Berit Bliesemann de Guevara and Florian P. Kühn, "'The International

Community Needs to Act': Loose Use and Empty Signalling of a Hackneyed Concept," *International Peacekeeping* 18, no. 2 (2011): 135–51.

41 Jarat Chopra and Thomas G. Weiss, "Sovereignty Is No Longer Sacrosanct: Codifying Humanitarian Intervention," *Ethics & International Affairs* 6 (1992): 95–117.

42 Larry Minear et al., *Humanitarianism Under Siege: A Critical Review of Operation Lifeline Sudan* (Trenton, NJ: Red Sea Press, 1991).

43 Thomas G. Weiss, *Humanitarian Intervention: Ideas in Action* (Cambridge: Polity Press, 2007).

44 See Gareth Evans, *The Responsibility to Protect: Ending Mass Atrocity Crimes Once and For All* (Washington, DC: Brookings Institution, 2008); Ramesh Thakur, *The United Nations, Peace and Security: From Collective Security to the Responsibility to Protect* (Cambridge: Cambridge University Press, 2006); and Alex J. Bellamy, *Responsibility to Protect: The Global Effort to End Mass Atrocities* (Cambridge: Polity Press, 2009).

45 The earliest published books on this topic are: Thomas G. Weiss, ed., *Humanitarian Emergencies and Military Help in Africa* (London: Macmillan, 1990); and Leon Gordenker and Thomas G. Weiss, eds., *Soldiers, Peacekeepers and Disasters* (London: Macmillan, 1991).

46 See, for example, a recent special section on "Critical Perspectives on R2P," *Journal of Intervention and Statebuilding* 4, no. 1 (2010): 35–107.

47 Robert J. Rummel, *Death by Government* (New Brunswick, NJ: Transaction Publishers, 1994), chapter 1.

48 International Commission on Intervention and State Sovereignty, *The Responsibility to Protect* (Ottawa: International Development Research Centre, 2001).

49 See Thomas G. Weiss and Don Hubert, *The Responsibility to Protect: Research, Bibliography, Background* (Ottawa: International Development Research Centre, 2001).

50 Gary J. Bass, *Freedom's Battle: The Origins of Humanitarian Intervention* (New York: Knopf, 2008), 382.

51 The phrase is Mary Kaldor's in *New and Old Wars: Organized Violence in a Global Era* (Stanford, Calif.: Stanford University Press, 1999). See also Mark Duffield, *Global Governance and the New Wars: The Merging of Development and Security* (London: Zed, 2001); and Robert Kaplan, "The Coming Anarchy," *Atlantic Monthly* (February 1994): 44–76 and *The Coming Anarchy: Shattering the Dreams of the Post-Cold War* (New York: Random House, 2000).

52 Thomas G. Weiss and Peter J. Hoffman, "The Fog of Humanitarianism: Collective Action Problems and Learning-Challenged Organizations," *Journal of Intervention and State-Building* 1, no. 1 (2007): 47–65.

53 Peter J. Hoffman and Thomas G. Weiss, *Sword & Salve: Confronting New Wars and Humanitarian Crises* (Lanham, Md.: Rowman & Littlefield, 2006).

54 Thomas G. Weiss with David A. Korn, *Internal Displacement: Conceptualization and its Consequences* (London: Routledge, 2006).

55 Michael Barnett and Thomas G. Weiss, eds., *Humanitarianism in Question: Politics, Power, Ethics* (Ithaca, NY: Cornell University Press, 2008); and Thomas G. Weiss and Michael Barnett, *Humanitarianism Contested: Where Angels Fear to Tread* (London: Routledge, 2011).

56 Thomas G. Weiss, *Military-Civilian Interactions: Humanitarian Crises and the Responsibility to Protect*, 2nd ed. (Lanham, Md.: Rowman & Littlefield, 2005, 1st ed. 1999). An earlier examination was Thomas G. Weiss and Cindy Collins, *Humanitarian Challenges and Intervention*, 2nd ed. (Boulder, Colo.: Westview, 2000, 1st ed., 1996).

57 Thomas G. Weiss, "Collective Spinelessness: U.N. Actions in the Former Yugoslavia," in *The World and Yugoslavia's Wars*, ed. Richard H. Ullman (New York: Council on Foreign Relations, 1996), 59–96.

58 A number of books grew from my collaboration with Larry Minear, including: Thomas G. Weiss and Larry Minear, eds., *Humanitarianism Across Borders: Sustaining Civilians in Times of War* (Boulder, Colo.: Lynne Rienner, 1993); Larry Minear and Thomas G. Weiss, *Humanitarian Action in Times of War: A Handbook for Practitioners* (Boulder, Colo.: Lynne Rienner, 1993); Larry Minear and Thomas G. Weiss, *Mercy Under Fire: War and the Global Humanitarian Community* (Boulder, Colo.: Westview, 1995); Larry Minear and Thomas

G. Weiss, eds., *Volunteers Against Conflict* (Tokyo: UN University Press, 1996); Larry Minear, Colin Scott, and Thomas G. Weiss, *The News Media, Civil War, and Humanitarian Action* (Boulder, Colo.: Lynne Rienner, 1996); and Thomas G. Weiss, David Cortright, George A. Lopez, and Larry Minear, eds., *Political Gain and Civilian Pain: Humanitarian Impacts of Economic Sanctions* (Lanham, Md.: Rowman & Littlefield, 1997). From the same period are also Robert Rotberg and Thomas G. Weiss, eds., *From Massacres to Genocide: The Media, Public Policy, and Humanitarian Crises* (Washington, DC: Brookings Institution, 1996); and Pamela Aall, Daniel Miltenberger, and Thomas G. Weiss, *Guide to IGOs, NGOs, and the Military in Peace and Relief Operations* (Washington, DC: U.S. Institute of Peace Press, 2001).

59 Nicholas J. Wheeler, *Saving Strangers: Humanitarian Intervention in International Society* (Oxford: Oxford University Press, 2000).

PART I

The United Nations,
Plus ça change

1

REINVIGORATING THE INTERNATIONAL CIVIL SERVICE

"People matter" is a central conclusion from the United Nations Intellectual History Project and the penultimate sentence of the first of 17 published volumes.[1] Yet critical contributions by individuals who work at the world organization are usually overlooked or downplayed by analysts who stress the politics of 192 member states and the supposedly ironclad constraints placed by them on international secretariats. However, I have devoted considerable professional energy to international administration, both as an analyst and as a civil servant.[2] My proposition is straightforward: the United Nations should rediscover the idealistic roots of the international civil service, make room for creative idea-mongers, and mark out career development paths for a twenty-first century UN Secretariat with greater turnover and younger and more mobile staff. This essay explores the origins of the concept, problems, the logic of reform, and specific improvements. Examples come from the UN's three main areas of activity—peace and security, human rights, and sustainable development.[3]

Overwhelming bureaucracy and underwhelming leadership: the "second UN"

If the conceptual UN is unitary, the real organization consists of three linked pieces. The "second UN" consists of heads of secretariats and staff members who are paid from assessed and voluntary budgets. Inis Claude long ago distinguished it from the arena for state decisionmaking, the "first UN" of member states. The "third UN" of nongovernmental organizations (NGOs), experts, commissions, and academics is a more recent addition to analytical perspectives.[4]

The possibility of independently recruited professionals with allegiance to the welfare of the planet, not to their home countries, remains a lofty but contested objective. During World War II, the Carnegie Endowment for International Peace sponsored conferences to learn from the "great experiment" of the League of Nations.[5] One essential item of its legacy, the international civil service, was purposefully included as UN Charter Article 101, calling for "securing the highest standards of efficiency, competence, and integrity."[6]

The second UN's most visible champion was Dag Hammarskjöld, whose speech at Oxford in May 1961, shortly before his calamitous death, spelled out the importance of an autonomous and first-rate staff. He asserted that any erosion or abandonment of "the international civil service . . . might, if accepted by the Member nations, well prove to be the Munich of international cooperation."[7] His clarion call did not ignore the reality that the international civil service exists to carry out decisions by member states. But Hammarskjöld fervently believed that UN officials could and should pledge allegiance to a larger collective good symbolized by the organization's light-blue-covered *laissez-passer* rather than the narrowly perceived national interests of the countries that issue national passports in different colors.

Setting aside senior UN positions for officials approved by their home countries belies that integrity. Governments seek to ensure that their interests are defended inside secretariats, and many have even relied on officials for intelligence. From the outset, for example, the Security Council's five permanent members have reserved the right to "nominate" (essentially select) nationals to fill the key posts in the Secretary-General's cabinet. The influx in the 1950s and 1960s of former colonies as new member states led them to clamor for "their" quota or fair share of the patronage opportunities, following the bad example set by major powers and other member states. The result was downplaying competence and exaggerating national origins as the main criterion for recruitment and promotion. Over the years, efforts to improve gender balance have resulted in other types of claims, as has the age profile of secretariats. Virtually all positions above the director level, and often many below as well, are the object of campaigns by governments, including the already rewarded permanent members of the Security Council.

How many people are in today's second UN? Professional and support staff number approximately 55,000 in the UN proper and in agencies created by the General Assembly, and 20,000 in the specialized agencies. This number includes neither temporary staff in peace operations (about 120,000 in 2008) nor the staff of the International Monetary Fund (IMF) and the World Bank group (another 15,000). These figures represent substantial growth from the approximately 500 employees in the UN's first year at Lake Success and the peak total of 700 staff employed by the League of Nations.[8]

I emphasize neglected personnel issues because individuals matter, for good and for ill. The second UN does more than simply carry out marching orders from governments. I thus disagree with three analysts who dismiss "the curious notion that the United Nations is an autonomous actor in world affairs that can and does take action independent of the will and wishes of the member governments."[9] This obviously is a truism for resolutions, but there is considerably more room for creativity and initiative in numerous activities than is commonly believed.

UN officials present ideas to tackle problems, debate them formally and informally with governments, take initiatives, advocate for change, turn general decisions into specific programs, and implement them. They monitor progress and report to national officials and politicians gathering at intergovernmental conferences and in countries in which the UN is operating.

None of this should surprise. It would be a strange and impotent national civil service that took no initiatives or showed no leadership, simply awaiting detailed instructions from the government in power. UN officials are no different except that formal decision makers are government representatives in boards meeting quarterly, annually, or even once every two years. With the exception of the Security Council, decision making and responsibility for implementation in most parts of the UN system, especially the development funds and specialized agencies, depend in large part on staff members as well as executive heads.

Problems in the international civil service

The composition, recruitment, promotion, and retention—and ultimately the disappointing performance—of international civil servants are a substantial part of what ails the world organization. Though writers like Brian Urquhart properly have long called for a dramatic change in the selection process for the Secretary-General and other senior positions,[10] the problems go much deeper. Moreover, the quality and impact of the staff are variables that can be altered far more easily, swiftly, and cheaply than such problems as state sovereignty, counterproductive North-South theater, and extreme decentralization that plague the organization. Examples from the main areas of UN activities highlight what is wrong and needs to be fixed.

International peace and security: the Oil-for-Food scandal and gender imbalance

The maintenance of international peace and security was the main justification for the UN's establishment. Many persons have served the world organization with distinction and heroism since 1945, including Sergio Vieira de Mello and 21other colleagues who lost their lives in Baghdad in August 2003, and the 17 UN staff who were killed in Algiers in December 2007. Like the 1961 death of Dag Hammarskjöld in a plane crash in the Congo, these high visibility sacrifices should not overshadow the less dramatic deaths of some 300 other civilian staff members[11] and almost 2,600 soldiers in UN service.[12] The award of the Nobel Peace Prize to UN peacekeepers in 1987 and to Kofi Annan and the Secretariat in 2001 reflects this reality.

Valor should not, however, blind us to such serious problems as those encountered in administering the Oil-for-Food Programme (OFFP) and in attempting to improve gender balance. The OFFP scandal was undoubtedly overblown and specifically linked to American domestic politics. Member states were responsible for quietly approving the bulk of the monies that found their way into Saddam Hussein's coffers and conveniently overlooked leakage to such key US allies as Jordan and Turkey. Nonetheless, the sloppy general management of this politically visible and crucial assignment tarnished the organization's reputation.

The OFFP was established in 1995 to allow Iraq to sell oil and purchase humanitarian relief items—primarily food and medicine—for ordinary Iraqis who were suffering the devastating effects of sanctions imposed by the Security Council after Iraq's 1990 invasion of Kuwait. The OFFP was regularly criticized as corrupt and inefficient for failing to address the basic needs of Iraqis while lining the pockets of officials. In 2004 the secretary-general finally appointed an Independent Inquiry Committee headed by the former chairman of the US Federal Reserve, Paul Volcker. The 2005 report pointed to the "ethically improper" conduct of the program's executive director and allegations about misconduct on the part of Kofi Annan's son Kojo. Subsequent dismissals of staff and criminal proceedings have resulted.

The main disconcerting details, however, related to an inattentive management system that was outmoded, inept, and quite out of its depth in administering a program of that size and complexity. While evolving from a forum for global policy discussions to leading substantial military and civilian operations worldwide (with costs four times larger than the core budget), advances in communications technology and modern management techniques had seemingly bypassed the Secretariat. Neither the people who had been hired to do the work nor the oversight systems in place were up to the job.

After years of hesitation by the General Assembly, Annan named the first deputy secretary-general in 1997. Rather than an all-purpose stand-in for the Secretary-General, this deputy should have a distinctly different job description. He or she should be an authorized chief operating officer for the organization. In this way, the management buck would stop short of the Secretary-General, who should remain the UN's chief politician, diplomat, and mediator. The Volcker team proposed that the deputy, like the Secretary-General, be nominated by the Security Council. Such a formality would require amending the UN Charter, but the objective could and should be accommodated by having the Security Council vet and informally approve a nominee.

The preface to the Volcker report could have been written by a Beltway neocon or perhaps US president Barack Obama: "The inescapable conclusion from the Committee's work is that the United Nations Organization needs thoroughgoing reform—and it needs it urgently."[13] Volcker continued: "Willing cooperation and a sense of legitimacy cannot be sustained without a strong sense that the Organization has both competence and integrity. It is precisely those qualities that have been called into question."[14] Such problems are not unusual but endemic; and "urgent" in UN parlance has a different meaning from any dictionary, since no significant change has followed.

One might have expected the UN to lead in integrating women into work compared with other institutions. The pace has been glacial. In her February 1946

"Open Letter to the Women of the World," Eleanor Roosevelt as first chair of the Commission on Human Rights made a direct appeal to bring women into peace efforts. Some three decades later, at the first UN-sponsored world conference on women in 1975 in Mexico City, governments signed the Declaration of Mexico, which proclaimed: "Women must participate equally with men in the decision-making processes which help to promote peace at all levels."[15] That same year, General Assembly resolution 3519 called upon women to participate in strengthening international peace and security.

However, the exclusion of women from the trenches and the bureaucracy continues at the beginning of the twenty-first century. As of April 2009, participation by women in UN peace operations was a paltry 2.7 percent.[16] Statistics about women elsewhere in the world organization also are disappointing. The representation of women in the professional and higher categories in the UN system is just over one-third. Only at the entry—P-1 and P-2—professional levels has gender balance been achieved. In the higher categories—D-1 and above—women only account for about a quarter of UN staff.[17] Moreover, in an arena with much flexibility—the appointment of special representatives of the secretary-general (SRSGs)—the results are remarkably poor.[18] As then US ambassador Swanee Hunt bluntly summarized on the world organization's sixtieth anniversary, "Two female SRSGs and one female Deputy SRSG in 26 peacekeeping missions is indefensible; a list of dozens of qualified women has sat on the Secretary General's desk for years."[19]

Human rights: individual courage and institutional cowardice

It seems justified to hold the international civil service to the highest standards of consistency because the UN has played an essential role in establishing human rights norms. The standard bearer should lead in implementing the standards set for others.

Following widespread allegations of sexual abuse and misconduct—including trading money and food for sex and engaging in sex with minors—on the part of UN troops in the Democratic Republic of the Congo in early 2005, the UN instituted systemwide reforms. When similar allegations surfaced later that same year in Burundi, Haiti, and Liberia, the UN was forced to acknowledge widespread abuse after downplaying problems. There is no UN discipline for troops because the command and control of UN troops are almost entirely in the hands of national commanders; and so reports of sexual misconduct by peacekeepers regularly continue to surface in spite of the "zero tolerance" policy adopted by Secretary-General Annan in 2006 and a UN-wide strategy to eradicate sexual abuse and exploitation agreed upon by UN and NGO personnel following the High-level Conference on Eliminating Sexual Exploitation and Abuse.

Moreover, two cases of unacceptable administrative reactions indicate a related lack of vigilance and appropriate support for staff from the UN's highest levels when visible senior personnel are caught in a vortex of sovereignty and human rights.

Perhaps the most searing example was when the force commander of the UN Assistance Mission for Rwanda, Roméo Dallaire, made repeated requests for assistance and authorization to try, even symbolically, to halt the fast-paced genocide. His *Shake Hands with the Devil* recounts how his pleas to the UN Department of Peacekeeping Operations (DPKO) for more combat troops and logistical support were denied before the April 1994 genocide.[20] Arguing that a force of 5,000 could have prevented the genocide—probably an overly optimistic assessment[21]—Dallaire's experience illustrates how the lack of leadership among those in key positions thwarted decisive personnel action.

The calls by the UN special representative to Sudan, Jan Pronk, for help to halt the slow-motion genocide in Darfur met with similar silence from New York in 2004–6. Governments and the Security Council were dragging their feet then as now, but should we not have expected outrage from UN headquarters when Khartoum expelled Pronk as *persona non grata* in late 2006? He had unflinchingly reported on the violence against civilians throughout his tenure and thus was accused of displaying "enmity to the Sudanese government and the armed forces" on his personal blog. Yet Annan recalled Pronk ahead of an expulsion deadline.[22] Failing to support him suggests an overly sensitive ear to the wishes of a sovereign state rather than to a special representative trying to hold the government in Khartoum responsible for its reprehensible violations of human rights subsequently highlighted by the International Criminal Court's March 2009 arrest warrant for President Omar Hassan al-Bashir.

All bureaucracies have their ups and downs, and the previous examples do not imply that there have not been numerous instances of outstanding behavior by UN officials. But the weight of the shackles of political correctness is a peculiar feature of the UN human rights machinery. What governments—be they major or minor powers—consider acceptable too often determines official policy. Such subservience reflects the outmoded concept of sovereignty without responsibility and builds a substantial structural flaw into the international civil service.

Sustainable development: politics trumps competence

The UN's reputation and performance in economic and social development are continually degraded when political machinations take precedence over competence. For instance, Ban Ki-moon selected Sha Zukang, a career Chinese diplomat who started as a translator and had virtually no exposure to development thinking and practice, as under-secretary-general to head the UN's Department of Economic and Social Affairs.

This was not an atypical appointment by the current secretary-general—his deputy's main asset is that she is a Tanzanian Muslim woman, and the main assets of the under-secretaries-general for political and humanitarian affairs were their closeness to George W. Bush and Tony Blair, respectively. Two of the most painful historical cases within the field of sustainable development concern the egregious incompetence of the director-general of the UN Educational, Scientific and

Cultural Organization (UNESCO) from 1974 to 1987, Amadou Mahtar M'Bow, and the director-general of the Food and Agriculture Organization (FAO) from 1976 to 1993, Edouard Saouma. Some institutions are headed always by a national of the same country—for instance, the World Bank by a US citizen, and the IMF by a European—whereas others have positions that are rotated among regions, including the UN Secretary-General. In M'Bow's and Saouma's cases, their elections were both because it was "Africa's and the Middle East's turn" at the helm of these organizations.

The result can be read in UNESCO's and FAO's decreased prominence in promoting development. During the period that M'Bow led UNESCO, rampant mismanagement resulted in continual budget deficits. His anti-Western bent—especially hostility toward a free press as called for in the New International Information Order—led the United States to withdraw in 1984, followed by the United Kingdom and Singapore in 1985. The withdrawals resulted in a major loss of funding for the organization, and many member countries breathed a sigh of relief when M'Bow announced that he would retire as director-general in 1987. Similarly, Saouma was lambasted by many, including the much-publicized criticism by Graham Hancock in *Lords of Poverty*. His corrupt and autocratic management practices, as well as his rigid control of public information during his 17-year tenure as FAO director-general, became an embarrassment.[23]

Again, while not gainsaying sterling contributions to development by such intellectual stalwarts as Raúl Prebisch and Helvi Sipilä, and operational ones as Jim Grant and Sadako Ogata, the selection criterion for senior appointments increasingly has become nationality, sometimes mixed with gender, rather than a demonstrated experience to do the job. Nationalistic politics and patronage thus get in the way of selecting personnel and ultimately of optimum performance and impact. Students of international relations and organization can hardly expect appointments to be "above politics." However, when purely political considerations so clearly trump competence and autonomy regarding the appointment of senior and more junior personnel, both member states and "We the peoples" suffer.

The logic of reinvigorating the second UN

The world organization's main expenditures (usually around 90 percent) are for its employees. These individuals are the UN's main strength and can be redirected and reinvigorated. The most essential and doable challenge for Ban Ki-moon and his successor is changing the way that the second UN and its chief executive do business, to go beyond the formulaic plea in the *World Summit Outcome Document* "to enhance the effective management of the United Nations."[24] Whereas Susan Strange and Robert Cox would argue that views from inside can only be orthodox and sustain the status quo,[25] I have a different view. The international civil service, properly constituted, can make a difference—not only in field operations but also in research and policy formulation.[26] Indeed, autonomous officials can and should provide essential inputs into UN discussions, activities, advocacy, and monitoring.

Significant change and not abolition is required. James O.C. Jonah, an international civil servant for over three decades, including a stint as head of personnel, tells us:

> It is a common practice of politicians to blame the civil service for their failures and inadequacies. More often than not, their citizens join them in complaining about the evils and sloppiness of bloated bureaucracies. The UN Secretariat is not immune to such criticisms, and over the years all and sundry have decried its waste and ineffectiveness. Despite these complaints about perceived defects, it would be inconceivable for member states to contemplate the dismantling of the Secretariat or parts of it. Surely, they would not abolish their own civil services despite their dissatisfaction?[27]

Knowing when to ignore standard bureaucratic operating procedures and to make waves is an essential part of effective leadership that can break down the UN system's bureaucratic barriers. For instance, former US congressman and later UN Development Programme (UNDP) administrator Bradford Morse and Canadian businessman Maurice Strong broke the rules of the feudal system when they headed the temporary Office for Emergency Operations in Africa in the mid-1970s. Their own experience, reputations, and independence permitted them to override standard operating procedures just as Sir Robert Jackson had done on numerous occasions. He applied the military skills and hierarchy that he used for defending Malta and with the Middle East Supply Centre during World War II to the United Nations Relief and Rehabilitation Administration in postwar Europe, parts of Africa, and the Far East—what may have been the biggest UN relief operation ever—and then in the Bangladesh emergency in 1971.[28]

The High-level Panel on Threats, Challenges and Change as well as the secretary-general proposed and the World Summit agreed to consider a onetime buyout to cut deadwood from the permanent staff.[29] No useful follow-up has resulted. Moreover, this long-standing proposal probably would not improve matters—enterprising and competent staff could take a payment and seek alternative employment while the real deadwood would remain. The more pertinent challenge is how to gather *new* wood for the Secretariat and ensure that the best and brightest are hired and promoted and then move to other international jobs.

Recruitment should return to the idealistic origins in the League of Nations and early UN secretariats. Competence should be the highest consideration rather than geographical origins—the primary justification for cronyism and patronage. Quotas, if they continue to exist, should reflect regions, not countries. In a globalizing world, origins as well as current nationality are relevant. Moreover, the onus should be put on governments to nominate only their most professionally qualified and experienced candidates—not just someone with contacts who fancies life in New York or Paris. And in contrast to the take-it-or-leave-it approach of the posts "reserved" for particular nationalities, several candidates should be nominated with the final selection by UN administrators.

It is possible to balance quality, independence, and representation. Special recruitment efforts can be focused on underrepresented nationalities, including the expanded use of standardized and competitive examinations for new entrants, without compromising overall quality. As with efforts to achieve better gender balance, priority can be given to nationals of underrepresented regions by casting the net widely enough to draw fully qualified candidates from those backgrounds but without resorting to cronyism. It is a fallacy that quality must suffer while moving toward more diversity. The real requirement is to limit outside influence and the pressures for patronage—which come from donors, friends, and family members of candidates from developed and Third World countries alike.

The beginning of a term for a Secretary-General is often a good moment for shaking up the second UN. Kofi Annan instituted significant managerial and technical improvements shortly after assuming the mantle in 1997 and again at the beginning of his second term in 2002—just as Boutros Boutros-Ghali had in 1992. Ban Ki-moon made no such visible effort to jump-start his administration. The next Secretary-General should make reinvigorating the international civil service a signature of her or his administration.

The clash between South and North at the end of Annan's term made it impossible to consider sensible proposals to place more authority over budgetary and personnel matters in the Secretary-General's hands. A relatively small number of countries in the global South are reluctant to move power away from the General Assembly, where by virtue of their numbers they call the shots. If more discretionary authority over personnel and power of the purse were placed in the UN administration, so the argument goes, it would be more subject to Western (and especially US) influence. The UK's minister with a portfolio for UN affairs, Mark Malloch Brown, noted with some puzzlement, "Taking a demotion to come over from UNDP to be Kofi Annan's chief of staff was a much bigger step down than I anticipated. . . . I found when it came to management and budgetary matters, he was less influential than I had been."[30]

Increased discretionary authority over budget and personnel decisions for the Secretary-General would be in the interests of developing countries whose populations and governments benefit most from UN operations. If the United Nations is to meet new and old challenges and be accountable, additional authority and responsibility at the top is required.

Specific improvements for the second UN

The residue from the Volcker Commission and sexual scandals are still very much with us, and there has been no implementation of *Investing in the United Nations*, the 2006 comprehensive report about personnel from the by-then lame-duck secretary-general, Kofi Annan. Sensible suggestions, like those in numerous other reports, remain in filing cabinets. It would be useful to explore experiments that worked and might be applied more generally to improve the second UN.

International peace and security: disciplining peacekeepers and resolution 1325

The problems discussed earlier—disciplining soldiers and better representation of women in peace operations—illustrate how slow change can be even after decisions are made. In response to allegations that emerged in 2004 of sexual misconduct among peacekeepers in the Democratic Republic of the Congo, the secretary-general invited Prince Zeid Ra'ad Zeid al-Hussein, then permanent representative of Jordan to the United Nations and currently its ambassador to Washington, to act as his "advisor on sexual exploitation and abuse by UN peacekeeping personnel." His hard-hitting 2005 report made a number of recommendations, including standard rules about sexual exploitation and abuse to apply to all peacekeeping personnel and the establishment of a professional investigative process to examine alleged abuses.[31]

The General Assembly adopted a "comprehensive strategy." The DPKO established conduct and discipline units to prevent, track, and punish gender-based crimes. The DPKO Conduct and Discipline Unit in 2006 joined with the Office for the Coordination of Humanitarian Affairs, UNICEF, and the UNDP to host a high-level conference. As a result, the "Statement of Commitment on Eliminating Sexual Exploitation and Abuse by UN and non-UN Personnel" contains ten commitments to "facilitate rapid implementation of existing UN and non-UN standards relating to sexual exploitation and abuse."[32]

The dominant national command and control structures within UN operations impose limits for international accountability. Usually, the worst that happens is for the soldiers in question to be sent home. Given the symbolic and actual importance of peace operations—in 2009, approximately 100,000 soldiers and 20,000 police and civilians, costing some $8 billion—tougher measures would be essential steps toward professionalism. UN accountability and punishment for individuals, rather than the "boys will be boys" attitude, certainly would enhance the UN's reputation and performance.

The world organization continues to struggle with underrepresentation of women at senior levels of the organization. In 2000, building on the momentum of the Millennium Declaration, the Fourth World Conference on Women held in Beijing in 1995, and the 1997 creation of the Office of the Special Advisor on Gender Issues and Advancement of Women, the Security Council approved resolution 1325. This marked a symbolic turning point in the UN's commitment to gender mainstreaming and addressing the impact of war on women as well as to appointing more women at all levels. A 2006 assessment of the resolution's implementation noted, however, that women remained underrepresented in senior positions at the UN, with still only one female special representative and one envoy.[33]

Ironically, certain member countries have done better and made conscious and public gestures to appoint women to decisionmaking positions in government. Liberia, led by Ellen Johnson-Sirleaf—the first democratically elected female head of state in Africa and a former international civil servant—has appointed women ministers of defense, finance, sports and youth, justice, and commerce, as well as chief of police and president of the Liberian Truth and Reconciliation Commission. The United Nations should follow her lead.

Human rights: "outside-insiders," rotation, and contracts

Using more outsiders, insisting on field rotation, and issuing fewer permanent contracts are desirable and plausible measures to improve the quality of personnel working on human rights and other issues as well. A considerable constraint on UN leadership is the status of full-time employees of the international civil service because member states are bound to be offended by human rights advocacy. With their jobs and family security on the line, officials often avoid not only robust public confrontation but also even one of a more gentle variety. Self-censorship is rife. Making no waves is usually a key to a successful career.

One possible solution is based on work by the senior official working on internally displaced persons, someone with a UN title and privileges but based outside without a salary.[34] Francis Deng's mandate (1992–2004) as the representative of the secretary-general was intertwined with the Project on Internal Displacement (PID) directed by him and Roberta Cohen at the Brookings Institution—and a similar arrangement has continued with Walter Kälin after 2004. The conceptualization of internal displacement was a notable contribution to contemporary thinking about international relations, in particular by reframing state sovereignty as responsibility. In addition, *Guidelines on Internal Displacement*, an important piece of soft law, was agreed; and UN institutions and NGOs established special programs for this ignored category of war victim.

Deng had a foot in two camps—taking advantage of being within the intergovernmental system of the United Nations *and* outside it. He made good use of having both official *and* private platforms. Richard Haass summed up the advantages of such an arrangement: "Many of us spend a lot of time figuring out how to get ideas into policy-makers' hands, but Francis had a readymade solution."[35] At the same time, PID's base at a public policy think tank working in tandem with universities provided a respectable distance from governments and from predictable multilateral diplomatic pressure, processes, and procedures. Moreover, a wide range of private and public donors expect the project's activities to extend the outer limits of what passes for conventional wisdom in mainstream diplomatic circles.

Although being on the "outside" has disadvantages—no guaranteed budget or access being among them—the role of outside-insider or inside-outsider offers advantages that should be replicated for other controversial issues when independent research is required, institutional protective barriers are high, normative gaps exist, and political hostility is widespread. More part-time senior officials pushing from independent bases outside the United Nations would strengthen policy formulation processes within the UN system, where a rule-breaking culture is in short supply.

Many students encounter the world organization through a tour at or pictures of headquarters in New York or Geneva or of specialized agencies like UNESCO in Paris or FAO in Rome. But the bulk of the UN's operations are in developing countries. A problem for staff morale and competence over the years has been that promotions are mainly the result of work and networks in pleasant headquarters settings, whereas the real challenges lie with delivery of services in the field. And the world organization is increasingly called upon to react to major crises by sending staff quickly to emergencies.

However, rewarding better fieldwork and applying a flexible personnel policy to meet the unforeseen, but expectable, demands of new crises poses real but not insurmountable challenges. In 1982, the Office of the UN High Commissioner for Refugees implemented the first formal rotation policy in order to promote burden-sharing among staff members and to ensure that all share in the postings to hardship duty stations where families are not permitted. All international professional staff are subject to rotation, a practice that the Joint Inspection Unit has cited as a model.[36] UNICEF and the UNDP also now have mandatory mobility and staff rotation policies; and similar ones should be a requirement across the UN system.

The mandatory rotation policy creates a sense of equity among staff members and ensures that they are exposed to field problems and acquire the management skills necessary in future emergencies. The secretary-general's 2006 *Investing in the United Nations* identified promotion and mobility among staff as key strategies. He also proposed that the majority of international professional posts be designated as rotational and that staff mobility between headquarters and the field be implemented as a matter of priority, describing this wrenching effort as "a radical overhaul of the United Nations Secretariat—its rules, its structure, and its systems and culture."[37] Indeed.

The League of Nations instituted permanent contracts, a practice continued by the United Nations, in order to protect staff from government pressure and arbitrary dismissal. Permanent contracts have the same justification as university tenure, and both have critics who argue that removing the possibility of being fired can also lead to coasting. There remains a widespread perception that such contractual arrangements do not stimulate but rather retard productivity because they impede hiring or retaining risk takers.

During Kofi Annan's decade at the helm, permanent contracts were increasingly phased out. Three types of contracts replaced them: short-term, up to a maximum of six months to meet specific short-term requirements; fixed-term, renewable up to a maximum of five years; and continuing, to be granted to staff who have completed a fixed-term contract and met the highest standards of efficiency, competence, and integrity.[38]

Though organizational memory may be enhanced by veteran officials, the number of persons with "continuing" contracts (basically the equivalent of "permanent") should be kept to a minimum. Currently about 13 percent,[39] they should be even fewer and reserved for a very limited number of administrators and avoided for substantive jobs, especially within controversial areas. Within the human rights field, in particular, an argument could be made that virtually no one should have a long-term contract. If a staff member, especially a senior one, was doing a job correctly, many member states would likely be irritated and ask for his or her head. Indeed, human rights officials with fixed assignments would provide an incentive to use public shaming to maximum effect and make a reputation in order to secure future employment in a government or an NGO.

There are more than enough qualified persons worldwide to fill UN posts for fixed periods. The possible loss of bureaucratic memory created by turnover would be outweighed by the benefits of attracting more idealistic and motivated personnel. Moreover, if mistakes are made in selection, as always is the case in any organization, the damage would be limited to five years. Of especial relevance is the guaranteed influx of younger and hungry staff anxious to make their mark and as a first step in a career in international affairs, rather than seeking the guaranteed benefits of a life-long UN position.

Sustainable development: ideas and the next generation

The bulk of the UN system's staff and resources are devoted to activities to foster sustainable development. Whether one believes glasses to be half full or half empty, the world body's efforts have contributed to genuine advances in human welfare since 1945, and there are ways to ensure that the liquid level rises. Two possible solutions suggest themselves for what ails the second UN that are drawn from this arena: better ideas and younger staff.

Ideas matter, for good and for ill; and so it is instructive to recall John Maynard Keynes's aphorism about so-called practical men and women who have no time to read but often are acting on the basis of theories from dead "scribblers" like the readers of this journal. He wrote that "the ideas of economists and political philosophers, both when they are right and when they are wrong, are more powerful than is commonly understood."[40]

Powerful minds are essential to the UN's performance. Intellectual contributions by such sharp minds as Hans Singer and W. Arthur Lewis (and eight other Nobel laureates in economics) are part of the world organization's history, to which can be added the more recent *Human Development Report*. Since 1990 this UNDP-subsidized report has put forth an annual unorthodox view of people-centered development. Participation, empowerment, equity, and justice are placed on an equal footing with the market and growth.

Mahbub ul Haq, the Pakistani UN economist whose vision animated the *Human Development Report*, died in 1998, but his approach continues.[41] A powerful tool consisting of three composite indicators for ranking countries for their performance on the Human Development Index remains: longevity, educational attainment, and access to a decent standard of living. In 2008, Iceland was number one, the United States was in fifteenth place, and the Central African Republic and Sierra Leone brought up the rear.

As might be imagined, calling a spade a shovel in numerical terms does not always make fans among governments that rank less well than they thought they should. As an outsider becoming a UN insider who insisted upon autonomy, ul Haq and others associated with the effort have taken political flak as well as resisted pressure from governments irritated with embarrassing publicity. Some resent that poorer neighbors get higher ratings because they make sensible decisions about priorities —for example, devoting limited resources to education and health instead of weapons. Some UNDP staff members, including its administrator William Draper, were keen on the approach, but the technical details were the work of minds of the quintessential outsider aided by scholars. Indeed, many governments disputed the appropriateness of Draper's approach using their financial contributions to commission research that produced embarrassing comparative data. Some rudely grumbled about "biting the hand that feeds." In spite of repeated pressures to halt it or tone it down, the UNDP has continued to subsidize and guarantee the independence of the team's work.

At all levels of the world organization, persons capable of such intellectual leadership should be on hand. And this is far more likely to come from the minds of fixed-term officials, specialized consultants, and academics on leave rather than permanent civil servants whose careers are dependent on reactions from superiors and governments, and who may not stay abreast of the literature. It should be possible to arrange for regular exchanges with university and think-tank personnel around the world, which would benefit secretariats while outsiders are in residence, and also benefit the research agendas of analysts once they return. In short, it is necessary to strengthen the institutional capacity to generate and disseminate original ideas, to fortify mechanisms that ensure creative thinking.

In the myriad of proposals for UN reform over the years, none has stressed the vital intellectual dimensions and reasons to invest in analytical capabilities. Honest evaluations are prerequisites for planning better, developing measurements of performance, and holding personnel accountable. The critical ingredient is up-to-date and well-grounded analysis. And producing, refining, and disseminating digestible research better prepares the United Nations for challenges, known and unknown.

Specific measures to strengthen this aspect of the second UN are not pie-in-the-sky aspirations. "Track II" reforms do not require constitutional changes or even additional resources but vision and courage by the Secretary-General and other heads of agencies. Two come to mind. First, all parts of the UN system should acknowledge that contributions to ideas, thinking, analysis, and monitoring in their areas of expertise should be a major emphasis of their work. An environment that encourages and rewards creative thinking along with first-rate staff is essential; and no compromise can be justified in ensuring the highest standards of competence and professional qualifications. Second, the mobilization of more financial support for research, analysis, and policy exploration should be a top priority. Not only are longer-term availability and flexibility necessary, but donors also should attach no strings in order to guarantee autonomy.

It is essential to attract young qualified staff. A 2000 report by the Joint Inspection Unit, for instance, identified the need to address "work-life" or "work-family" issues.[42] The UNDP in the 1960s launched the Junior Professional Officer (JPO) program, which provides some 13 percent of the UNDP's international staff.[43] JPOs are selected and sponsored (i.e., fully funded) by their governments to work for a fixed period of time—usually two to three years. The program has become the key entry point for an international career and has been adopted by numerous other UN agencies, including UNICEF, the UNHCR, and the World Food Programme. Other agencies have adopted similar programs under different titles —e.g., the International Monetary Fund's Economist Program and the Asia Development Bank's Young Professional Program.

There are no silver bullets—indeed, some observers criticize JPO programs as jump-starts for the careers of nationals from wealthy countries. Shortcomings could be overcome, and in some cases have been, by funding individuals from developing countries. Essential, however, is finding the means to lower the average age at the professional entry level (currently 37) and the average age of the Secretariat as a whole (currently 46) over the next five years when at least 15 percent of the staff reach retirement age.

Adlai Stevenson once joked that work at the United Nations involves "protocol, Geritol and alcohol."[44] Little can be done to reduce diplomatic procedures and the consumption of fermented beverages, but sclerosis in the Secretariat guarantees mediocrity. And the world organization should find ways to infuse continually new blood.

Conclusion: the way forward

The international civil service is not the UN's most virulent illness—the myopia of Westphalian member states wins that award—but the crucial health of the second UN could and should be improved. Luckily, the world organization's residual legitimacy and the ideal of international cooperation keep a surprisingly large number of competent people committed to its work. The likes of Kofi Annan and Margaret Joan Anstee indicate that autonomy and integrity are not unrealistic expectations of international civil servants who are recruited as junior officials without government approval and have distinguished careers. The fact that both Ralph Bunche and Brian Urquhart joined the Secretariat originally on loan from national government service also suggests that government clearance need not entail subservience to national perspectives.[45] The potential is far from realized.

In a series of follow-up reports for *Investing in the United Nations*, Kofi Annan lamented the "silos" that characterize staff appointments and promotions and spelled out his back-to-the-future "vision of an independent international civil service with the highest standards of performance and accountability. The Secretariat of the future will be an integrated, field-oriented, operational organization."[46] The so-called Four Nations (Chile, South Africa, Sweden, and Thailand) Initiative (4NI) sought to come up with consensus proposals for improved governance and management of the Secretariat. Though it originally did not have human resources on the agenda, that subject necessarily "came to the fore" during conversations with other member states. Predictably, the 4NI expressed concern with "geographical representation," but the main thrust of its 2007 recommendations pointed to "merit-based" recruitment and the use of "expert hearings" for the most senior positions that "should not be monopolized by nationals of any state or group of states."[47]

The stereotype of a bloated and lumbering administration overlooks many talented and dedicated individuals; but the composition, recruitment, promotion, and retention policies certainly constitute a fundamental but fixable part of what ails the world body. Successes usually reflect personalities and serendipity rather than conscious recruitment of the best persons for the right reasons and institutional structures designed to foster collaboration and maximize output. Staff costs account for the lion's share of the UN's budget. People are not only the principal cost item but also represent a potential resource whose composition, productivity, and culture could change, and change quickly. It is time to reinvigorate the international civil service.

Notes

1 Louis Emmerij, Richard Jolly, and Thomas G. Weiss, *Ahead of the Curve? UN Ideas and Global Challenges* (Bloomington: Indiana University Press, 2001), 214. The capstone volume is Richard Jolly, Louis Emmerij, and Thomas G.Weiss, *UN Ideas That Changed the World* (Bloomington: Indiana University Press, 2009). Other details are available at www.unhistory.org.

2 This ACUNS swan song revisits my first book and doctoral dissertation (done under the supervision of my dear friend and mentor Leon Gordenker) along with one of my most recent books, on which this article draws—*What's Wrong with the United Nations and How to Fix It* (Malden, Mass.: Polity, 2009). See also *International Bureaucracy: An Analysis of the Operation of Functional and Global International Secretariats* (Lexington, Mass.: D.C. Heath, 1975).

3 These pillars provide the framework for the UN textbook by Thomas G. Weiss, David P. Forsythe, Roger A. Coate, and Kelly-Kate Pease, *The United Nations and Changing World Politics*, 6th ed. (Boulder, Colo. Westview, 2010).

4 Inis L. Claude Jr., *Swords Into Plowshares: The Problems and Prospects of International Organization* (New York: Random House, 1956); and "Peace and Security: Prospective Roles for the Two United Nations," *Global Governance* 2, no. 3 (1996): 289–98. See also Thomas G. Weiss, Tatiana Carayannis, and Richard Jolly, "The 'Third' United Nations," *Global Governance* 15, no. 1 (2009): 123–42.

5 Egon Ranshofen-Wertheimer, *The International Secretariat: A Great Experiment in International Administration* (Washington, DC: Carnegie Endowment for International Peace, 1945).

6 See, for example, Leon Gordenker, *The UN Secretary-General and Secretariat*, 2nd ed. (London: Routledge, 2010).

7 Dag Hammarskjöld, "The International Civil Servant in Law and in Fact," lecture delivered to Congregation at Oxford University, 30 May 1961, reprinted by Clarendon Press, Oxford, quotes at 329 and 349. Available at www.un.org/depts/dhl/dag/docs/internationalcivilservant.pdf.

8 Thant Myint-U and Amy Scott, *The UN Secretariat: A Brief History (1945–2006)* (New York: International Peace Academy, 2007), 126–8.

9 Donald J. Puchala, Katie Verlin Laatikainen, and Roger A. Coate, *United Nations Politics: International Organization in a Divided World* (Upper Saddle River, NJ: Prentice Hall, 2007), x.

10 See, for example, Brian Urquhart and Erskine Childers, *A World in Need of Leadership: Tomorrow's United Nations* (Uppsala, Sweden: Dag Hammarskjöld Foundation, 1990).

11 An astounding 291 UN civilian staff members have died as a result of malicious acts in the period since reporting began in 1992 through July 2008: *Safety and Security of Humanitarian Personnel and Protection of UN Personnel*, Report of the Secretary-General, UN doc. A/63/305, 18 August 2008.

12 Fatalities of 2,591 resulted from 1948 through 31 May 2009 as compiled by the UN Department of Peacekeeping Operations, available at www.un.org/en/peacekeeping/fatalities.

13 Paul A. Volcker, Richard J. Goldstone, and Mark Pieth, *The Management of the Oil-for-Food Programme*, vol. 1, 7 (September 2005), 4–5, available at www.iic-offp.org.

14 Paul A. Volcker, "Introduction," in a summary version of the principal findings done by two staff members, Jeffrey A. Meyer and Mark G. Califano, *Good Intentions Corrupted: The Oil-for-Food Scandal and the Threat to the UN* (New York: Public Affairs, 2006), xii, x.

15 Quoted by Devaki Jain, *Women, Development, and the UN: A Sixty-year Quest for Equality and Justice* (Bloomington: Indiana University Press, 2005), 72.

16 There were 2,474 women out of a total 92,655 peacekeepers worldwide. See DPKO, "Gender Statistics by Mission," 30 April 2009, available at www.un.org/Depts/dpko/dpko/contributors/gender/2009gender/apr09.pdf.

17 Office of the Special Adviser to the Secretary-General on Gender Issues and Advancement of Women, "The Status of Women in the United Nations System and in the Secretariat," October 2008, available at www.un.org/womenwatch/osagi/wps/factsheet%206%20oct%2008.pdf.

18 "Special and Personal Representatives and Envoys of the Secretary-General," Department of Peacekeeping Operations, available at www.un.org/Depts/dpko/SRSG/table.htm.

19 Ambassador Swanee Hunt's Remarks to the UN Security Council on UN Resolution 1325 and the Status of Women's Inclusion in Peace Processes Worldwide at the Initiative for Inclusive Security (25 October 2005), available at www.huntalternatives.org/download/253_10_25_05_hunt_haf_statement_to_un_security_council_on_resolution_1325.pdf.

20 Roméo Dallaire, *Shake Hands with the Devil: The Failure of Humanity in Rwanda* (New York: Carroll and Graf, 2004). See also Samantha Power, *"A Problem from Hell": America and the Age of Genocide* (New York: Harper, 2003); and Michael Barnett, *Eyewitness to Genocide: The United Nations and Rwanda* (Ithaca, NY: Cornell University Press, 2003).

21 Alan J. Kuperman, *The Limits of Humanitarian Intervention: Genocide in Rwanda* (Washington, DC: Brookings Institution, 2001).

22 Warren Hoge, "Khartoum Expels UN Envoy Who Has Been Outspoken on Darfur Atrocities," *New York Times*, 23 October 2006.

23 Graham Hancock, *Lords of Poverty: The Power, Prestige, and Corruption of the International Aid Business* (New York: Atlantic Monthly Press, 1989).

24 *2005 World Summit Outcome*, UN doc. A/60/1, 24 October 2005, para. 163.

25 See, for example, Susan Strange, *The Retreat of the State: The Diffusion of Power in the World Economy* (Cambridge: Cambridge University Press, 1996); and Robert C. Cox, *The New Realism: Perspectives on Multilateralism and World Order* (New York: St. Martin's Press, 1997).

26 See Ramesh Thakur and Thomas G. Weiss, "United Nations 'Policy': An Argument with Three Illustrations," *International Studies Perspectives* 10, no. 2 (2009): 18–35.

27 James O.C. Jonah, "Secretariat: Independence and Reform," in *The Oxford Handbook on the United Nations*, ed. Thomas G. Weiss and Sam Daws (Oxford: Oxford University Press, 2007), 171.

28 James Gibson, *Jacko, Where Are You Now?* (Richmond, UK: Parsons Publishing, 2006), 247–80.

29 High-level Panel on Threats, Challenges and Change, *A More Secure World: Our Shared Responsibility* (New York: United Nations, 2004); and Kofi A. Annan, *In Larger Freedom: Towards Development, Security, and Human Rights for All* (New York: UN, 2005).

30 Mark Malloch Brown, "Can the UN Be Reformed?" *Global Governance* 14, no. 1 (2008): 10.

31 Zeid Ra'ad Zeid al-Hussein, *A Comprehensive Strategy to Eliminate Future Sexual Exploitation and Abuse in United Nations Peacekeeping Operations*, UN doc. A/59/710, 24 March 2005.

32 Available at www.icva.ch/doc00001962.html.

33 "Peace and Security: Implementing UN Security Council Resolution 1325," Global Conflict Prevention Pool, UK Commonwealth Secretariat, Canadian International Development Agency, Gender Action for Peace and Security, 30 May–2 June 2006, 4.

34 See Thomas G. Weiss and David A. Korn, *Internal Displacement: Conceptualization and Its Consequences* (London: Routledge, 2006), chapter 8.

35 Interview with author, 30 November 2005.

36 *Staff Mobility in the United Nations*, prepared by Even Fontaine Ortiz and Guangting Tang, Joint Inspection Unit, UN doc. JIU/REP/2006/7, Geneva, 2006.

37 Kofi Annan, *Investing in the UN: For a Stronger Organization Worldwide* (New York: UN, 2006).

38 "Human Resources Management Reform: Report of the Secretary General— Addendum: Contractual Arrangements," UN doc. A/59/263/Add.1, 9 September 2004.

39 Myint-U and Scott, *The UN Secretariat*, 127.

40 John Maynard Keynes, *The General Theory of Employment, Interest, and Money* (London: Macmillan, 1936), 383.

41 See Craig Murphy, *The United Nations Development Programme: A Better Way?* (Cambridge: Cambridge University Press, 2006). See also Khadija Haq and Richard Ponzio, eds., *Pioneering the Human Development Revolution: An Intellectual Biography of Mahbub ul Haq* (Delhi: Oxford University Press, 2008).

42 Francesco Mezzalama, *Young Professionals in Selected Organizations of the United Nations System: Recruitment, Management, and Retention* (Geneva: United Nations Joint Inspection Unit, 2000), v–vi.

43 See www.jposc.org.

44 Quoted in "Thoughts on the Business of Life," *Forbes* 171, no. 2 (January 2003): 120.

45 Thomas G. Weiss, Tatiana Carayannis, Louis Emmerij, and Richard Jolly, *UN Voices: The Struggle for Development and Social Justice* (Bloomington: Indiana University Press, 2005), 315–43. See also *The Complete Oral History Transcripts from UN Voices* CD-ROM (New York: United Nations Intellectual History Project, 2007).

46 Annan, *Investing*, 3.

47 Four Nations Initiative Secretariat, *Towards a Compact: Proposals for Improved Governance and Management of the United Nations Secretariat* (Stockholm: 4NI, 2007), 32–3.

2

HOW UN IDEAS CHANGE
THE WORLD

Ideas are a main driving force in human progress and also one of the world organization's most important contributions over the last six and a half decades, which
is the central finding by the independent United Nations Intellectual History Project
(UNIHP).[1] The project's 17 volumes and oral history archive provide substantive
accounts of the UN's work in major areas of economic and social thinking and
action, as well as in related areas where the boundaries of peace and development
intersect—namely, human security, human rights, preventive diplomacy, and
global governance.[2]

This research has breathed new life into the UN's overlooked history, its intellectual leadership and values-based framework for dealing with the global challenges
of our times. The project's decade-long effort has explored areas omitted or under-
valued in textbooks or press accounts—namely, the ideas, norms, and principles
that permeate the world body's atmosphere. This finding flies in the face of UN
bashing, a favorite sport not just in Washington's Beltway but elsewhere. Unlike
popular wisdom—graciously stimulated by the mass media—the United Nations
is more than a rigid bureaucracy without sparkle, wit, or creativity. Nor is it merely
a traveling circus, a talk shop, and paper-pusher. These images and on-and-off-again
tales of corruption sustain an unbalanced view even if elements of such criticism
strike close to home on First Avenue in Manhattan. But we cannot judge a portrait
of Boeing or Airbus that stresses its employees' globe-trotting, internet surfing, or
wasting of resources without mentioning the quality of products, the bottom-line,
and plans for the future. A fair depiction of an enterprise or an international organization is misleading without a discussion of its goals and achievements, including
intellectual leadership.

International organizations live or die, thrive or shrivel up, by the quality and
relevance of the policy ideas that they put forward and sustain. This essay begins
by examining the nature of UN ideas—the good, the bad, and the ugly—while

recognizing that most have multiple origins and various carriers, and it continues by assessing impact. The UN's under-appreciated role in changing the world through ideas is suggested by examining two counterfactuals: a world without the world organization and its ideas as well as with a more creative institution. The conclusion explores how to improve the UN's intellectual output and punch.

The nature of ideas

To most people, the United Nations is unitary; but the real organization consists of three linked components that interact. Inis Claude long ago distinguished the arena for state decision making, the "first UN" of member states,[3] from the "second UN" of staff members and secretariat heads who are paid from assessed and voluntary budgets. The "third UN" of nongovernmental organizations (NGOs), experts, commissions, and academics is a more recent addition to conceptual perspectives.[4] This broad embrace is not only a more accurate reflection of reality but also crucial to understanding the itinerary of ideas. UN history to date essentially excludes the private, for-profit sector that has been missing in action in relationship to the UN's past. A foundation for a "fourth UN" has been laid with the Global Compact and other traditional ones like employers at the International Labour Organization (ILO), which will undoubtedly be a more substantial part of a future intellectual history.

What do we—in this essay, my use does not connote the 'royal' first-person but rather my close collaboration with Richard Jolly and Louis Emmerij and our collective responsibility for what follows—mean by ideas? Ideas are notions and beliefs held by individuals and institutions that influence their attitudes and actions, in this case, toward economic and social development. They mostly arise as the result of social interactions among people or groups within any of the three United Nations or among them. Often ideas take more definite shape over time, sometimes as the result of research or debate or challenges, other times through efforts to transform them into policy as well as experiment by putting them into practice.

Three types of UN ideas—*positive*, *normative*, and *instrumental*—are worth parsing. Positive ideas are those resting on hard evidence, open to challenge and verifiable. That the countries of the Organization for Economic Co-operation and Development's Development Assistance Committee (OECD/DAC) spent about 0.3 percent of their gross national income (GNI) on development assistance in 2009 is an example. Normative ideas are beliefs about what the world should look like. That these countries ought to implement the long-standing UN target of spending 0.7 percent of GNI on development assistance or that there should be a more equitable allocation of world resources are examples. Instrumental (which some might label "causal") ideas are often about what strategy will have what result or what tactic will achieve a desirable outcome, usually less verifiable and with a normative veneer. At the United Nations, instrumental ideas often take operational form—for instance, the calculation that over 0.5 percent of gross national income will be needed as official development assistance (ODA) to realize the Millennium Development Goals (MDGs). They may be specific but rarely are full-blown theories.[5] For example, if we were to begin with the sweeping ethical proposition that the world should be more just, then the idea of a more equitable allocation of resources can be both a normative idea as well as one causal way to improve international justice.

UN ideas have set past and present international agendas within economic and social arenas and will do so for future ones. The lack of attention to the UN's role in generating or nurturing ideas is perplexing, as Ngaire Woods tells us: "In short, ideas, whether economic or not, have been left out of analyses of international relations."[6]

Many political scientists steeped in the dominant North American approaches are *re*discovering the role of ideas in international policymaking. While relatively new in international relations and organization, ideas are a more common bill-of-fare for American historians, philosophers, students of literature, and economists—that is, analysts who see forces at work besides sovereign states selfishly calculating their interests. Ideas also have customarily been more central for the so-called English School. Most readers of these pages undoubtedly are more comfortable with the role of ideas than counterparts among colleagues and graduate students in the United States.[7]

The political science literature on the role of ideas that informs this inquiry can be grouped into three broad categories. The first is institutionalism—such as Judith Goldstein's and Robert Keohane's analyses of foreign policy[8] and Kathryn Sikkink's on developmentalism in Latin America[9]—and is concerned with how organizations shape the policy preferences of their members. Ideas can be particularly important for policymaking during periods of upheaval. In thinking about the end of World War II or of the Cold War or post–September 11th challenges, for instance, ideas provided a conceptual road map that can be used to understand changing preferences and definitions of vital interests for state and non-state actors alike. This approach helps to situate the dynamics at work among ideas, multilateral institutions, and national policies. It also enables us to begin thinking about how the UN influences elite and popular images, as well as how opinion makers affect the world organization.

The second category focuses on the approaches and interactions of various groups, including Peter Haas's epistemic communities,[10] Peter Hall's Keynesian economists,[11] Ernst B. Haas's purveyors of knowledge and power,[12] as well as Margaret Keck and Kathryn Sikkink's more amorphous transnational networks of activists.[13] These approaches examine the role of intellectuals in creating ideas, of technical experts in diffusing them and making them more concrete and scientifically grounded, and of all sorts of people in influencing the positions adopted by a wide range of actors, especially governments. The UN's Intergovernmental Panel on Climate Change (IPCC), the network of world-class volunteer scientists from several disciplines who translate scientific findings into language comprehensible by policymakers, is a powerful illustration of such influence.

Networks of experts influence a broad spectrum of international politics through their ability to interact with policymakers irrespective of location and national boundaries. Researchers working on climate change or HIV/AIDS, for instance, can have an impact on policy by clarifying an issue from which decision makers may explore what is in the interests of their administrations. Researchers also can help to frame the debate on a particular issue, thus narrowing the acceptable range of bargaining in international negotiations. They can introduce standards for action. These networks can help provide justifications for alternatives, and often build national or international coalitions to support chosen policies and to advocate for change. In many ways, efforts by the Intergovernmental Panel on Climate Change to shed light on human impact on the natural environment borrow from Thomas Kuhn's often-cited work on the nature of scientific revolutions.[14]

The third category consists of so-called constructivists such as Alexander Wendt[15] and John G. Ruggie.[16] They seek to determine the potential for individuals acting on their own but especially as members of governments and international institutions to be active agents for change rather than robots whose behavior merely reflects previous theories and accumulated experience. Also relevant are the critical approaches of those influenced by Antonio Gramsci and the Italian school of Marxism, such as Robert Cox and his followers.[17] They view the work of all organizations, including the United Nations, as heavily determined by material conditions and supportive of the status quo.

Irrespective of one's theoretical orientation, individuals and organizations and their ideas matter. The UN system has spawned or nurtured a large number that have called into question conventional wisdom as well as reinforced it. Indeed, the very definition of what passes for "conventional" at a particular point in time in various regions of the world is part of the puzzle that we have only begun to address.

In addition, numerous questions typically circulate about the importance of ideas. First, which comes first, the idea or policy and action? Most approaches do not explain the sources of ideas but rather their effects. They rarely explain how ideas emerge or change, with the exception of pointing to technological innovations. By ignoring where ideas come from and how they change, cause and effect are uncertain. Do ideas shape policy, or do they merely serve, after the fact, as a convenient justification for a policy or a decision? Or does policy push existing ideas forward, and perhaps even generate new ones that may emerge in response to that policy or action? Quentin Skinner raised these issues forty years ago: "[T]he social context, it is said, helps to cause the formation and change of ideas; but the ideas in turn help to cause the formation and change of the social context. Thus the historian ends up presenting himself with nothing better that the time-honored puzzle about the chicken and the egg."[18] There is little pay-off from this endless bickering, and so we are comfortable being agnostic and eclectic and simply moving on.

Second, are ideas mere products, or do they have a life of their own? For us, it is the latter; and our volumes have tried to trace the trajectory of ideas within the UN and examine how individual leadership, coalitions, and national and international bureaucratic rivalries within the UN have generated, nurtured, distorted, and implemented particular ideas. At the same time, it is crucial to discern whether and how ideas, in and of themselves, have helped to shape policy outcomes at the United Nations.[19]

Third, should an idea be analyzed in light of the historical and social context within which it emerged and evolved? For our part, we argue that economic and social ideas at the United Nations cannot be properly understood if examined on their own, divorced from historical and social circumstances. The birth and survival of ideas within the UN—or their death and suppression—invariably reflect events and are contingent upon world politics and the global economy.

Fourth, when should one begin to trace the trajectory of a particular idea? Could anyone disagree with Woods that "Very few ideas are very new"?[20] At what point in its life or in which of its many possible incarnations should one begin to study an idea? Frederick Cooper and Randall Packard point out that postwar modernization theory aimed to transform individuals from "superstitious and status-oriented beings to rational and achievement-oriented beings."[21] But the idea of creating a new person could be traced back to the efforts of the earliest missionaries, the Enlightenment, and Karl Marx, or to God with Adam's rib in the Garden of Eden. Why worry about origins, which usually are irrelevant to determining impact?

Fifth, what about copyrights and patents? Analysts are still arguing whether Charles Darwin or Alfred Russel Wallace should be foremost credited with the theory of natural selection, and whether Alexander Graham Bell deserves credit for inventing the telephone because so many others were toying with the idea at about the same time. The difficulty of identifying a single individual or institution responsible for the creation of an idea is even more manifest in the complex world of multilateralism. An idea evolves and ownership becomes more widely shared through group processes. Within multilateral institutions, anonymous documents or ones ghost-written for organizational heads are the rule; and widespread ownership is a goal of deliberations.[22] Hence, it seems futile to undertake the type of historical analysis pioneered by A.O. Lovejoy who sought to trace an idea "through all the provinces of history in which it appears."[23] Rather, it is more pragmatic merely to pick up an idea at the time it intersected with the United Nations.

Sixth, what is the influence of ideas versus the carriers of ideas?[24] There is little consensus about which—in this case, the ideas or the key individuals from the three United Nations—are more influential. Yet, Thomas Risse's framing seems on target, "ideas do not float freely."[25] Or for Sheri Bermann, ideas "do not have any independent impact by themselves, as disembodied entities floating around in a polity."[26] They need institutions, actors, and opportunities. This is particularly relevant for our treatment of experts and the outside-insiders of the third UN, many of whom go through the revolving door with experiences in government, secretariats, and the private sector. It can be argued that the more influential the members of an expert group or the greater their access to governmental policymakers, the greater the odds that their ideas will be adopted, irrespective of their inherent value. The impacts of ideas (for good or ill) presuppose agents, and at the UN they cannot be divorced from agency—which is one reason that we documented through oral histories the role of individuals in the evolution of international economic and social development.

In short, our comparative advantage is not as philosophers or patent attorneys. The important fact is that an idea exists and has entered into the arena of the United Nations. The bottom line results from analyzing the evolution and impact of key ideas, especially how international economic and social concepts have been nurtured, refined, and applied under UN auspices. They exist, and they matter.

Assessing the impacts of UN ideas

It is essential to examine how UN ideas exert influence, and how and when they fall flat. The late Barbara Ward wrote: "Ideas are the prime movers of history. Revolutions usually begin with ideas."[27] From elsewhere on the political spectrum, Irving Kristol claimed that all modern politics are fundamentally about ideology because the battle is over "who owns the future."[28] Political theorist Daniel Philpott's study of sovereignty demonstrated that revolutions for even this building block of international studies too are driven primarily by the power of ideas.[29] For instance, few would dispute that the international system is in the midst of an upheaval in which state sovereignty is becoming more contingent on upholding basic human rights values, in which states have obligations and not just rights.

Ideas lead to action in many ways. While the process is rarely linear, the steps run from the creation of a new idea to dissemination to decisions by policymakers to implementation and on to impact and results. We can observe how UN ideas exert influence:

* changing the ways that issues are perceived and the language used to describe them;
* framing agendas for action;
* altering the ways that key groups perceive their interests—and thus altering the balance of forces pressing for action or resisting it; and
* becoming embedded in institutions, which thus adopt responsibility for carrying the idea forward and become a focus for accountability and monitoring.

The formulation of statistical norms and guidelines provides a concrete example of how the four ways usually operate simultaneously but not necessarily in tandem when setting standards. In *Quantifying the World*, the late Michael Ward traced the development in the early 1950s of the System of National Accounts (SNA), which provided guidelines that even today enable and encourage countries to calculate gross national product (GNP) and other core economic indicators in a standardized way—thereby providing the stylized facts for longitudinal data sets that are helpful bases for policy and decision making. Agendas are thus defined in country-after-country, which in turn has unleashed pressures for better use of economic resources as well as for more attention to social and other indicators.

The SNA was embedded in the work of the UN Statistical Commission (UNSC) and UN Statistical Office (UNSO). Thus in all four ways, the UN's early work on the SNA has sustained its influence over the following decades. Ward concludes that "the creation of a universally acknowledged statistical system and of a general framework guiding the collection and compilation of data according to recognized standards, both internationally and nationally, has been one of the great and mostly unsung successes of the UN Organization."[30]

Another example is the formulation and adoption of goals for development. Since the launching of the First Development Decade in 1961, the world organization has debated, adopted, promoted, supported, and monitored a succession of quantified and time-circumscribed goals, serving as both national and international guidelines for economic and social development. In total, some fifty such goals have been agreed, the first being for educational expansion and acceleration of economic growth. Later goals for subsequent decades have covered reductions in child mortality, improvements in human welfare, efforts in sustainable and equitable development, and support for these efforts by the expansion of development assistance. The most well-known probably are the so-called Millennium Development Goals for poverty reduction by the year 2015.

A review of performance shows that many such goals have had considerable impact, more than most people realize. The idea of setting objectives and standards is, of course, not new. But setting internationally agreed targets as a means to foster economic and social development is a singular UN achievement. The results have been far from complete successes but rarely total failures. A few like the goal in 1966 for the eradication of smallpox or in 1980 for a worldwide reduction of infant mortality and for increases in life expectancy have registered resounding successes—"complete achievement" in the case of small pox eradication and "considerable achievement" in the other two.[31]

The most serious failures have been in sub-Saharan Africa and the least developed countries. The other weakest performances have been in levels of development aid among the industrialized countries of the global North. Except for Denmark, the Netherlands, Norway, and Sweden—and in the last few years, Luxembourg—developed countries have consistently failed to achieve the 0.7 target for concessional transfers to developing countries in general and fallen short of the specific targets for aid to the least developed countries. But even here, the existence of the goal helped bureaucrats and do-gooders in some countries striving to reach the target and also resulted in their putting pressure on or at least trying to embarrass their stingier Western partners.

Have goals altered the ways that development is perceived? Here the answer changes over time. The UN Educational, Scientific, and Cultural Organization (UNESCO) in the 1960s set early goals for education, which were in part preaching to the converted—countries newly independent or about to be independent, already with demands for educational expansion high on their political agenda. The UNESCO goals for rapid expansion at all levels did not so much shift perceptions of development as give international legitimacy to national ambitions that might otherwise have been treated by colonial powers as unrealistic and even unjustified. The goals for economic expansion of the First Development Decade were certainly treated as over-ambitious when first set—even though, like educational goals, in many countries they were exceeded.

Expectations about performance in the 1960s raised the stakes in later decades, and economic performance increasingly fell below the most ambitious economic targets. By the 1980s, UN economic goals were sidelined by the shift of economic power and influence to the Bretton Woods institutions (the World Bank and International Monetary Fund, IMF), which introduced programs of structural adjustment and stressed economic and financial targets at the country level rather than social outcomes. Given the disastrous declines in rates of economic growth and levels of economic performance that followed, it is startling that considerable improvements nonetheless took place in health, water, sanitation, and child mortality if not in education. These experiences, especially the failures of economic adjustment in the 1980s and early 1990s and the accusation that they were imposed from outside rather than adopted by countries themselves, accounts for the shift by industrialized countries and the Bretton Woods institutions in the late 1990s toward accepting outcome goals and the adoption of the MDGs in particular.

These illustrations show how UN goals have influenced the ways that development has been perceived and influenced agendas for action by governments and their aid agencies, by local and international NGOs, by foundations and corporations. Goals have also served over the years as a focus for mobilizing coalitions of interested partners. This is clear with respect to the MDGs but other goals have also served the same purpose: for instance, goals for expanding aid toward the 0.7 percent target, for debt forgiveness, and for priorities for women and children.[32]

New ideas and priorities have also led to the creation of new institutions to emphasize previously ignored issues—the UN Conference on Trade and Development (UNCTAD) for trade, the UN Industrial Development Organization (UNIDO) for industrial development, the UN Environment Programme (UNEP) for sustainability, the UN Development Fund for Women (UNIFEM) for gender, and so on. And new ideas have also led to new emphases within existing organizations, usually called "mainstreaming"—the insertion of new thinking into existing institutions and programs or significant restructuring of an existing institution to make room for a new idea.

Nonetheless, generating and promulgating ideas is a necessary but insufficient condition for meaningful change. Sometimes UN ideas have spread but often with too little effect. Why do some ideas gain traction while others do not? Morten Bøas and Desmond McNeill have analyzed their evolution among international institutions. New ideas may spread, especially if they are gaining support from governments and the third UN. Indeed, that is the objective of advocates of ideas. But in doing so, they are likely to be adapted and modified by the institutions into which they are moving—to fit their existing priorities, programs of work, and paradigms. As Bøas and McNeill demonstrate, the processes of adaptation, negation, and distortion of ideas to make them fit existing agendas has often led to perceptions of change rather than to genuine transformation. "CANDID"—the Creation, Adoption, Negation and Distortion of Ideas in Development—is the label for their effort and summarizes the key positive and negative elements of the process.[33]

Adopting more recent work by McNeill and Asunción Lera St. Clair about moral variables,[34] five factors seem pertinent in giving some ideas clout and largely sidelining others: international consensus and legitimacy; professional endorsement and interest; nongovernmental support; and financial backing. The fifth—and perhaps the most important for the longer run and certainly the most criticized in anti-UN circles—is the extent to which the UN organizations or institutions in which the idea is embedded take responsibility and initiatives for implementation. Here, even a critical theorist like Robert Cox, who spent twenty-five years in the ILO, suggests that the very existence of new institutions could challenge the rigidity of existing norms. "I guess the reason why new institutions are created," he states, "is that those people who feel that the new idea is important are doubtful that they are going to be able to put it into action through the existing institutions. It is the rigidity of existing institutions that leads to the idea that if you want to start something new, you have to create another institution."[35]

Rarely do all five factors come together in the United Nations with 192 member states and multiple moving parts. Perhaps the main occasions were at the beginning, when the very idea of founding the world organization stirred official and non-governmental enthusiasm and received strong financial backing from the richest country in the world. At that juncture, the politics within deliberative bodies were less divisive. The Cold War was raging; but the West and, at the time, supportive partners in Latin America were on the same ideological page as Washington. Thereafter, the influx of newly independent states in Africa and Asia along with the evolution of Latin America away from a decidedly pro-American stance changed the dynamics, and the North-South divide made many ideas highly controversial, even toxic.

The creation of the SNA described above is a case where Cold War divides, though disruptive, were insufficient to prevent or even slow ideas and action. The staff of the Statistical Commission was mostly drawn from developed Western countries, including all the directors, and drew heavily on leading statisticians and economists. Not surprisingly—and most professionals would argue properly —the guidelines matched the priorities of industrialized rather than developing countries; and the priorities of market economies dominated those of the non-market economies of the Soviet bloc, although the UNSO published analyses on how comparisons could be made. Thus, backed by a dominant international majority with professional and financial support, the proposed SNA spread rapidly ahead in most parts of the world.

Other ideas that arose within the United Nations have not had such backing, especially following the establishment of the Group of 77 in the lead-up to the first UNCTAD in 1964.[36] Work on trade policy, debt relief, transnational corporations, and the formulation of targets for aid and the needs of the least developed countries had little clout in spite of being derived from detailed analyses. Proposals were strongly backed by developing countries while the main developed countries distanced themselves. NGOs often provided support and, since the 1980s, increasingly so. But clout has been feeble because the main donor countries and, often, mainstream professional economists resisted.

The phenomenon of opposition or weak support for UN ideas on economic and social policy from the mainstream of the economics profession requires reflection. Even before the current crisis, many have thought of economics as the "dismal science," although among the social sciences it has been esteemed because of its robust theory, evidence base, and ever more sophisticated econometric techniques. Whatever one's bottom line, it is safe to say that mainstream development economists have mostly stuck to the tools and perspectives of neo-liberal analysis. Outside this mainstream, there has been a vocal professional minority, especially in developing countries and somewhat in Europe, sometimes economists and social scientists working within other disciplines or multidisciplinary frameworks.

The Bretton Woods institutions mostly have navigated within this mainstream— to some, explained by their overlapping interests with those of industrialized countries that provide the bulk of the funding. Although all such generalizations present problems, it is fair to say that the United Nations has mostly approached development issues by swimming outside of mainstream economics, in part reflecting the political priorities and broader interests of the majority of its member states from the global South. Another important factor has been a much greater pressure of non-economic professions in many UN organizations—the medical professions in the World Health Organization (WHO), agriculturalists in the Food and Agriculture Organization (FAO), labor experts in the ILO, a diversity of educationalists and other scientists in UNESCO, and professionals of a wide variety of backgrounds and country experience with children in the UN Children's Fund (UNICEF), of nutrition in the World Food Programme (WFP), and of management administration in the UN Development Programme (UNDP). This diversity has meant that the UN system as a whole has approached development from wider perspectives than the economists working for the Bretton Woods institutions.

At its best, the result of pulling together different professions has challenged received wisdom and improved thinking about international policy options. And sometimes, as with the UN's early economic work on the need for concessional finance for poorer countries and the proposals for the Special United Nations Fund for Economic Development (SUNFED), the world organization's work persuaded more orthodox economists at the World Bank or the IMF to think again. But on other occasions, as with *Adjustment with a Human Face* for which UNICEF and the Economic Commission for Africa clamored in the 1980s, adoption by the Bretton Woods institutions has been slow and lukewarm.[37]

Nine UN ideas that changed the world

Space here does not permit doing more than enumerating the nine ideas in which UN efforts have altered the ways that global issues are perceived and addressed.

The argument in *UN Ideas That Changed the World* draws on the evidence from one or more of the commissioned volumes. Hopefully the chapter titles provide a sufficient flavor to whet the reader's appetite to examine, or even buy, the project's volumes about these significant ideas: "Human Rights: From Aspiration to Implementation"; "Gender and Women's Rights: From Empowerment to Equality"; "Development Policies: From National and Regional Perspectives to Beyond"; "International Economic Relations: From National Interests to Global Solidarity"; "Development Ideologies: From Planning to Markets"; "Social Development: From Sectoral to Integrated Perspectives"; "Sustainability: From Protecting the Environment to Preserving Ecological Systems"; "Peace and Human Security: From States to Individuals"; and "Human Development: From Narrower to Broader Horizons."

The UN's contributions to broadening the content of economic and social development range from early concerns with human rights and gender to priorities and perspectives of national and international development to the management of global resources and the need to develop sustainable development strategies. The sub-titles of the chapters also indicate that ideas are not static but evolve considerably and continually. For instance, more recent UN calls for action combine development with preserving the world's eco-systems from the consequences of greenhouse gases, global warming, and climate chaos.[38] Moreover, as mentioned already, the analysis necessarily goes beyond the economic, the social, and the environmental because development, human rights, and human security intersect.

Our overall balance sheet maintains that the UN has often led the charge with pioneering ideas. Admittedly, the "three United Nations" enlarges what we count as the world organization's specific contributions. However, that is the reality of the contemporary international system, of fledgling global governance.[39] Many key ideas are those that were often initially formulated or articulated by distinguished experts as members of UN panels or as work commissioned by UN staff or by governments. Examples are the first fledgling ideas about the construction of a global and consistent economic order that came out of the three committees that reported between 1949 and 1951,[40] or more recently those on climate change presented by the Intergovernmental Panel on Climate Change,[41] or in between by Hans Singer on the terms of trade or UNCTAD staff on debt problems. In other cases, the UN's contributions have been less in providing the initial spark of creativity than in challenging the way a problem is framed—as with the ILO missions on basic needs in the 1970s.

Many times and on many occasions, UN contributions have been multiplied by widely disseminating and promoting ideas. The UNDP's annual *Human Development Report* and reports by UNICEF on the *State of the World's Children* or by the UN High Commissioner for Refugees (UNHCR) on *The State of the World's Refugees* achieved part of their global visibility and impact by being subsidized and disseminated widely—hundreds of thousands of copies in English, French, and Spanish and other languages as well. There were also media launches in the 100 or so countries in which the UN system has country offices. Other than a few academic blockbusters by the likes of Joseph Stiglitz, Jeffrey Sachs, or Paul Collier, few scholarly publications could have achieved such outreach. This global dissemination was increasingly reinforced by UNDP support for national and regional reports, taking the human development methodology and applying it to specific problems and situations—another illustration of how ideas matter to monitoring moves forward or backward.

If the nature and impact of UN ideas are not clear enough, it is instructive to situate the overall balance sheet by asking two questions: Where would the world be without the UN and its ideas in the economic and social arena? Could the UN have done better, in follow-up or in crafting the ideas themselves? *UN Ideas That Changed the World* provides answers for the nine ideas and demonstrates the extent to which UN ideas have had influence. Here it is useful to think through two counterfactuals.[42]

Counterfactual # 1: the world without the UN and its ideas?

One way of considering the impact of UN ideas is to imagine where the planet might be without the world organization or with one set up solely as a passive convener, with no capacity for generating or nurturing independent ideas. It would be a markedly different United Nations, with a minimum of staff, presumably only ex-diplomats to bring groups with differences together and help to resolve them but with few ideas of their own. It would be a strange and impotent international body although not totally different from the type that extreme critics, including such members of the flat-earth society as former American UN ambassador John Bolton, put forward as their preference. Such a stripped-down United Nations would be more limited even than the League of Nations, which had staff members in a number of specialist areas, including some who did pioneering work on nutrition and food security as well as on economics.[43]

In this counterfactual, what might have happened to the ideas that the United Nations has framed, massaged, and sometimes put into practice? In the economic arena, the need for rules and regulation to facilitate international trade and other economic transactions would have generated a more limited range of institutions, not so different from the Organization for Economic Co-operation and Development, the European Union, and other regional organizations. If the world organization did not exist, it would have been invented, if not in 1945 then about 1960 with decolonization, or in the 1970s with the floating of the dollar and the surge of oil prices. A series of ad hoc meetings to cope with wide-ranging issues of vital economic importance only for the wealthiest of industrialized countries would rapidly be seen to be inadequate and something permanent with universal representation would have been created.

The evolution of the Group of Eight (G-8) into the Group of 20 (G-20) reflects the fact that wider not narrower membership is a necessary feature of world politics. Whatever the advantages of economic consultations among the upgraded G-20 that account for 90 percent of the world's GDP, only the United Nations can formulate global norms, set global standards, make global law, and eventually enforce global treaties. The G-20 certainly is more representative and potentially effective than the Security Council for which there are endless proposals for reform that go nowhere. The new G-20 encompasses 4.2 billion people (instead of 900 million in the G-8), but another 2.6 mainly poor people are left out. And they and their governments are a prerequisite for solving most global problems. The G-192 has advantages that the upgraded G-20, ad hoc coalitions of the willing, and various proposals for "leagues of democracies" do not. The policy preferences of the countries that count will need to be endorsed globally. The range of links between the G-20, on the one hand, and the universal United Nations, on the other hand, represents a potentially rich research vein.

Cynics might comment that a narrower focus would have been little different from the General Agreement on Tariffs and Trade or its replacement, the World Trade Organization (WTO), which indeed have commanded the respect and support of industrialized countries. However, the WTO at present employs over 600 staff, just shy of the dimensions of the League of Nations in the 1930s. Most of the staff are economists and lawyers, many engaged in producing research and statistical reports in areas in which the UN over a much broader field is also engaged. The WTO takes the rules of the game as fixed and tries to interpret and enforce them while the UN tries to produce alternate policy ideas for new situations. The notion that international organizations engaged solely in facilitating interactions rather than contributing substantively—including questioning the fairness of the rules of the game and who sits at the gaming table as well as whether it is level—is unviable for an international institution that has universal membership.

But beyond the economic imperatives required for facilitating trade and the functioning of global markets, some of what the United Nations does in other areas would also be required and need to be re-created. Two examples could illustrate this reality, namely the UN's work in international public goods as well as human rights and humanitarian concerns.

Providing public goods in the form of rule setting and regulation would be required in such areas as health, food, and agriculture, weather and meteorology, civil aviation, and maritime law. Economists describe them as such because they are needed for individual countries and for the international system.[44] At the same time, global public goods are beyond the capacity of the marketplace because individual countries lack the incentives and the capacity to provide them on the scale required—in part because of the classic "free rider" problem. To ensure public goods, many specialized functional organizations would need to have been invented if they were not already part of the UN system. Indeed, many such institutions were created long before the current generation of postwar organizations. Examples include the Pan American Sanitary Bureau, which was founded in 1902 and transformed into the Latin American arm of the WHO in 1948 and renamed PAHO, the Pan American Health Organization; and earlier international organizations like the Universal Postal Union and International Telecommunications Union, whose origins are in the mid-nineteenth century.[45]

Certainly, some of what the United Nations does in areas with a values-orientation would have had to be re-created. The human rights arena clearly illustrates how the world would be poorer without the United Nations.[46] Even a world focused solely on economic efficiency and free markets would be under public pressure to invent an organization to embrace some rights. The United Nations, however, embraces the entire gamut of human rights—from civil and political to economic, social, and cultural—not for reasons of economic efficiency or political necessity but as a reflection of the vision and humanity of its founders.

Such vision and idealism are also reflected in the mandates and work of the UN funds and specialized agencies—for instance, UNICEF and UNIFEM, the UNDP and the WFP as well as UNESCO, the WHO, the FAO, and the ILO. They are also at the core of the work of the offices of the UNHCR as well as of the Office of the High Commissioner for Human Rights (OHCHR). Work on the rights of minorities and indigenous peoples as well as the prevention of torture and genocide are important and visible efforts in the forefront of the world organization's work. And because their mandates put human values ahead of economic concerns and market efficiency, these bodies often clash with the dominant interests of governments and market priorities, and they often call for more political and financial support than governments are prepared to provide.

Anyone familiar with my past writing about the world organization is aware that I am anything except an apologist: UN institutions are riddled with bureaucratic and coordination problems; and implementation lags quite far behind rhetoric.[47] But the fact that human values are emphasized and sometimes placed ahead of economic concerns and market efficiency is far from trivial. One undoubtedly can imagine a world without such concerns. But it would be much poorer and much less human than the one to which the United Nations aspires and, at its best, achieves.

Counterfactual #2: a more creative UN?

Recalling the lofty vision and ideas of the United Nations offers no defense for its inefficiencies or a justification for its weaknesses. Nor is it a reason for suggesting that the world organization could not have done far better in formulating ideas or in ensuring their follow-up. UNIHP's volumes and oral history interviews of nearly eighty individuals contain specific suggestions for ways in which the UN could indeed have done much better.[48] Here, three substantive ones are highlighted that provide food for thought regarding the "what if" of a more intellectually creative world organization.

First, more creative work could have been done on political economy in areas in which the international system is manifestly failing. Economic weaknesses about how the global system limits opportunities for the poorest countries is one such crucial area that has become even more pressing as a result of the ongoing global economic and financial crisis. Inadequate progress toward the goals of sustainable development and environmental protection is another, which seems ever more acute. Biases in aid along with the lack of coherence in the global trade system and the failures of industrialized countries to make good on their public commitments to a free and open international economic system are issues that remain critical as does the lack of incentives for measures of disarmament and development.

Across all these areas, more sustained attention could have been given to measures required to achieve a more egalitarian international system and to pursue national policies that combine redistribution with growth. It may sound hopelessly naïve even to utter the acronym "NIEO" (New International Economic Order). Nonetheless, the sentiments that motivated the quest for framing an alternative to the global economic order in the 1970s and a fairer distribution of global wealth and the benefits of growth can hardly be ignored in today's world. Glaring inequalities are even worse than three decades ago; and the economic and financial meltdown of 2008 has hurt most those on the bottom who already had too little.

Second, far more work could have been done on the conditions to create stability in weak and failing states—a crucial requirement, especially in Africa. Even if international inequities were reduced, far more fulsome efforts also are required to address glaring inequalities within countries. Since 2006, the effort to pull together UN inputs in the Peacebuilding Commission is an encouraging sign that preventing a return to war has emerged as a priority, but here too glaring inequalities within fragile states continue to menace any return to stability.

Third, better promotion of UN ideas would have helped in *all* areas of its work. Production of new ideas is one task, but the distribution and dissemination of key UN reports to academics, policy analysts, and the media is also crucial. Outreach, including translation and subsidies, for high-visibility reports has sometimes been impressive, but too many quality analyses languish on book shelves or in filing cabinets. Following the UNDP's example of disseminating its annual *Human Development Report*, the world organization as a whole should have ensured far greater outreach for the part of its work where it has originality and comparative advantage—work outside the box of neoclassical economic orthodoxy. The encouragement of wide discussions of multidisciplinary work is especially essential in areas in which economic issues interact with human rights, human security, and human development. The UN could and should have engaged in a broader debate over the weaknesses of Bretton Woods dogma and the Washington consensus. Even those persuaded that such approaches are broadly correct now recognize that the UN's past work often led to crucial new insights into the weaknesses of mainstream thinking.

The world organization, of course, also spawned many bad ideas that fortunately had short shelf-lives. Such notions as halting the brain-drain by limiting migration or taxing beneficiary countries or prohibiting containers in ports in poor countries seem laughable in a globalizing world. Brian Urquhart's candidate for worst idea was Julian Huxley's early UNESCO project to study "sex at high altitudes."[49] But as anyone associated with a university knows, such poor meanderings are the price of doing business; and in the UN they pale in comparison with productive ideas.

And to return to the point of this counterfactual, the United Nations could have been better and done more in many areas. There is still time. How could this happen?

Improving UN intellectual output

Part of the reason for UN failures to fulfill mandates or achieve goals is that they are too visionary, or at least go far beyond where most governments are prepared to go. Meanwhile, the vast majority of analysts in international studies focus on one obvious explanation, the lack of political will among member states.

Throwing up our hands in despair is unacceptable; rather we should examine where change is possible, and an essential component of the preceding counter-factual consists of improving the intellectual quality of the second United Nations.[50] Inefficiency and weak institutions and staff do less than they might, and governments provide less finance than required. We could have a more effective world organization if there were more intellectual firepower and less interference from governments in the process of recruitment and promotion.[51]

The most visible champion of the second UN was Dag Hammarskjöld, whose speech at Oxford in May 1961, shortly before his calamitous death, spelled out the importance of an autonomous and first-rate staff. He asserted that any erosion or abandonment of "the international civil service . . . might, if accepted by the Member nations, well prove to be the Munich of international cooperation."[52] His clarion call did not ignore the reality that the international civil service exists to carry out decisions by member states. But Hammarskjöld fervently believed that UN officials could and should pledge allegiance to a larger collective good symbolized by the organization's light-blue-covered *laissez-passer* rather than the narrowly perceived national interests of the countries that issue national passports in different colors.

The long-standing policy of setting aside UN positions for officials approved by their home countries belies integrity. Governments seek to ensure that their interests are defended inside secretariats, and many have even relied on officials for intelligence. The influx in the 1950s and 1960s of former colonies as new member states led them to clamor for "their" quota or fair share of the patronage opportunities, following the bad example set by major powers and other member states. The result was downplaying competence and exaggerating national origins as the main criterion for recruitment and promotion. Over the years, efforts to improve gender balance have resulted in other types of claims, as has the age profile of secretariats. Virtually all positions above the director level, and often many below as well, are the object of campaigns by governments.

How many people are we speaking about? Professional and support staff number approximately 55,000 in the UN proper and in agencies created by the General Assembly, and another 20,000 in the specialized agencies. This number includes neither temporary staff in peace operations (about 120,000 in 2008) nor the staff of the IMF and the World Bank group (another 15,000). These figures represent substantial growth from the approximately 500 employees in the UN's first year at Lake Success and the peak total of 700 staff employed by the League of Nations.[53]

Neglected personnel issues are relevant because people like ideas matter, for good and for ill. In spite of its slavish image, international secretariats do more than simply carry out marching orders from governments. Thus, it is clear that this position differs with three analysts who dismiss "the curious notion that the United Nations is an autonomous actor in world affairs that can and does take action independent of the will and wishes of the member governments."[54] There is considerably more room for creativity and initiative than is commonly believed. UN officials can present ideas to tackle problems, debate them formally and informally with governments, take initiatives, advocate for change, turn general decisions into specific programs, and implement them. They monitor progress and report to national officials and politicians gathering at intergovernmental conferences and in countries in which the UN is operating.

Thinking through the counterfactual of a more creative United Nations requires us to imagine what the world organization would be if it aggressively maintained its ability to produce or nurture world-class public intellectuals, scholars, thinkers, planners, and practitioners who could aspire to Nobel and other prizes. Members of UN secretariats are typically considered second-class citizens in comparison with the researchers, thinkers, and practitioners from the World Bank and the IMF. This notion partially reflects vastly differing resources devoted to research as well as their respective cultures, media attention, dissemination outlets, and the use of the research in decision making.

The reality is often different. Nine persons with substantial experience within the UN and its policy formulation processes have won the Nobel Prize in economic sciences—Jan Tinbergen, Wassily Leontief, Gunnar Myrdal, James Meade, W. Arthur Lewis, Theodore W. Schultz, Lawrence R. Klein, Richard Stone, and Amartya Sen—whereas only one from the World Bank, Joseph Stiglitz, has done so. But he resigned in protest and is now deeply associated with the United Nations in New York. And this list is in addition to 15 UN organizations and individual Nobel Peace Prize winners who worked for years as staff members of the United Nations: Ralph Bunche, Dag Hammarskjöld, Kofi Annan, Mohammed ElBaradei, and Martti Ahtisaari. No other institution can rival this performance.

In short, the UN requires ideas and the people who produce them to be taken more seriously. Improved research, analysis, and policy work would permit the Secretary-General and the system as a whole to play more important roles in world political, economic, social, and environmental decision making. To this effect, the world organization should implement three changes in human resources management.

First, human resources policy should do more to foster an environment that encourages creative thinking, penetrating analysis, and policy-focused research of the highest intellectual caliber. The quality of staff members is essential and will depend on improvements and better professional procedures in recruitment, appointment, promotion, and organization of responsibilities. Some progress has been made, such as the establishment of a system of national competitive examination for entry-level recruitment as well as internship and junior professional officer programs—but even here competence is hardly the most essential criterion for those who have passed exams or applied for training. There could also be a continual infusion of young or senior scholars for fixed periods to the UN, which could result from regular exchange procedures with universities and think tanks around the world, not just from the West. It would benefit not only the United Nations while these visitors were in residence but also the future research agendas of scholars once they returned to their university bases.

Second, independent research and analysis requires space within the institution. Whenever the UN pursues a bold agenda, it is unable to please all 192 member states all of the time. Calling into question conventional or politically correct wisdom requires longer-term funding that sympathetic donors should provide. A less skewed allocation of international resources toward the IFIs is a place to start. The terms on which such finance is provided are of crucial importance, not only to ensure availability but sustained multi-year commitments without strings. Encouragement of free thinking and policy exploration is vital but not cheap.

Typically, messages are watered down to satisfy the lowest common intergovernmental denominator. The experience with the *Human Development Report* illustrates how independent teams could be liberated from the purported obligation to check analyses before publication with boards or donors.[55] Given the current "culture" of the world body and the reluctance of its Secretary-General to ruffle any diplomatic feathers, "safety zones" are required within UN organizations—where serious and independent analyses can take place, freed from daily urgent matters and where controversy is tolerated. It could also be accomplished by subcontracting UN projects to such autonomous think tanks as London's Chatham House or Cape Town's Centre for Conflict Resolution.

Third, the United Nations should seek as many alliances as possible with as well as borrow personnel from centers of expertise and excellence—in academia, think tanks, government policy units, and corporate research centers. A prominent location for dialogue and for knitting together the international cooperative fabric, the UN also should be a place to network outstanding thinking. Independent international commissions beginning with the 1969 Pearson report on *Partners in Development* as well as the more recent High-level Panel on Threats, Challenges and Change have had research secretariats,[56] and this kind of independent staff borrowed from universities and think tanks but loosely affiliated with the UN should become a permanent feature of the organization but with frequent and regular turnover in personnel. Another possible route would be to replicate the experience with climate change by the IPCC and pool world-class expertise from a variety of disciplines for such global challenges as pandemics, finance, proliferation, and terrorism. Basic research is best done in universities, but many elements of applied research can and should be undertaken within the United Nations in collaboration with world-class research institutions.

Conclusion

Even the harshest critic would admit that the UN's intellectual work could have been poorer. It could have been totally smothered by caution and controlled by secretaries-general who allowed no scope for creativity by members of the Secretariat, lacked any vision, and were dogmatic. This could have happened so early in the world organization's life that many non-state actors became definitively disillusioned and discouraged about the UN's potential for social change.

In fact, the world organization has attracted participation and commitment from many people with outstanding intellectual or leadership capabilities to work for the second UN as well as engage actively with relevant parts of the first and the third United Nations. At each stage of its life, individuals and some governments have argued passionately for maintaining the original vision and for applying its inspirational values to the contemporary but ever-evolving international system. The UN could have gone the way of the League of Nations; it did not.

The UN's achievements have helped, including the impact of its ideas. Throughout its six-and-a-half decades, many of the world organization's core ideas have had remarkable impact; and even those that have been rejected, sidelined, or adopted only rhetorically after long periods of time have emerged, not unscathed but intact. Politically unacceptable to many powerful countries at first, they often later became part of mainstream international discourse. Readers should, for example, recall everything from climate change to gender equality; from concessional loans, debt relief, and other special measures for least developed countries to putting people at the center of development; from the role of a high commissioner for human rights to human security and removing the license to kill from the attributes of sovereign states.

Moreover, timing is everything; and an idea's time may not have come. If so, the UN's role may be to persevere with a notion—even so seemingly far-fetched as world government.[57] The fact that such ideas may have failed to change the world and have little chance to be implemented immediately is not a reason to give up the good fight for more solidarity and a better and less conflict-ridden world. The UN's effectiveness cannot fairly be judged from a short-term perspective. Today's visions sometimes are tomorrow's commonplace. The idea of a new world war seems absurd, but until 2008–9 so too did the idea of a worldwide economic and financial collapse of the 1930s variety.

Perhaps as much as any recent event, the ongoing global financial and economic meltdown, which the late John Kenneth Galbraith might well have dubbed "the great crash 2008,"[58] made even clearer what many previous crises had not—namely the risks, problems, and enormous costs of a global economy without adequate international institutions, regulation, democratic decision making, and powers to bring order, spread risks, and enforce compliance.

The world body's role as an idea-monger provides some "good news" that deserves to be better known and understood. Its contributions to economic and social thinking, policymaking, and action have been more successful than generally appreciated, or "ahead of the curve" as the title of the UN Intellectual History Project's first volume puts it.[59] In short, the United Nations has distinctly influenced the ways that we as academics and, more importantly, states think and talk about issues, frame agendas for action, and constitute coalitions as well as the ways that both new and reformed public and private institutions deal with global problems.

That is how UN ideas have changed the world.

Notes

1 This article draws on Richard Jolly, Louis Emmerij, and Thomas G. Weiss, *UN Ideas That Changed the World* (Bloomington: Indiana University Press, 2009). Published with permission.

2 See S. Neil MacFarlane and Yuen Foong-Khong, *Human Security and the UN: A Critical History* (Bloomington: Indiana University Press, 2006); and Bertrand G. Ramcharan, *Preventive Diplomacy at the UN* (Bloomington: Indiana University Press, 2008). All the project's volumes are cited in this article and are published by Indiana University Press with the exception of Thomas G. Weiss and Sam Daws, eds., *The Oxford Handbook on the United Nations* (Oxford: Oxford University Press, 2007). Full details are available at www.unhistory.org.

3 Inis L. Claude, Jr., *Swords Into Plowshares: The Problems and Prospects of International Organization* (New York: Random House, 1956), and "Peace and Security: Prospective Roles for the Two United Nations," *Global Governance* 2, no. 3 (1996): 289–98.

4 Thomas G. Weiss, Tatiana Carayannis, and Richard Jolly, "The 'Third' United Nations," *Global Governance* 15, no. 1 (2009): 123–42.

5 Morten Bøås and Desmond McNeill, *Global Institutions and Development: Framing the World?* (London: Routledge, 2004).

6 Ngaire Woods, "Economic Ideas and International Relations: Beyond Rational Neglect," *International Studies Quarterly* 39 (1995): 164.

7 See, for example, Martin Wight, *Systems of States* (Leicester, UK: Leicester University Press, 1977) edited with an introduction by Hedley Bull; Gabriele Wight and Brian Porter, ed., *International Theory: The Three Traditions* (Leicester, UK: Leicester University Press, 1977) with an introduction by Hedley Bull; Hedley Bull, *The Anarchical Society: A Study of Order in World Politics* (New York: Columbia University Press, 1977); and John Vincent, *Human Rights and International Relations* (New York: Cambridge University Press, 1986). Ideas also were strong influences on Alfred E. Zimmern, *The League of Nations and the Rule of Law, 1918–1935* (London: Macmillan, 1936).

8 Judith Goldstein and Robert O. Keohane, eds., *Ideas and Foreign Policy* (Ithaca, NY: Cornell University Press, 1993).

9 Kathryn Sikkink, *Ideas and Institutions: Developmentalism in Argentina and Brazil* (Ithaca, NY: Cornell University Press, 1991).

10 Peter M. Haas, "Introduction: Epistemic Communities and International Policy Coordination," *International Organization* 46, no. 1 (1992): 1–36; and Peter M. Haas, Robert O. Keohane, and Marc A. Levy, eds., *Institutions for the Earth: Sources of Effective International Environmental Protection* (Cambridge, Mass.: MIT Press, 1992).

11 Peter A. Hall, ed., *The Political Power of Economic Ideas: Keynesianism Across Nations* (Princeton, NJ: Princeton University Press, 1989).

12 Ernst B. Haas, *When Knowledge is Power: Three Models of Change in International Organizations* (Los Angeles: University of California Press, 1994); and see Peter M. Haas and Ernst B. Haas, "Learning to Learn: Improving International Governance," *Global Governance* 1, no. 3 (1995): 255–84.

13 Margaret Keck and Kathryn Sikkink, *Activists Beyond Borders: Advocacy Networks in International Politics* (Ithaca, NY: Cornell University Press, 1998).

14 Thomas S. Kuhn, *The Structure of Scientific Revolutions*, 2nd ed. (Chicago: University of Chicago Press, 1970).

15 Alexander Wendt, *Social Theory of International Politics* (Cambridge: Cambridge University Press, 1999).

16 John G. Ruggie, *Constructing the World Polity* (New York: Routledge, 1998).

17 See, for example, Robert W. Cox, ed., *The New Realism: Perspectives on Multilateralism and World Order* (New York: St. Martin's Press, 1997); Robert W. Cox with Timothy J. Sinclair, *Approaches to World Order* (Cambridge: Cambridge University Press, 1996); and Quentin Hoare and Geoffrey N. Smith, eds. and trans., *Selections From the Prison Notebooks of Antonio Gramsci* (London: Lawrence and Wishart, 1971).

18 Quentin E. Skinner, "Meaning and Understanding in the History of Ideas," *History and Theory* 8 (1969): 42.

19 See Ramesh Thakur and Thomas G. Weiss, "United Nations 'Policy': An Argument with Three Illustrations," *International Studies Perspectives* 10, no. 2 (2009): 18–35.

20 Woods, "Economic Ideas and International Relations," 168.

21 Frederick Cooper and Randall Packard, eds., *International Development and the Social Sciences: Essays on the History and Politics of Knowledge* (Berkeley: University of California Press, 1997), 17.

22 See Ramesh Thakur, ed., *What is Equitable Geographic Representation in the Twenty-first Century* (Tokyo: UN University, 1999).

23 Arthur O. Lovejoy, *The Great Chain of Being* (New York: Torchbook, 1960).

24 See Albert Yee, "The Causal Effects of Ideas on Policies," *International Organization* 50 (1996): 69–108.

25 Thomas Risse-Kappen, "Ideas Do Not Float Freely: Transnational Coalitions, Domestic Structures, and the End of the Cold War," *International Organization* 48, no. 2 (1994): 185–214.

26 Sheri Bermann, *The Social Democratic Moment: Ideas and Politics in the Making of Interwar Europe* (Cambridge, Mass.: Harvard University Press, 1998), 22.

27 Cited by Mahbub ul Haq, *Reflections on Human Development* (New York: Oxford University Press, 1995), 204.

28 Irving Kristol, *Reflections of a Neoconservative* (New York: Basic Books, 1983), 253–6.

29 Daniel Philpott, *Revolutions in Sovereignty: How Ideas Shaped Modern International Relations* (Princeton, NJ: Princeton University Press, 2001).

30 Michael Ward, *Quantifying the World: UN Contributions to Statistics* (Bloomington: Indiana University Press, 2004), 2.

31 By the year 2000, 138 countries had brought infant mortality to below 120 and 124 countries had raised life expectancy to 60 years or more, two of the goals set in 1980. A full assessment of the achievements in relation to the fifty goals are found in "The Record of Performance," in *UN Contributions to Development Thinking and Practice*, by Richard Jolly, Louis Emmerij, Dharam Ghai, and Frédéric Lapeyre (Bloomington: Indiana University Press, 2004), chapter 10. Differences among regional thinking can be found in Yves Berthelot, ed., *Unity and Diversity in Development Ideas: Perspectives from the UN Regional Commissions* (Bloomington: Indiana University Press, 2004).

32 See Olav Stokke, *The UN and Development: From Aid to Cooperation* (Bloomington: Indiana University Press, 2009); and Devaki Jain, *Women, Development, and the UN: A Sixty-Year Quest for Equality and Justice* (Bloomington: Indiana University Press, 2006).

33 Bøas and McNeill, eds., *Global Institutions and Development*.

34 Desmond McNeill and Asunción Lera St. Clair, *Global Poverty, Ethics and Human Rights: The Role of Multilateral Organisations* (London: Routledge, 2009).

35 Thomas G. Weiss, Tatiana Carayannis, Loius Emmerij, and Richard Jolly, *UN Voices: The Struggle for Development and Social Justice* (Bloomington: Indiana University Press, 2005), 420.

36 See John Toye and Richard Toye, *The UN and Global Political Economy: Trade, Finance, and Development* (Bloomington: Indiana University Press, 2004). See also Tagi Sagafi-nejad

in collaboration with John Dunning, *The UN* and *Transnational Corporations: From Code of Conduct to Global Compact* (Bloomington: Indiana University Press, 2008).

37 For a trenchant analysis, see Robert Wade, "Japan, the World Bank and the Art of Paradigm Maintenance: The East Asian Miracle in Political Perspective," *New Left Review* I/217 (1996). For a critique from a former insider, see Joseph Stiglitz, *Globalization and Its Discontents* (New York: Norton, 2003).

38 Nico Schrijver, *From Destruction to Development: The UN and Global Resource Management* (Bloomington: Indiana University Press, 2010).

39 See Thomas G. Weiss and Ramesh Thakur, *The UN and Global Governance: An Unfinished Journey* (Bloomington: Indiana University Press, 2010).

40 United Nations, *Measures for Full Employment* (New York: UN, 1949); *Measures for the Economic Development of Under-Developed Countries* (New York: UN, 1951); and *Measures for International Economic Stability* (New York: UN, 1951).

41 See especially IPCC, *Summary for Policymakers of the Synthesis Report of the IPCC Fourth Assessment Report of the IPCC* (Geneva: IPCC, 2007).

42 This is not the place to examine the pluses and minuses of the technique, which are the subject of Philip E. Tetlock and Aaron Belkin, eds., *Counterfactual Thought Experiments in World Politics: Logical, Methodological, and Psychological Perspectives* (Princeton, NJ: Princeton University Press, 1996); Niall Ferguson, ed., *Virtual History: Alternatives and Counterfactuals* (New York: Basic Books, 1999); and Ned Lebow, *Forbidden Fruit: Counterfactuals and International Relation* (Princeton, NJ: Princeton University Press, 2010).

43 See Jolly et al., *UN Contributions*, 169–219.

44 See, for example, Scott Barrett, *Why Cooperate? The Incentive to Supply Global Public Goods* (Oxford: Oxford University Press, 2007); and Inge Kaul, Isabelle Grunberg, and Marc A. Stern, eds., *Global Public Goods: International Cooperation in the 21st Century* (New York: Oxford University Press, 1999).

45 See Craig Murphy, *International Organization and Industrial Change: Global Governance since 1850* (Cambridge: Polity Press, 1994).

46 Roger Normand and Sarah Zaidi, *Human Rights at the UN: The Political History of Universal Justice* (Bloomington: Indiana University Press, 2008).

47 See Thomas G. Weiss, *What's Wrong with the United Nations and How to Fix It* (Cambridge: Polity, 2009).

48 Excerpts are in Weiss et al., *UN Voices*, but the complete transcripts of the oral history interviews are available on CD-ROM: United Nations Intellectual History Project, *The Complete Oral History Transcripts from "UN Voices"* (New York: UNIHP, 2007).

49 Weiss et al., *UN Voices*, 323.

50 See Thomas G. Weiss, Tapio Kanninen, and Michael K. Busch, *Creating Sustainable Global Governance for the 21st Century: The United Nations Confronts Economic and Environmental Crises Amidst Changing Geopolitics* (Berlin: Friedrich Ebert Stiftung, 2009), Occasional Paper No. 40.

51 This argument is based on Thomas G. Weiss, "Reinvigorating the International Civil Service," *Global Governance* 16, no. 1 (2010): 39–57.

52 Dag Hammarskjöld, "The International Civil Servant in Law and in Fact," lecture delivered to Congregation at Oxford University, 30 May 1961, reprinted by Clarendon Press, Oxford, quotes at 329 and 349. Available at www.un.org/depts/dhl/dag/docs/internationalcivilservant.pdf.

53 Thant Myint-U and Amy Scott, *The UN Secretariat: A Brief History (1945–2006)* (New York: International Peace Academy, 2007), 126–8.

54 Donald J. Puchala, Katie Verlin Laatikainen, and Roger A. Coate, *United Nations Politics: International Organization in a Divided World* (Upper Saddle River, NJ: Prentice Hall, 2007), x.

55 See Craig Murphy, *The UN Development Programme: A Better Way?* (Cambridge: Cambridge University Press, 2006), 232–62; and Khadiha Haq and Richard Ponzio, eds.,

Pioneering the Human Development Revolution: An Intellectual Biography of Mahbub ul Haq (New Delhi: Oxford University Press, 2008).

56 See Commission on International Development, *Partners in Development* (New York: Praeger, 1969); and High-level Panel on Threats, Challenges and Change, *A More Secure World: Our Shared Responsibility* (New York: United Nations, 2004).

57 See, for instance, Thomas G. Weiss, "What Happened to the Idea of World Government?" *International Studies Quarterly* 53, no. 2 (2009): 253–71; and Alexander Wendt, "Why a World State is Inevitable," *European Journal of International Relations* 9, no. 3 (2003): 491–542.

58 John Kenneth Galbraith, *The Great Crash, 1929* (Boston: Houghton Mifflin, 1954).

59 Louis Emmerij, Richard Jolly, and Thomas G. Weiss, *Ahead of the Curve? UN Ideas and Global Challenges* (Bloomington: Indiana University Press, 2001).

3

WHAT HAPPENED TO THE IDEA OF WORLD GOVERNMENT?

Le machin (the thing) is what Charles de Gaulle scornfully called the United Nations, thereby dismissing multilateral cooperation as frivolous in comparison with the real red meat of world politics, national interests, and realpolitik. He conveniently ignored—as many amateur and professional historians have since—that the formal birth of "the thing" was not the signing of the UN Charter on 26 June 1945, but rather the adoption of the "Declaration by the United Nations" in Washington, DC, on 1 January 1942. The same twenty-six countries of the powerful coalition that defeated fascism and rescued France also anticipated the formal establishment of a world organization as an essential extension of their war-time commitments. After the failure of the League of Nations, states did not view the second generation of universal international organizations in the form of the UN system as a liberal plaything but rather a vital necessity for postwar order and prosperity.

Numerous other politicians and pundits since have made careers by questioning the UN's relevance and calling for its dismantlement. Mine, in contrast, has revolved around trying to strengthen the world organization. Thus, the 50th Annual Meeting of the International Studies Association (ISA) in the city that hosts UN headquarters provides me with an opportunity to revisit the United Nations from a particular angle: the desperate requirement for a third generation of inter-governmental organization that moves beyond the "anarchy" and absence of overarching authority that Hedley Bull and virtually all ISA members take as a point of departure for international studies.[1]

Will it take a calamity on the scale of World War II to demonstrate the abject poverty of our current thinking? Is such a disaster necessary to catalyze a transformation of the current feeble system of what many of us now call "global governance"—the patchwork of formal and informal arrangements among states, international organizations, and various public-private partnerships—into something with at least some attributes of a world federal government? A negative reply to these questions and hope for transformed multilateral organizations requires a real stretch of the imagination, especially in the United States where the term is a four-letter word and rarely uttered in polite company. Robert Jenkins summarizes: "Once a staple of informed debate on international affairs, the term is almost never uttered in mainstream political discussion, unless it is to dismiss those who advocate the idea as hopelessly naïve, or to demonize those suspected of secretly plotting the creation of a global leviathan."[2]

This article traces what happened to the idea of a world government and its replacement by "global governance." My colleague, the American historian David Nasaw, reminded me that the 13 original states during the American Revolution were operating under the weak Articles of Confederation but sought in 1787 a "more perfect union" in Philadelphia. The world and the weak confederation of 192 UN member states require a "Philadelphia moment." First, however, I examine why and how we arrived at the notion of global governance as well as its pluses and minuses.

Background to contemporary thinking about world order

It is commonplace to state that many of the most intractable contemporary problems are transnational, ranging from climate change, migration, and pandemics to terrorism, financial instability, and proliferation of weapons of mass destruction (WMDs); and that addressing them successfully requires actions that are not unilateral, bilateral, or even multilateral but rather global. At the same time, the policy authority and resources necessary for tackling such problems remain vested in individual states rather than collectively in a universal institution; the classic collective action problem is how to organize common solutions to common problems and spread costs fairly. The fundamental disconnect between the nature of a growing number of global problems and the current inadequate structures for international problem-solving goes a long way toward explaining the fitful, tactical, and short-term local responses to challenges that require sustained, strategic, and longer-run global perspectives and action.

In preparation for the world organization's 60th anniversary in 2005, then UN secretary-general Kofi Annan's dramatic wake-up calls included references to "forks in the road"[3] and "a new San Francisco moment."[4] The *New York Times* lead editorial after the September 2005 World Summit was closer to the truth: "A once-in-a-generation opportunity to reform and revive the United Nations has been squandered."[5] At first viewed as a window of opportunity to revisit the UN in light of changes in world politics since 1945, instead negotiations exposed the very debilitating political and bureaucratic conflicts that regularly paralyze the organization. Ironically, the deliberations among prime ministers, presidents, and princes highlighted the indecisiveness and pettiness that the summit was supposedly convened to address.[6]

In spite of the ongoing mantra of reform and the obvious need for a drastic overhaul, the state-centric world organization continues to limp along much as it has since its establishment. Decolonization with its massive membership expansion as well as other fundamental geopolitical and technological changes have changed the agenda to be sure, but the UN's basic structure is fundamentally intact, a formidable bastion of state sovereignty. Unlike earlier cataclysms, today's narrow misses have not yet led to any transformation of the structures of international cooperation. Shortly after leaving his post as deputy-secretary-general and prior to becoming the UK's minister for Africa, Asia, and the United Nations, Mark Malloch Brown commented that while no topic, not even sex, was more popular than reform, neither governments nor Secretary-General Ban Ki-moon understood "the scale of change required." Member states "would have to rise above their own current sense of entrenched rights and privileges and find a grand bargain to allow a new more realistic governance model for the UN." But, he continued, "That may take a crisis."[7]

On the one hand, it is safe to say that the framers of the UN Charter would today have trouble recognizing many activities because of extensive adaptations and changes since 1945, when such contemporary topics as global warming, HIV/AIDS, and gender inequality were not on the international agenda. On the other hand, and in spite of the almost quadrupling in membership, the founders would certainly find the familiar state-centric and decentralized institutional approach to problem solving that is incapable of addressing many of today's life-threatening global challenges.

The generic label for the organizational chart is "UN system," a term implying more coherence and cohesion than is characteristic of the world body's actual behavior. Frequent use is made of the "UN family," a preferable image because like many families the United Nations is dysfunctional and divided. "The orchestra pays minimum heed to its conductor,"[8] long ago wrote Brian Urquhart and Erskine Childers. The UN cannot be compared to the vertical and hierarchical structures of national governments, corporations, or militaries. In 1969 Sir Robert Jackson, in his customary picturesque fashion, was charged to evaluate the UN's efforts in development and began the *Capacity Study*: "Governments created this machine which is . . . unmanageable in the strictest use of the word . . . like some prehistoric monster."[9] His lumbering dinosaur is now 40 years older and certainly not better adapted to the climate of the twenty-first century.

In fact, Rube Goldberg could not have come up with a better design for futile complexity than the current array of agencies focusing on a substantive area often located in a different country or continent from other relevant UN partners and with separate budgets, governing boards, and organizational cultures as well as independent executive heads. Whatever contemporary issue is of greatest concern— be it terrorism, climate change, migration, pandemics, or WMDs—we require transnational perspectives and efforts across sectors with some central direction, none of which the UN supplies.

The usual explanation for this sorry state of affairs and institutional disarray is great power politics or classic collective action problems, but blame also should be apportioned to us scholars for our lack of imagination. In struggling with the conclusion for my latest book, *What's Wrong with the United Nations and How to Fix It*,[10] I recalled with some discomfort what the Quaker economist and former ISA president Kenneth Boulding repeated often, "We are where we are because we got there."[11]

We analysts of international organization have strayed away from paradigmatic rethinking. We have lost our appetite for big and idealistic plans because so many previous ones have failed: the Concert of Europe flopped; Tsar Alexander's Hague conferences failed to end war: the Kellogg-Briand Pact was never a serious proposition; and Immanuel Kant's and Woodrow Wilson's collective security visions were incorporated in the moribund League of Nations and were still-born in the ineffective United Nations. Consequently, we no longer regard the challenges of thinking about drastically different world orders as part of the job description for serious scholars.

What is global governance?

Over the ISA's lifetime, mainstream thinking has shifted decidedly away from strengthening the United Nations and other intergovernmental organizations toward "global governance." Ramesh Thakur and I have struggled to understand the origins and itinerary of this idea for the United Nations Intellectual History Project,[12] which we trace to an offspring of a marriage between academic theory and practical policy concerns in the 1990s. James Rosenau and Ernst Czempiel's theoretical *Governance without Government* was published in 1992, just about the same time that the Swedish government launched the policy-oriented Commission on Global Governance under the chairmanship of Sonny Ramphal and Ingmar Carlsson. The 1995 publication of its report, *Our Global Neighbourhood*,[13] coincided with the first issue of *Global Governance: A Review of Multilateralism and International Organization*, the journal of the Academic Council on the United Nations System.

While a cottage industry of "prevention" has emerged since the publication of the Carnegie Commission's final report in 1997,[14] anticipating problems before they overwhelm us is not the strength of our species. About the best that we can hope for is playing catch-up in the face of life-menacing threats. Dramatic climate change and environmental deterioration, weapons proliferation and run-away technology, massive poverty and pandemics, ethnic cleansing and destabilizing financial flows nudge states to react, cope, and eventually agree under duress to construct the feeble intergovernmental organizations that we have.

Perhaps they have always been too few in number, and perhaps they have always arrived too late on the scene and with too little punch. But as we approach the second decade of the twenty-first century, the collective problems threatening the planet require building far more robust intergovernmental organizations with far greater scope and resources, and very soon indeed. US civil rights champion Martin Luther King, Jr., in his 1967 address at Riverside Church, reminded us: "Over the bleached bones and jumbled residues of numerous civilizations are written the pathetic words: 'Too late.'"[15]

The market will not graciously provide global institutions to ensure human survival with dignity. Adam Smith's "invisible hand" does not operate among states to solve problems any more than it does within states; the supply of global public goods lags far behind the demand. The state remains essential for national, regional, and global problem-solving; but states and their creations, in the form of the current generation of intergovernmental bureaucracies, cannot address many actual and looming trans-border problems.

We thus have embraced the idea of global governance. "Governance" represents the range of both informal *and* formal values, norms, practices, and institutions that provide better order than if we relied purely upon formal regulations and organizations. Confusion enters because the Latin root *gubernare* is the same for all the units that we study as political scientists. "Governance" is closely associated with "governing" and "government"—that is, with political authority, institutions, and effective control. The failure to distinguish clearly enough among terms such as global governance, world government, and cosmopolitanism is analytically very unhelpful.[16]

Applying "governance" to the planet is fundamentally misleading. It captures the gamut of interdependent relations in the *absence* of any overarching political authority and with international institutions that exert little effective control.[17] Quite a distinction exists, then, between the national and international species of governance. At the national level, we have governance *plus* government which, whatever its shortcomings in Mexico or the United States, together can usually and predictably exert effective authority and control. At the international level, we have governance *minus* government, which means virtually no capacity to ensure compliance with collective decisions.

"Global governance" refers to collective efforts to identify, understand, or address worldwide problems that go beyond the capacities of individual states to solve; it reflects the capacity of the international system at any moment in time to provide government-like services in the absence of world government. Global governance encompasses an extremely wide variety of cooperative problem-solving arrangements that may be visible but informal (e.g., practices or guidelines) or result from temporary units (e.g., coalitions of the willing). Such arrangements may also be more formal, taking the shape of hard rules (laws and treaties) as well as constituted institutions with administrative structures and established practices to manage collective affairs by a variety of actors, including state authorities, intergovernmental organizations, nongovernmental organizations, private sector entities, and other civil society actors.

As is worth repeating, at the national level we have governance plus government. And, despite well-known weaknesses, lapses, and incapacities, the expectation in Berlin, New Delhi, Brasilia, and Johannesburg is that existing institutions are routinely and predictably expected to exert authority and control. For the globe, we have only the feeblest of imitations—institutions that routinely help ensure postal delivery and airline safety, to be sure, but that routinely do far too little to address such life-threatening problems as climate change and ethnic cleansing.

Why did global governance emerge?

Three explanations exist for the appearance of the notion of global governance. The first is that, beginning in the 1970s, interdependence and rapid technological advances fostered the recognition that certain problems defy solutions by a single state. The development of a consciousness about the human environment and especially the 1972 and 1992 UN conferences in Stockholm and Rio de Janeiro are usually seen as key events in this evolution. Although other examples abound, sustainability is especially apt to illustrate why we are in the same listing boat. It simply is impossible—in spite of laudable environmental legislation in California or wind farms in the Netherlands—to halt global warming or acid rain with isolated actions.

The second explanation for the growing interest in global governance is the sheer expansion in numbers and importance of non-state actors, both civil society and for-profit corporations. Such growth has been facilitated by the so-called third wave of democratization,[18] including institutional networks similar enough to facilitate greater transnational and transgovernmental interactions described by Anne-Marie Slaughter.[19] That intergovernmental organizations like the UN no longer occupy center stage for students of international organization was symbolized by establishing the Global Compact at the Millennium Summit of 2000. The private sector—both the for-profit and the not-for-profit species—was recognized as a necessary partner for the world organization. State-centric structures—states themselves as well as their creations in the form of intergovernmental organizations—no longer enjoy a monopoly over collective efforts to improve international society and world order. They share the crowded governance stage with many other actors.

To borrow an image from James Rosenau, a "crazy quilt"[20] of authority is constantly shifting, and the patchwork of institutional elements varies by sector and over time. Perhaps even better images can be adapted from non-scholars, however, including Gertrude Stein's characterization of Oakland—"there's no there, there"—or the Cheshire cat in *Alice in Wonderland*, a grinning head floating without a body or substance. Contemporary global governance is highly uneven, often giving the impression of coverage but usually without much effect. Moreover, appearances can be deceiving and dangerous; a well-populated institutional terrain can mask a lack of coherence, substance, and accomplishment. We may feel virtuous and persuade ourselves that we are making progress when we are merely treading water or, worse, wasting time and energy rather than moving from danger toward safety. Informal, loose global governance is insufficient even were it to be accompanied by strengthened international institutions.

This brings me to the third reason for the emergence of global governance and the motivation behind this essay, namely that many of us are embarrassed with the seemingly simplistic and overly idealistic notion of supranationality. While Europe proceeds apace to move, in the late Ernst Haas's formulation, "beyond the nation-state,"[21] apparently the planet is different. Although the European Union was once thought to be a model for what could happen in the international system, currently a world federal government or even elements of one is not only old-fashioned, it is commonly thought to be the preserve of lunatics.

What happened to the idea of world government?

According to Craig Murphy's masterful history of "global governance" *avant la lettre*, since their growth began in the nineteenth century, international organizations customarily are viewed as "what world government we actually have."[22] Murphy is right, but the problem lies elsewhere. At the national level we have the authoritative structures of government *supplemented* by governance; but internationally we simply have governance with some architectural drawings that are seven decades old and not up to present building codes, along with unstable ground and shifting foundations under existing structures.

The United Nations is a makeshift expedient, what we and preceding generations have been able to concoct for addressing global problems. Not conceived as a world government, of course, the UN also was not the creation of pie-in-the-sky idealists. "Its wartime architects bequeathed us this system as a realist necessity vital in times of trial," one historian notes, "not as a liberal accessory to be discarded when the going gets rough."[23]

Unlike earlier generations of international organization scholars, however, the goal of contemporary proponents of global governance is *no longer* the creation of world government.[24] This is a dramatic change from the past when such thinking was not beyond the pale and actually not even far from the mainstream.

Beginning with Dante's *Monarchia* at the beginning of the fourteenth century, there is a long tradition of criticizing the existing state system and replacing it with a universal government.[25] The idealist tradition includes Hugo Grotius, the Dutch jurist whose *On the Laws of War and Peace* (1625) usually qualifies him as the "father" of international law; Emeric Cruce, the French monk who died in the same year as the Peace of Westphalia and who had dreamed of a world court, a place for nations to meet and work out disputes, and disarmament; and, of course, Immanuel Kant whose *Perpetual Peace* (1795) envisioned a confederation of democratic and pacific states (though he stopped short of world government). Finally, demonstrating that these ideas are not the monopoly of Western thoughts, Derek Heater has found contemplations about "world government" in Chinese and Indian philosophies.[26]

The late Harold Jacobson noted that the march toward a world government was woven into the tapestries decorating the walls of the *Palais des Nations* in Geneva—now the UN's European Office but once the headquarters of the League of Nations. He observed that they

> picture the process of humanity combining into ever larger and more stable units for the purpose of governance—first the family, then the tribe, then the city-state, and then the nation—a process which presumably would eventually culminate in the entire world being combined in one political unit.[27]

Today it is hard to imagine a United States in which discussions about the topic depicted in that tapestry would be possible. Yet there once was a sizable group of prominent American supporters from every walk of life, reflected by resolutions passed by 30 of 48 state legislatures, supporting a US response to growing interdependence and instability that would pool American sovereignty with that of other countries.

September 11th and the Bush administration turned customary wariness toward international organizations—or the ups and downs of what Edward Luck has called "mixed messages"[28]—into visceral hostility toward the United Nations. One now requires unknown powers of imagination to envision a Washington, DC, where the idea of world government would be a staple of public policy analysis. Yet a 1949 sense of Congress resolution, House Concurrent Resolution 64, argued in favor of "a fundamental objective of the foreign policy of the United States to support and strengthen the United Nations and to seek its development into a world federation." It was sponsored by 111 representatives, including two future presidents, John F. Kennedy and Gerald Ford, as well as such other future prominent politicians as Mike Mansfield, Henry Cabot Lodge, Abraham Ribicoff, Christian Herter, Peter Rodino, Henry Jackson, and Jacob Javits. About the same time, the Senate Foreign Relations Sub-committee was considering several similar motions to recommend to President Harry Truman.[29] Throughout the 1940s, it was impossible in the United States to read periodicals, listen to the radio, or watch newsreels and not encounter the idea of world government.

We now conveniently ignore how many prominent groups in the interwar years and during World War II pushed the idea.[30] One of the first such organizations was the Campaign for World Government, founded in 1937 by peace and women's rights activist Rosika Schwimmer. Clarence Streit, a *New York Times* reporter in Geneva who reported on the League of Nations in the 1930s, published a 1939 best-seller, *Union Now*,[31] that proposed a global federal union of liberal democracies. Schwimmer criticized Streit because the inclusion of former enemies, in her view, would be necessary if the new experiment was to be accepted as a veritable world government and not dismissed as a continuation of a wartime alliance.[32]

Neither persuaded the Roosevelt administration to include the idea of world government in American proposals in San Francisco, but peace movements of various stripes raised the profile of supra-nationality. The cause had an unusual hero, the defeated 1940 Republican presidential candidate, Wendell Wilkie, who was Franklin and Eleanor Roosevelt's goodwill ambassador and published in 1943 another unlikely hit that spent four months in the first position on the *New York Times* best-seller list, *One World*.[33] It sold some two million copies and at least attenuated the Republican Party's isolationism and helped secure bipartisan approval of the United Nations.

Shortly before the nuclear age began, the June 1945 signing of the Charter in San Francisco diminished the punch of those pushing for a world federation because at least there was a new universal institution; but it far from satisfied world-government advocates because the United Nations, except for an occasional Security Council decision, could not act independently from its member states and enforce decisions. And so the world organization's establishment in part whetted the appetites of a numerically small lobby seeking to avoid a nuclear World War Three. The legacy of wartime activism was the United World Federalists, founded in 1947. Its 50,000 members were inspired by another best-seller, Emery Reves's *The Anatomy of Peace*,[34] which was serialized in *Reader's Digest* and argued that the United Nations of member states had to be replaced by the rule of law for the world. Grenville Clark, a Wall Street lawyer and friend of Roosevelt's, teamed up with Harvard Law School Professor Louis Sohn to burnish these ideas in what later was expanded in their classic textbook *World Peace through World Law*.[35] Simultaneously, financier Bernard Baruch devised a visionary plan to place the nuclear fuel cycle under the United Nations at a time when the United States still enjoyed the atomic monopoly. Led by its president Robert M. Hutchins, the University of Chicago from 1945 to 1951 sponsored a prominent group of scholars in the Committee to Frame a World Constitution.

The movement drew support not only from a scientific luminary like Albert Einstein but also from such visible entertainers as E.B. White, Oscar Hammerstein, and—Ripley, believe it or not—Ronald Reagan. Future senators Alan Cranston and Harris Wofford sought to spread the UWF's message among university students, and the Student Federalists became the United States' largest nonpartisan political organization. Other prominent individuals associated with the world government idea included Kurt Vonnegut, Walter Cronkite, H. G. Wells, Peter Ustinov, Dorothy Thompson, Supreme Court justices William Douglas and Owen Roberts, Senator Estes Kefauver, and future vice-president Hubert Humphrey. And the list goes on.

By the early 1950s, the world government idea was hidden by the Iron Curtain, overshadowed by the Cold War, and eclipsed by Senator Joseph McCarthy's witch hunt. On the right wing, this jump-started the engines of the black helicopters that are still whirling and fostered labeling advocates for world government as communist fellow travelers; and more recently on the left wing, the idea has encountered fears of top-down tyranny in a dystopia.[36]

In Europe, the attention of most intellectuals was on reconstruction although a few individuals pursued the universal federal ideal, including historian Arnold Toynbee as well as Aldous Huxley, Bertrand Russell, and John Boyd Orr (the first head of the UN's Food and Agriculture Organization and 1949 Nobel Peace Prize laureate). Led by the French banker Jean Monnet, Europeans shifted to a regional federal idea for the continent and away from one for the globe.

Most of the countries in what we now call the "global South" were still colonies at this time, and local independence struggles and solidarity in decolonization efforts were far more pressing than distant world orders. Nonetheless, aspirations for a world federal government were not absent from public discourse in, for example, newly independent India. In an address to the General Assembly as late as December 1956,

Jawaharlal Nehru, no utopian, argued: "In spite of the difficulties and the apparent conflicts, gradually the sense of a world community conferring together through its elected representative is not only developing but seizing the minds of people all over the world." He continued, "The only way to look ahead assuredly is for some kind of world order, One World, to emerge."[37]

In short, the United States became obsessed with anticommunism; Europe focused on the construction of a regional economic and political community; and the burgeoning number of postcolonial countries shifted their preoccupations toward nonalignment and Third World solidarity.

In any case, this "ancient history" of world government now seems quaint. ISA members thinking about it are almost extinct. From time to time a contemporary international relations theorist like Alexander Wendt suggests that "a world state is inevitable"[38] or Daniel Deudney wishes one were because war has become too dangerous.[39] Or, an international lawyer like Richard Falk calls for an irrevocable transfer of sovereignty upwards.[40] When someone like Campbell Craig notes the "resurgent idea of world government," this has more to do with the buzz about "global governance" and less with the serious discussion of world government per se.[41] In short, the idea of world government has been banned in sober and sensible discussions of global affairs and certainly is absent from classrooms. In fact, I cannot recall a single undergraduate or graduate student inquiring about the theoretical possibility of a central political authority exercising elements of universal legal jurisdiction. The surest way to secure classification as a crackpot is to mention a world government as either a hypothetical or, worse yet, desirable outcome.

Occasionally a mainstream academic utters "world government" for one of two reasons. First, the author wishes to demonstrate her realistic approach and scholarly credentials by spelling-out clearly what she is *not* doing. At the outset of her insightful book, *A New World Order*, Anne-Marie Slaughter stressed that "world government is both infeasible and undesirable."[42] No reader would have mistaken her convictions without this disclaimer. But "new world order" seems ominously close to a slippery slope between international cooperation and an embryonic world government; and so the author or publisher or both felt compelled apparently to formally distance the book from the entirely discredited literature about world government. Second, the term may be invoked as a functional equivalent for Pax Americana—for instance, Michael Mandelbaum's book on US hegemony, *The Case for Goliath: How America Acts as the World's Government in the Twenty-first Century*, or Niall Ferguson's book on America as an empire, *Colossus: The Price of America's Empire*.[43] They discuss the many global public goods that the United States provides (or should provide) and especially its role as the world's policeman, making it the functional equivalent of a world government.

Changes from earlier thinking

After his archival labors to write a two-volume history of world federalism, Joseph Barrata observes that in the 1990s "the new expression, 'global governance,' emerged as an acceptable term in debate on international organization for the desired and practical goal of progressive efforts, in place of 'world government.'" He continues that scholars

> wished to avoid using a term that would harken back to the thinking about world government in the 1940s, which was largely based on fear of atomic bombs and too often had no practical proposals for the transition short of a revolutionary act of the united peoples of the world.[44]

Most analysts of global governance see world government as atavistic idealism that is beyond the pale. To investigate or support such a policy is seen as naïveté at best, and lunacy at worst. And certainly no younger scholar would wish to cut short her career by exploring such a thought for a dissertation.

Global governance is a half-way house between the international anarchy underlying Realist analysis and a world state. The current generation of intergovernmental organizations undoubtedly helps lessen transaction costs and overcome some structural obstacles to international cooperation as would be clear to anyone examining international responses to the 2004 tsunami or ongoing humanitarian crises for which we see a constellation of helping hands—soldiers from a variety of countries, UN organizations, large and small NGOs, and even Wal-Mart.

Global governance certainly is not the continuation of traditional power politics. It also is not the expression of an evolutionary process leading to the formation of institutional structures able to address contemporary or future global threats. Moreover, to speak of "governance" and not "government" is to discuss the product and not the producer. Agency and accountability are absent.

Most of us certainly are not complacent about what is at stake or satisfied that global governance can accomplish what global government could. Rather, our approach reflects a judgment about how to spend limited analytical energies in the immediate term. Even those considered modestly engaged, however, are no longer even imagining anything more than institutional tinkering. The disappearance of any passion for more robust intergovernmental organizations appears to be the accompanying downside in the pursuit of global governance.

Two important features distinguish global governance from earlier thinking about collective responses to international problems; and they have serious implications for how we act because they restrict our thinking and advocacy. First, many analysts formerly viewed the development of international organization and law not only as a step in the right direction and as more effective than unilateral efforts and the law of the jungle. But they also viewed the march of a growing web of international institutions as an unstoppable progression.

However, even a rabid world federalist had to admit that a powerful state could solve most problems on its own, or at least could insulate itself from their worst impacts. Efforts to eradicate malaria within a geographic area and to prevent those with the disease from entering a territory should be seen as qualitatively different from halting terrorist money-laundering, avian flu, or acid rain. Today, no state, no matter how powerful, can labor under the illusion that it can guarantee success in protecting its population from such threats. Earlier problems could be constrained by a rich state within its borders by constructing effective barriers, whereas a growing number of contemporary challenges to world order consist of what former UN secretary-general Kofi Annan calls "problems without passports."[45]

Paradoxically, when states still could solve or attenuate most problems, the idea of a world government remained plausible over the longer term and was part of the mainstream. Now when states visibly cannot address a growing number of threats, world government is unimaginable; and even more robust international organizations are often looked upon askance.

Second, earlier conceptual efforts emphasized the state and grudgingly admitted the presence and capacities of other actors. But starting in the 1980s, and earlier in some cases, both civil society and market-oriented groups were recognized as having a crucial impact and reach. They became an increasingly integral part of solutions either promulgated or actually undertaken by the United Nations and many of its member states.

This shift in perspective has, however, led us to go overboard in our enthusiasm for non-state actors and their potential for problem solving. Burgeoning numbers of NGOs and corporations clearly have resources and energy; but why are more robust intergovernmental organizations viewed as an afterthought if even thought about at all? The current generation of such organizations is so obviously inadequate that we have to do more than throw up our hands and hope for the best from norm entrepreneurs, activists crossing borders, profit-seeking corporations, and transnational social networks. To state the obvious, NGOs and multinational corporations will not eliminate poverty, fix global warming, or halt murder in Darfur.

In the early postwar period, it should be recalled that such prominent US realists as Hans Morgenthau and Reinhold Niebuhr had already (albeit uneasily) concluded that a "world state" was logically necessary in light of the nuclear threat.[46] Neorealists subsequently viewed the absence of central authority as an unalterable fact of life[47] and even favored a system of sovereign states over a world government.[48] Hence rereading E.H. Carr[49] is valuable in that he warned readers in the interwar years that blending utopia and power in thinking was necessary in order to avoid stagnation and despair. In other words, the father of realism understood that a vision of where ideally we should be headed is necessary to avoid getting mired and going nowhere. Oscar Wilde said it more poetically: "A map of the world that does not include Utopia is not worth looking at."[50]

Without a long-term vision, we accept the contours of the current and unacceptable international system, including the feeble United Nations. By not even struggling to imagine a fundamentally different system, we make the continuation of the current lackluster one inevitable.

The pluses and minuses of global governance

Global governance is a useful analytical tool—if I were choosing an expensive word, I would say a good "heuristic" device—to understand what is happening in today's world. At the same time, it lacks prescriptive power to point toward where we should be headed and what we should be doing. It is a process, not an entity, which assembles any stakeholder with an interest in whatever topic is at hand. To repeat, in the domestic context governance adds to government, implying shared purpose and goal orientation *in addition to* formal authority and police or enforcement powers. For the planet, governance is essentially the whole story, what Scott Barrett describes as "organized volunteerism."[51]

We are obliged to ask ourselves whether we can approach anything that resembles effective governance for the world without institutions with some supranational characteristics at the global level. At a minimum, we require more creative thinking about more robust intergovernmental organizations. We also need more passionate (or less embarrassed) advocacy for steps leading toward elements of supranationality rather than hoping somehow that the decentralized system of states and a pooling of corporate and civil society efforts will ensure human survival and dignity.

Proponents of global governance—and it would be difficult to say that I am not in this category, having edited the journal with that title from 2000 to 2005—make a good-faith effort to emphasize how to best realize a stable, peaceful, and well-ordered international society in the absence of a unifying global authority. But this pragmatism also reflects an assumption that no powerful global institutions will appear any time soon, amounting to a self-fulfilling prophecy of sorts. But agency is essential; and better problem solving will not simply materialize without more muscular intergovernmental organizations, first and foremost those of the United Nations system.

Paradoxically, intergovernmental organizations seem more and more marginal to our thinking at exactly the moment when enhanced multilateralism is so sorely required. And ironically, this reality coincides with a period when globalization—and especially advances in information and communication technologies along with reduced barriers to transnational exchanges of goods, capital, and services, of people, ideas, and cultural influences—makes something resembling institutions with at least some characteristics of supranationality appear feasible. As Daniel Deudney and John Ikenberry tell us, "the relentless imperatives of rising global interdependence create powerful and growing incentives for states to engage in international cooperation."[52] However, what gets lost as we struggle to comprehend an indistinct patchwork of authority is that current intergovernmental organizations are insufficient in scope and ambition, inadequate in resources and reach, and incoherent in policies and philosophies.

It is humbling to realize how much our aspirations have diminished, how feeble our current expectations are in comparison with earlier generations of analysts who did not shy away from world government or at least robust intergovernmental bodies. At Bretton Woods in 1944, John Maynard Keynes and the British delegation proposed a monetary fund equal to half of annual world imports while Harry Dexter White and the American side proposed a smaller fund with one-sixth of annual world imports. As the late Hans Singer sardonically noted: "Today's Fund is only 2 percent of annual world imports. The difference between Keynes's originally proposed 50 percent and the actual 2 percent is a measure of the degree to which our vision of international economic management has shrunk."[53]

While it is true that a denser network of institutions exists now than when Keynes was writing, the tasks that he sought to accomplish remain—indeed, the ongoing financial and economic crisis make the lacunae more obvious by the day. We must ask ourselves why we are satisfied that the contemporary intergovernmental organization with supposedly the sharpest economic enforcement teeth is such a pale imitation of what the twentieth century's greatest economist thought desirable and plausible. While his big plans never panned out, what is required is not thinking bigger but making a quantum shift in thinking, not just an institutional thickening of the current international order but a different order.

Article 109 of the UN Charter foresaw a constitutional review of the world organization no later than 1955, but a two-thirds quorum has never been assembled to convene such a gathering. There were those who hoped that ten years would be sufficient to demonstrate that the UN was not up to the challenges facing the international system. So it may seem hazardous, and the epithet "Pollyannaish" undoubtedly will come my way, to assert that we now have reached a point that states will understand the need to federate in some fashion.

Nonetheless, it is time to reaffirm a belief that human beings are as strong as the problems that they have created, that they can pull together more powerful intergovernmental institutions. Craig Murphy encourages us, "the longer history of industry and international organizations indicates that the task of creating the necessary global institutions may be easier than many of today's liberal commentators believe."[54] His contention mirrors a poetic encouragement by the UN's second secretary-general, Dag Hammarskjöld: "Never measure the height of a mountain until you have reached the top. Then you will see how low it was."[55]

Are anomalies no longer anomalous?

In *The Structure of Scientific Revolutions*, Thomas S. Kuhn outlined the process by which a dominant scientific paradigm—or "ways of seeing the world"—is replaced by a new one.[56] Being on the outlook for unanticipated results creates both an awareness of possible deficiencies in a theory or existing paradigm. Puzzling anomalies have to be addressed through the generation of auxiliary hypotheses in order to explain an anomaly within that existing paradigm. If too many anomalies and too messy a web of auxiliary hypotheses arise, a new paradigm is required when "the anomalous has become the expected."[57] Kuhn's classic example was the shift from Ptolemy's model of planets rotating around a fixed Earth to the one introduced by Copernicus. It occurred when the old model simply could not explain what was going on let alone predict what was going to happen and provide prescriptive guidance.

We are not yet at a Copernican moment for state sovereignty because anarchy still predicts much of international relations albeit amidst a growing number of disconnects. Like Copernicus, however, we should stare at the same sun and planets that others have seen but reframe the relations among them. Rarely do international systemic changes evolve in a linear fashion, but rather they usually are accompanied by discontinuities and contradictions.[58] The malfunctioning of today's international system has not yet led to a new paradigm but rather to global governance, which helps us to understand what *is* happening but does not push us to determine what *should* happen. Many of us are willing to admit that we are living in a "post-Westphalian" moment—a label much like "post–Cold War"—which accurately indicates that we are leaving behind the era begun in 1648 but provides neither a catchy nor an accurate label for what follows.

Like the United Nations itself, global governance is a bridge between the old and the as yet unborn. It cannot solve those pesky problems without passports that are staring us in the face—global warming, genocide, nuclear proliferation, migration, money laundering, terrorism, and worldwide pandemics like AIDS.

If someone is a Westphalian pessimist—an image I borrow from Richard Falk[59]—she should feel free to eat, drink, and be merry as nuclear apocalypse is inevitable shortly before or after the planet's average temperature increases by several degrees. And if someone is a post-Westphalian pessimist, he might as well do the same because globalization's inequities and proliferation of lethal technologies will lead to a different kind of chaos and undermine or even doom civilization as we know it.

Nonetheless, I still firmly believe that human beings can organize themselves to solve global problems. There are numerous ways to think about an eventual supranational global entity, and human agency is an essential element for everyone. Westphalian optimists consist of those who believe that the state system can be adapted and eventually modified; they possess a basic Kantian faith in the warming of international relations. For them, the combined spread of trade and economic progress along with the consensual strengthening of existing international organizations ultimately will result in a world state. David Held is the best example of a Westphalian optimist, whose vision is more humanistic and less militaristic than those of other observers.[60]

Post-Westphalian optimists like Peter Singer see globalization as creating a context for global unity in which sovereign states no longer will represent the outer limits of political community and ethical obligations—and his version, like Wilkie's and Nehru's, is called "one world."[61] Over time, there will be voluntary actions by governments and peoples—akin to what is happening in the European Union—and this gradual process could eventually result in important elements of a world federal government. Singer recognizes the dangers of a lumbering institutional behemoth and potential tyranny—indeed, even the existing UN is anathema to extremist libertarians, some of whom still imagine it as a plot to take over the world and destroy individual freedoms. He nonetheless sees the growing influence of transnational social forces as making possible a different kind of post-Westphalian global unity.

As either a Westphalian or a post-Westphalian optimist—I vacillate between the two—global government rather than global governance is the missing component of future analytical perspectives. If, as Kenneth Boulding told us, we are where we are because we got there, then we will remain there without an alternative vision. A clear link exists between our aspirations, on the one hand, and our policies, institutions, and accomplishments, on the other. My late friend Sergio Vieira de Mello, who died in the attack on UN headquarters in Baghdad in August 2003, put it differently: "Unless we aim for the seemingly unattainable, we risk settling for mediocrity."[62]

Perhaps as much as any recent event, the global financial and economic meltdown that began last year, which the late John Kenneth Galbraith might well have dubbed "the great crash 2008,"[63] made even clearer what many less serious previous crises had not—namely the risks, problems, and enormous costs of a global economy without adequate international institutions, democratic decision-making, and powers to bring order, spread risks, and enforce compliance. "The global financial and political crises are, in fact, closely related," no less an observer than Henry Kissinger wrote on President Barack Obama's Inauguration Day, but the financial collapse "made evident the absence of global institutions to cushion the shock."[64]

Most countries, and especially the major powers, are not ready to accept the need for elements of global government and the inroads that this would entail for their own autonomy. Nonetheless, the logic of interdependence and a growing number of system-wide and life-threatening crises place this possibility more squarely on the international agenda and make parts of a world federal government an idea that is both necessary and possible.

Conclusion

We need a big international vision from the Obama administration.[65] In nominating his confidante Susan Rice as ambassador to the United Nations and by restoring the post's cabinet status, Obama not only announced that the United States has rejoined the world and is ready to re-engage with all member states, but also he acknowledged what is evident to most people on the planet who were not in the ideological bubble of the Bush administration, namely "that the global challenges we face demand global institutions that work."[66]

The new president excels in political imagination and the articulation of his vision for "change," and he should draw on his skills for two communications challenges in the United States. First, he understands one of the major tenets of democracy, which is essential to building the next world order as well, namely that disagreements over priorities and policy choices have to be resolved through consensus on process. Some criticize his willingness to negotiate with domestic adversaries. This is not a sign of weakness; and internationally, it is a prerequisite to moving beyond evaporating American hegemony. With power shifting, the United Nations is no longer a detour that delays but rather a destination that enriches US options and influence.

Second, he also must help overcome what can only be described as the lamentable public ignorance, including especially members of Congress, about why the UN agglomeration works the way that it does. Why, despite its weaknesses, does it have a presence in every trouble spot and in every emerging issue that anyone can spot? In the contemporary world, US diplomats as well as the public need to understand the usefulness of setting goals, seeking cooperative programs (even those that never are executed as is hardly unknown in governments, militaries, and businesses), and thinking of global policies as a better way of keeping alive than trotting out the tanks.

It is not enough that the United Nations be made to work; it must be seen to work for all. And Obama may be the leader who makes Americans and other citizens of the world agree on the need for a new grand bargain, a third generation of international organizations. The choreography of a grand bargain is delicate. It happens in stages, with each side giving up something to get something. The era of unending US gains through the application of unilateral power is over, but there can be addition by subtraction. Compromises that preserve a substantial degree of US persuasiveness in the long term are worth giving up some power in the short term.

There are of course still many members of the contemporary flat-earth society, the John Boltons and John Yoos for whom the mere mention of even "the benignly labeled 'global governance'" is anathema.[67] However, those whose ears do not pick up any humming noise of black helicopters but rather a loud collective sigh of relief with the prospect for enhanced international cooperation under the Obama administration are obliged to ask ourselves whether anything that resembles effective global governance can occur without something that looks much more like government at the global level. We certainly should respect subsidiarity, the commonsensical principle that higher levels of society should not take on tasks and functions that can be accomplished better at lower levels. At a bare minimum, however, we require more creative thinking about more robust intergovernmental organizations. It is certainly not far-fetched to imagine that over the coming decades we will see a gradual advance of intergovernmental agreements and powers along the lines that Europe has nurtured since World War II. Who would not have been denounced as a crank seven decades ago for thinking that political and economic union were possible among France, the United Kingdom, Germany, and other European states?

And the scent of reinvention is beginning to be in the air. For example, in January 2008 British prime minister Gordon Brown argued before business leaders in New Delhi:

> To succeed now and in the future, the post-war rules of the game, the post-war international institution, fit for the Cold War and for a world of just 50 states, must be radically reformed to fit our world of globalization where there are 200 states, an emerging single marketplace, unprecedented individual autonomy and the increasing power of informal networks across the world.[68]

In the midst of the ongoing financial crisis, President George W. Bush pulled together a "G-20" because the G-7/8 did not include the countries that now account for most of world economic growth or credit. The Council on Foreign Relations has begun a program on International Institutions and Global Governance, World Order in the 21st Century. In December 2008, the Carnegie Endowment for International Peace hosted "Present at the Creation 2.0: How Reinventing the International System Could Become One of the Central Legacies of the Obama Administration." Richard Hormats and David Rothkopf, two mainstays at Beltway seminars, argued that "the United States cannot effectively or affordably achieve its goals without restoring, renovating, or in some cases reinventing the multilateral mechanisms available to it in each major policy area."[69]

The reference to Dean Acheson's autobiography is especially apt because Washington was not only present at the creation[70] of but also led the post–World War II efforts to construct a second generation of international organizations to promote peace and prosperity after the collapse of the League of Nations and the Great Depression. Now, we urgently need to establish the next generation of international institutions or at least to revise the largely outmoded architectural drawings for existing ones and introduce twenty-first century building-codes.

Looking back on a "remarkable generation of leaders and public servants," Sir Brian Urquhart recalls earlier US leaders who

> were pragmatic idealists more concerned about the future of humanity than the outcome of the next election; and they understood that finding solutions to postwar problems was much more important than being popular with one or another part of the American electorate.[71]

Could that same far-sighted political commitment dawn again under the Obama administration, if not in 2009 at least by the end of a second term?

Notes

1 Hedley Bull, *The Anarchical Society* (New York: Columbia University Press, 1977). Research about the United Nations system is not idiosyncratic among past presidents of this association. A quick overview of my forty-eight distinguished predecessors shows that over one-quarter of them have written at least a book and major articles on the UN or part of the system, and three-quarters have at least a few articles touching upon the United Nations. Among those from whom I have learned a lot who have held this job in the last thirty years and who have devoted a considerable portion of their scholarly attention to the United Nations are: Craig Murphy, Charles Kegley, the late Hayward Alker, Bob Keohane, David Singer, James Rosenau, Bruce Russett, the late Harold Jacobson, and Chadwick Alger. I am grateful to Anoulak Kittikhoun for his research assistance.
2 Rob Jenkins, "What the U.N. Might Have Been: World Government Movements in 1940s America," *BBK Magazine*, January 2006. I have benefited enormously from conversations with him and from his comments as well as his book manuscript.
3 Kofi A. Annan, "Secretary-General Address to the General Assembly given 23 September 2003," available at: www.un.org/webcast/ga/58/statements/sg2eng030923.htm.

4 Kofi A. Annan, "In Larger Freedom: Decision Time at the UN," *Foreign Affairs* 84, no. 3 (2005): 65.

5 "The Lost U.N. Summit Meeting," *New York Times*, 14 September 2005.

6 See Thomas G. Weiss and Barbara Crossette, "The United Nations: Post-Summit Outlook," in *Great Decisions 2006*, ed. Foreign Policy Association (New York: Foreign Policy Association, 2006), 9–22.

7 Mark Malloch Brown, "Can the UN Be Reformed?" *Global Governance* 14, no. 1 (2008):1–12, quotes from 7–8.

8 Erskine Childers with Brian Urquhart, *Renewing the United Nations System* (Uppsala, Sweden: Dag Hammarskjöld Foundation, 1994), 32.

9 United Nations, *A Capacity Study of the United Nations Development System* (Geneva: UN, 1969), volume I, iii.

10 Thomas G. Weiss, *What's Wrong with the United Nations and How to Fix It* (Cambridge: Polity Press, 2009).

11 Interview with Elise Boulding in Needham, Massachusetts by the author, 16 April 2001. See *The Complete Oral History Transcripts from UN Voices*, CD-ROM (New York: United Nations Intellectual History Project, 2007).

12 See Ramesh Thakur and Thomas G. Weiss, *The UN and Global Governance: An Unfinished Journey* (Bloomington: Indiana University Press, 2010). For other books in the series, see www.unhistory.org.

13 Commission on Global Governance, *Our Global Neighbourhood* (Oxford: Oxford University Press, 1995).

14 Carnegie Commission on the Prevention of Deadly Conflict, *Preventing Deadly Conflict* (New York: Carnegie Corporation, 1997).

15 Martin Luther King, Jr., "Beyond Vietnam," Address delivered to the Clergy and Layment Concerned about Vietnam, Riverside Church, 4 April 1967, available at: www.ratical. org/ratville/JFK/MLKapr67.html.

16 See, for example, Campell Craig, "The Resurgent Idea of World Government," *Ethics & International Affairs* 22, no. 2 (2008): 133–42.

17 Ernst-Otto Czempiel, "Governance and Democratization," in *Governance without Government: Order and Change in World Politics*, ed. James N. Rosenau and Ernst-Otto Czempiel (Cambridge: Cambridge University Press, 1992), 250–71. Also see Leon Gordenker and Thomas G. Weiss, "Pluralizing Global Governance: Analytical Approaches and Dimensions," in *NGOs, the UN, and Global Governance*, ed. Leon Gordenker and Thomas G. Weiss (Boulder, Colo.: Lynne Rienner, 1996), 17–47.

18 Samuel P. Huntington, *Third Wave: Democratization in the Late Twentieth Century* (Norman: University of Oklahoma Press, 1991).

19 See Anne-Marie Slaughter, "America's Edge: Power in the Networked Century," *Foreign Affairs* 88, no. 1 (2009): 94–113, which updates and expands *A New World Order* (Princeton, NJ: Princeton University Press, 2004).

20 James N. Rosenau, "Toward an Ontology for Global Governance," in *Approaches to Global Governance Theory*, ed. Martin Hewson and Timothy J. Sinclair (Albany: State University of New York, 1999), 293.

21 Ernst B. Haas, *Beyond the Nation-State: Functionalism and International Organization* (Palo Alto, Calif.: Stanford University Press, 1964).

22 Craig N. Murphy, "Global Governance: Poorly Done and Poorly Understood," *International Affairs* 76, no. 4 (2000): 789.

23 See Dan Plesch, "How the United Nations Beat Hitler and Prepared the Peace," *Global Society* 22, no. 1 (2008): 137–58, quote at 137.

24 For an alternative view, see James A. Yunker, *Rethinking World Government: A New Approach* (Lanham, Md.: University Press of America, 2005). See also Robert Latham, "Politics in a Floating World: Toward a Critique of Global Governance," in *Approaches to Global Governance Theory*, 23–53.

25 Craig N. Murphy, *International Organization and Industrial Change: Global Governance Since 1850* (Cambridge: Polity Press, 1994), 1.

26 Derek Heater, *World Citizenship and Government: Cosmopolitan Ideas in the History of Western Political Thought* (New York: St. Martin's Press, 1996).

27 Harold K. Jacobson, *Networks of Interdependence: International Organizations and the Global Political System*, 2nd ed. (New York: Knopf, 1984), 84.

28 Edward C. Luck, *Mixed Messages: American Politics and International Organization 1919– 1999* (Washington, DC: Brookings Institution, 1999).

29 Paul Boyer, *By the Bomb's Early Light: American Thought and Culture at the Dawn of the Atomic Age* (New York: Pantheon, 1985).

30 For an exhaustive summary and key primary documents, see Joseph Preston Barrata, *The Politics of World Federation*, 2 volumes (Westport, Conn.: Praeger Publishers, 2004). Some examples here draw on his thorough research.

31 Clarence K. Streit, *Union Now* (New York: Harper & Brothers, 1939).

32 Rosika Schwimmer, *Union Now, For Peace or War? The Danger in the Plan of Clarence Streit* (New York: author, 1940).

33 Wendell L. Wilkie, *One World* (New York: Simon and Schuster, 1943).

34 Emery Reves, *The Anatomy of Peace* (New York: Harper & Brothers, 1946).

35 Grenville Clark and Louis B. Sohn, *World Peace through World Law* (Cambridge, Mass.: Harvard University Press, 1958).

36 Richard Falk, *Achieving Human Rights* (London: Routledge, 2009), 13–24; and *On Humane Governance: Toward a New Global Politics* (Cambridge: Polity, 1995).

37 Jawaharlal Nehru, "Towards a World Community," in *India at the United Nations*, ed. S. K. Madhavan, vol. I (New Delhi: APH Publishing Corporation, 1949), 61–4.

38 Alexander Wendt, "Why a World State Is Inevitable," *European Journal of International Relations* 9, no. 4 (2003): 491–542. See Vaughn P. Shannon, "Wendt's Violation of the Constructivist Project: Agency and Why a World State Is Not Inevitable," *European Journal of International Relations* 11, no. 4 (2005): 581–7; and Alexander Wendt, "Agency, Teleology and the World State: A Reply to Shannon," *European Journal of International Relations* 11, no. 4 (2005): 589–98.

39 Daniel H. Deudney, *Bounding Power: Republican Security Theory from the Polls to the Global Village* (Princeton, NJ: Princeton University Press, 2006).

40 Richard Falk, "International Law and the Future," *Third World Quarterly* 27, no. 5 (2006): 727–37.

41 See Craig, "The Resurgent Idea of World Government."

42 Slaughter, *A New World Order*, 8.

43 Michael Mandelbaum, *The Case For Goliath: How America Acts as the World's Government in the Twenty-first Century* (New York: Public Affairs, 2006); and Niall Ferguson, *Colossus: The Price of America's Empire* (New York: Penguin Press, 2004).

44 Baratta, *The Politics of World Federation*, vol. 2, 534–5.

45 Kofi A. Annan, "What Is the International Community? Problems Without Passports," *Foreign Policy*, no. 132 (Sept.-Oct. 2002): 30–1.

46 See Campbell Craig, *Glimmer of a New Leviathan: Total War in the Realism of Niebuhr, Morgenthau, and Waltz* (New York: Columbia University Press, 2003), 166–73; Hans Morgenthau, *Politics Among Nations* (New York: Knopf, 1960), ch. 27, 29; Hans Morgenthau, *The Restoration of American Politics* (Chicago: Chicago University Press, 1962), 174–5; and Rienhold Niebuhr, *Structure of Nations and Empires: A Study of the Recurring Patterns and Problems of the Political Order in Relation to the Unique Problems of the Nuclear Age* (New York: Scribner, 1959).

47 John Mearsheimer, *The Tragedy of Great Power Politics* (New York: Norton, 2001).

48 Kenneth N. Waltz, *Theory of International Politics* (New York: McGraw-Hill, 1979), 111–12.

49 Edward Hallett Carr, *The Twenty Years' Crisis, 1919–1939* (New York: Harper Torchbooks, 1964), 108.

50 Oscar Wilde, "The Soul of Man Under Socialism," in *Selected Essays and Poems* (London: Penguin, 1954), 34.

51 Scott Barrett, *Why Cooperate? The Incentive to Supply Global Public Goods* (Oxford: Oxford University Press, 2007), 19.

52 Daniel Deudney and G. John Ikenberry, "The Myth of the Autocratic Revival: Why Liberal Democracy Will Prevail," *Foreign Affairs* 88, no. 1 (2009): 77–93 at 79.

53 Hans Singer, "An Historical Perspective," in *The UN and the Bretton Woods Institutions: New Challenges for the Twenty-First Century*, ed. Mahbub ul Haq, Richard Jolly, Paul Streeten, and Khadija Haq (London: Macmillan, 1995), 19.

54 Murphy, *International Organization and Industrial Change*, 9.

55 Dag Hammarskjöld, *Markings*, translated by Leif Sjoberg and W.H. Auden (New York: Knopf, 1965), 7.

56 Thomas S. Kuhn, *The Structure of Scientific Revolutions*, 2nd ed. (Chicago: University of Chicago Press, 1970), 4.

57 Ibid., 53.

58 See Charles Jencks, *The Architecture of the Jumping Universe, A Polemic: How Complexity Science is Changing Architecture and Culture* (New York: Wiley, 1997).

59 These terms are Richard Falk's in "International Law and the Future."

60 See David Held, *Global Covenant: The Social Democratic Alternative to the Washington Consensus* (Cambridge: Polity, 2004).

61 Peter Singer, *One World: The Ethics of Globalization*, 2nd ed. (New Haven, Conn.: Yale University Press, 2004).

62 Sergio Vieira de Mello, "Their Dignity Will Be Mine, As It Is Yours," in *The Role of the United Nations in Peace and Security, Global Development, and World Governance*, ed. Michaela Hordijk, Maartje van Eerd, and Kaj Hofman (Lesiston, NY: Edwin Mellen Press, 2007), 9.

63 John Kenneth Galbraith, *The Great Crash, 1929* (Boston: Houghton Mifflin, 1954).

64 Henry Kissinger, "The World Must Forge a New Order or Retreat into Chaos," *The Independent*, 20 January 2009.

65 This argument is based on Thomas G. Weiss, "Indispensable and Imperfect, the United Nations and Obama's UN Policy," *Washington Quarterly* 32, no. 3 (2009): 141–62.

66 "Announcement of National Security Team," 1 December 2008.

67 John R. Bolton and John Yoo, "Restore the Senate's Treaty Power," *New York Times*, 5 January 2009.

68 "Speech at the Chamber of Commerce in New Delhi, 21 January 2008," available at www.number10.gov.uk/Page14323.

69 Robert Hormats and David Rothkopf, "Present at the Creation 2.0: Discussion Document," Prepared for the Carnegie Endowment Strategy Roundtable, 1 December 2008, 1.

70 Dean Acheson, *Present at the Creation: My Years in the State Department* (New York: Norton, 1969). See also James Chase, *Acheson: The Secretary of State Who Created the American World* (New York: Simon & Schuster, 1998).

71 Brian Urquhart, "The New American Century," *New York Review of Books*, 11 August 2005, 42.

4

MOVING BEYOND NORTH-SOUTH THEATER

Beginning in the late 1940s and gaining speed during the 1950s and 1960s, decolonization reflected Cold War politics. Former colonies coalesced in the Non-Aligned Movement (NAM) and the Group of 77 (G-77) to articulate their perceived security and economic interests vis-à-vis the major powers. Thus, in addition to the East-West rivalry, another rigid dichotomy was mapped onto the globe—the so-called North-South divide. While the East-West split disappeared with the implosion of the Soviet Union, the division of the world into camps representing the North and South has survived despite its increasing irrelevance in the contemporary world. The politics of the UN system—not just the highly politicized principal organs of the Security Council and General Assembly but even such more "technical" organizations as the World Health Organization and the Universal Postal Union—continue to reflect the global division between the so-called wealthy, industrialized North and the less advantaged, developing South.

This is hardly news to the readers of *Third World Quarterly*, but my objective for the thirtieth anniversary of the journal is to push us beyond these banal categories because in my own area of scholarly interest—the behavior and misbehavior of the United Nations system—NAM and the G-77 remain the only way to organize international debates and negotiations.[1] My contention is that the North-South divide is counterproductive to the generation of norms and policies geared toward ensuring human security in a globalizing world. Moreover, developing countries productively abandon Southern solidarity when it is in their perceived interests to do so.

Conor Cruise O'Brien aptly described the United Nations as "sacred drama."[2] This essay first provides an historical introduction to the geographical terms describing the two main groups of countries and then examines how the various constructed roles on the international stage in the global theater are played by actors from the two major troupes, North and South. It concludes with some encouraging examples of changed stances within the supposedly ironclad categories.

UN geography, mathematics, and lexicon

Amateur geographers may have trouble without a special compass. During the Cold War, the "East" consisted of the Soviet Union and its allies in Central and Eastern Europe while the "West" consisted of the industrialized countries (North America, Western Europe, Japan, Australia, and New Zealand). These were also called the "Second World" and "First World," respectively, to contrast with what at the outset of the 1950s Alfred Sauvy had labeled *le tiers monde* (the Third World). Whatever their actual hemispheric locations—for instance, New Zealand and Australia are in the "North," Taiwan is nowhere (i.e., is not a member of the UN), and Israel is usually a member of what is now called the "Western and Other Group"—the "developed" countries of East and West constituted the "North," and the rest of the planet of "developing" countries the "South." In more recent years the adjective "global" has been inserted in front of South.[3] "All terms used to denote countries needing 'development' have shortcomings," notes Maggie Black. "Axis descriptors—developing/developed, nonindustrialized/industrialized, rich/poor—are crude and value-laden."[4] This may partially explain the continued popularity of "North" and "South," which, however inaccurate, apparently have the fewest pejorative connotations.

To understand the North-South divide within the United Nations, it is helpful to go back to the beginning. The first visible manifestation was at the Asian-African Conference—the momentous political gathering held in Bandung, Indonesia, in April 1955. "It was the kind of meeting that no anthropologist, no sociologist, no political scientist would ever have dreamed of staging," wrote African-American novelist Richard Wright. It cut "through the outer layers of disparate social and political and cultural facts down to the bare brute residues of human existence: races and religions and continents."[5] The key figures at the conference were the giants of that first generation of Third World leaders: Indonesia's president and host, Sukarno; Indian prime minister Jawaharlal Nehru; and Egyptian president Gamal Abdel Nasser. Also present were Ho Chi Minh, leader of the Democratic Republic of Vietnam; Kwame Nkrumah, the future prime minister of Ghana; and Zhou Enlai, foreign minister and then prime minister of the People's Republic of China.

The original motivation for the Bandung gathering was to find a way to steer between the Soviet Union and the United States within the confines of the world organization. Specifically, many newly independent countries were fed-up with the logjam resulting from their inability to secure UN membership, which had become enmeshed in the rivalry between the two superpowers. By 1954, no new members had been admitted since Indonesia in January 1950 because neither Moscow nor Washington would agree to permit a member from the other's camp to join; the veto was in evidence.

Eventually, Bandung led to the formation of NAM—representing those countries claiming to be aligned neither with the Soviet Union nor the United States. Following the 1955 conference, the African-Asian Peoples' Solidarity

Organization was founded at a meeting in Cairo, and then a more moderate group gathered in Belgrade in September 1961, the First Conference of the Heads of State or Government of Non-Aligned Countries. Despite rhetoric, it would be hard to contradict Marc Berger who, as a guest editor of this journal, wrote "most nationalist movements and Third World regimes had diplomatic, economic, and military relations with one or both of the superpowers."[6] Indeed, confused geographers could find soul-mates among amateur lexicographers having problems in finding a commonsensical dictionary entry for "nonaligned" that included such Soviet lackeys as Fidel Castro's Cuba and such American ones as Mobutu Sese Seko's Zaire.

Working in parallel with NAM but concentrating on economic issues, another conglomeration of developing countries became known as the "Group of 77,"[7] and amateur mathematicians require a special calculator. Established in June 1964, the G-77 was named after two new members joined the original 75 members (which included New Zealand) in a working caucus that gathered to prepare for the first UN Conference on Trade and Development (UNCTAD). The numbers continued to grow, and New Zealand left. Although their numbers now are over 130, the label stuck.

The crystallization of developing countries into a single bloc for the purposes of international economic negotiations represented a direct and, at first, useful challenge to industrialized countries.[8] The Third World's "solidarity" resulted in cohesion for purposes of early international debates. It meant that developing countries were in a better position collectively to champion policies that aimed to change the distribution of benefits from growth and trade,[9] just as they were better able to create some middle ground on security issues through NAM.

The well-known divisions between East and West during the Cold War have disappeared, but the United Nations continues to struggle with member states that align themselves along regionally-defined ideological and economic divisions, especially the North-South axis. The predictable antics between the industrialized North and global South continue to impede any sensible regrouping of the majority of voices, which should change from issue to issue. As Stephen Lewis has lamented, "Alas, man and woman cannot live by rhetoric alone."[10]

Dramatic and largely symbolic and theatrical confrontations rather than a search for meaningful partners is the usual way to proceed. With a push toward consensus as the operating principle—the preferred route for UN discussions— lowest common denominators are one way to have 192 states (the current UN membership) agree on a resolution, work program, or budget. The other is for each country to interpret a resolution in the way that it sees fit or to participate or ignore programs that it dislikes. It should be obvious that neither is the best collective way to solve global problems.

Why North-South categories are problematic

This first section discusses two crucial security issues: terrorism, which has been on the UN's agenda for decades; and the composition of the Security Council, the world body's preeminent security organ, which has preoccupied international deliberations since the ink was drying on the signatures penned on the UN Charter in June 1945.[11] The former issue demonstrates the extent to which North–South divisions have stifled conceptual consensus and consequently practical progress on combating a fundamental threat to international peace. The latter issue illustrates the substantive emptiness of the groupings when narrow interests trump collective ones. While much of the most recent debate on Security Council reform, centering on the 2005 World Summit and its aftermath, supposedly concerns divisions between the overrepresented North and underrepresented South, actual country positions have virtually nothing to do with these categories.

Definitions of terrorism

While the jury is still out regarding whether a paradigm shift in international relations took place after the tragic attacks of September 11, 2001, the topic of terrorism clearly has moved front and center, at UN headquarters and elsewhere. Yet UN discussions over decades have been bogged down by North–South bickering. Two main sticking points prevent agreement on a working definition of "terrorism."[12] The first is captured by the expression "your terrorist is my freedom fighter"—that is, many developing countries justify armed violence by those fighting for national liberation. The second is whether "state terrorism" should be included in any definition agreed by member states—the use of force by Israeli and more recently US forces, for many, is mentioned in the same breath as suicide bombers. The sticking points remain because of vacuous North–South disputes.

Appointed by Secretary-General Kofi Annan in 2003 after the contentious start of the Iraq war, the High-level Panel on Threats, Challenges and Change (HLP) confronted head-on these traditional stumbling blocks: "Attacks that specifically target innocent civilians and non-combatants must be condemned clearly and unequivocally by all."[13] The secretary-general chimed in, "the proposal has clear moral force."[14] Yet the final text from the 2005 World Summit contains no such clear definition of terrorism. For the first time in UN history, however, the heads of state and government at least agreed to "strongly condemn terrorism in all forms and manifestations, committed by whomever, wherever and for whatever purposes."[15] The final text eliminated earlier and clearer language asserting that the targeting of civilians could not be justified because the G-77 could not agree as a group to drop an exemption for movements resisting occupation.

On balance, the summit added a bit of momentum to the secretary-general's evolving counter-terrorism strategy, which was adopted in September 2006 by General Assembly resolution 60/288. Whether or not the assembly "concludes a comprehensive convention on international terrorism" in the near future as was hoped, the summit's clear condemnation of violence against civilians was a small step forward. The September 2006 resolution marked the first time that member states agreed to a framework since the issue came before the League of Nations in

1934. There is an ethical content, which contains the basis for a convention and places the UN near the center of the fight against terrorism.

Nonetheless, for meaningful progress to occur, a prerequisite is to have defectors from the mindless support in the South for "freedom fighters" and the equally mindless rejection in the North of a consideration of state terrorism. This is ironic, to say the least, as a group of experts pulled together by the Stanley Foundation argues: "There is a widespread feeling inside and outside of UN circles that global counterterrorism initiatives are primarily of importance to the 'Northern' states while, in fact, the majority of deaths from terrorism are South–South rather than South–North in nature."[16] Addressing this threat requires a holistic approach, not vacuous divisions into warring camps with empty and predictable confrontations and equally empty and predictable outcomes.

Security Council reform

From the outset, the clearest candidate for inaction and paralysis at the World Summit was the Security Council. In proposing reforms, both the HLP and the secretary-general made tactical blunders by making changes in the council's numbers and procedures the *sine qua non* of their sales pitches. Of course, the Security Council reflects the world of 1945 and not the twenty-first century's distribution of power. Every potential solution, however, brings as many problems as it solves. And no amount of diplomatic theater can eliminate that reality, which has almost nothing to do with the divisions into North and South.

The debate about the Security Council presents a microcosm of a perpetual problem: the UN is so consumed with getting the process right that it neglects consequences. Allowing the Security Council to expand into a "rump" General Assembly of two dozen or more members, as some states demanded, would not stimulate activism by the body. The council would be too large to conduct serious negotiations but too small to represent the membership as a whole. None of the possible changes would foster decision making about the use of nonconsensual measures in cases such as Darfur or Myanmar—they would no doubt inhibit it.

The High-level Panel proposed two alternatives for a 24-member council, an expansion from the current permanent five (P-5)—the United States, the United Kingdom, France, Russia, and China—plus 10 nonpermanent members elected to two-year terms.

> Model A provides for six new permanent seats . . . and three new two-year–term nonpermanent seats . . . . Model B provides for no new permanent seats but creates a new category of eight four-year renewable-term seats and one new two-year-term nonpermanent (and nonrenewable) seat.

In both, the veto remains the exclusive prerogative of the P-5, and seats are divided among the major regional areas. Article 23 of the Charter never specified diversity as a criterion for membership but rather sought a willingness of council members to contribute to the maintenance of international peace and security. The HLP wished to revive the largely ignored criteria of financial, military, and diplomatic contributions as part of the selection and reelection qualifications of those aspiring to membership.

Everyone can agree that the council's decisions would have greater political clout and legitimacy if they had broader support. How to get there from here has always been the conundrum. Significantly, no other previous blue-ribbon international group had ever tried to disguise their lack of agreement by presenting two options as a "recommendation." If the 16 individuals who composed the HLP in their personal capacities could not find a way to formulate a single way forward, how could almost 200 states and their parliaments? Even a single individual, namely the secretary-general, did not take a stand, urging "member states to consider the two options . . . or any other viable proposals."

Against a backdrop of anti-Japan street demonstrations, fueled in part by Tokyo's campaign to secure a permanent seat on the Security Council, China dealt a peremptory blow to the notion of expansion. Beijing told the General Assembly in April 2005 that it was unwilling to rush a decision. The next day, Washington echoed the sentiment with specific references to "artificial deadlines."

Nonetheless, three more options were put on the table in mid-July. Germany and Japan, ever more impatient about their roles as ATMs for UN budget short-falls, joined forces with Brazil and India in the "G-4"—the "Group of 4" or, less affectionately, the "Gang of 4." They initially appeared willing to push for a showdown in the General Assembly in the hopes of a symbolic but pyrrhic victory of 128 votes—that is, two-thirds of the member states present and voting—on their proposal to add 10 new seats (four nonpermanent and six permanent, including the four for themselves and two for Africa).

Meanwhile, a group of their regional rivals—Argentina, Mexico, Italy, Pakistan, and South Korea among others—which had been caucusing for years as the "Coffee Club," rechristened themselves "Uniting for Consensus." Taking umbrage with the G-4's claim to permanent status, they proposed instead increasing Security Council membership to 25 by adding 10 new two-year nonpermanent seats with provision for reelection, but no new permanent members. Simultaneously, following a regional summit in Libya, African states proposed 26 council seats with six new permanent seats with veto power (including two for Africa, but without specifying among Nigeria, South Africa, or Egypt) along with five new non-permanent seats, with two earmarked for Africa. At the same time, other options were also being floated, including a 21-member council with six longer-term, "double-digit" (that is, 10-year or longer) renewable seats, and a host of ways to alter working methods.

Because of insufficient support, the G-4 switched gears. They first dropped a demand for a veto but then sought to woo the 53 members of the African Union, which was still insisting that the veto be given to new permanent members. Late in July 2005, the foreign ministers of the G-4 met at UN headquarters with 18 counterparts from Africa to reconcile the irreconcilable. Shortly thereafter in

Addis Ababa, African states met and nine out of ten rejected the no-veto proposal. At that point, the secretary-general postponed any vote in order not to sink the coming summit ship totally.

In the end, the heads of state and government could merely agree to "support early reform of the Security Council" and "continue to adapt its working methods." The cacophony, jealousies, and vested interests that had plagued this issue since the world organization's 50th anniversary in 1995 remained intact through the 2005 summit. And they have since—as they will for the foreseeable future. The inability to move ahead has nothing to do with North-South divisions. It is not clear, for instance, whether some of the most serious candidates will agree to take half a loaf: a permanent seat with no veto. While the G-4 backed off, Africans became firmer about no second-class permanent membership.

Moreover, it is not clear that Britain and France will accept the inevitable discussion of giving one permanent seat to the European Union originally proposed for a 15-year review in 2020. It is also not clear that the United States will agree to consider a body with 24, 25, or 26 members. Washington's rare public pronouncements indicate a preference for at most 19 or 20 members, with perhaps two additional permanent seats. Nor is it clear that some of the main "losers" (the Italys, Algerias, Mexicos, Pakistans, Canadas, and Nordic countries) will drop the very issues to which they have consistently objected, or whether Arab or Central European states would agree to a formula that makes no specific membership allocation to them.

Most important, it is not clear how any of the recommended changes would improve the chances for reaching consensus regarding the use of force. "[T]he enlargement of the Security Council is the least urgent element in the reform proposals on the table," laments Venezuela's former UN ambassador, Diego Arria, who helped institute several innovations in the council's working methods in the mid-1990s. "[T]he opposition and divisiveness that it has generated worldwide guarantees that the council's composition will remain unaltered." Moreover, he emphasizes the importance of successful experiments becoming traditions rather than being formally codified, which is the usual view emanating from the South. For example, it would be a mistake to spell out any procedures for the Arria formula, which permits NGOs and other private parties to brief the council in informal sessions. Unlike philosophers who are worried when what works in practice does not in theory, Arria cited with respect the philosophy of former baseball hero Yogi Berra: "If it ain't broke, don't fix it."[17]

Diplomatic clashes over the last decade, however, have contributed to a permissive environment that facilitated the pragmatic modifications favored by Arria in working methods by opening up closed discussions to permit: inputs from troop contributors and belligerents; briefings from UN officials; informal sessions with NGOs and experts; and first-hand exposure to missions. These have injected more openness, accountability, and diverse inputs into council deliberations. They have not removed the problem of decision making based on national interest, but neither would UN Charter amendments.

Will the inability to move ahead with dramatic reforms compromise UN credibility? Not more than in the past. Will North-South groupings facilitate debate and agreement? Clearly not. If coalitions for and against various reform possibilities contain members from every region and every level of development, the North-South split has very limited value as a structure for debates about Security Council reform as for other UN issues, as demonstrated in the following sections.

Encouraging signs of change

The disappearance of the North-South dichotomy and the generation of new partnerships that transcend the confines of these simplistic categories is essential. The medicine is hard to swallow for long-time UN hands. Benedict Anderson's use of "imagined communities" also applies to large groupings of states;[18] they no less ferociously defend their group's constructed identities than do individual countries or nations.

There have been occasions when the protective fortifications around the North-South camps have been breached. They portend other types of coalitions of the willing that might unclog deliberations within the United Nations. Specifically, it is useful to examine the unusual approaches to two critical security issues, negotiations for treaties on landmines and the International Criminal Court (ICC).

Ottawa treaty to ban landmines

In the late 1990s, an intriguing alternative pattern for diplomatic negotiations took place for an important disarmament issue. This section examines the constellation of like-minded states—from both the North and the South—and NGOs that formed partnerships and triumphed in the face of hostility from some major powers. The Ottawa Process that brought about in 1997 the convention banning antipersonnel landmines is a prominent case of new partnerships that cross anachronistic categories.

The 1997 Nobel Peace Prize was awarded to the International Campaign to Ban Landmines (ICBL), led by Jody Williams. It always makes for good journalism to associate a single face with a move forward in international relations. However, the problem of landmines mobilized a very diverse group of countries across the usual North-South divide as well as global civil society under the leadership of the World Federalist Movement and the usually reticent International Committee of the Red Cross.

What was there about this issue that broke down the typical divisions? The indiscriminate use of antipersonnel landmines—especially in the late Cold War for the armed conflicts in Afghanistan, Kampuchea (Cambodia), and Angola—led to a ghastly number of deaths and amputees. Moreover, the presence of these munitions also impeded enormously complicated post-conflict transitions and peace-building. Yet many states and many belligerents viewed antipersonnel mines as war-fighting essentials. Meanwhile, non-state actors normally have little lobbying leverage in areas of military policy and national security, and they tend to be allergic to working with governments.

After the end of the Cold War, movement on this issue suddenly seemed possible. The broadly-based ICBL was formed to advocate a comprehensive ban on the production, export, and use of antipersonnel landmines. Seemingly from nowhere, the ICBL not only mobilized grassroots activists and public opinion but also effectively lobbied a wide range of sympathetic governments. In spite of US opposition, an eclectic mix of lesser powers moved ahead and managed to have the Landmines Convention signed in December 1997. Don Hubert tells us why:

> While much of the credit for the successful banning of landmines has deservedly gone to the ICBL and to NGO advocates, the success of the campaign can be explained only through an examination of three other sets of actors: the International Committee of the Red Cross, the United Nations, and key governments.[19]

There are many lessons to be learned from this case, but the most important one for our purposes is that the coalition of like-minded states—including Canada and South Africa, France and Burkina Faso—ignored the usual boundaries between North and South and focused instead on substance.[20] Canada and its energetic foreign minister Lloyd Axworthy led the "Ottawa process," but the UN was an important and legitimating player; and breaking down the barriers of the UN's negotiating blocs was essential to advancing debate.

Rome Statute

A group of reluctant or hostile countries led by the United States not only have failed to ratify the 1998 Rome Statute establishing the ICC but also have actively tried to sabotage this international legal step forward. Nonetheless, over the past decade, a broad-gauged coalition of NGOs has worked in tandem with like-minded states across the North-South chasm. As a result, the ICC has proven to be more robust and has also moved ahead to implement its mandate faster than many had initially predicted.

The court came into being on 1 July 2002 when the Rome Statute entered into force with the requisite 60 ratifications. As of October 2010, there are 114 state members of the ICC allied in permanent efforts to prosecute individuals for genocide, crimes against humanity, war crimes, and crimes of aggression. Over 30 other countries have signed but not ratified; but, a number of important states (including China and India) have done neither; and, symbolically, the United States and Israel have both done what previously had been an unthinkable legal step—in 2002, they revoked their signatures.

The ICC can prosecute offenses committed after 1 July 2002 but only when a crime is committed on the territory of a state party or by one of a state party's citizens, or when a case is referred to it by the Security Council. While the non-signatories are uneasy about jurisdiction, the court complements rather than replaces national legal systems and can act only when national courts are unwilling or unable to investigate or prosecute crimes. With its headquarters in The Hague and led by Chief Prosecutor Luis Moreno-Ocampo, who in mid-2008 made headlines by asking for an indictment of Sudan's president Omar al-Bashir, and subsequently had an arrest warrant issued, the ICC has also opened investigations into the situations in Northern Uganda, the Democratic Republic of the Congo, and the Central African Republic upon the requests of those countries' governments, and into the situation in Darfur upon the request of the Security Council.[21]

How did this precedent-setting organization get off the ground? Answering this question is especially important because of the deep hostility from the globe's most powerful country.[22] Many find it puzzling, except on almost mindless ideological grounds, to understand the position in Washington from the former traditional standard-bearer for human rights. Indeed, the United States originally led the charge in the 1948 General Assembly to establish such a permanent court following large-scale atrocities against civilians in World War II and the trials in Nuremberg and Tokyo; and it was an active participant in negotiations leading up to the draft of the Rome Statute in 1998.

In the wake of the end of the Cold War, the idea was again championed and received an additional push after the establishment of the ad hoc International Criminal Tribunals for the former Yugoslavia and for Rwanda.[23] The scale of atrocities—in Europe and in Africa—demonstrated the need for international justice in the 1990s just as it had earlier. And the shortcomings in the ad hoc tribunals (including costs and the burden of evidence) demonstrated the need for creating a permanent court that could also act as a deterrent for future thugs.

By the middle of the 1990s, governments across the North and the South as well as NGOs had formed coalitions to lobby for the creation of what would become the ICC.[24] This "like-minded group" began with a modest hope, namely to bring together a kind of consensus at a preliminary diplomatic conference in Rome in July 1997. When the official UN Conference of Plenipotentiaries on the Establishment of an International Criminal Court—known informally as the Rome conference—convened a year later, the 60-country like-minded group represented a formidable and persuasive coalition that joined forces with the 700 members of the NGO Coalition for an International Criminal Court.

The momentum was such that the actual formal Rome conference itself in 1998—which, unlike the landmines treaty, was negotiated under the auspices of the United Nations—moved toward a decision in spite of strong opposition from several members of the P-5. Afterward, the signature and ratification process also moved on a fast track.

Lessons

The need to set aside country-group cookie-cutters becomes clear when examining these two tough cases on the high politics of international security. Progress resulted specifically from ignoring the theatrical and automatic ideological divisions of

North and South. While no two campaigns are identical, the efforts to agree on the Convention on Landmines and the ICC reflect two tactical advances: the agreement to move ahead without universal support; and a broad-based working coalition of NGOs and states from both the North and the South. Rather than digging the chasm deeper and wider, like-minded partners found a way to build bridges. As Teresa Whitfield notes, a host of small and "ad hoc, informal, issue-specific mini-coalitions of states or intergovernmental organizations that become involved in and provide support for resolving conflicts and implementing peace agreements" have "become a critical element of an incipient system of post-Cold War global security governance."[25]

Analogously, an expert group assembled in June 2007 by the Stanley Foundation to discuss counterterrorism made a recommendation for this fraught security problem: "Narrow the gap of understanding between the G-8 and G-77 on substantive issues."[26] Yet, David Malone and Lotta Hagman describe why this remains so implausible: "The political ecology of the UN, and especially of the General Assembly, often seems stuck in the past, with North-South polemics all too often paralyzing action . . . [and] threatens the UN with irrelevance and redundancy."[27] Many diplomats in New York claim that the current atmosphere is as toxic as it was in the mid-1970s.

It is necessary to find different roles, different actors, different scripts, and different stages in order to move beyond the empty North-South theater that often paralyzes deliberations and actions. The results-oriented negotiations on landmines and the ICC suggest the benefits of a more pragmatic and less ideological approach to international deliberations and that such reorientations are not impossible. A similar argument applies to debates about human rights and sustainable development.

Conclusion: future performances

Political differences and contestation are inevitable and desirable in an institution with 192 member states and tens of thousands of staff members and soldiers. Descriptions of the United Nations are equally wide-ranging and as accurate or inaccurate as John Godfrey Saxe's fable "The Blind Men and the Elephant":

> It was six men of Indostan, to learning much inclined
> *Who went to 'see' the elephant, though all of them were blind.*
> The first approached the elephant and happening to fall
> Against his broad and sturdy side at once began to bawl,
> 'This wonder of an elephant is very like a wall.'

Perhaps Indostan should become a UN member state? There is no consensus among scholars, governments, civil servants, journalists, nongovernmental organizations, and others as to whether the world organization is really more like a wall, spear, or snake. Is the United Nations the potential solution to pressing global problems or rather a pathetic reflection of the inability of human beings to attack the problems that threaten their very survival and dignity? The collective attempts to describe the animal create not an elephant, but a "theologic war." Analyses of UN affairs and recommendations about its future are similar in that narrow perspectives impede the perception that we are experiencing this elephant together. Transforming the current United Nations into an institution capable of addressing the challenges that threaten human survival poses a similar challenge: the diagnosis of what ails the UN reflects a wide variety of perceptions—indeed, a variety of realities depending on the viewers' analytical lenses.

The end of the Cold War allowed scholars and some diplomats to begin to look more objectively at alliances within the world body. But as we have seen, many of the labels and mindsets from the former era remain although it is now commonplace to point out the economic, ideological, and cultural heterogeneity among developing countries.[28] In the past, it was politically more correct to speak of the Third World as if it were homogeneous, with little hesitation in grouping Singapore's and Chad's economies or Costa Rica's and North Korea's approaches to military affairs. If one probes a bit deeper and adds a dash of cynicism, the problem is that the governments of the powerful states in both the North and the South are comfortable maintaining this fiction because it permits them to avoid any substantial democratization of international relations. They embrace fixed roles and oppose any global democratic means for dealing with most of the problems generated by globalization—the North because global democracy would challenge its privilege, and the South because global democracy would require local democracy.

On some issues—like emphasizing the importance of the General Assembly, where each state has one vote—developing countries demonstrate consistently common positions. In such instances, the North-South divide continues to be salient. Frequently, developing countries subdivide according to the issue before the UN: between radicals and moderates; between Islamic and non-Islamic; between those in a region and outside; between maritime and landlocked; between those achieving significant economic growth and those suffering from stagnation or decline. Even within the Western group, there have always been numerous differences, which have come more to the fore with the abrupt disappearance of East-West tensions. Divisions among and within all groups over the pursuit of war against Iraq in 2003 clearly illustrated this phenomenon.

So, where are we after so many performances? The artificial division of the world into a global North and global South is a simplification; and, like all simplifications, it overlooks substantial parts of reality. But it is the default option because no other template is readily available. The previous discussion suggests that the rigid categories are more helpful to diplomats hoping to write a clear and simple script than for analysts and decision makers attempting to move beyond the paralysis and sterile confrontation that characterizes UN deliberations.

The UN is moving in largely uncharted international waters and cannot rely on the compass provided by North-South orthodoxy. We clearly need to move beyond the sterile performances guided by the tired script-writers from North and South that virtually guarantee a poor and hackneyed production, and ultimately failure.

Notes

1 This essay draws upon Thomas G. Weiss, *What's Wrong with the United Nations and How to Fix It* (Cambridge: Polity Press, 2009). Printed with permission.

2 Conor Cruise O'Brien, *United Nations: Sacred Drama* (London: Hutchinson & Company, 1968).

3 Jacqueline Ann Braveboy-Wagner, *Institutions of the Global South* (London: Routledge, 2008).

4 Maggie Black, *The No-Nonsense Guide to International Development*, 2nd ed. (Oxford: New Internationalist, 2007), 16.

5 Richard Wright, *The Color Curtain* (Jackson, Miss.: Banner Books, 1956), 13–14.

6 Mark T. Berger, "After the Third World? History, Destiny and the Fate of Third Worldism," *Third World Quarterly* 25, no. 1 (2004): 13. Interested readers may also wish to consult such standard works as: R. Malley, *The Call From Algeria: Third Worldism, Revolution and the Turn to Islam* (Berkeley: University of California Press, 1996); and G. Lundeestad, *East, West, North, South: Major Devleopments in International Politics Since 1945* (New York: Oxford University Press, 1999). Older references include: R. Abdulgani, *Bandung Spirit: Moving on the Tide of History* (Djakarta: Prapantja, 1964); C. P. Romulo, *The Meaning of Bandung* (Chapel Hill: University of North Carolina Press, 1956); and, P. Worsley, *The Third World* (London: Weidenfeld and Nicolson, 1964).

7 Georges Balandier and Alfred Sauvy, *Le "Tiers-Monde," Sous Développement et Développement* (Paris: Presse Universitaire de France, 1961).

8 Joseph S. Nye, "UNCTAD: Poor Nations' Pressure Group," in *The Anatomy of Influence: Decision Making in International Organization*, ed. Robert W. Cox and Harold K. Jacobson (New Haven, Conn.: Yale University Press, 1973), 334–70.

9 See Ian Taylor and Karen Smith, *United Nations Conference on Trade and Development (UNCTAD)* (London: Routledge, 2007); John Toye and Richard Toye, *The UN and Global Political Economy: International Trade, Finance, and Development* (Bloomington: Indiana University Press, 2004); Thomas G. Weiss, *Multilateral Development Diplomacy in UNCTAD: The Lessons of Group Negotiations, 1964–84* (London: Macmillan, 1986); Michael Zammit Cutajar, ed., *UNCTAD and the South-North Dialogue: The First Twenty Years* (London: Pergamon, 1985); Robert L. Rothstein, *Global Bargaining: UNCTAD and the Quest for a New International Economic Order* (Princeton, NJ: Princeton University Press, 1979); Branislav Gosovic, *UNCTAD: Compromise and Conflict* (Leiden, Netherlands: Sijthoff, 1972); Diego Cordovez, *UNCTAD and Development Diplomacy: From Conference to Strategy* (London: Journal of World Trade Law, 1970); and Kamal Hagras, *United Nations Conference on Trade and Development: A Case Study in UN Diplomacy* (New York: Praeger, 1965).

10 Stephen Lewis, *Race against Time* (Toronto: Anansi Press, 2005), 145.

11 This discussion is based on Thomas G. Weiss and Barbara Crossette, "The United Nations: The Post-Summit Outlook," in *Great Decisions 2006* (New York: Foreign Policy Association, 2006), 9–20.

12 M. J. Peterson, "Using the General Assembly," in *Terrorism and the UN: Before and After September 11*, ed. Jane Boulden and Thomas G. Weiss (Bloomington: Indiana University Press, 2004), 173–97.

13 High-level Panel on Threats, Challenges and Change, *A More Secure World: Our Shared Responsibility* (New York: UN, 2004), para. 161.

14 Kofi Annan, *In Larger Freedom: Towards Development, Security and Human Rights for All* (New York: UN, 2005), para. 91.

15 *2005 World Summit Outcome*, UN document A/60/L.1, 15 September 2005, para. 81.

16 The Stanley Foundation, *Implementation of the UN Global Counterterrorism Strategy* (Muscatine, Iowa: Stanley Foundation, 2007), 2.

17 In a letter to Russian ambassador Sergey Lavrov, dated 23 October 1997.

18 Benedict Anderson, *Imagined Communities: Reflections on the Origin and Spread of Nationalism* (London: Verso, 1983).

19 Don Hubert, *The Landmine Ban: A Case Study in Humanitarian Advocacy*, Occasional Paper #42 (Providence, RI: Watson Institute, 2000), xviii. He will examine these cases in greater depth in *Human Security* (London: Routledge, forthcoming).

20 Richard Price, "Reversing the Gun Sights: Transnational Civil Society Targets Landmines," *International Organization* 52, no. 3 (1998): 613–44.

21 Germain Katanga, the former chief of staff of the Patriotic Force of Resistance in Ituri (FRPI), the military wing of the Front for National Integration (FNI) militia, was transferred from the DRC to The Hague on 18 October 2007. Thomas Lubanga, former leader of the Union of Congolese Patriots, was transferred to the court on 17 March 2006.

22 See Program in Law and Public Affairs, *The Princeton Principles on Universal Jurisdiction* (Princeton, NJ: Princeton University, 2001); and Council on Foreign Relations, *Toward an International Criminal Court?* (New York: Council on Foreign Relations, 1999); and Steven R. Ratner and James L. Bischoff, eds., *International War Crimes Trials: Making a Difference?* (Austin: University of Texas Law School, 2004).

23 Richard Goldstone, "International Criminal Court and Ad Hoc Tribunals," in *The Oxford Handbook on the United Nations*, ed. Thomas G. Weiss and Sam Daws (Oxford: Oxford University Press, 2007), 463–78. See also Richard Goldstone and Adam Smith, *International Judicial Institutions: The Architecture of International Justice at Home and Abroad* (London: Routledge, 2008).

24 Fanny Benedetti and John L. Washburn, "Drafting the International Criminal Court Treaty," *Global Governance* 5, no. 1 (1999): 1–38.

25 Teresa Whitfield, *Friends Indeed? The United Nations, Groups of Friends, and the Resolution of Conflict* (Washington, DC: US Institute of Peace, 2007), 9 and 2.

26 Stanley Foundation, *Implementation of the UN Global Counterterrorism Strategy*, 7.

27 David M. Malone and Lotta Hagman, "The North–South Divide at the United Nations: Fading at Last?" *Security Dialogue* 33, no. 4 (2002): 410–11.

28 Soo Yeon Kim and Bruce Russett, "The New Politics of Voting Alignments in the United Nations General Assembly," *International Organization* 50, no. 4 (1996): 629–52. See also Evan Luard, *A History of the United Nations: The Years of Western Domination* (London: Macmillan, 1982).

5

WORLD POLITICS

Continuity and change since 1945

With Sam Daws

Since its establishment in 1945, the United Nations Organization, as well as the universal agencies that form part of the UN system, has been central to international relations. The main story is one of continuity and change—the UN is over 60 years old and 60 years young. It faced specific opportunities and difficulties during the Cold War; and these were followed with a radically different set of inter-pretations, fears, hopes, and policies in the confusion of the post–Cold War era. That same description could again be used to characterize the briefer period since 11 September 2001.

But behind these macro-political changes lies a startling reality that was very much in evidence at the largest-ever global summit at UN headquarters in September 2005. Over 150 presidents, prime ministers, and princes encountered the same problems that have restricted international cooperation since the launch-ing of the current generation of global institutions that replaced the defunct League of Nations—indeed since the beginning of modern experiments with multilateral cooperation in the nineteenth century.[1]

New challenges to international peace and security and human survival have arisen. New non-state actors have appeared on the world stage, and older ones have occasionally been transformed. New conventions and norms have proliferated. New intergovernmental initiatives and institutions have been established. On the other hand, decision making in world politics and international organizations remains dominated by states.

Hence, nothing has altered the validity of Adam Roberts and Benedict Kingsbury's evaluation in *United Nations, Divided World*: "international society has been modified, but not totally transformed."[2] The UN does not exist in isolation from the world that it is attempting to serve. Many scholars and practitioners resist the notion that there has been a fundamental change in world politics. Essentially, they are right in claiming that the more things change the more they stay the same.

Certainly the fundamental units of the system—sovereign states—are here to stay. They are still organized to pursue their perceived national interests in a world without any meaningful overall authority.

The world thus still reflects what Hedley Bull and virtually all political scientists call "anarchy,"[3] or the absence of a central global authority. In spite of the construction of a seemingly ever-denser web of international institutions, there is nothing like a world government in the offing. Although it would be inaccurate to ignore the extremes—ranging from fractious political authority in failed states to the supranational integration of the European Union—it still is accurate to point to a fundamental continuity: state sovereignty remains the core of international relations.

Change and continuity

The clear recognition of this fundamental continuity pervades the chapters in *The Oxford Handbook on the United Nations*, as it does world politics; but it would be hard to argue that substantial change has not also marked the world organization since 1945. This *Handbook* is thus a contribution to greater analytical precision and historical reflection about the balance between change and continuity within the United Nations. The most pertinent changes can be conveniently grouped under four headings: the emergence of new threats; the increasing role of non-state actors; the reformulation of state sovereignty; and the emergence of a single "hyperpower." What follows is an overview of the nature and role of each of these in today's international system.

The rise of new threats

The first category of change consists in the proliferation of new threats and challenges to the well-being of states and their citizens that surpass the ability of individual states, however powerful, to address on their own. Some readers may find it hard to imagine that many of the problems central to this *Handbook* were not even on the international radar screen in 1945. For instance, environmental degradation, population growth, urbanization, and women's rights came onto the international agenda during the global conferences of the 1970s,[4] and the AIDS pandemic and the need for human development and human security appeared in the 1980s and 1990s. Moreover, other challenges that have long languished on the agenda—terrorism and self-determination come immediately to mind—have taken on a different urgency with the proliferation of weapons of mass destruction (WMDs).

In short, war, human rights abuse, and poverty have persisted throughout the last six decades. Judgments about the relative success or failure of the UN in addressing such perennial blights on the human condition can only be made with the recognition that many of these "old" threats have themselves changed in nature over time, and that praise for success or criticism for failure cannot simply be placed at the door of the organization.

The threat of armed conflict was foremost in the minds of the architects of the UN Charter, the Preamble to which pledged members "to save succeeding generations from the scourge of war." This threat endures or, to paraphrase Inis Claude's classic early UN textbook, too few swords have been turned into plough-shares.[5] There has been, however, a significant change in the patterns of political violence. While interstate war is not yet a thing of the past—as demonstrated by the decision of the United States and United Kingdom to go to war against Iraq in 2003—the UN's original focus on war between states has largely given way to the dominant reality of intrastate warfare.

Intrastate—or "civil" or "non-international"—wars (i.e., taking place primarily within the borders of a state and involving indigenous armed factions) accounted for over 90 percent of all armed conflicts in the 1990s that resulted in more than 1,000 deaths.[6] It is conventional wisdom that civilians have become the main victims in such civil wars—estimated at 90 percent in the turbulent 1990s, itself a notable reversal from the early twentieth century when soldiers accounted for that percentage.[7] However, new evidence raises questions about such statistics. Direct killing of civilians through armed conflict may have in fact declined significantly in the early 2000s although it remains difficult to calculate the indirect effects of war-exacerbated disease and malnutrition.[8] Whether or not these wars are truly "new" is debatable, but clearly many of the usual dynamics have altered or been exaggerated. "Changed" is probably a more accurate characterization of the trans-formation at hand as history demonstrates comparable dynamics.[9]

The woes of our planet are obvious. Egregious human rights violations have continued over six decades, and many of the moves toward national independence have ended in brutal dictatorship. Despite economic growth, the world has been left, at the opening of the new millennium, with widening gaps in wealth distribution (the world's 500 richest individuals' combined wealth is greater than that of the poorest 416 million), and almost half the global population (some 2.5 billion) survive on incomes equivalent to less than two dollars a day. These prob-lems too have been with us for some time, but their magnitude continues to grow as does our real-time exposure to the plight of those who suffer.

The importance of new actors?

The second type of substantial change that is reflected in many of this *Handbook*'s chapters is the burgeoning role of actors other than states. The proliferation of "uncivil" actors—from belligerents and warlords to "spoilers" and criminals whose interests are served by continued armed conflict[10]—is certainly a factor behind the ugly reality of civil war. However, the UN as an arena has also traditionally provided space for what is increasingly called "global civil society" to interact with states, articulate demands and solutions, and pursue their own interests.

Charter Article 71 carved out space for nongovernmental organizations (NGOs) to engage with the United Nations. But during the Cold War, the Soviet bloc and many developing countries with totalitarian regimes resisted the intrusion of independent and dissident voices. Since the thawing of East-West relations in the mid-1980s, however, human rights advocates, gender activists, developmentalists, and groups of indigenous peoples have become ever more vocal, operational, and important in contexts that were once thought to be the exclusive preserve of states.

The sheer growth in NGO numbers has been nothing short of remarkable. The Union of International Associations estimates the number of international NGOs (operating in more than two countries) at about 25,000.[11] A more cautious estimate is some 13,000, all but one-quarter of which have been created since 1990.[12] National NGOs have grown faster still in the South than in the North. Throughout the Third World, grassroots organizations are said to number in the millions.

For-profit businesses and the media are key nongovernmental sectors that relate directly to the United Nations. Corporations have always been an important lobbying presence. In addition, their potential contribution to the UN's work—as well as their labor, social, and environmental obligations—have been recognized in Kofi Annan's Global Compact initiative. The media's influence is widely acknowledged. Indeed, Secretary-General Boutros Boutros-Ghali suggested that they effectively constitute a "16th member of the Security Council" for some decisions.

Hence, it is no longer disputed that NGOs play a prominent role on the world stage and that we are unable to fully understand contemporary international relations without looking at such non-state actors. What is insufficiently known is that their rate of growth has surpassed intergovernmental organizations (IGOs). By 2006, IGOs had shrunk to 238 (down from a peak of over 300 at the outset of the 1980s), which means that a quarter of a century ago, "the ratio of NGOs to IGOs stood at 15:1, whereas today the relation is 28:1."[13] The presence of alternative voices has become integral to the UN system's processes of deliberation[14] and of world politics more generally. International discussions are more pluralistic, and international decisions necessarily reflect a wider array of perspectives.

Indeed, and as a result, the term "international community" can be confusing when it is used in relationship to the UN system and multilateralism more broadly. While international lawyers continue to use it to refer narrowly to the "community of peace-loving states," other observers frequently employ it far more loosely and expansively. Some include not merely states but also their creations in the form of intergovernmental bodies, while still other observers also use the term to embrace some of the non-state actors that are contributing to the resolution of global problems. In these pages, we restrict the use of the term to the narrow legal sense, but the expanded cast playing roles on the UN's stage is a crucial part of the analysis in virtually every chapter in this volume.

Reinforced or reduced state sovereignty?

Reflecting the proliferation of threats and actors is the third dominant element of change—the reformulation of state sovereignty. Paradoxically, the UN has been responsible for both the triumph *and* the erosion of state sovereignty. There are almost four times as many member states at the outset of the twenty-first century as signed the Charter in June 1945. The Charter emphasized self-determination in response to colonialism, and decolonization is virtually complete. And since the collapse of the Soviet Union in 1991 and the implosion of the former Yugoslavia the following year, the idea of the sovereign state has attained virtually universal resonance.

At the same time, however, sovereignty has never been as sacrosanct and unchangeable as many believe. Stephen Krasner went so far as to describe it as "organized hypocrisy."[15] The recasting of state sovereignty over the UN's lifetime is rooted in three factors.

The first is that technology and communications have remolded the nature of the global economy and economic aspirations.[16] There is great controversy over the oft-used and confused term "globalization."[17] Some observers argue that it has been occurring since the earliest trade expeditions (e.g., the Silk Road); and despite the current obsession, the process itself is not fundamentally new. Others suggest that the current era of globalization is unique in the rapidity of its spread and the intensity of the interactions that result. It is difficult to deny the processes of increased interconnectivity across the planet and the worldwide dimensions of human, financial, commercial, and cultural flows that require no passport. For the latter, the UN's normative efforts have been combined with technology to produce what one analyst called "the end of geography."[18]

Wherever one stands in the debate about globalization's reach, pace, and impact on state sovereignty, it is clear that definitions of vital national interests—often called *raisons d'état*—are expanding and being continually redefined. Their pursuit is not exclusive because sometimes state actors are playing in a non-zero-sum game; the European Union is often cited as an example of sovereignty being recast if not transcended, a process long-ago described by Ernst Haas as moving "beyond the nation-state."[19] Globalization creates losers as well as winners, and it entails risks as well as opportunities. The rapid growth of global markets has not seen the parallel development of social and economic institutions to ensure their smooth and efficient functioning, and the global rules on trade and finance produce asymmetric effects on rich and poor countries, very often to the detriment of the latter. This too means that some states are more or less "sovereign" than others.

The second factor explaining the paradox is that the content of sovereignty itself has expanded to accommodate human rights. Underlying this is an unresolved tension in the Charter between respect for the domestic jurisdiction of states and the imperatives of individual rights. In his 1992 *An Agenda for Peace*, Secretary-General Boutros Boutros-Ghali summarized: "The time for absolute and exclusive sovereignty, however, has passed; its theory was never matched by reality."[20]

Of course, for some time states have chosen to shed bits of sovereignty in signing international conventions or trade pacts—some 1,500 multilateral treaties were in existence in 1995 when a prominent legal group made the effort to count them.[21] But for human rights in particular, the trade-off is not always a conscious choice but rather involves a blurring of domestic and international jurisdictions over time. This became particularly clear with the willingness to override sovereignty by using military force for humanitarian purposes in the 1990s. The rationale came from Frances M. Deng and Roberta Cohen's notion of "sovereignty as responsibility," which they developed to protect internally displaced persons; from Secretary-General Annan's articulation of "two sovereignties;" and from the norm of the "responsibility to protect," elaborated and advocated by the International Commission on Intervention and State Sovereignty (ICISS).[22]

As a result, the four characteristics of a sovereign—territory, authority, population, and independence—spelled out in the 1934 Montevideo Convention on the Rights and Duties of States have been complemented by another, a modicum of respect for human rights. Sovereignty has become contractual or conditional rather than absolute. Indeed, with the possible exception of the prevention of genocide in the first years after World War II, no idea has moved faster in the international normative arena than "the responsibility to protect." The basic idea is that human beings should count more than the rigid sovereignty enshrined in Charter Article 2 (7) with its emphasis on nonintervention in the internal affairs of states. Or, as Kofi Annan graphically told a 1998 audience at Ditchley Park, "state frontiers . . . should no longer be seen as a watertight protection for war criminals or mass murderers."[23]

The third part of an explanation for the paradox of the UN's contribution to both strengthening and weakening sovereignty is that experience, beginning in the 1990s, suggests that states can be born *and* die—sovereign entities can, in the popular language of the day, "fail."[24] A number of other euphemisms have arisen —for instance, "weak" and "fragile"—while the "on-the-ground" reality varies from the situation in Somalia,[25] where there has been no effective central authority since 1992, to the former Yugoslavia, which no longer exists as a unitary state. Charter Article 2 (1) is clear: "The Organization is based on the principle of the sovereign equality of all its Members." This essentially means that all states have equal sovereignty, but not that they are equal in nature. Fictions abound in world politics, including the pretence within the UN of treating member states that are not de facto sovereign as equal to functioning members, and the fiction of treating China and Chad or Venezuela and Vanuatu on a par in the General Assembly despite their vast inequalities in size and power.

In short, the notion of state sovereignty seems considerably less sacrosanct today than in 1945. Borders still are crucial considerations in international relations, but their significance is very different than at the outset of the United Nations.

US hegemony?

The fourth remarkable disjuncture is the preeminence of the United States—what former French foreign minister Hubert Védrine dubbed the *hyper-puissance*. On the one hand, major power politics have always dominated the deliberations of the world organization. The bitter East–West divide of the Cold War and the North–South clashes of the 1960s and the 1970s provide extensive evidence of this reality. On the other hand, there is no modern precedent for America's current military, economic, and cultural preponderance. Much of contemporary UN debate could be compared with the Roman Senate's effort to control the emperor.

Scholars speculate about the nuances of economic and cultural leverage in the international system resulting from US soft power,[26] but the hard currency of international politics undoubtedly remains military might. Before the war on Iraq, the "hyper-power" was already spending more on its military than the next highest-spending 15–25 countries combined (depending on who was counting). With additional appropriations for Afghanistan and Iraq, Washington began spending more than the rest of the world's militaries combined. And even in the domain of soft power, the United States remains without challenge on the world stage for the foreseeable future although some analysts see the hegemony as more Western than American.[27]

Yet at this moment, there are two world "organizations." The United Nations is global in membership, and the United States is global in reach and power. While many observers emphasize the peculiarly "go-it-alone" character of the George W. Bush administration, American unilateralism is not new.[28] This reality creates acute difficulties for card-carrying multilateralists. For example, UN-led or UN-approved operations with substantial military requirements take place only when Washington approves or at least acquiesces. In other issue areas, moving ahead without the United States is problematic, although experiments are underway—for example, the 1998 Rome Statute establishing the International Criminal Court and the 1997 Convention on the Prohibition of the Use, Stockpiling, Production and Transfer of Anti-Personnel Mines and on Their Destruction.

Whether the US presence and power are overrated and will wane in the coming decade remains to be seen. Even if, as Joseph Nye claims, "the world's only super-power can't go it alone,"[29] US power and Washington's willingness to resort to unilateralism may well dominate, for some years, every level of UN affairs—normative, legal, and operational.[30]

The confluence among these four types of change along with the dominant continuity of an anarchical international system is such that very few contemporary UN watchers can imagine anything like a world government emerging in their lifetimes. We should nonetheless recall that such a notion was at least at the back of the minds of not only world federalists but many of the framers of the UN Charter. While pointing to the rise of "networks of interdependence," an earlier formulation of global governance, the late Harold Jacobson noted a fitting image for the older view of world government in the tapestries in the Palais des Nations in Geneva—the headquarters of the League of Nations and now the UN's European Office. He noted that they

> picture the process of humanity combining into ever larger and more stable units for the purpose of governance—first the family, then the tribe, then the city-state, and then the nation—a process which presumably would eventually culminate in the entire world being combined in one political unit.[31]

That dream—Alexander Wendt still argues that "a world state is inevitable"[32]— of a world government has been replaced by the contemporary idea of global governance.[33] Even the most enthusiastic proponents of national interests or those least sympathetic toward the United Nations are cognizant of the need for multilateral efforts in some sectors to address problems that spill beyond borders. "Governance" refers to purposeful systems and rules or norms that ensure order beyond what occurs "naturally." In the domestic context, governance is usually more than government, implying shared purpose and goal orientation as well as formal authority or police powers.

The origins of this idea in the 1990s reflect an interesting marriage between academic and policy concerns. James Rosenau and Ernst Czempiel's theoretical *Governance without Government* was published in 1992, and the policy-oriented Commission on Global Governance's *Our Global Neighbourhood* was published three years later.[34] The first issue of the journal *Global Governance*, whose subscribers are both scholars and practitioners, also appeared in 1995. And the literature has burgeoned since that time.

Distinctions are not always made between the species of national and global governance. For example, UNDP's *Human Development Report 1999* argued that "Governance does not mean mere government."[35] In a national context, this is perfectly correct because governance is government plus additional nongovernmental mechanisms that contribute to order and predictability in problem solving. For the planet, however, governance essentially is close to the whole story because there is no world government—hence, the sum of nongovernmental mechanisms but minus an input from a central authority because there is none. In many instances, the network of institutions and rules at the global level provides the appearance of partially effective governance, but normally without the actual desired effects.

So global governance is not a supplement to global government but rather a *faute de mieux*. It is a surrogate for transnational authority and enforcement in the contemporary world. However useful as a heuristic device to explain some kinds of complex multilateral cooperation and transnational interactions, the basic question remains: can global governance without a global government adequately address the range of problems faced by humanity in the new millennium?

Evaluating UN efforts at problem-solving

Our point of departure in this *Handbook* is neither defensive nor celebratory—the UN's record should be viewed and analyzed empirically but in context.[36] The need to avoid repetition of two world wars and the massive global recession of the 1930s—as well as the failure of the League of Nations—sharply focused the thoughts of those who created the United Nations. In particular, they had very much in mind what the father of the international relations approach later dubbed "realism." E.H. Carr's sweeping interwar analysis of the catastrophic results of ill-considered idealism led to a very different generation of international organizations.[37] The basic structures, sketched during World War II and in the first decade or two afterward, were all directed toward pragmatic ends.

But what made the UN's design and establishment so remarkable was its broader ambitions—for human rights on a global scale, for sovereign independence and freedom and democracy in all parts of the world, for improvements in standards of living worldwide. While such lofty idealism is often derided, more of that original vision has been achieved than is often recognized. No period in human history has seen so many people benefiting from advances in life expectancy, health, education, and living standards as in the UN's lifetime. The organization cannot claim credit for all the progress that has been made, any more than it can be blamed for the lack thereof.

At the same time, the UN's contribution is far from negligible. The globe undoubtedly would have been in a sadder state of affairs without the world organization's efforts. Successes have arguably surpassed the initial hopes and expectations of the delegates who first gathered at the San Francisco Conference on International Organization in April 1945, and of those attending the opening session of the first General Assembly in London in January 1946. For instance, there has been no world war. Although military spending has broken all records and tens of thousands of nuclear weapons still threaten the survival of the human race, deaths from war since 1945 have been markedly fewer than those in the first half of the twentieth century. In spite of the Cold War, indeed because it was mostly cold rather than hot, barely a fifth of the twentieth century's 110 million war-related deaths took place in the 55 years after the UN's creation, compared with some 85 million prior.

The *Human Security Report 2005* suggests that the surge of international activities after the end of the Cold War, aimed at stopping ongoing wars and preventing new ones, actually achieved considerable success. Spearheaded by the United Nations, these activities included a sixfold increase in the world body's preventive diplomacy missions and a fourfold increase in its peacemaking missions. This upsurge in international activism coincided with a decrease in crises and wars, despite the real and much publicized failures. While the UN did not act alone, the report asserts that there is evidence from a number of sources that the UN's initiatives were directly linked to quantifiable progress in the reduction and resolution of conflicts. This is, at the very least, a plausible proposition.

The end of colonization and the achievement of sovereign independence came within a decade or two, whereas in 1945 many observers expected that the decolonization process might well take a century. Today 192 countries are members of the UN, compared with the initial 51. About two-thirds of them now have governments chosen through multiparty elections, a substantial shift from the situation in the early 1960s in the immediate aftermath of decolonization and throughout the Cold War when the vast majority of governments were anything except democratically elected.

Economic and social development has been impressive in many instances. In developing countries, average life expectancy has increased to double the estimated level of the late 1930s. Child mortality has been lowered by more than three-quarters. Nearly three-quarters of the world's population over the age of 18 are now literate, and some 85 percent of the world's children benefit from education. Malnutrition has been reduced in all regions of the world except Africa. Smallpox has been eradicated; and yaws, guinea worm, and polio—a worldwide scourge in the early postwar world—virtually eliminated. UNDP's 2005 edition of its annual *Human Development Report* noted that, since the first such report was issued in 1990, "On average, people in developing countries are healthier, better educated and less impoverished—and they are more likely to live in a multiparty democracy."[38]

Progress in human rights has also been nothing short of extraordinary, starting with the 1948 approval of the Universal Declaration of Human Rights. Beginning in the 1980s, a surge of ratifications of human rights conventions occurred along with increasing implementation of many measures and greater public outrage over abuses. While ratification and implementation are not always correlated as closely as we would like, it nonetheless is significant that almost a hundred countries, over half of UN member states, have now ratified six of the seven major human rights instruments, each of which has a committee of experts to monitor implementation; and some of which are supplemented by optional protocols. Moreover, about three-quarters of member states have ratified the International Covenants on Civil and Political Rights and on Economic, Social and Cultural Rights, and over 80 percent of countries the International Convention on the Elimination of All Forms of Racial Discrimination as well as the Convention for the Elimination of All Forms of Discrimination Against Women, a kind of international bill of rights for women.

Three analytical problems

The preceding rapid summary is fleshed out in far greater detail in the chapters of this *Handbook*. In weighing elements of continuity and change and evaluating the UN's efforts to solve problems in spite of the obvious constraints on its operations, our authors adopt a variety of perspectives. In examining the evidence in each chapter, we urge readers to keep in mind three distinct analytical problems: defining the nature of change; determining the nature of success and failure; and tracking the ups and downs of world politics.

Defining "change"

The first analytical concern regards defining what constitutes "change." Kalevi Holsti's *Taming the Sovereigns* probes the concept of change and ways of measuring it: "These include change as novelty or replacement, change as addition or subtraction, increased complexity, transformation, reversion, and obsolescence."[39]

Change thus can be analyzed in quantitative or qualitative ways. If we think simply in terms of the growing scale and scope of international secretariats and staff or their budgets, there would be no debate. If change can be additive or subtractive and thus measured quantitatively, on any conceivable measure, the UN system has expanded exponentially.

We have already noted some of the data, such as the near quadrupling of the world body's membership. When the United Nations was born in 1945, there were 51 members, comprised mostly of European and Latin American countries. By 1975, the number of states sitting in the General Assembly had nearly tripled, as decolonization proceeded rapidly in the wake of the mass destruction wrought by World War II, in conjunction with the tide of nationalist independence movements that rippled across what became known as the Third World. Less than two decades later, the implosion of the Soviet Union (or formally the Union of Soviet Socialist Republics, USSR) and Yugoslavia gave birth to 20 new states. As of early 2007, the world body is comprised of 192 members. The number of democracies has quintupled.[40]

Other figures help illustrate quantitative change, such as the number of peacekeeping operations, also briefly discussed above. From the launch of the first peacekeeping operation in 1948 until 1978, only 13 missions were deployed. For almost a decade thereafter, the Security Council approved no new operations with UN blue helmets. The political realities of the East–West split rendered launching such operations politically impossible. New operations resumed in 1988, when the Soviet Union dramatically altered its foreign policy position toward the world body. Since the thawing of the Cold War, the UN has undertaken 47 peacekeeping operations. In mid-2006, for instance, the world body had boots on the ground in more than 15 countries; with some 80,000 troops deployed, collectively a larger overseas military presence than any country except the United States. In July 2007, when it authorized hybrid operations in Lebanon and the Darfur region of Sudan, the Security Council approved, in principle, a 50 percent increase in the number of UN soldiers and total peacekeeping expenditures.

Change in the intensity of UN activity can also be illustrated with figures pertaining to the number of resolutions passed in the Security Council. During the Cold War, from 1946 to 1986, the council passed 593 resolutions; in less than half the length of time, between 1987 and 2005, this figure amounted to 1,010.[41]

Another indication of change in multilateral cooperation more broadly can be illustrated with the number of treaties regulating state conduct. Between 1946 and 1975, the number of international treaties in force more than doubled from 6,351 to 14,061.[42] They spanned a broad gamut of issues—genocide, human rights, terrorism, the environment, and narcotics.[43]

Along with the greater extensiveness of its reach and membership, the UN's budget has grown to meet the ever increasing demands of a more interdependent and complex world. In 1946, the regular budget was $21.5 million;[44] some three decades later, the resources at the disposal of the world body amounted to $307 million,[45] while in 2006 the regular budget reached $1.8 billion. This regular budget, which is debated endlessly because of its significance for control and direction of the United Nations, represents only 20 percent of total spending. In 2005, the peacekeeping budget alone amounted to another $5 billion, and extra-budgetary contributions another $2.8 billion.

In addition to financial wherewithal, the human resources on which the daily operations of the UN depend also have increased substantially. In 1945, the UN Secretariat itself was a small family while the entire system had some 1,500 people. Early in the millennium, the UN with its global reach relies on some 15,000 employees (7,500 are paid from the regular budget) from approximately 170 countries. The UN system as a whole—including the World Bank and International Monetary Fund—employs some 61,000 staff.

These quantitative indicators of growth, however, should be placed in context. Measured in comparison with the challenges to be overcome or in relationship to national expenditures, the UN's statistics could be considered almost trivial. Over the 60-year period, the regular budget appears to have increased eighty-eight times; however, when the figures are adjusted for inflation, the increase corresponds approximately to 16 times the 1946 budget. This amounts to an allocation of about $0.30 per human being alive in 2006; even with the peacekeeping budget included, this figure is only about $1.07.

Total global procurement by the UN, about 85 percent of which arises from peacekeeping, grew from about $400 million in 1997 to $1.6 billion in 2005. However, even the record-breaking expenditure on UN peacekeeping operations worldwide in 2005 was the equivalent of only one month of US expenditures in Iraq in that same year.

Writing in the mid-1990s, Erskine Childers and Brian Urquhart pointed out a number of relevant comparisons to challenge the commonplace impression of a "vast, sprawling bureaucracy." They wrote: "The entire UN system world-wide, serving the interests of some 5,500,000,000 people in 184 countries [now 6.5 billion in 192 countries], employs no more workers than the civil service in the American state of Wyoming, population 545,000 . . . and less than the combined civil services of the Canadian Province of Manitoba and its capital city of Winnipeg." They further noted that the budgets for the whole system's regular activities ($6.5 billion) amounted to about the same that US citizens spent annually on cut flowers and potted plants, while the total worldwide expenditure of the UN system—$10.5 billion—was three-and-a-half times *less than* the amount that UK citizens spend on alcoholic beverages per year. Moreover, the total budgetary portion allocated to the UN proper (some $4.1 billion) was no more than the budgets of the New York City fire and police departments together. In another quantitative comparison, Childers and Urquhart noted that the UN's "giant paper factory" producing documents in six languages is also a myth in that "the *New York Times* consumes more paper in one single Sunday edition than the United Nations consumes in all its documents in a whole year."[46]

However, the more intriguing and perhaps controversial questions relate to qualitative change. And here too the UN has changed dramatically since 1945. One qualitative means is to conduct a historical analysis and trace great events. International relations scholars typically trace movements from one historical period to another in terms of wars in general and great power wars in particular. World War II and the founding of the UN itself followed by the Cold War qualify as do many of the crises over the last 60 years in which the world organization has been involved—in security ones from the division of Palestine to the Cuban Missile Crisis and the implosion of the Balkans; in human rights from McCarthyism to Rwanda's genocide; and in development from the influx of newly independent countries to the Asian financial crisis of 1997–98. By commission or omission, many such events are viewed as seminal for the UN and defining moments for international cooperation.

Qualitative change can be defined as difference in kind. Novelty and replacement are types of qualitative change. The presumption is of rupture, or a clear break between what once was and what currently is.[47] To that extent, we are looking for discontinuities, when new forms replace old ones, which is pretty much the story of the United Nations—including, for instance, the creation of peacekeeping and the return to peace enforcement; the introduction of gender and other types of human rights mainstreaming; the change from protecting the environment to sustainable development.

Holsti notes that change is quite different for someone playing today's stock market or for those of us trying to understand it in international relations where recent events are not of interest unless they have a demonstrable effect on how diplomatic, military, or humanitarian work is actually done. "This is the Hegelian and Marxist problem: at what point," he asks, "does quantitative change lead to qualitative consequences?"[48] In other words, we can also characterize as "new" a tipping point[49] at which quantitative change is so substantial that it constitutes something qualitatively "new."

Many of the arguments about the shifts that have occurred over the last twenty years about the nature of humanitarian agencies, for example, are claims that the environment, the relationships among actors, and the process of delivery of relief itself have become more complex.[50] In many respects, the sum of such changes in quantitative trends have combined in such a way as to have "system effects,"[51] the equivalent of qualitative change. The growing involvement of states, for instance, has had a series of important consequences on the organization of humanitarian action. The use of the military for human protection purposes is undoubtedly the clearest example.[52]

In many instances, the contemporary international order is in turmoil. The mere quantity of developments may strike readers—it certainly does the editors—as the equivalent of qualitative change. In presenting his reform proposals to the General Assembly in March 2006, Secretary-General Annan summarized: "Today's United Nations is vastly different from the Organization that emerged from the San

Francisco conference more than 60 years ago."[53] In short, he was pointing to the obvious, namely a significant shake-up in the way that the UN does business is essential to keep pace with the significantly altered circumstances six decades after its founding.

Determining "success" and "failure"

A similar complication arises and constitutes a second analytical problem for readers who may be struggling to decide whether international cooperation through particular institutions has been a "success" or a "failure." In this effort, they should keep in mind the often-ignored distinction between the "two United Nations"[54]—one being the forum in which states make decisions and the other being the international civil service. Which UN is behind what is viewed as a success or failure, and to what extent?

The success or failure of the "first UN," of course, depends upon governments' perceptions of their vital interests and the accompanying political will, or lack thereof, to move ahead within a multilateral framework. It is this United Nations that is most often the locus of evaluation by the public and scholars alike. But throughout the pages of this *Handbook* we show that the "second UN" is capable, under certain circumstances, of leadership and influence that alter international outcomes. We maintain that individuals matter—for international secretariats as for all human endeavors. Success or failure in implementing policy is, of course, not independent of governments, resources, and political support. Yet there is more room for maneuver and autonomy for members of the international civil service, particularly in the intellectual and advocacy realms, than is often supposed.

The old adage comes to mind here—success has numerous parents, but failure is an orphan. States are often unwilling to dilute their sovereignty through multilateral cooperation and diplomacy, but they rarely are willing to blame themselves for breakdowns in international order and society. The "first UN" has a convenient scapegoat in the "second UN," and vice versa. Conor Cruise O'Brien described the "sacred drama" of these two entities whose creation was designed to appeal to the imagination. As such, he undoubtedly is correct in noting that "its truths are not literal truths, and its power not a material power."[55]

The stage for the drama by these two United Nations has, over the last six decades, become increasingly crowded with a diversity of other actors.[56] States are still the dominant players in the UN, and national interests have not receded as the basis for making decisions; and secretariats sometimes make a difference. However, there is substantial evidence that what might be called the "third UN"—or perhaps the "complementary" UN—is becoming increasingly salient. This consists in a host of important players who are part of a parallel world of independent experts and consultants whose job descriptions include research, policy analysis, and idea-mongering. They work along with NGOs, the private sector, and other non-state actors. These voices too appear in many of our chapters because they are playing more prominent roles in the United Nations. Thus, deciding who is responsible for what portion of the blame for failure or what contribution to success is an increasingly complex task—for our readers as for our authors.

The UN's changing fortunes in world politics

The third variety of analytical problem reflects a common oversight: too many observers forget the ebb and flow of world politics. In trying to wrap their minds around the previous two problems, an additional complicating factor is a pattern of reactions to experiments with international organization—high hopes followed by disillusionment, which in turn has an impact on the performance of the United Nations.[57] In the past, however, the disappointment often set in after a war or major cataclysm accompanied by the collapse of institutions—for example, the Concert of Europe or the League of Nations. Even without US participation in the latter, for example, the defections by important states took place over a decade and a half.

In the post–Cold War era, however, the disillusionment/euphoria roller coaster seems to be accelerating, with highs and lows exchanged with greater frequency. Because often the UN's business is tied to this morning's headlines, maintaining some perspective is a challenge. National and international reactions to the performance of the world organization follow an up-and-down pattern. The changing fortunes of the UN are continual—sometimes it is viewed as an essential player in international society, and then suddenly it is marginalized.

It is essential, for instance, in evaluating the debate of the 1990s about humanitarian intervention and multilateralism to search for historical baselines, even in the recent past, against which subsequent changes can be gauged. Shortly after the 1991 Gulf War and the allied efforts in Iraqi Kurdistan, the word "renaissance" was ubiquitous. Apparently, there was nothing that the organization could not do. However, by 1994 there was nothing that it could do to halt the murder of 800,000 people in Rwanda's nightmare. From that nadir, 1999 was then either an *annus mirabilis* or *horribilis* for the UN, depending on one's views, with interventions in East Timor and Kosovo. And then following Washington and London's decision in March 2003 to wage war in Iraq without explicit Security Council approval, the world organization was once again headed toward the "dark ages" and confronted widespread disillusionment—there was nothing it could do to halt US hegemony, or there was nothing it could do to enforce decisions against the rogue regime of Saddam Hussein. Even seasoned observers of UN affairs seemed out of breath in attempting to gauge exactly the nature of the world organization's standing —not just in the United States but in "new" and "old" Europe, and virtually everywhere.

We would characterize the lead-up to the sixtieth anniversary of the UN, for example, as a reflection of a distinctly ahistorical perspective. A good place to begin is the dramatic imagery of the secretary-general's famous "fork in the road" speech,[58] which formed the basis for convening the High-level Panel on Threats, Challenges and Change.[59] The secretary-general urged that "the UN must undergo the most sweeping overhaul in its 60-year history."[60] The outcome of the September 2005 UN World Summit inevitably failed to live up to such high expectations. But neither were the cynics who predicted a dismal failure proved entirely right. The World Summit's outcome and the initial follow-up indicated the tenacity of the organization with its ability to survive, grow, and adapt, but also that it achieves progress only through historical cycles of modest adaptation and change.

Its member states, throughout this process, continue to cling to the prerogatives of sovereignty while pursuing a predictable pattern. They find reasons to characterize the most incremental reforms in radiant hues, but they then begin again to bemoan the state of the world organization and assert that profound changes in the planet's situation necessitate sweeping structural renovations in it.

Despite these rhetorical sleights of hand, the UN's advances, while sometimes checkered, continue. Whether we consider more abstract advances in norm setting or concrete gains in the areas of conflict resolution, poverty alleviation, and human rights and democratization, the world organization—the first, second, and third United Nations—struggles to make the planet at least a little more habitable and hospitable.

We are reminded of a cautionary quip attributed to Dag Hammarskjöld: "The UN was not created to take humanity to heaven, but to save it from hell." Our view, which is reflected throughout the chapters in this *Handbook*, is that the relatively feeble power of the UN system will have to be augmented if many of the current threats to human survival and human dignity are to be adequately addressed. One reason that we are not in the netherworld already is the existence of the United Nations.

Notes

1 Craig Murphy, *International Organization and Industrial Change: Global Governance since 1850* (Cambridge: Polity, 1994).
2 Adam Roberts and Benedict Kingsbury, "Introduction: The UN's Roles in International Society since 1945," in *United Nations: Divided World*, 2nd ed., ed. Adam Roberts and Benedict Kingsbury (Oxford: Oxford University Press, 1993), 1.
3 Hedley Bull, *The Anarchical Society: A Study* (New York: Columbia University Press, 1977). A more recent treatment is Robert Jackson, *The Global Covenant: Human Conduct in a World of States* (Oxford: Oxford University Press, 2000).
4 Michael G. Schechter, *United Nations Global Conferences* (London: Routledge, 2005).
5 Inis L. Claude, Jr., *Swords into Plowshares: The Problems and Prospects of International Organization* (New York: Random House, 1956).
6 This is the definition used to determine whether a particular war was tabulated. Peter Wallensteen and Margareta Sollenberg, "Armed Conflict, 1989–2000," *Journal of Peace Research* 38, no. 5 (2001): 632. Some have argued that there has been an upswing in the number, intensity, and duration of civil wars, particularly since 1989. However, data indicate that the quantity of overall conflicts decreased while negotiated settlements increased over the 1990s. See Swedish International Peace Research Institute, *SIPRI*

Yearbook 1998: Armaments, Disarmament, and International Security (Oxford: Oxford University Press, 1998), 17. This SIPRI data is shortened and updated annually by Wallensteen and Sollenberg in the *Journal of Peace Research*.

7 UNDP, *Human Development Report 2002* (New York: Oxford University Press, 2002), 85.

8 Andrew Mack et al., *Human Security Report 2005: War and Peace in the 21st Century* (Oxford: Oxford University Press, 2005).

9 Mary Kaldor, *New & Old Wars: Organized Violence in a Global Era* (Palo Alto, Calif.: Stanford University Press, 1999); Mark Duffield, *Global Governance and the New Wars: The Merging of Development and Security* (London: Zed Books, 2001); and Peter J. Hoffman and Thomas G. Weiss, *Sword & Salve: Confronting New Wars and Humanitarian Crises* (Lanham, Md.: Rowman & Littlefield, 2006).

10 Stephen John Stedman, "Spoiler Problems in Peace Processes," *International Security* 22, no. 2 (1997): 5–53.

11 See Union of International Associations, "International Organizations by Type (Table 1)," in *Yearbook of International Organizations* (Brussels: Union of International Associations, 2006).

12 Helmut Anheier, Marlies Glasius, and Mary Kaldor, "Introducing Global Civil Society," in *Global Civil Society 2001*, ed. Helmut Anheier, Marlies Glasius, and Mary Kaldor (Oxford: Oxford University Press, 2001), 4.

13 Kerstin Martens, *NGOs and the United Nations: Institutionalization, Professionalization and Adaptation* (Basingstoke, UK: Palgrave Macmillan, 2005), 2.

14 See Johan Kaufmann, *United Nations Decision Making* (Alphen aan den Rijn: Sijthoff & Noordhoff, 1980).

15 Stephen Krasner, *Sovereignty: Organized Hypocrisy* (Princeton, NJ: Princeton University Press, 1999).

16 Andrew Chadwick, *Internet Politics: States, Citizens, and New Communication Technologies Politics* (New York: Oxford University Press, 2006).

17 For example, see David Held and Anthony McGrew, with David Goldblatt and Jonathan Perraton, *Global Transformations: Politics, Economics, and Culture* (Palo Alto, Calif.: Stanford University Press, 1999).

18 Richard O'Brien, *Global Financial Integration: The End of Geography* (London: Pinter, 1992).

19 Ernst B. Haas, *Beyond the Nation-State: Functionalism and International Organization* (Palo Alto, Calif.: Stanford University Press, 1964).

20 Boutros Boutros-Ghali, *An Agenda for Peace* (New York: UN, 1992), para. 17.

21 Paul Szasz, "General Law-Making Processes," in *United Nations Legal Order*, ed. Oscar Schachter and Christopher Joyner (Washington, DC: American Society of International Law, 1995), 35 and 59.

22 See, for example, Frances M. Deng et al., *Sovereignty as Responsibility: Conflict Management in Africa* (Washington, DC: Brookings, 1996); Kofi A. Annan, *"We the Peoples": The United Nations in the 21st Century* (New York: UN, 2000); and International Commission on Intervention and State Sovereignty, *The Responsibility to Protect* (Ottawa: International Commission on Intervention and State Sovereignty, 2001).

23 Kofi A. Annan, *The Question of Intervention: Statements by the Secretary-General* (New York: United Nations, 1999), 7.

24 Gerald B. Helman and Steven R. Ratner, "Saving Failed States," *Foreign Policy*, no. 89 (1992–93): 3–20.

25 Martin Meredith, *The State of Africa: A History of Fifty Years of Independence* (London: Free Press, 2005).

26 See Joseph E. Nye, Jr., *The Paradox of American Power: Why the World's Only Superpower Can't Go It Alone* (Oxford and New York: Oxford University Press, 2002).

27 Donald J. Puchala, "The United Nations and Hegemony," *International Studies Review* 7, no. 4 (2005): 571–84.

28 Edward C. Luck, *Mixed Messages: American Politics and International Organization 1919–1999* (Washington, DC: Brookings, 1999).

29 Nye, *The Paradox of American Power*.

30 For a variety of interpretations, see: Rosemary Foot, S. Neil MacFarlane, and Michael Mastanduno, eds., *US Hegemony and International Organizations: The United States and Multilateral Institutions* (Oxford: Oxford University Press, 2003); Steward Patrick and Shepard Forman, eds., *Multilateralism & U.S. Foreign Policy: Ambivalent Engagement* (Boulder, Colo.: Lynne Rienner, 2002); David M. Malone and Yuen Foong Khong, eds., *Unilateralism & U.S. Foreign Policy: International Perspectives* (Boulder, Colo.: Lynne Rienner, 2003); and Michael Byers and Georg Nolte, eds., *United States Hegemony and the Foundations of International Law* (Cambridge: Cambridge University Press, 2003).

31 Harold K. Jacobson, *Networks of Interdependence: International Organizations and the Global Political System*, 2nd ed. (New York: Knopf, 1984), 84.

32 Quoted by J. Martin Rochester, *Between Peril and Promise: The Politics of International Law* (Washington, DC: CQ Press, 2006), 27.

33 See Ramesh Thakur and Thomas G. Weiss, *The UN and Global Governance: An Idea and its Prospects* (Bloomington: Indiana University Press, 2010), chapter 1. See also Michael Barnett and Martha Finnemore, *Rules for the World: International Organizations in Global Politics* (Ithaca, NY: Cornell University Press, 2004); and Margaret P. Karns and Karen A. Mingst, *International Organizations: The Politics and Processes of Global Governance* (Boulder, Colo.: Lynne Rienner, 2004).

34 James N. Rosenau and Ernst-Otto Czempiel, *Governance Without Government: Order and Change in World Politics* (Cambridge: Cambridge University Press, 1992); and Commission on Global Governance, *Our Global Neighbourhood* (Oxford: Oxford University Press, 1995).

35 UNDP, *Human Development Report 1999* (New York: Oxford University Press, 1999), 8.

36 The following draws on Louis Emmerij, Richard Jolly, and Thomas G. Weiss, *Ahead of the Curve? UN Ideas and Global Challenges* (Bloomington: Indiana University Press, 2001), 17–19; and *The Power of UN Ideas: Lessons from the First 60 Years* (New York: United Nations Intellectual History Project, 2005), 3–4.

37 Edward Hallett Carr, *The Twenty Years' Crisis, 1919–1939: An Introduction to the Study of International Relations* (London: Macmillan, 1939).

38 UNDP, *Human Development Report 2005: International Cooperation at a Crossroads: Aid, Trade and Security in an Unequal World* (Oxford: Oxford University Press, 2005), 3.

39 Kalevi J. Holsti, *Taming the Sovereigns: Institutional Change in International Politics* (Cambridge: Cambridge University Press, 2004), 12–13.

40 Freedom House, *Democracy's Century: A Survey of Global Political Change in the 20th Century* (New York: Freedom House, 1999).

41 This information is updated from David M. Malone, ed., *The UN Security Council: From the Cold War to the 21st Century* (Boulder, Colo.: Lynne Rienner, 2004).

42 David Held, Anthony McGrew, David Goldblatt, and Jonathan Perraton, *Global Transformations: Politics, Economics and Culture* (Palo Alto, Calif.: Stanford University Press, 1999), 53.

43 José E. Alvarez, *International Organizations as Law-makers* (Oxford: Oxford University Press, 2005), 273–337.

44 Erskine Childers with Brian Urquhart, *Renewing the United Nations System* (Uppsala, Sweden: Dag Hammarskjöld Foundation, 1994), 143.

45 This figure represents approximately half of the biennial 1974–75 budget. See UN, General Assembly resolution 3551, 17 December 1975.

46 Childers and Urquhart, *Renewing the United Nations System*, 28–30, 143.

47 The related distinction between evolutionary and revolutionary change also is germane, as is the analytical distinction between punctuated equilibrium and evolution. See John

Campbell, *Institutional Change and Globalization* (Princeton, NJ: Princeton University Press, 2004), 34.

48 Holsti, *Taming the Sovereigns*, 8.

49 Malcolm Gladwell, *The Tipping Point: How Little Things Can Make a Big Difference* (Boston: Little Brown, 2002).

50 See Michael Barnett and Thomas G. Weiss, eds., *Humanitarianism in Question* (Ithaca, NY: Cornell University Press, 2008).

51 Robert Jervis, *System Effects: Complexity in Political and Social Life* (Princeton, NJ: Princeton University Press, 1999).

52 Thomas G. Weiss, *Civilian-Military Interactions: Humanitarian Crises and the Responsibility to Protect*, 2nd ed. (Lanham, Md.: Rowman & Littlefield, 2004).

53 Kofi A. Annan, "Investing in the United Nations: For a Stronger Organization Worldwide" UN document A/60/692, 7 March 2006, 1.

54 Inis L. Claude, Jr., "Peace and Security: Prospective Roles for the Two United Nations," *Global Governance* 2, no. 3 (1996): 289–98.

55 Conor Cruise O'Brien, *The United Nations: Sacred Drama* (London: Hutchinson, 1968), book jacket.

56 See Robert W. Cox and Harold K. Jacobson, eds., *The Anatomy of Influence: Decision Making in International Organization* (New Haven, Conn.: Yale University Press, 1973).

57 Francis. II. Hinsley, *Power and the Pursuit of Peace* (Cambridge: Cambridge University Press, 1963).

58 The UN Secretary-General's Address to the General Assembly, as delivered on 23 September 2003, available at www.un.org.

59 High-level Panel on Threats, Challenges and Change, *A More Secure World: Our Shared Responsibility* (New York: United Nations, 2004).

60 Kofi A. Annan, "In Larger Freedom: Decision Time at the UN," *Foreign Affairs* 84, no. 3 (2005): 66. This is the title of his own summary document for the summit: *In Larger Freedom: Towards Development, Security and Human Rights for All* (New York: UN, 2005).

6

AN UNCHANGED SECURITY COUNCIL

The sky ain't falling

Birthdays are often moments to take stock and then change. However, the results of the UN's fiftieth anniversary in 1995 and the Millennium Summit in 2000 lead to profound skepticism about any major overhaul in September 2005 for the world organization's sixtieth anniversary. The agenda will advance modestly, but there is no evidence of Secretary-General Kofi Annan's "fork in the road," the justification for the High-level Panel (HLP) on Threats, Challenges and Change.[1]

Indeed, an interesting reversal of roles is taking place around the three documents before member states from the HLP, the Millennium Project, and the secretary-general.[2] Usually it is outside scholars who rant and rave about the untenable status quo. Once these have made the case for dramatic reforms, if not revolution, practical folks in foreign ministries or international secretariats habitually point to geopolitics, throw cold water, and call instead for incremental changes.

This time, we are witnessing the opposite. The refrain from many diplomats, secretariat officials, and members of august commissions resembles that of Chicken Little, and their hyperbolic rhetoric amounts to "it's now or never." Meanwhile, academics are scratching their heads and injecting some historical perspective into the secretary-general's plea that "the UN must undergo the most sweeping overhaul in its 60-year history."[3] It seems as though many observers share the worst negative judgments of current multilateralism put forward by Washington's neocons.

The UN's business is excessively tied to this morning's headlines. It is essential, for instance, in evaluating the debate about humanitarian intervention and multilateralism to recall even the recent past. Shortly after the 1991 Gulf War and allied efforts in Kurdistan, the word "renaissance" was ubiquitous. Apparently, there was nothing the world organization could not do. But in 1994 there was nothing that it could do to halt the murder of 800,000 people in Rwanda's nightmare. From that nadir, 1999 was the *annus mirabilis* or *horribilis*, depending on one's views, with interventions in East Timor and Kosovo. And then, following the decision in March 2003 by Washington and London to wage war in Iraq without UN approval and the disingenuous morphing into a humanitarian justification, we were once again in the "dark ages."

This roller-coaster is the essence of international relations, not an aberration. Yet the dramatic climate of so-called paradigm changes in the post-9/11 world characterized the High-level Panel's deliberations and report. The latter has many positive building blocks: the definition of terrorism, thoughts about disarmament and non-proliferation, the Peacebuilding Commission, an intellectual framework linking security and poverty reduction. Nonetheless, it also has at least two basic problems. The first is the lengthy shopping list of recommendations—unkindly known as the "101 Dalmatians." Supposedly, these constitute a "grand bargain" to which member states are to vote thumbs-up or thumbs-down. The secretary-general also speaks of a "package."

Former US president Bill Clinton contended that in his student days he smoked but did not inhale. The HLP and the secretary-general, however, seem to have done both. International negotiations always occur item-by-item. Only a very limited number of the HLP's recommendations will be accepted as is; perhaps a few more will be modified and approved; but the vast majority will be debated and left for further deliberation down the road.

The clearest candidate for no action is a reformed Security Council, and the second key problem is the HLP's tactical blunder of having recommended changing the council's numbers and procedures as the linchpin of its sales pitch. This political correctness was dead in the water.

Of course, the Security Council reflects the world of 1945 and not the twenty-first century's distribution of power, but every solution brings as many problems as it solves. Since its establishment in 1993, the entity with the lengthiest name in the annals of multilateral negotiations—the "Open-Ended Working Group on the Question of Equitable Representation and Increase in the Membership of the Security Council and Other Matters Related to the Security Council"—risks also setting a record for continuing to go nowhere for the longest period of time.

Reform efforts are a microcosm of a perpetual problem: the UN is so consumed with getting the process right that it routinely neglects consequences. The HLP argues for increased legitimacy but ignores the third component, because it is composed of not only process and purpose but performance as well. A Security Council that grows into a "rump" General Assembly would not stimulate activism. It would be too large to conduct serious negotiations, but too small to represent the membership as a whole. The recommended changes would do nothing to foster decision making about the use of force in Darfur or Congo—indeed, they would inhibit it.

The High-level Panel proposes two alternatives for an expanded 24-member council. In addition to the permanent five (P-5) and ten elected members, "Model A provides for six new permanent seats . . . and three new two-year term non-permanent seats. . . . Model B provides for no new permanent seats but creates a new category of eight four-year renewable term seats and one new two-year term non-permanent (and non-renewable) seat." In both, the veto remains the exclusive prerogative of the P-5, and seats are divided among the major regional areas. Article 23 of the UN Charter never specified diversity as a criterion for membership, but rather the willingness of council members to contribute to the maintenance of international peace and security. The HLP would like to revive the largely ignored criterion of financial, military, and diplomatic contributions as part of the selection and re-election qualifications of those aspiring to membership. The panel suggests a full review in 2020.[4]

Everyone can agree that the council's decisions would have greater political clout if they had broader support. How to get there from here has always been the conundrum. The HLP's so-called recommendation is a superb illustration of why there will be no movement. Never has a major independent international commission or panel made a "recommendation" that is an option rather than a clear-cut pronouncement. If 16 individuals cannot come up with a single way ahead, how will 191 states and their parliaments? Even the secretary-general by himself did not decide. He urged "Member States to consider the two options . . . or any other viable proposals"[5]—one more indication of the absence of political convergence.

In early April, and undoubtedly spurred by popular protest against Japan's campaign for a permanent seat, China dealt a peremptory blow to the notion of expansion and told the General Assembly that Beijing was unwilling to rush a decision. The next day, the United States echoed the sentiment with specific references to "artificial deadlines."

If past is prelude, there will be no substantial changes anytime soon in the Security Council, and certainly not in September 2005. Rhetorical fireworks over the last decade have contributed to a permissive environment that facilitated pragmatic modifications in working methods. These have injected more openness, accountability, and diverse inputs into council deliberations and should be expanded.[6] They have not made a dent in the national-interest decision making, but neither would UN Charter changes.

Will the inability to move ahead with dramatic reforms compromise UN credibility on matters related to the future use of force? The answer is: not more than in the past.

Notes

1 The UN Secretary-General's Address to the General Assembly, as delivered on 23 September 2003, available at www.un.org.
2 High-level Panel on Threats, Challenges and Change, *A More Secure World: Our Shared Responsibility* (New York: UN, 2004); Millennium Project, *Investing in Development: A Practical Plan to Achieve the Millennium Development Goals* (New York: United Nations Development Programme, 2005); and Kofi A. Annan, *In Larger Freedom: Towards Development, Security and Human Rights for All* (New York: UN, 2005).

3 Kofi A. Annan, "In Larger Freedom: Decision Time at the UN," *Foreign Affairs* 84, no. 3: 63–74, quote at 66.

4 *A More Secure World*, para. 244–60.

5 Annan, "In Larger Freedom," 43.

6 See Thomas G. Weiss and Karen Young, "Compromise and Credibility: Security Council Reform?" *Security Dialogue* 36, no. 2 (June 2005): 131–54; and Thomas G. Weiss, *Overcoming the Security Council Impasse: Envisioning Reform* (Berlin: Friederich Ebert Stiftung, 2005), occasional paper 14. This would also conform with the secretary-general's earlier thinking in Kofi A. Annan, "The Quiet Revolution," *Global Governance* 4, no. 2 (April-June 1998): 123–38.

PART II

Non-state actors and global governance

7

THE "THIRD" UNITED NATIONS

With Tatiana Carayannis and Richard Jolly

Research and oral histories from the United Nations Intellectual History Project (UNIHP) demonstrate that ideas, one of the UN's most important legacies, have made a substantial contribution to international society.[1] This work also suggests that the concept of a "third UN" should be added to our analytical toolkit in order to move beyond Inis Claude's classic twofold distinction between the world organization as an intergovernmental arena and as a secretariat.[2]

This "additional" UN consists of certain nongovernmental organizations (NGOs), external experts, scholars, consultants, and committed citizens who work closely with the UN's intergovernmental machinery and secretariats. The third UN's roles include advocacy, research, policy analysis, and idea mongering. Its elements often combine forces to put forward new information and ideas, push for new policies, and mobilize public opinion around UN deliberations and operations. Critics might disagree and regard our perspective as quite orthodox.[3] However, in our view, informed scholars, practitioners, and activists have a value-added and comparative advantage within intergovernmental contexts to push intellectual and policy envelopes. These circles—a third UN—are independent of and provide essential inputs into the other two UNs. Such "outside-insiders" are an integral part of today's United Nations. What once seemed marginal for international relations now is central to multilateralism.

We begin by situating the notion of a third UN among broader scholarly efforts to reconceptualize multilateralism before briefly examining Claude's two traditional components. We then consider the contributions of the third UN concept by exploring key definitional questions and parsing its membership and interactive dynamics in the world organization. Finally, we spell out why the idea of a third UN is significant for the theory and practice of international organization and propose an agenda for future research.

New multilateralisms and public policy networks

The notion of a three-faceted UN is a contribution to the challenge of theorizing contemporary global governance. It builds on a growing body of work that calls for a conception of "multiple multilateralisms."[4]

Why bring forward this idea now? After all, networks of diplomats and professionals are hardly new. Although major governments have resisted the influence of non-state actors and, particularly, civil society organizations, parts of the UN system have long engaged them and drawn on academic expertise located outside the system. The International Labour Organization has incorporated representatives of trade unions and the business sector into its tripartite structure since 1919. NGOs have been significant for advances in ideas, norms, and policies at the UN beginning with advocacy for the inclusion of human rights in the UN Charter in 1945 and for the adoption of the Universal Declaration of Human Rights three years later. The United Nations Children's Fund (UNICEF) has long had close interactions with civil society groups for a wide range of children's issues and for fund-raising and advocacy. The United Nations Educational, Scientific and Cultural Organization and the United Nations Development Fund for Women have interacted with national committees consisting of academics and NGOs. Indeed, most parts of the UN have drawn on academic or professional expertise located outside the system.

A growing number of authors have attempted to conceptualize the phenomenon of non-state actors, especially NGOs, as they intersect with the United Nations.[5] The number of nonofficial groups involved has grown dramatically, while the density of globalization has meant that communications and technological developments have increased the reach of their voices as well as their decibel levels.

Adopting the notion of the third UN is a sharper way to depict interactions in and around the world organization than employing the usual threefold vocabulary of state, market, and civil society. This terminology resonates for students of international organization who were raised on Claude's framework. Moreover, beyond the United Nations there could also be a third European Union (EU), a third Organisation for Economic Co-operation and Development (OECD), and so on. However, the data and argument presented here relate more specifically to the UN.

Why have analysts relatively neglected—or often resisted addressing—something that seems so obvious? Part of the answer lies in difficult definitional questions about an amorphous, fluid, and ill-defined group of actors who engage with the United Nations at various levels, at various times, and on various issues. Patterns are hard to grasp, and many of the interactions are ad hoc. Which groups should be included? Should one examine all NGOs and all academics? Where does one draw the line? Would it make more sense to focus on policy orientations rather than on sectors of actors? Once in, are actors forever part of the third UN, or do they move in and out depending on the issue, their influence, or the calendar? This article is another step in conceptualizing global governance in terms of free-flowing networks rather than rigid formal structures.[6]

Most social scientists—development economists, students of comparative politics, sociologists, and anthropologists—have long recognized the empirical and theoretical importance of non-state actors. However, this insight largely eluded international relations (IR) specialists who, with their preoccupation with issues of sovereignty and with the UN's being composed of member states, tended to minimize or even ignore interactions with non-state actors and their influence on decision making. Beginning in the 1970s with Robert Keohane and Joseph Nye,[7] the growing presence and activities of actors other than states have gradually forced many mainstream IR theorists to pry open the lid on the black box of state-centric theories of international organization. Realists remain unreconstructed in this regard. But with issues as varied as gender and climate change moving into the limelight on the international agenda, largely as a result of efforts by non-state actors, and despite the recalcitrance of many states and international civil servants, it is imperative to better understand the impact of the third UN.

The first and the second UN

Unsurprisingly, the "first UN" and the "second UN" have long provided the principal grist for analytical mills about the world organization. After all member states—51 in June 1945 and 192 today—establish the priorities and pay the bills, more or less, thus determining what the world body does. International civil servants would not exist without member states, nor could a permanent institution of member states operate without a secretariat.

Michael Barnett and Martha Finnemore distinguish five roles for the first UN: "as an agent of great powers doing their bidding; as a mechanism for interstate cooperation; as a governor of international society of states; as a constructor of the social world; and as a legitimation forum."[8] States pursue national interests in this arena, which varies from "high politics" in the Security Council to "low politics" in the boards and governing councils of UN funds and specialized agencies. States caucus in regional groups for the General Assembly and in smaller groups for numerous issues. Notions of the first UN find a home in virtually all IR theory: for a realist emphasizing self-interested states within an anarchical system; for a liberal institutionalist looking for a stage where states pursue mutual interests and reduce transaction costs; for a proponent of the English School seeking to foster shared norms and values in an international society; for a constructivist looking for a creative agent for ideational change and identity shaping; and for a pragmatist seeking a place to legitimate specific values and actions.

The second UN is also a distinct sphere, consisting of career and long-serving staff members who are paid through assessed and voluntary contributions. This international civil service is a legacy of the League of Nations. Article 101 of the UN Charter calls for a core of officials to tackle international problems. A leading advocate for the second UN was Dag Hammarskjöld. His May 1961 speech at Oxford does not ignore the reality that the international civil service exists to carry out decisions made by states; but it emphasizes that a UN official could and should pledge allegiance to striving for a larger collective good, rather than defending the interests of the country that issues his or her passport.[9] The practice of reserving senior UN positions for former high-level officials approved by their home governments undermines the integrity of secretariats. Moreover, a shadow today hangs over the UN Secretariat as a result of corruption in the Oil-for-Food Programme, sexual exploitation by peacekeepers, and the Staff Council's vote of no-confidence in the secretary-general in May 2006.

Nonetheless, a basic idealism continues to animate the second UN. The likes of Ralph Bunche and Brian Urquhart indicate that autonomy and integrity are realistic expectations of international civil servants.[10] Today's professional and support staff number approximately 55,000 in the UN proper and another 20,000 in the specialized agencies. This number excludes temporary staff in peace operations (about 100,000 in 2007) and the staff of the International Monetary Fund and the World Bank Group (another 15,000). These figures represent substantial growth from the 500 employees in the UN's first year at Lake Success and the peak total of 700 staff employed by the League of Nations.[11]

The second UN does more than simply carry out marching orders from governments. UN officials also present ideas to tackle problems, debate them formally and informally with governments, take initiatives, advocate for change, turn general decisions into specific programs of action, and work for implementation. None of this should surprise. It would be a strange and impotent national civil service whose staff took no initiatives or showed no leadership, simply awaiting instructions from the government in power. The second UN is no different, except that the formal decision makers are government representatives on boards meeting quarterly, annually, or even biennially. With the exception of the Security Council, decision making and responsibility for implementation in most parts of the UN system, especially the development funds and specialized agencies, depend in large part on the executive head or a staff member of the second UN.

What is the third UN?

From the outset, non-state actors have been active in UN corridors and field projects. The Charter's 1945 Preamble opened with a clarion call from "We the Peoples of the United Nations," when one might have expected "We the Representatives of Sovereign Member States." Article 71 explicitly made room for NGOs in UN debates. Nonetheless, the extent to which non-state actors are now routinely part of what passes for "international" relations by "intergovernmental" organizations is striking.

Involvement of NGOs has been a routine part of all UN-sponsored global conferences since the 1972 Stockholm Conference on the Human Environment, when the conference secretary-general, Maurice Strong, insisted on their presence. NGO parallel meetings, usually called "forums," have become a prominent fixture of deliberations and have been an important force in pressing for more forward-looking policies. For the Millennium Summit and the 2005 World Summit, special hearings involving NGOs were organized in advance.

Although the terminology may sound odd, it is appropriate to refer to such networks as a "third United Nations." Many individuals who have played an essential role in the world organization's intellectual and norm-building activities were neither government officials nor international civil servants. Moreover, many key contributors to ideas as members of the first and the second UN had significant prior associations with a university, a policy think tank, or an NGO—or joined one after leaving government or UN service. Many individuals have served as members or chairs of independent panels and commissions that examined emerging problems not yet on the international radar screen. The Intergovernmental Panel on Climate Change is a prominent example. Many also served as staff or board members of NGOs, and most have attended ad hoc global conferences that pull together a range of actors on the international stage.

We define the third UN as comprising NGOs, academics, consultants, experts, independent commissions, and other groups of individuals that routinely engage with the first and the second UN and thereby influence UN thinking, policies, priorities, and actions. The key characteristic for this third sphere is its independence from governments and UN secretariats. Thus, legislators in Parliamentarians for Global Action as well as local governmental officials in United Cities and Local Governments would be part of the third UN by virtue of their position outside the executive branch of government.

Deciding who is in or out of the third UN depends on the issue and the period in question. But the third UN consists of "outsiders"—that is, persons who are not on the regular payroll of a government or a secretariat—who complement the "insiders" of the other two United Nations in collective efforts to generate, debate, implement, and disseminate ideas and programs. That said, the distinction between outsiders and insiders can blur in the case of many prominent individuals who move in and out of institutions through a "revolving door."

At the same time, it is essential to distinguish persons who are neither government representatives nor international civil servants when they make certain contributions to the UN. Outsiders are often better placed to be more adventuresome and critical. Anyone who has attended a UN-sponsored global conference is quite aware that Secretariat staffers who organize these meetings are joined not only by representatives of governments who make decisions, but also by a legion of NGOs, think tanks, and academics. The Beijing conference on women in 1995 perhaps illustrated this interaction most visibly.[12] The same is true of the board meetings of many UN funds, programs, and specialized agencies.

In spite of the Global Compact and other schemes for "corporate social responsibility" we do not include the for-profit sector in the third UN. The primary focus of business is not on any larger community of interests, but on financial bottom lines. Companies also have relatively little direct interaction with the first and the second UN in the context of the organization's policy formulation and project execution.[13] Business groups that promote fair trade or microcredit, for instance, are better considered as NGOs. The same holds for corporate-centered NGOs such as the World Business Council for Sustainable Development and the World Economic Forum.

The mass media that follow UN activities often have an impact on international thinking and action. However, their primary role as a category of actors in global governance is to report on and not to alter policy. For this reason we do not include media organizations within the third UN. On the other hand, investigative journalists and columnists who are in the opinion business can be aptly considered part of the third UN as influential individuals, like scholars and policy analysts.

In brief, then, three main groups of nonofficial actors compose the third UN: nongovernmental organizations; academics and expert consultants; and independent commissions of eminent persons. None of these subgroupings is monolithic. The importance of particular individuals and organizations in multiactor policymaking or project execution varies by issue and over time. Thus "membership" in the third UN is temporary and contingent.

Eight roles played collectively by the first, second, and third UNs can be summarized as: providing a forum for debate; generating ideas and policies; legitimating ideas and policies; advocating for ideas and policies; implementing or testing ideas and policies in the field; generating resources to pursue ideas and policies; monitoring progress in the march of ideas and the implementation of policies; and occasionally burying ideas and policies. As is elaborated in subsequent sections, the importance of each role and the importance of each of the three UNs in those roles varies depending on how new a particular policy approach is at a given moment, and how much it flies in the face of strong national or regional interests and received wisdom.

Intellectual energies among the three UNs blend. Indeed, there is often synergy. A revolving door turns as academics and national political actors move inside to take staff positions in UN secretariats, or UN staff members leave to join NGOs, universities, or national office and subsequently engage from outside, but are informed by experience inside. Primary loyalties to, or location in, one of the three UNs provide strategic and tactical advantages and disadvantages, which give these analytical distinctions their importance.

Nongovernmental organizations

In the last six decades, there has been a dramatic growth in the role and influence of NGOs in UN corridors as elsewhere. The result is a qualitatively different debate than would take place without their inputs. "I think life would be duller without the NGOs, and there would probably be much less point to it also," said Viru Dayal, the former chef de cabinet of two UN secretaries-general. "Besides, civil society knows where the shoe pinches. They know when to laugh and they know when to cry."[14]

Most UN global meetings attract NGO participants, and in large numbers. Usually the scenario does not resemble the Seattle Ministerial Conference of the World Trade Organization in late 1999, when tens of thousands of protesters filled the streets. In fact, most involvements by the third UN are more peaceful and more supportive of the other two UNs. While estimates vary because of different ways that delegates are counted, the orders of magnitude are striking. The Earth Summit in Rio in 1992 had some 17,000 nongovernmental participants, the Fourth World Conference on Women in Beijing in 1995 drew some 32,000 (including 5,000 Chinese), and UNICEF's World Summit for Children in New York in 1990 stirred over a million people worldwide to join in candlelight vigils.[15]

Commentators rightly emphasize the last few decades of NGO growth, but the phenomenon has been gaining momentum over two centuries, beginning with the antislavery movement late in the eighteenth century.[16] Before and during the San Francisco conference in 1945, US-based private actors of the third UN were especially visible, including 42 consultants officially recognized by Washington, plus some 160 other observers from diverse NGOs, including religious groups.[17]

The Cold War slowed the growth of non-state actor participation in the UN. The communist bloc and many totalitarian developing countries resisted independent and dissident voices. NGOs in such places were essentially an extension of the state and its views, which prompted the ugly acronym GONGO (government-organized NGO). Indeed, there are still so-called NGOs in repressive countries that are anything but *non*governmental. Purists would also point to problems when democratic governments provide substantial funding to NGOs, even if few visible strings are attached. Moisés Naim's proposal for a credible rating agency to evaluate the backers, independence, goals, and track records of NGOs is intriguing,[18] as is the signature in 2006 of an Accountability Charter by 11 of the world's leading international NGOs in the fields of human rights, environment, and social development.[19] Since the thaw in East-West relations and the changing balance between markets and states, human rights advocates, gender activists, development specialists, and groups of indigenous peoples have become more vocal, operational, and important in contexts that were once thought to be the exclusive prerogatives of states or international secretariats.

Since the 1990s, the sheer growth in NGO numbers has prompted Lester Salamon to discern an "associational revolution" that has been largely driven by communications technology and funding availability.[20] The Union of International Associations currently estimates international NGOs (those operating in more than two countries) to number 25,000.[21] Not all of these organizations are active in UN matters, but the size of the phenomenon is clear. Much NGO engagement with the first and second UNs occurs at headquarters, where some 2,870 NGOs now have "consultative status" and are routinely joined by others without such status. In the field, meanwhile, outsourcing and subcontracting to members of the third UN also reflect the changing balance between markets and states in global governance. Executing predetermined activities as subcontractors is not the same as shaping policy, but many dual-purpose NGOs use field experience in advocacy and vice versa. In fact, NGOs had already become substantial executors of projects funded by the second UN by the time that the Economic and Social Council agreed to more flexible NGO accreditation standards in 1996.

NGOs in the third UN are not always appealing bodies. Much has been made of the ugly elements of local civil society in the genocides in Rwanda and Sudan. NGOs with direct links to the UN also include "nasty" social movements,[22] or what Cyril Ritchie has called "criminals, charlatans and narcissists."[23] For instance, the National Rifle Association hardly pursues a human security agenda that most NGOs with consultative status at the UN would support. In humanitarian emergencies, a number of mom-and-pop organizations as well as larger operations proselytize and/or have agendas that reflect the biases of government funders—especially evident in Afghanistan and Iraq—that are anathema to most NGOs in the third UN. But despite such shortcomings in some cases, NGOs have become integral to UN processes and to global governance more generally.

Academics, consultants, and think tanks

The bulk of scholarship about the United Nations and the main substantive issues on the world organization's agenda emanates from universities, specialist research institutes, and learned societies in North America and Western Europe.[24] During World War II, the notion that the UN would be a major instrument of Washington's foreign policy attracted support from US foundations. For example, the Carnegie Endowment for International Peace actively followed and promoted research on the new organization by scholars and by officials from the League of Nations. Such support has continued in fits and starts since then, including the $1 billion gift from the business leader Ted Turner in 1997 to create the UN Foundation and Better World Fund. Other external policy research organizations with intimate links to UN affairs include the Stanley Foundation, the International Peace Institute, the Center for International Cooperation, and the Center for Humanitarian Dialogue. Two professional associations, the Society for International Development (founded in 1967) and the Academic Council on the United Nations System (founded in 1987), emerged as part of policy research networks focused on the UN and the international system.

"Knowledge networks"[25] have become an analytical concern for students of global governance because they create and transfer knowledge and influence policymakers irrespective of location. These networks often frame debate on a particular issue, provide justifications for alternatives, and catalyze national or international coalitions to support chosen policies and advocate change. What Peter Haas called "epistemic communities" influence policy, especially during times of uncertainty and change when the demand for expertise increases.[26] Much literature relates to scientific elites with particular expertise in areas such as the HIV/AIDS pandemic and the environment.[27] A related approach to knowledge networks is Peter Hall's earlier study of the cross-national dissemination of ideas among experts in the postwar period, when Keynesianism spread largely because it "acquired influence over the economic policies of a major power and was exported as that nation acquired increasing hegemony around the world."[28]

Three panels of experts in the late 1940s and early 1950s—not then called "knowledge networks"—produced pioneering reports for the United Nations that launched the world organization's use of external expertise: *National and International Measures for Full Employment, Measures for the Economic Development of Under-Developed Countries,* and *Measures for International Economic Stability.*[29] These groups permitted the entry of outside expertise—including prescient thinking by such later Nobel laureates as W. Arthur Lewis and Theodore W. Schultz—as parts of teams of prominent economists from different parts of the world, supported by professionals within the UN Secretariat.

In the 1960s, the Committee for Development Planning (since 1999, "Policy" has replaced "Planning" in the acronym, CDP) was created and initially chaired by Jan Tinbergen, who later won the first Nobel Prize in Economic Sciences. The CDP usually comprised 24 economists, all unpaid and appointed in their personal capacities by the UN Secretary-General, without nomination by governments. The CDP met a few times a year to bring external expertise into the UN regarding development and international economic policy.

A strong ethical dimension was present among such teams—pursuing a world of greater economic and social justice with less poverty and a more equitable income distribution. Nobel economics laureate Lawrence Klein, an eloquent member of the third UN on disarmament and development, observed, "I believe that it would be quite valuable if the UN had a better academic world contact."[30] Indeed, the import of new thinking, approaches, and policies from scholars in the third UN remains vital to the world organization, as suggested by recent reports from Jeffrey Sachs and the UN Millennium Project.[31]

The UN Research Institute for Social Development (UNRISD) was the first of a handful of United Nations think tanks, and the core 14 research entities of the UN University are now collectively the largest. While the staffs of these units have somewhat more autonomy than most international civil servants, UNRISD and UNU remain part of the second UN because their research agendas are subject to subtle and not-so-subtle financial pressure from governments. However, they often provide a backdoor channel for external academic and analytical expertise.

Independent commissions

In addition to NGOs and experts, some of the loudest and most challenging voices in the third UN come from "eminent persons." For example, as part of the lead-up to the UN's sixtieth anniversary, Secretary-General Kofi Annan convened the High-level Panel on Threats, Challenges and Change. As part of the follow-up to the September 2005 World Summit, Annan pulled together the High-level Panel on System-wide Coherence in the areas of development, humanitarian aid, and the environment.

This tradition goes back to the late 1960s and the panel, headed by former Canadian prime minister Lester B. Pearson, that produced *Partners in Development*

(1969). The so-called Pearson Commission was followed by a host of others, including commissions on development issues chaired by former German chancellor Willy Brandt (1980 and 1983); on common security by former Swedish prime minister Olof Palme (1982); on environment and development by serving Norwegian prime minister Gro Harlem Brundtland (1987); on humanitarian problems by Iranian and Jordanian princes Sadruddin Aga Khan and Hassan bin Talal (1988); on South-South cooperation by serving Tanzanian president Julius Nyerere (1990); on global governance by former Swedish prime minister Ingvar Carlsson and the Commonwealth secretary-general Shridath Ramphal (1995); on humanitarian intervention and state sovereignty by former Australian minister of external affairs Gareth Evans and former Algerian ambassador to the UN Mohamed Sahnoun (2001); on human security by Sadako Ogata and Amartya Sen (2003); and on civil society by former Brazilian president Fernando Henrique Cardoso (2004). There are also commissions that are recalled more by their sponsors' names rather than those of their chairs—for example, the Club of Rome (1972) and the Carnegie Commission on Preventing Deadly Conflict (1997).

This type of expertise—combining knowledge with political punch and access to decision makers—has been influential in nourishing ideas. Commissioners speak in their individual capacities and can move beyond what passes for received wisdom in governments and secretariats. The reports are normally presented to the Secretary-General, who can point to multinational composition and a variety of perspectives behind a consensus and thus use the findings and recommendations more easily than ideas emanating from inside the Secretariat, which many governments believe should not go beyond established intergovernmental positions. Research teams are often led by academics and usually located "outside" the UN but sometimes temporarily in the employ of the second UN. The researchers play an important role not only by supporting the commissioners' deliberations with necessary documentation, but also by providing an entry point for ideas that eventually get carried forward by the commissioners and the published panel reports.

These examples indicate the utility for international deliberations of a mechanism that takes visible individuals who made careers as senior governmental or intergovernmental officials, or both, but who subsequently—as independent and usually prominent elders—are willing to voice criticisms at higher decibel levels and make more controversial recommendations than when they occupied official positions. These commissions are a key part of the third UN even if they are established and bankrolled by the first or the second UN. They can formulate ideas beyond what passes for political correctness in governments and secretariats.

Interactions among the three UNs

Understanding the interactions among the three United Nations is crucial in the analysis of global policy processes. It is a difficult task in view of the increasing ease of movement by talented people who contribute to UN deliberations and actions from several vantage points during their careers. In the contemporary world, it is common for leading policy figures to have significant exposure to all three United Nations. For instance, Adebayo Adedeji was a junior academic working on UN issues before becoming a government minister, before taking over as the head of the Economic Commission for Africa (ECA), and before setting up his own UN-related NGO in Nigeria after his retirement from the ECA secretariat in Addis Ababa. Bernard Chidzero was about to start as an academic, then became a UN official, and finally, after Zimbabwe's independence, became a member of parliament, minister of economic planning and development, and then senior minister of finance. Julia Taft ran the emergency program of the United Nations Development Programme (UNDP), after having been the CEO of InterAction— a consortium of some 165 US development and humanitarian NGOs—while being a member of a UN committee coordinating emergency operations, and after having headed the US State Department's Bureau of Population, Refugees, and Migration. Boutros Boutros-Ghali earned a reputation as a professor of international law and a government minister in Egypt before spending five years at the helm of the United Nations. He subsequently headed two NGOs in Europe after his failed bid for reelection as the UN's top civil servant.

Figure 7.1 depicts the three United Nations as separate circles whose overlaps convey interactive space. This article focuses on where the three come together (D),

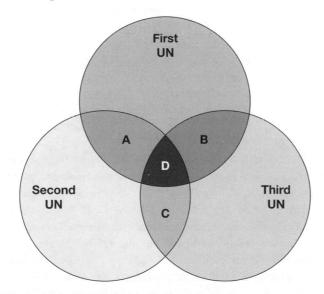

A International and national civil servants' interactions
B State-civil society interactions
C Secretariat-civil society interactions
D The networked space within which individuals and private organizations interact with the first UN and the second UN to influence or advance UN thinking, policies, priorities, or actions

Figure 7.1 Interactions among the three United Nations

but also addresses where the third and the second interact (C), because these networked spaces have been underexplored in the literature and help explain shifts in ideas, policies, priorities, and practices. The universe of UN activities is illustrated by these interplays in combination with the interactions between the first and the second United Nations (A) as well as between the first and the third (B), spaces that have received more significant scholarly scrutiny. The interactions between governments and secretariats have constituted the bulk of UN studies over the past six decades, while those between governments and non-state actors have become prevalent as an explanation for influencing many international policy outcomes.

In terms of advancing ideas, the most obvious target is the first UN, since member states make policies, sign treaties, deploy soldiers to halt mass murder or keep the peace, and establish priorities and budgets. Ideas can also emanate from visionary individuals within the first UN. Examples include Canadian foreign minister Lester B. Pearson's call for the first peacekeeping effort in 1956 and the Swedish government's decision to organize the first ad hoc global conference on the human environment in 1972.

In addition, influential ideas sometimes gravitate from the second UN to the first UN. An intriguing example is the notion of declining terms of trade, a thesis formulated by Hans Singer in 1949 at UN headquarters in the Department of Economic Affairs and rapidly further developed and applied by Raúl Prebisch at the UN Economic Commission for Latin America.[32] The two intellectual stalwarts were highly influential members of the second UN who pulled together the initial data and argument. They then publicized the problems created by the tendency of the terms of trade to move against primary commodities, thus creating persistent balance-of-payments problems for poor countries and slowing their economic growth. This argument, radical at the time, framed debates on economic development for the 1960s and 1970s and led to the establishment in 1964 of the United Nations Conference on Trade and Development.

However, this article focuses on the third UN, whose members often launch or doggedly pursue notions about which important players in the first or the second UN are less than enthusiastic. "Sovereignty as responsibility," which Francis M. Deng and Roberta Cohen deftly designed in the late 1980s and early 1990s to help foster international assistance and protection for internally displaced persons,[33] in turn was made more visible and palatable in 2001 by the report of the International Commission on Intervention and State Sovereignty, *The Responsibility to Protect*.[34] For decades, few members of the first or the second UN embraced the notion of international responsibility to enforce basic human rights standards because of sacrosanct Article 2 (7) of the Charter. When Secretary-General Kofi Annan dared to speak out in 1998–99,[35] many member states were livid and many staff members were baffled. Nonetheless, this emerging norm figured in the consensus of the 2005 World Summit, where it was one of the few issues on which progress was made.[36]

In many instances, various constellations of the first, the second, and the third UN constitute a like-minded partnership to move ahead on issues, with or without some member states, including major powers. One prominent case was the coming together of like-minded governments, UN officials, analysts, and NGOs in the Ottawa Process, which in 1997 produced the convention banning antipersonnel landmines.[37] A similarly diverse coalition led to the adoption of the 1998 Rome Statute, which established the International Criminal Court.[38]

In another variation, members of the second UN may sometimes turn to the third UN to formulate ideas that are controversial but propitious to place on the agenda and pursue when they come from non-state actors. One of the clearest examples is the idea of "human development" which UNDP administrator William Draper imported through the work of Mahbub ul Haq and Amartya Sen. The concept has seen continual refinements since the publication of the first *Human Development Report* in 1990.[39] Certainly, some UNDP staff members were keen on the notion, but the technical details were the work of minds outside the Secretariat. These outside-insiders also took the political flack from governments that were irritated with the publicity given to their embarrassing positions in the rankings. Indeed, many governments at first disputed the appropriateness of paying the bill for such research, a complaint arising from disgruntled governments as viewed in the research about international commissions as well.[40]

A research agenda

Too little is known about the precise roles and impact of the third UN. In particular, future research should aim to fill three lacunae: mapping networks; tracing movements of individuals; and measuring relative influence in specific settings.

Mapping networks

The first pressing task is the rather unexciting, though necessary, exercise of systematic data gathering in order to acquire thick descriptions of the loose networks of individuals and groups across the three UNs. Lacking such data, we cannot move beyond black boxes and sweeping generalizations as explanations for action or inaction. Anne-Marie Slaughter, for instance, has done ground-breaking work in tracking transgovernmental networks, for which the building blocks are not "states but parts of states: courts, regulator agencies, ministries, legislatures."[41] Other scholars have dissected networks of transnational activists organized to "multiply channels of access to the international system,"[42] transnational movements to end the Cold War,[43] and knowledge-based networks.[44]

Multi-actor policymaking networks for the United Nations are less precisely defined, which poses a substantial analytical challenge. However, the basic notion that transnational actors contribute to changes in thinking and policy is similar to that put forward by Slaughter. As such, social network analysis holds the promise of better being able to capture complex relationships among the three UNs.[45] This research method focuses on the patterns of interactions among actors rather than on the attributes of individual units. Some networks have informal, decentralized, and horizontal relationships, while others have a more hierarchical organization. There is little definitional consensus about networks, given wide variations in structures. However, network analysts do agree that, regardless of the type of structure, the nodes (or actors) in these networks are interdependent. They are therefore "not seen as acting in isolation, but within complex linkages with other actors that influence decision making."[46]

Social network analysis potentially can help explain which portions of which networks are more important than others under specified circumstances. Key individuals are so embedded in diplomatic, policy, research, and other social networks that separating them for analytical purposes is extremely challenging, but nonetheless it is a critical part of the contemporary puzzle of international cooperation and global governance. The next step is to move the discussion beyond *which* non-state actors matter toward determining more precisely *how* each matters in the UN's policy-shaping process.

Tracing individuals' trajectories

The second research area involves mapping the movements of key individuals who are active in UN policymaking. In view of the increasing ease of movement by policy professionals, a proposition to be tested is that prominent individuals may be more influential, internationally or nationally, because of their firsthand exposure to a wide variety of institutions. Many individuals are, in effect, "cross-dressers" whose membership at any moment in one of the three UNs reflects the extent to which they are embedded in larger social networks.

As Barnett and Finnemore observe, "Many UN staff and field personnel have varied careers and move back and forth between UN appointments, jobs within their own governments at home, and positions in the private sector, universities, and NGOs." They go on to note that work by sociologists, anthropologists, and scholars of organizational behavior indicates that such backgrounds are important in explaining flows of information and individual behavior. "Good network analysis and good ethnographic work on the UN would contribute greatly to our understanding of its behavior."[47] While privacy legislation applying to personnel files may be an obstacle to obtaining relevant data, a pertinent research task is to track career movements and to explore whether exposure to the culture of an international secretariat, for instance, is an asset in career development in government or NGO service, and vice versa.

Weighing influence

Distinguishing forums for state decision making, international secretariats, and the outside-insiders are essential to determine which UN is behind which policy or action, and to what extent they are responsible for desirable outcomes to be emulated or for undesirable results to be avoided. Analysts of global governance are obliged to design better empirical indicators to move beyond the adage that success has numerous parents, but failure is an orphan.

States rarely are willing to blame themselves for breakdowns in international order and society; and UN secretariats often indiscriminately fault governments for their lack of political will. The first UN has a convenient scapegoat in the second UN, and vice versa. Sometimes the third UN adds to this confusion, blaming or praising the world organization in general. But in other cases—say, the influence of the Bretton Woods institutions on structural adjustment policy or the slowness of developed country governments to finance debt relief—members of the third UN have pointed fingers with more precision and effect.

Agency is crucial, but students of global governance know too little about the relative influences of the actors in what Conor Cruise O'Brien aptly called the "sacred drama" of the United Nations.[48] The stage with Claude's two United Nations has, over the last six decades, become increasingly crowded with other actors who play more than bit parts. States are still the most prominent actors, and national interests have not receded as the basis for decision making; and international secretariats still largely serve these state masters but with margins for independence and maneuver. And there is substantial evidence that the third UN is increasingly salient—sometimes in the wings or dressing room, sometimes in the limelight. Hence, numerous individuals and institutions that are neither states nor their creation in the form of intergovernmental bureaucracies contribute to and circumscribe virtually every deliberation, decision, and operation by either of the other two UNs.

Deciphering what Robert Cox and Harold Jacobson long ago called "the anatomy of influence"[49] requires identifying the strengths and weaknesses of a seemingly ever growing number of actors. A third research task involves identifying better criteria to measure which actors have contributed to "success" and which to "failure" within the United Nations. And a comparable research task for global governance would apply to other intergovernmental arenas—for example the "third EU" and the "third OECD."

Conclusion

A special section of the journal *Foreign Policy* in fall 2002 was titled, "What Is the International Community?"[50] The lead-in quipped, "Invoking the international community is a lot easier than defining it." It no longer makes sense to use the term restrictively to refer to states alone, because non-state characters are playing essential roles with respect to virtually every global challenge to human survival and dignity. International lawyers conceive of the international community narrowly in terms of "peace-loving states"—that is, euphemistically, the first UN. Other observers employ the concept more expansively and also include the creations of states in the form of intergovernmental secretariats—that is, the second UN. Still other commentators also embrace non-state actors operating internationally—that is, the third UN.

We hazard a step in this wider direction by beginning to parse the contemporary international community in terms of interactions among three United Nations. Filling the glaring gaps in global governance[51] leads us to urge that "the UN"—first, second, and third—continue to pool energies and make maximum use of its comparative advantages.

The value of the third UN, in practice as well as in theory, is clear. States and intergovernmental organizations cannot adequately address threats to human security. Whether the UN is seen as a convener, a norm entrepreneur, or an operator, we the peoples require all the helping hands we can get—and many of those are toiling in the third United Nations.

Notes

1 Richard Jolly, Louis Emmerij, and Thomas G. Weiss, *The Power of UN Ideas: Lessons from the First Sixty Years*, available along with other information at www.unhistory.org. See also Robert J. Berg, "The UN Intellectual History Project," *Global Governance* 12, no. 4 (2006): 325–41. For the capstone book in the series, see Richard Jolly, Louis Emmerij, and Thomas G. Weiss, *UN Ideas That Changed the World* (Bloomington: Indiana University Press, 2009).
2 Inis L. Claude Jr., *Swords Into Plowshares: The Problems and Prospects of International Organization* (New York: Random House, 1956); and Inis L. Claude Jr., "Peace and Security: Prospective Roles for the Two United Nations," *Global Governance* 2, no. 3 (1996): 289–98.
3 Susan Strange, *The Retreat of the State: The Diffusion of Power in the World Economy* (Cambridge: Cambridge University Press, 1996); and Robert C. Cox, *The New Realism: Perspectives on Multilateralism and World Order* (New York: St. Martin's Press, 1997).
4 Barry Carin, Richard Higgott, Jan Aart Scholte, Gordon Smith, and Diane Stone, "Global Governance: Looking Ahead," *Global Governance* 12, no. 1 (2006): 1–6. Other authors have begun to speak of "new multilateralism" (Michael G. Schechter, ed., *Innovation in Multilateralism* [Basingstoke, UK: Palgrave Macmillan, 1999]); "complex multilateralism" (Robert O'Brien, Anne Marie Goetz, Jan Aart Scholte, and Marc Williams, *Contesting Global Governance: Multilateral Economic Institutions and Global Social Movements* [Cambridge: Cambridge University Press, 2000]); "polylateralism" (Geoffrey Wiseman, "'Polylateralism' and New Modes of Global Dialogue," Discussion Paper No. 59 [Leicester, UK: Leicester Diplomatic Studies Programme, 1999]); and "plurilateralism" (Philip G. Cerny, "Plurilateralism: Structural Differentiation and Functional Conflict in the Post-Cold War World Order," *Millennium: Journal of International Studies* 22, no. 1 (1993): 27–51).
5 Thomas G. Weiss and Leon Gordenker, eds., *NGOs, the UN, and Global Governance* (Boulder, Colo.: Lynne Rienner, 1996); Peter Willetts, ed., *The "Conscience" of the World: The Influence of Non-Governmental Organisations in the UN System* (Washington, DC: Brookings Institution Press, 1996); Bob Deacon, *Global Social Policy and Governance* (London: Sage, 2007); and Jan Aart Scholte, *Civil Society Voices and the International Monetary Fund* (Ottawa: North-South Institute, 2002).
6 Wolfgang R. Reinicke, *Global Public Policy: Governing Without Government?* (Washington, DC: Brookings Institution, 1998); Wolfgang R. Reinicke, Francis M. Deng, Thorsten Benner, and Jan Martin Witte, *Critical Choices: The United Nations, Networks, and the Future of Global Governance* (Ottawa: IDRC Publishers, 2000). Jan Aart Scholte has suggested that it may be more useful to distinguish between "conformist," "rejectionist," "reformist," and "transformist" orientations rather than focus on sectors, in *Democratizing the Global Economy: The Role of Civil Society* (Coventry, UK: Centre for the Study of Globalisation and Regionalisation, 2004).

7   Robert Keohane and Joseph Nye, eds., *Transnational Relations and World Politics* (Cambridge, Mass.: Harvard University Press, 1971).
8   Michael Barnett and Martha Finnemore, "Political Approaches," in Thomas G. Weiss and Sam Daws, eds., *The Oxford Handbook on the United Nations* (Oxford: Oxford University Press, 2007), 42.
9   Dag Hammarskjöld, "The International Civil Servant in Law and in Fact," reprinted by permission of Clarendon Press, Oxford; quotes at 329 and 349.
10 Thomas G. Weiss, Tatiana Carayannis, Louis Emmerij, and Richard Jolly, *UN Voices: The Struggle for Development and Social Justice* (Bloomington: Indiana University Press, 2005). See also *The Complete Oral History Transcripts from UN Voices*, CD-ROM (New York: United Nations Intellectual History Project, 2007).
11 Thant Myint-U and Amy Scott, *The UN Secretariat: A Brief History (1945–2006)* (New York: International Peace Academy, 2007), 126–8.
12 Devaki Jain, *Women, Development, and the UN: A Sixty-Year Quest for Equality and Justice* (Bloomington: Indiana University Press, 2005).
13 John G. Ruggie, "global_governance.net: The Global Compact as Learning Network," *Global Governance* 7, no. 4 (2001): 371–8. See also Tagi Sagafi-nejad, in collaboration with John Dunning, *The UN and Transnational Corporations: From Code of Conduct to Global Compact* (Bloomington: Indiana University Press, 2008).
14 Weiss, Carayannis, Emmerij, and Jolly, *UN Voices*, 387.
15 UNRISD, *UN World Summits and Civil Society Engagement*, UNRISD Research and Policy Brief 6 (Geneva: UNRISD, 2007), 2. See also Michael G. Schechter, *United Nations Global Conferences* (London: Routledge, 2005).
16 Steve Charnowitz, "Two Centuries of Participation: NGOs and International Governance," *Michigan Journal of International Law* 18, no. 2 (1997): 183–286.
17 Stephen Schlesinger, *Act of Creation: The Founding of the United Nations* (Boulder, Colo.: Westview, 2003), 122.
18 Moisés Naim, "Democracy's Dangerous Impostors," *Wall Street Journal*, 21 April 2007.
19 "INGO Accountability Charter," available at www.ingoaccountabilitycharter.org.
20 Lester M. Salamon, Helmut K. Anheier, Regina List, and S. Wojciech Sokolowski and Associates, *Global Civil Society: Dimensions of the Nonprofit Sector* (Baltimore, Md.: Johns Hopkins Center for Civil Society Studies, 1999).
21 Data available at the website of the Union of International associations: www.uia.be/stats.
22 Peter Waterman, "Global Civil Society: A Concept Worth Defining: A Terrain Worth Disputing," see the Network Institute for Global Democratization (www.nigd.org).
23 Civil Society Development Forum 2007 General Report, "Overview by Cyril Ritchie, General Rapporteur, Secretary of CONGO," available at www.ngocongo.org/index.php?what = doc&id = 1121.
24 W. Andy Knight, S. Neil MacFarlane, and Thomas G. Weiss, "Swan Song," *Global Governance* 11, no. 4 (2005): 527–35; and Leon Gordenker and Christer Jönsson, "Knowledge," in *The Oxford Handbook on the United Nations*, 82–94.
25 Diane Stone, *Global Knowledge Networks and International Development* (London: Routledge, 2005); and Janice Gross Stein, Richard Stren, Joy Fitzgibbon, and Melissa MacLean, *Networks of Knowledge: Collaborative Innovation in International Learning* (Toronto: University of Toronto Press, 2001).
26 Emanuel Adler and Peter M. Haas, "Epistemic Communities, World Order, and the Creation of a Reflective Research Program," *International Organization* 46, no. 1 (1992): 367–90.
27 For example, Leon Gordenker, Roger A. Coate, Christer Jönsson, and Peter Söderholm, *International Cooperation in Response to AIDS* (London: Pinter, 1995); Peter M. Haas, Robert O. Keohane, and Marc A. Levy, eds., *Institutions for the Earth: Sources of Effective International Environmental Protection* (Cambridge, Mass.: MIT Press, 1992).
28 Peter A. Hall, "Introduction," in *The Political Power of Economic Ideas: Keynsianism Across Nations*, ed. Peter A. Hall (Princeton, NJ: Princeton University Press, 1989), 26.

29 Louis Emmerij, Richard Jolly, and Thomas G. Weiss, *Ahead of the Curve? UN Ideas and Global Challenges* (Bloomington: Indiana University Press, 2001), 26–42.

30 Weiss, Carayannis, Emmerij, and Jolly, *UN Voices*, 373.

31 *Investing in Development: A Practical Plan to Achieve the Millennium Development Goals*, and ten reports from thematic task forces, available at www.unmillenniumproject.org.

32 John Toye and Richard Toye, *The UN and Global Political Economy: Trade, Finance, and Development* (Bloomington: Indiana University Press, 2004), 110–36.

33 Roberta Cohen and Francis M. Deng, *Masses in Flight: The Global Crisis of Internal Displacement* (Washington, DC: Brookings Institution, 1998); and Roberta Cohen and Francis M. Deng, eds., *The Forsaken People: Case Studies of the Internally Displaced* (Washington, DC: Brookings Institution, 1998).

34 International Commission on Intervention and State Sovereignty, *The Responsibility to Protect* (Ottawa: International Development Research Centre, 2001).

35 Kofi A. Annan, *The Question of Intervention: Statements by the Secretary-General of the United Nations* (New York: UN, 2000).

36 Thomas G. Weiss, *Humanitarian Intervention: Ideas in Action* (Cambridge: Polity, 2007).

37 Don Hubert, *The Landmine Ban: A Case Study in Humanitarian Advocacy* (Providence, RI: Watson Institute, 2000), Occasional Paper No. 42; Richard Price, "Reversing the Gun Sights: Transnational Civil Society Targets Landmines," *International Organization* 52, no. 3 (1998): 613–44; and Motoko Mekata, "Building Partnerships Toward a Common Goal: Experiences of the International Campaign to Ban Landmines," in *The Third Force: The Rise of Transnational Civil Society*, ed. Ann M. Florini (Washington, DC: Carnegie Endowment, 2000), 143–76.

38 Fanny Benedetti and John L. Washburn, "Drafting the International Criminal Court Treaty," *Global Governance* 5, no. 1 (1999): 1–38.

39 Craig N. Murphy, *The United Nations Development Programme: A Better Way?* (Cambridge: Cambridge University Press, 2006), 232–62.

40 Ramesh Thakur, Andrew F. Cooper, and John English, *International Commissions and the Power of Ideas* (Tokyo: UN University Press, 2005).

41 Anne-Marie Slaughter, *A New World Order* (Princeton, NJ: Princeton University Press, 2004), 5.

42 Margaret E. Keck and Kathryn Sikkink, *Activists Without Borders: Advocacy Networks in International Politics* (New York: Cornell University Press, 1998), 1.

43 Matthew Evangelista, *Unarmed Forces: The Transnational Movement to End the Cold War* (Ithaca, NY: Cornell University Press, 1999).

44 Stein, Stren, Fitzgibbon, and MacLean, *Networks of Knowledge*, 2.

45 Stanley Wasserman and Katherine Faust, *Social Network Analysis: Methods and Applications* (Cambridge: Cambridge University Press, 1994).

46 Tatiana Carayannis, "The Complex Wars of the Congo: Towards a New Analytic Approach," *Journal of Asian and African Studies* 38, no. 2–3 (2003): 236.

47 Barnett and Finnemore, "Political Approaches," 54.

48 Conor Cruise O'Brien, *United Nations: Sacred Drama* (London: Hutchinson & Company, 1968).

49 Robert W. Cox and Harold K. Jacobson, eds., *The Anatomy of Influence: Decision Making in International Organization* (New Haven, Conn.: Yale University Press, 1973).

50 *Foreign Policy*, no. 132 (September-October 2002): 28–46.

51 Ramesh Thakur and Thomas G. Weiss, *Global Governance and the UN: An Unfinished Journey* (Bloomington: Indiana University Press, 2009).

8

FRAMING GLOBAL GOVERNANCE, FIVE GAPS

With Ramesh Thakur

There is no government for the world. Yet, on any given day, mail is delivered across borders; people travel from one country to another via a variety of transport modes; goods and services are freighted across land, air, sea, and cyberspace; and a whole range of other cross-border activities take place in reasonable expectation of safety and security for the people, groups, firms, and governments involved. Disruptions and threats are rare—indeed, in many instances rarer in the international domain than in many sovereign countries that should have effective and functioning governments. That is to say, international transactions are typically characterized by order, stability, and predictability. This immediately raises a puzzle: How is the world governed even in the absence of a world government in order to produce norms, codes of conduct, and regulatory, surveillance, and compliance instruments? How are values allocated quasi-authoritatively for the world, and accepted as such, without a government to rule the world?

The answer, we argue, lies in global governance. It is the sum of laws, norms, policies, and institutions that define, constitute, and mediate relations between citizens, societies, markets, and states in the international system—the wielders and objects of the exercise of international public power.

That said, at the time we write this, the world is suffering the worst financial and economic crisis since the Great Depression that began in 1929 and continued into the 1930s. The "normal" periods of calm, stability, order, and predictability are interspersed with periodic bouts of market volatility, disorder, and crisis, as well as internal, regional, transnational, and international armed conflict and warfare on the peace and security side. Where the Asian financial crisis of 1997–98 proved the perils of crony capitalism, the 2007–8 US subprime and financial crises showed the pitfalls of unbridled capitalism. Governments may be fallible, but markets too are imperfect. Both the Asian crisis of a decade ago and the 2008 US market collapse demonstrate the need for efficient, effective, and transparent regulatory and surveillance instruments and institutions. The state has an essential role to play. Those countries where the state has not abandoned the market to its own supposedly self-regulating devices are seemingly better placed to weather the current crisis of confidence in capitalism.

In other words these are crises of governance in terms of the proper role of governments and market institutions as well as the appropriate balance in the relationship between them. The second and equally important point to note is that they are crises of domestic governance. The causes of the crises lie in domestic governance imperfections and the solutions entail domestic government and market responses. The role for global governance institutions is restricted to containing the contagion. Global governance can play a facilitative and constraining role, but rarely a determinant and predominant role. The authority and capacity for the latter is vested almost exclusively in domestic public authorities.

As the number of international actors and the frequency and intensity of their interactions have grown, so has the requirement for institutionalized cooperation among them. States are, and for the foreseeable future are likely to remain, the primary actors in world affairs; and state sovereignty is the bedrock principle on which their relations are based and organized. Intergovernmental organizations help states to cooperate in the pursuit of shared goals and to manage competition and rivalry. Arising from this, the *problématique* of global governance in our times may be simply stated: the evolution of intergovernmental organizations to facilitate robust international responses lags well behind the emergence of collective problems with trans-border, especially global, dimensions. This is the true significance of the worldwide financial and banking crisis.

The *problématique* of global security governance consists of the disconnect between the distribution of authority within existing intergovernmental institutions and the international distribution of military power. Similarly, there is a "growing gap between the distribution of authority within existing international institutions and the international distribution of economic power."[1] Historically, global financial governance focused on mediating exchanges between national markets. However, capital can no longer be parsed as national or international—it has become truly global. Accordingly, apprehending the regulation of capital and the provision of economic stability demands examining the global reach of powerful actors and institutions. While not so long ago finance essentially flowed from corporations based in states with some transnational links, today it is essentially global with some local characteristics. And it is not self-governing. Instead, "stability in financial markets requires the judicious exercise of public authority."[2] Moreover, maximizing allocative efficiency for the globe cannot be the only goal of international financial and economic policy more generally. Questions of legitimacy, distributive justice, and social safety nets are as important as efficacy, currency convertibility, or capital mobility. Yet there is nothing remotely resembling an overarching authority for global financial governance to help facilitate stability or reduce the social costs of contemporary economic developments.

This essay begins by probing the idea of global governance before parsing five "gaps" in contemporary global governance that we believe are the best way to understand the strengths and weaknesses of the UN's past, present, and future roles. We then discuss the 2004 tsunami and global climate change to illustrate how this analytical lens works when examining a specific event and an issue-area.

The idea of global governance and globalization

"Good governance" incorporates participation and empowerment with respect to public policies, choices, and offices; rule of law and independent judiciary to which the executive and legislative branches of government are subject along with citizens and other actors and entities; and standards of probity and incorruptibility, transparency, accountability, and responsibility. It includes also institutions in which these principles and values find on-going expression. Good governance thus can be considered a normative definition concerned with laudable standards.

"Global governance"—which can be good, bad, or indifferent—refers to collective[3] problem-solving arrangements for challenges and threats that are beyond the capacity of a single state to address. Both formal and informal, such arrangements provide more order and stability for the world than would occur naturally. Another way to think of global governance is as purposeful systems of rules or norms with imperfections and major limitations—in a phrase, international cooperation without world government—within which states pursue their own national or regional interests and only limited and often ineffective measures to require compliance with internationally agreed rules, regulations, and decisions.

Traditionally, and this is the source of some confusion, governance has been associated with "governing," or with political authority, institutions and, ultimately, control. Governance in this sense denotes formal political institutions that both aim to coordinate and control interdependent social relations and that also possess the capacity to enforce decisions. In recent years, however, some authors have used "governance" to denote the regulation of interdependent relations in the absence of overarching political authority, such as in the international system.[4] Through informal as well as formal mechanisms and arrangements, collective interests are articulated, rights and obligations are established, and differences are mediated on the global plane.

In addition to interdependence and a growing recognition of problems that defy solutions by a single state, the other explanation for a growing interest in understanding global governance stems from the sheer growth in numbers and importance of non-state actors (civil society and market), which also are conducting themselves or combining themselves in new ways. Society has become too complex for citizens' demands to be satisfied solely by governments at national, regional, and global levels. Instead, civil society organizations play increasingly active roles in shaping norms, laws, and policies. The growing influence and power of civil society actors means that they have effectively entered the realm of policy-making. They are participants in global governance as advocates, activists, and policymakers, which in turn poses challenges of representation, accountability, and legitimacy both to governments and back to the civil society actors. In an increasingly diverse, complex, and interdependent world, solutions to collective-action problems are attainable less and less at any one level or by just state actors. Instead, we have partnerships between different actors and levels of governance, and issue-specific and contingent choices between them on other issues. With influence over policy should come responsibility for the consequences of policy.

Global governance entails multilevel and networked relations and interactions[5] in order to deal with the linkages across policy levels and domains. As the planet's most representative organization, the United Nations has unparalleled legitimacy even if it cannot displace the responsibility of local, state, and national governments; but it can and should be the locus of multilateral diplomacy and collective action to solve problems shared in common by many countries. "Good" global governance implies, not exclusive policy jurisdiction, but an optimal partnership between the state, regional, and global levels of actors, and between state, intergovernmental, and nongovernmental categories of actors.

The other concept necessary to this analysis is "globalization," a process of increased interconnectivity throughout the world. Many regard it as both a desirable and an irreversible engine of commerce that will underpin growing prosperity and a higher standard of living throughout the world. Others recoil from it as the soft underbelly of corporate imperialism that plunders and profits on the basis of unrestrained consumerism. Some observers have argued that globalization has been occurring since the earliest trade expeditions (e.g., the Silk Road); international trade, as a proportion of total production in the world economy, was about the same in the 1980s as in the last two decades of the Gold Standard (1890–1913);[6] and, despite the current obsession, the process itself is not fundamentally new. Still others have suggested that the current era of globalization is unique in the rapidity of its spread and the intensity of the interactions in real time that result.[7]

Globalization creates losers as well as winners, and entails risks as well as provides opportunities. As an International Labour Organization blue-ribbon panel noted, the problems lie not in globalization per se, but in the "deficiencies in its governance."[8] The deepening of poverty and inequality—prosperity for a few countries and people, marginalization and exclusion for many—has implications for social and political stability, again among as well as within nations. That is, for governance, both domestic and global.[9] The rapid growth of global markets has not seen the parallel development of social and economic institutions to ensure their smooth and efficient functioning; labor rights have been less assiduously protected than capital and property rights; and the global rules on trade and finance are unfair to the extent that they produce asymmetric effects on rich and poor countries.

"Gaps" in global governance

The clearest way to comprehend the relevance of using the lens of global governance is by examining what we dub the five "gaps" between concrete global problems and feeble global solutions. Knowledge, normative, policy, institutional, and compliance gaps are discussed below separately as a prelude to pulling them together in the subsequent discussion of the December 2004 tsunami and climate change.

Knowledge gaps

The first analytical lens consists of the "knowledge gap." With or without institutions and resources, there often is little or no consensus about the nature, gravity, and magnitude of a problem, either about the empirical information or the theoretical explanation. And there is often similar—and sometimes even more bitter—disagreement over the best remedies and solutions to these problems. Two good examples are global warming and nuclear weapons, neither of which was known when the UN Charter was signed. What is the best "mix-and-match" strategy for combating the threat of global warming, for instance, the severity and causes of which remain in political if not scientific dispute, which minimizes present disruption while also minimizing future risks and damage? Or for preventing the proliferation of nuclear weapons while also trying to encourage the elimination of existing stockpiles and avoiding their use in the meantime?[10] Can we get beyond ideology and let information, data, experience, and science guide us?

We adopt a "whole-of-cycle" approach to gaps with respect to knowledge, norms, policy, institutions, and compliance. At least partially filling the knowledge gap is essential for dealing with the other gaps in global governance—normative, policy, institutional, and compliance. If we can recognize that there is a problem and agree on its approximate dimensions, then we can take steps to solve it. A critical gap in any of the five stages can cause the entire cycle to collapse. A UN-relevant knowledge gap arises from a lack of knowledge about the existence, scale, location, causes of, or possible solutions to an international policy problem. How is knowledge of new problems and issues acquired or created? How is it transmitted to the policy community? And how do solutions get formulated and adopted? Thus, the first step in eventually addressing a problem that goes beyond the capacity of states to solve is actually to recognize its existence, to understand that there is a problem. Next, it is necessary to collect solid data that challenge the consensus about the nature of the problem, to diagnose its causes—in short, to explain the problem.

One under-appreciated comparative advantage of the United Nations is its convening capacity and mobilizing power. UN-sponsored world conferences, heads of government summits, and blue-ribbon commissions and panels have been used for framing issues, outlining choices, making decisions; for setting, even anticipating, the agenda; for framing the rules, including for dispute settlement; for pledging and mobilizing resources; for implementing collective decisions; and for monitoring progress and recommending midterm corrections and adjustments.[11]

Normative gaps

Once a threat or problem has been identified and diagnosed, the next step is to help solidify a new norm of behavior. To refer to the same two examples again:

in the decades since 1945, the norms of environmental protection and nuclear abstinence have become firmly established. How were the existing gaps filled? There are enormous difficulties in reaching consensus about universally acceptable norms, for example, the "emerging norm" of human rights can be (and has been) culturally deconstructed to cast doubts upon the universality of even long-agreed principles. Here again, the source of ideas to fill in normative gaps is now more likely than ever to be civil society. At the same time, the United Nations is an essential and unequalled arena in which states codify norms in the form of resolutions and declarations (soft law) as well as conventions and treaties (hard law). That is, the United Nations offers the most efficient forum for processing norms—standards of behavior—into laws—rules of behavior. Again, the notion of global governance helps us to see how, despite the absence of overarching global authority, fledgling steps take place that on occasion enhance international order and stability and consolidate what Hedley Bull called "international society" more than would otherwise occur without the world organization.[12]

Norms matter because people—citizens as well as politicians and officials—care about what others think of them. This is why approbation, and its logical corollary, shaming, can be effective in regulating social behavior.[13] It is also why the United Nations and its secretaries-general, sometimes called a "secular pope," have often relied upon the bully pulpit.[14] Like Josef Stalin's characterization of the papacy— "How many divisions does the pope have?"—the power of the UN's ideas and moral voice is often underestimated. In the Ottawa Treaty banning landmines, for example, norm-generation by Western middle powers was underpinned by norm-advocacy from NGOs and reinforced by norm-promoting standard-setting by the UN Secretary-General when he endorsed the Ottawa process as the negotiating track, and the convention that resulted from it.[15]

A relatively recent effort at UN norm building was the Global Compact that grew from the 2000 Millennium Summit. Principle 10 ("Businesses should work against all forms of corruption, including extortion and bribery") attempts to answer the questions: What is corruption? Why is it wrong? What can be done about it? Adequate answers to these questions suggest that filling the normative gap requires first at least partially filling the knowledge gap; there is usually a lag because norms reflect an agreement about the state of affairs as a basis for building a consensus about the most appropriate ways to frame an issue and future action.

As a universal organization, the United Nations is an ideal forum to seek consensus about normative approaches that govern global problems and would work best with a worldwide application of a norm. The host of problems ranging from reducing acid rain to impeding money laundering to halting pandemics clearly provide instances for which universal norms and approaches are emerging.

At the same time, the UN is a maddening forum because dissent by powerful states or even coalitions of less powerful ones means either no action occurs, or agreement can be reached only on a lowest common denominator. For instance, the avoidance of meaningful action against a white-minority regime in South Africa until the 1990s reflected mainly US and British refusals, which were backed by their vetoes in the Security Council. Similarly, widespread dissent even by a minority of countries can also slow normative progress. For instance, cultural differences can complicate the emergence of norms that strike most people in most parts of the world as "no-brainers." The unholy alliance of the Vatican and Islamic fundamentalists against women's reproductive rights is a clear illustration.

As elsewhere in the story of global governance, the proliferation of actors is vital. The presence and work of civil society is essential in terms of identifying normative gaps and in proposing ways to reduce them. Examples of individuals and institutions come immediately to mind: Raphael Lemkin's efforts to coin the term "genocide" and his role in the formulation and adoption of the UN Genocide Convention; Henri Dunant and the Red Cross movement in the field of international humanitarian law; Peter Benenson and Amnesty International's pursuit of human rights; and Jody Williams and the International Campaign to Ban Landmines.

Once information has been collected and knowledge gained that a problem is serious enough to warrant attention by the international policy community, new norms in which the newly acquired knowledge is embedded need to be articulated, disseminated, and institutionalized. For example, once we know that HIV/AIDS is transmitted through unprotected promiscuous sexual activity, the norm of safe sex follows logically. Or as we gain information about the sexual activities of personnel deployed in the field in UN peace operations, the norm of no sexual contact or no paid sex between UN personnel and the local population might be articulated by the UN Secretariat.

In spite of the obvious problems of accommodating the perspectives of 192 countries, the UN provides an essential, even unique, arena to permit the expression of official views from around the planet on international norms. The crucial question is how contested norms become institutionalized both within and among states, and the interactive dynamics of the process of insitutionalization at the national, regional, and global levels. International norms can be transmitted down into national politics through incorporation into domestic laws or into the policy preferences of political leaders through elite learning. It is only through state structures, through governments, that international norms can be integrated into domestic standards. Norm diffusion is not in itself, therefore, about the state withering away. Indeed, the United Nations can be considered the last bastion of sovereignty. It provides a forum that has promulgated norms with the consent of most member states with a view toward sustaining, not eroding, the prerogatives of sovereigns.

Policy gaps

By "policy" we mean the articulated and linked set of governing principles and goals, and the agreed programs of action to implement those principles and achieve those goals. Thus, the Kyoto Protocol, the Nuclear Nonproliferation Treaty (NPT) and the Comprehensive Test Ban Treaty may be seen as examples of policies for combating the threats of global warming and nuclear weapons.

That said, is "international" policy made and implemented by international organizations, or by national authorities meeting and interacting in international organizational forums?[16] To what extent is the evident policy paralysis over Darfur the result of a policy gap on the part of the UN as opposed to weak political will among key member states?

A second set of questions arises about possible disconnects between the numbers and types of actors playing ever-expanding roles in civil, political, and economic affairs within and among nations, and the concentration of decision-making authority in intergovernmental institutions. Where, for example, are operational ideas (such as measures to counter climate change) coming from? The source of ideas to fill policy gaps is likely to be governments and intergovernmental organizations. When policy is made in the absence of institutions, it takes on an ad hoc character. Such an approach can lead to fragmented and incompatible policies that become incoherent over time.

UN policymakers are the principal political organs, the Security Council and the General Assembly, and the member states collectively. But all of these are intergovernmental forums. That is, the people making the decisions in the form of adopting resolutions that set out new governing principles, articulate goals, and authorize programs of action to achieve those goals, do so as delegates of national governments from the UN's member states. And they make these choices within the governing framework of their national foreign policies, under instructions, on all important policy issues, from their home governments. Or member states may make the policy choices directly themselves, for example at summit conferences. That being the case, it is not always clear just what might be meant by "United Nations" policy, policymaking, and policymakers.

The responsibility for implementation of most "UN policy" does not rest primarily with the United Nations itself, but devolves to member states. But even UN policy, in the form of policy resolutions and actions adopted and authorized by the Security Council and the General Assembly or summit decisions made by member states directly, may exhibit regulative, distributive, and redistributive characteristics.

Based on these considerations, we conclude that some resolutions adopted by the General Assembly are the equivalent of policy declarations, in that they articulate broad principles and goals and/or call for programs of action for the attainment of these goals. One of the clearest examples of such a resolution is General Assembly resolution 2922 of 15 November 1972 reaffirming apartheid as a crime against humanity. This policy became a staple of UN resolutions over many years until the liberation of South Africa and the replacement of the apartheid regime with an elected black majority government formed by the African National Congress with Nelson Mandela as the first president.

A second set of "UN policy" documents might be goals, plans of action, and desirable codes of conduct embedded in international treaties and conventions. Good examples include the Genocide Convention; the Universal Declaration of

Human Rights; the two Covenants on Civil and Political and Social, Economic and Cultural Rights; the NPT; and the UN Convention on the Law of the Sea.

Clearly, as new problems emerge and new norms arise, they will highlight gaps in policy that also need addressing. United Nations policy might be to promote awareness about the gravity and causes of HIV/AIDS, encourage educational campaigns by member governments, or declare zero tolerance of sexual exploitation by UN peacekeepers.

Institutional gaps

If there is a problem that is relatively well known and/or a range of agreed-upon policy, what is the machinery that will put such a policy into effect? For example, one may have determined that democratic states are less likely to go to war and that increasing their numbers is valuable, and hence a policy could be announced to hold elections after peace has broken out in a protracted conflict. However, this has little meaning unless there also are institutions such as a local election commission along with outside observers to register voters and to arrange for poll workers, polling stations, printing of ballots, verification of rolls, and tallying of results. Often, institutional gaps can exist even when knowledge, norms, and policies are in place.

If policy is to escape the trap of being ad hoc, episodic, judgmental, and idio-syncratic, it must be housed within an institutional context. This refers to the fact that there is either no overarching global institution (or such a flimsy one as to be the equivalent) or capability to address a problem with trans-border dimensions. In such cases, even the most "powerful" institutions such as the Security Council, the World Bank, or the International Monetary Fund,[17] often lack either the appropriate resources or authority or both.

We use "institution" here in two senses of the term: both formal, organizational entities as well as regimes, or recurring and stable patterns of behavior around which actor expectations converge. For example, the "coalition of the willing" and the Proliferation Security Initiative are stable patterns even though the membership is variable. It is easier to identify formal institutions that have treaties and budgets, but the messier and more informal variety are just as essential to our analysis of gaps.

Institutional gaps can refer to the fact that there may be no overarching global institution, in which case many international aspects of problem-solving may be ignored, for example, the control of nuclear weapons. Or it may be impossible to address a problem because of an institutional gap of missing key member states— e.g., the World Trade Organization (WTO) before China's entry or the League of Nations without the United States—or simply because resources are incom-mensurate with the magnitude of a problem.

Institutions that are most effective often are those that deal with well-known areas with well-embedded norms and consensus among member states: the UN Children's Fund (UNICEF) and the World Health Organization (WHO), to name but two. Many issues treated by such organizations are seen as having little controversial political content—there is nothing in them that impacts a state's interests, and that would therefore lead to conflict. Therefore, these issues can safely be turned over to experts for resolution.[18] Positive examples thus should figure in contemporary discussions along with laments about those that fall short, for example the late but little lamented UN Commission on Human Rights as well as its successor, the Human Rights Council. These institutions may work well because they focus on specific problems and are "functional"—that is, part of their work and part of the bureaucracy deals with narrowly defined issues and technologies.

Institutions are another example of the impact of ideas. Sixty years into the UN's history, there are very few issues that do not have some global institutions working on them. Actors in world politics can and do cooperate, and they do so more often than they engage in conflict. The problems involved in cooperation include the difficulty of coordination due to the lack of reliable information about what other actors are doing. Actors thus form institutions to mitigate such problems by sharing information, reducing transaction costs, providing incentives for concessions, providing mechanisms for dispute resolution, and establishing processes for making decisions. Institutions can facilitate such problem solving even though they do not possess coercive powers. In particular, intergovernmental institutions can increase the number of productive interactions among their member states that can in turn help build confidence and bridges for other relations. Once created, because they promise benefits in one arena of technical cooperation, organizations formed by states can sow the seeds for additional cooperation—in short, they can take on a personality and life of their own.

The less formal relationships are called "regimes" in political science. As John Ruggie has explained, "international regimes have been defined as social institutions around which actor expectations converge in a given area of international relations," which create "an intersubjective framework of meaning."[19] Regimes are important because power alone cannot predict the type of order created. Change can come from power or from social purpose (or sense of legitimacy). Just as with more formal institutions, "international regimes alter the relative costs of transactions."[20]

Compliance gaps

The "compliance gap" may usefully be divided into implementation (including monitoring) and enforcement gaps. Recalcitrant or fragile actors may be unwilling or unable to implement agreed elements of international policy, for example a ban on commercial whaling, the acquisition of proliferation-sensitive nuclear technology and material, or the cross-border movement of terrorist material and personnel. Even if an institution exists, or a treaty is in effect, or many elements of a working regime are in place, there is often a lack of political will to rely upon or even provide resources for the previously established institutions or processes. Second, confronted with clear evidence of noncompliance by one or more members amidst them, the collective grouping may lack the strength of conviction or commonality of interests to enforce the norm. How do we monitor the implementation records of states who have signed on to Kyoto and the NPT? How do we enforce treaty obligations on signatory states (e.g., the NPT and Iran and North Korea, on the one hand, with respect to nonproliferation, and all five legally recognized nuclear powers with respect to disarmament on the other)? And on non-signatory states (e.g., nonproliferation and India, Israel, and Pakistan)—not to mention non-state actors who lie outside the jurisdiction of any formal normative architecture?

Enforcement is a subset of compliance, especially difficult at the international level in an anarchic society of sovereign states. The past six-and-a-half decades have been the story of the never-ending search for better compliance mechanisms. While looking for better institutions, the trick has been to develop governance for the world, but not world government, for powers that rival those of domestic governments in the areas of security, justice, and general welfare—the analogues of peace and security, human rights, international trade and development, and environment and sustainability.

The cumulative challenge of filling the gaps in global governance is demonstrated by the extreme difficulty in ensuring compliance—indeed, this last gap often appears as a complete void as there is actually no way to enforce decisions, certainly not to compel them. For example, in the area of international peace and security, even though the UN Charter calls for them, there are no standing UN military forces and never have been. The UN has to beg and borrow troops, which are always on loan, and there is no functioning Military Staff Committee (called for in Charter Article 47) and never has been. Perhaps even more tellingly in terms of crisis response, the UN has no rapid reaction capability, which is not because of a lack of ideas or policy proposals—Trygve Lie's proposal was first made in 1947, and the latest proposal comes from the Brahimi report in 2000.[21] As for the crucial issue of nuclear proliferation, the compliance gap has been more than evident with Iran thumbing its nose at the International Atomic Energy Agency and the Security Council.

In the area of international trade and finance, the WTO is considered a relatively effective enforcement mechanism although it is among the youngest intergovernmental organizations. In the area of human rights, whether it is hard or soft law, there is often no enforcement capability. Although the use of ad hoc tribunals and the creation of the International Criminal Court were important institutional steps that led to some indictments and convictions, there is precious little enforcement capacity in this arena.[22] For example, there has been universally accepted knowledge about, as well as norms and institutions regarding, genocide since 1948. There is credible evidence that the general prohibition of genocide is a universally accepted norm: there is substantial agreement that it is wrong, there is even a treaty/institution prohibiting it: the Genocide Convention of 1948 (hard law), which came into effect in 1951.

In the area of environment and sustainability, the 1997 Kyoto Protocol created binding emission targets for developed countries, a system whereby they could obtain credit toward their emission targets by financing energy-efficient projects in less-developed countries (known as "joint implementation"), clean-development mechanisms, and emissions trading (trading the "right to pollute"). Backtracking began almost before the ink was dry on the signatures. As the world's climate changes at breakneck speed, there is no way to ensure that even the largely inadequate agreements on the books are respected.

A policy still needs to be implemented, and shortcomings might show up in implementation. The zero-tolerance policy toward sexual exploitation by UN soldiers has been in existence for some time, yet the problem continues.[23] Inevitably, even with full knowledge, adequate norms, and policy and operations to back them up, there will always be the problem of some individuals or groups who cheat, challenge, and defy the norms and laws of the broader society and community. This is why all societies have mechanisms in place to detect violators and outlaws, subject them to trial, and punish convicted offenders. The goal is both punishment of outlaws so justice is seen to be done, and deterrence of future violations. For these goals to be achieved the modalities and procedures for enforcing compliance with community norms and laws must be efficient, effective, and credible.

An event: the 2004 tsunami and gaps in global governance

The worldwide response to the 2004 Indonesian earthquake and the resulting Indian Ocean tsunami, whose death toll climbed to 280,000, provides us with global governance in microcosm—how an enormous trans-border problem can be addressed in a decentralized world. On 26 December 2004, an earthquake that registered magnitude 9.0 on the Richter scale occurred off the west coast of the Indonesian island of Sumatra. The earthquake and the resulting tsunami spread mind-boggling devastation across the Indian Ocean, affecting 12 countries, some as far away as the Horn of Africa. Public attention was transfixed by the images: waves swallowing islands and cities whole, creating scenes of apocalyptic destruction. The most frequently used adjectives to describe the tragedy were "biblical" and "nuclear."

The globalizing effect of innovations in transportation and communications were obvious. Thousands of tourists from Western developed nations and from around the region were vacationing in the area with video cameras in tow. Their homemade footage began to appear on international television news and the Internet making the scope of the disaster clear. In addition, technology also made it possible to mobilize humanitarian assistance for rescue, relief, assistance, and reconstruction almost in real time. The United Nations can deploy physically to humanitarian emergencies anywhere in the world within 24 hours, barring any political or bureaucratic hurdles—or so at least it claims.

The tsunami was an illustration, first, of the thesis that many problems are truly transnational and multinational, and that solutions to them are global in scope and require substantial resource mobilization. The location of the initial earthquake was in Indonesia, but the resulting tsunami affected the entire perimeter of the Indian Ocean. Moreover, because of the time of the year, it caught thousands of holidaying Westerners in its deathly grip as well. And emergency humanitarian aid and disaster relief assistance, medium-term reconstruction and rebuilding, as well as longer-term preventive and ameliorative measures, required a coordinated effort on a global scale by a multitude of actors across all levels of analysis, from the local to the global, governmental, intergovernmental, and nongovernmental.

The effort generated by the tsunami also illustrates the remaining gaps that we have briefly sketched: knowledge, normative, policy, institutional, and compliance. Previously, for example, there was local knowledge about tsunamis in East Asia, but there was no system to dispense it: what causes them, what the warning signs are, and what the damage could be. We still lack the capacity to predict earthquakes and so prevent the death and destruction caused by tremors directly. But predictive knowledge about tsunamis generated by earthquakes is common and reliable. One of the authors, based in Japan for nine years, is only too familiar with routine statements following any significant earthquake about whether or not to expect a tsunami and, if so, where, when, and how powerful. This knowledge has been integrated into an early warning system around the Pacific which is integrated into the UN system.

Yet the Indian Ocean had no such system in place. Public authorities were no more knowledgeable than ordinary people about the potent symptoms of tsunamis, with the result that many people rushed to see and photograph the strange sight of water being sucked out to sea by powerful currents: a telltale symptom of a tsunami made famous in Japanese paintings and prints. Nor had knowledge about natural barriers to absorb and blunt the power of tsunamis, such as mangroves which were being systematically destroyed, been integrated into disaster prevention planning schemes.

After the tsunami occurred, normatively, no one questioned that there was a responsibility to protect individuals, and that if governments could not manage the disaster and its consequences, outsiders should exert pressure and come to the rescue. The United Nations has been preaching the culture of prevention with regard to disasters, natural as well as those caused by ecologically damaging patterns of human and social activity, as much as conflicts. In his millennium report, the Secretary-General noted that the cost of natural disasters in 1998 alone had exceeded the cost of all such disasters in the 1980s.[24] But the norm of disaster prevention had not been internalized by the governments around the Indian Ocean rim.

In consequence, there was a critical policy gap. Of course, policymakers faced competing priorities: should they divert resources to coping with a once-in-a-century tsunami, or invest in preparations for dealing with more regular floods and earthquakes? Should there be a tsunami warning system in the Indian Ocean (which rarely experienced tsunamis), or would the money be better spent elsewhere? The point is not that the lower policy priority given to tsunami warning and response systems is not understandable. Rather, the point is that given the existing state of knowledge in other countries and within the UN, not to invest in adequate systems to provide early warning and response mechanisms was a conscious policy choice.

How else can we explain the deaths caused by the tsunami on the African continent hours after the earthquake?

That such a warning system is in place for the Pacific points also to the critical institutional gap for the Indian Ocean. Institutionally, the UN is not the main avenue for implementation, which is still seen as the primary responsibility of states and civil society. However, the tsunami highlighted that the UN was the institution of choice when it came to coordinating the response to a disaster of such enormity. Finally, with regard to compliance gaps, both dimensions of compliance may be highlighted. The political will to provide immediate assistance and help for the longer term was instantly mobilized, especially as in some cases citizens dipped into their pocket books more generously than their governments which were then shamed into increasing their pledges. But there were operational failures, or implementation gaps, with aid agencies often competing with one another, and some also proving inadequate to the challenges. The disaster also highlighted another major and recurring gap, namely between pledges and delivery of the promised funds and resources. There simply is no enforcement mechanism for holding governments or other donors to their word. One of the strongest methods of enforcing compliance seems to be the UN's moral authority to call down shame on niggardly or non-cooperative actors, which was used to nudge Western donors to substantially increase their initial contributions.

In short, and in spite of the absence of any overarching authority or established pool of financial and relief resources, ideas and experiments that had circulated for years resulted in a "crazy quilt" of responses that impressed even the UN's harshest critics. The UN, through its Office for the Coordination of Humanitarian Affairs (OCHA), orchestrated the relief effort across the 12 affected countries. OCHA's Situation Reports, posted on a daily basis, represented the information-gathering activity of the UN on a country-by-country basis, and had such useful information as a situation summary, requirements including a breakdown of provision by sector, agency, and dollar amount, the UN's response, and the national response. Through the ReliefWeb Internet site, OCHA was able to inform the world both what survivors' immediate needs were, what was being done to meet those needs, and the help aid workers required, such as transportation and communications equipment. The relief effort showed the UN's centrality and ability to convene and foster multi-constituency processes, and its ability to provide global leadership, as well as earlier discussions and actual experiences in human-made as well as natural disasters. The UN-coordinated response to the 2004 tsunami thus was far better than one might assume without any overarching global authority.

An issue area: climate change and gaps in global governance

Almost uniquely among the major current, life-threatening, global challenges, the United Nations has made a singular contribution to global governance through the work of the Intergovernmental Panel on Climate Change (IPCC). The UN has been the single most authoritative actor in assembling and advancing the state of knowledge with respect to the reality, gravity, and urgency of climate change, both causes and consequences. It has been the most authoritative agent in articulating and globalizing the norm of environmental protection, in particular through the innovative global governance modality of world conferences that incorporated civil society actors and the scientific community, and the principal site for converting the norm into a legislative agenda by negotiating a series of treaties and conventions in which NGOs also have had a voice not easily silenced or unheard.

But, as with many other areas of its work, the organization has not been vigorous or effective in ensuring compliance with the global norms and regimes, with weak surveillance and enforcement mechanisms and still weaker collective will to do so. In a clash between national and international interests with respect to the environment, no less than in other areas, the logic of collective inaction has usually triumphed over that of collective action.

By the end of 2007 with respect to climate change at least, the award of the Nobel Peace Prize jointly to the IPCC and former US vice president Al Gore for his tireless advocacy for tackling climate change, including his documentary film *An Inconvenient Truth*, reflected that the political equation seemed to be shifting toward effective action through the UN framework to forestall one of the gravest threats to the Earth and all its life forms, including human beings. Whether this will prove to be too little and too late, only time will tell.

The UNDP's *Human Development Report 2007/2008* focused on climate change as its special theme.[25] With respect to knowledge gaps, it warned that the world was approaching a tipping point on climate change that could lock millions of the poorest people in the world's poorest countries in a downward spiral facing malnutrition, water scarcity, and loss of livelihoods. The responsibility for having created the problem through carbon-intensive growth and profligate consumption patterns, and therefore for the solutions, rests largely with the rich countries who have far deeper carbon footprints and also the financial and technological capabilities to undertake the necessary action. The three worst greenhouse gas (GHG) emitters per capita are the United States, Canada, and Australia. If the whole world adopted US and Canadian levels of production, consumption, and waste generation per person, we would need nine planets Earth to sustain them; with Australian levels, seven would do. Yet while the responsibility for causing climate change rests largely with the rich countries, it is the poor people who will be the hardest hit by worsening drought, weather volatility, and extremes, and a rising sea level. The cost of stabilizing GHG at 450 particles per million could be limited to an average of 1.6 percent of world GDP to 2030. It repeats the Stern report warning that even the economic costs of inaction, let alone the social and human costs, will be much more.[26]

Climate change could lead to a breakdown in many parts of the world with increased drought exposure, rising temperatures, and erratic rainfall. An estimated additional 600 million could face malnutrition. By 2060, the semi-arid regions of sub-Saharan Africa could face productivity losses of more than one-quarter. By 2080, almost two billion people more could have to face water scarcity. Glacial retreat and changed rainfall could produce an ecological crisis in large swathes of northern China and southern Asia. Intensified flooding and storms could displace an additional 330 million people in coastal and low-lying areas (including 70 million in Bangladesh, 22 million in Vietnam, 6 million in Egypt). Droughts, floods, and storms are already among the most powerful drivers of poverty and inequality as they wipe out assets, lead to malnutrition, and impede literacy as children are withdrawn from school. Moreover, existing studies show that those exposed to drought in early childhood are one-third more likely to be malnourished.

The publication of its *Fourth Assessment Report* showed that the IPCC with its worldwide network of 3,000 leading scientists is the most authoritative and influential body for collecting, collating, synthesizing, and pronouncing on the current scientific consensus in filling the knowledge gaps. Moreover, during its short lifetime the panel has become increasingly more confident that global warming is occurring, climate change is real and substantial, and human activity is the principal cause. The norms of emissions reductions, adaptation, mitigation, and developed/developing country equity ("common but differentiated responsibility") have also been promoted most aggressively by the UN system. The policy gaps were addressed at the Kyoto (1997) and Bali (2007) conferences.

Gaps remain in the state of our knowledge with respect to climate change. In part this is due to different assumptions regarding fossil fuel use and GHG emissions; and in part due to the existing limits to understanding of how clouds, oceans, and aerosols mix and interact. Within this margin of uncertainty, the twin scientific conclusion that climate change is occurring, and that human activity has caused and continues to contribute to it, has been provided authoritatively by the United Nations through the work and voice of the IPCC. Simply put, weather patterns will continue to fluctuate across regions from day to day and season to season. But the statistical distribution—means, ranges, and extremes—will shift with dramatic acceleration. The panel has also provided assessments of the impacts of climate change, the options to policymakers, and the costs of the different options. While the Earth's warming is a global phenomenon, its impact will be neither uniform nor equal between countries and socioeconomic groups. The main forum for conducting negotiations and reaching agreements about policies to address climate change is the UN Framework Convention on Climate Change. According to Han Seung-soo, one of the special envoys of the UN Secretary-General on climate change, "The Convention . . . and the Kyoto Protocol are the pillars of the international climate change regime that is currently in effect."[27]

Building on the norm of protecting the human environment, the 2007/2008 HDR addressed fundamental policy gaps. It called for global warming in the twenty-first century to be limited to less than 2°C above the pre-industrial levels. The present global level is 0.7°C above the pre-industrial level and on current trends the world is set to breach 4°C.

Other policy gaps can be filled through the twin-track approach of stringent mitigation and strengthened international cooperation on adaptation. The forthcoming UN negotiations to continue the tough bargaining that was suspended in December 2007 in Bali provide the opportunity to convert the norm into an international convention or treaty. To that extent the report was more a call for international action than a counsel of global despair.

On policy, the four parameters are adaptation, mitigation, technology transfers, and financial transfers. Only the United Nations has the authority to convene and the capacity to mobilize the necessary resources for the enhanced global response that is required, and required with urgency. But actual implementation will require tough decisions by sovereign states and collaborative partnerships between them, international organizations, civil society, business, and even individual citizens with respect to changed behavior and lifestyle patterns.

On mitigation, the industrial countries have to own up to their historical responsibility and take the lead in cutting their 1990 GHG levels by 30 percent by 2020 and 80 percent by 2050. This can be done through a mix of carbon taxation; more stringent cap-and-trade programs; energy regulatory standards on vehicle emissions, buildings, electrical appliances, etc; and greater recourse to renewable energies and carbon capture and storage.

Developing countries have lesser responsibility for having created the climate change problem and a lesser capacity for both mitigation and adaptation. They therefore need more transition time, financing for low-carbon technology transfer and assistance with adaptation. Their target should be set at cutting emissions by 20 percent of 1990 levels by 2050, starting from 2020 and supported by international transfers of finance and low-carbon technology. The HDR recommends the creation of a climate change mitigation facility to provide $25–50 billion annually toward incremental low-carbon energy investments in developing countries. China—which in 2007 probably surpassed the United States in the dubious race to be the world's largest producer of greenhouse gases—and India because of their size and recent growth rates, are in a different category.

Even with stringent mitigation, warming will continue at least until 2050. Adaptation is necessary to cope with the implications and as insurance against the threat of insufficiently stringent mitigation. Here again, differential capacity between the rich and poor countries carries the risk of a developing "adaptation apartheid."[28] The spending to date on multilateral mechanisms on adaptation total a mere $26 million, with high transaction costs associated with such low levels of financing. Additional annual financing for adaptation, for example for climate proofing infrastructure and building resilience, will require $86 billion by 2015.

With respect to institutional gaps, the IPCC has helped to collate and disseminate to the public as well as policy elite the scientific consensus on the state of existing knowledge, to transform our conceptions of the timescale within which the norm of halting and then reversing global warming has to move to policy and action, and to alter our conception of the use of science as an aid to policy.[29]

With respect to compliance gaps, the report points out that the developed countries have failed to align stated climate security goals with concrete energy policies and thus far have fallen well short of achieving even the modest Kyoto Protocol goals of around 5 percent reductions from 1990 levels. On current trends, CO_2 emissions are calculated to increase by 50 percent by 2030. Sustainability requires an urgent realignment of the global energy system with the Earth's ecological system.

The defining feature of global environmental governance—the strengths and achievements as well as the frailties and shortfalls—has been the development of multilateral environmental agreements at UN initiative or under UN auspices.[30] The largely UN-centered system of international environmental governance has generated and disseminated increasing volumes of data and information on environmental trends; improved the systematic monitoring and assessment of the state of the global environment; and resulted in numerous legally binding and voluntary instruments that provide norms, principles, procedures, guidelines, and codes of conduct on environmental issues. At the same time, serious gaps and problems persist regarding the continuing deterioration of the environment, "an alarming discrepancy between commitments and action and an inadequate level of integration of environmental considerations into mainstream decision making for economic and social development."[31] To put it bluntly, international commitments have failed to shape national environment policies to the same decisive extent as other policy areas like trade.

Global governance is both multi-actor and multi-level. The United Nations has acted as the node of interacting clusters of the different drivers of global environmental governance, including states, international organizations, regional organizations, NGOs, and epistemic communities of scientists.[32] An increasingly important actor will have to be the business community. Industry accounts for about 40 percent of the world's GHG emissions.[33] Business engagement with the international environmental governance is therefore crucial. And many businesses are vigorously engaged in the debate on "greening" their industry, reducing environmental footprints and embracing corporate social responsibility. This is why on 11 January 2007, the International Chamber of Commerce issued a statement that "a strong, efficient and effective" United Nations in "environmental management is central to the interests of business."[34]

Conclusion

With respect to multi-level governance, a recurring refrain in our story is how, even if the most pressing problems are global in scope and require global solutions, the policy authority for addressing them remains vested in states. One can go further and argue that formal engagement with the forums of international policy making is not a good indicator of domestic policy development or emissions reductions, even for a good international citizen like Canada, let alone for the United States.[35]

For most countries, the different contexts of intergovernmental relations within national jurisdictions and the varying resources available to sub-state levels of governments for policy development and implementation are at least as important, if not more so, than international commitments. This is especially the case because an issue like climate change cuts across so many conventional policy and agency lines. In addition, there is a need to examine both the domestic "push" factors alongside the international "pull" factors in any explanation of states' engagement with global commitments and norms.[36]

As mentioned at the outset, "governance" refers to purposeful systems of rules or norms that ensure order beyond what occurs "naturally." In the domestic context, governance is usually more than government, implying shared purpose and goal orientation as well as formal authority or police powers. For the planet, however, governance is the whole story because there is no world government, hence the additional mechanisms absent government.

Understanding the mechanics of global governance is crucial because it attempts to channel behavior by all relevant actors through the creation of knowledge, norms, policies, and institutions that can together create sufficient pressure to secure greater compliance from states parties to abide by concrete measures to address problems that Kofi Annan described as "problems without passports."[37] A growing number of problems are clearly without passports and are recognized as such. Policy authority and the requisite resources for tackling problems remain vested in states, while the source and scope of the problems are increasingly global and require the globalization of the process of policymaking solutions without passports.

Progression toward better global governance is rarely linear. It moves in fits and starts, is messy, and rarely happens on a first attempt. Politics, context, and unanticipated consequences all play a role in a trial-and-error process that leads to an always imperfect but hopefully ever-improving system of governance for the planet. The world is interdependent in areas as diverse as financial markets, infectious diseases, climate change, terrorism, product safety, food supply, and water tables. Our collective capacity to manage these interdependencies throughout pooled or coordinated policy responses has fallen farther and farther behind the rise in the numbers and intensity of interdependent sectors.

To borrow language from the climate change context, all countries have a common but differentiated responsibility for the stability of the global economic and financial systems. Countries like China and India have limited access to current global decision-making channels and sharing the responsibility for managing the global order. The idea that they will continue to integrate with the world order on terms and following norms set by the West is quaint and archaic. In order to be made responsible stakeholders in the management of the regime and the outcomes that come from it, they need ownership of the process.

As stated by US treasury secretary Henry Paulson, "If you look at the global financial architecture, I don't think it reflects the global economy today."[38] He was responding to a question whether the Group of 7 (G-7)—the United States, Britain, Canada, France, Germany, Italy, and Japan—should be expanded to include developing powers such as China, India, Russia, Brazil, and Mexico. "It's a big world, and it's a lot bigger than the G-7," he added.

The idea was quickly taken up by Prime Minister Gordon Brown of the UK and supported by several other G-7 leaders. They called for a major global meeting to redesign the world's finance system and rewrite the rulebook of global capitalism. Writing in the *Washington Post*, Brown argued that while the "old post-war international financial institutions are out of date," "the same sort of visionary internationalism is needed to resolve the crises and challenges of a different age" as had been demonstrated at Bretton Woods back in 1944. He proposed

> cross-border supervision of financial institutions; shared global standards for accounting and regulation; a more responsible approach to executive remuneration that rewards hard work, effort and enterprise but not irresponsible risk-taking; . . . the renewal of our international institutions to make them effective early-warning systems for the world economy

and a rejection of "the beggar-thy-neighbor protectionism that has been a feature of past crises."[39] Earlier, at a briefing on 14 October, he had warned that "We are in the first financial crisis of the new global age . . . . We need to recognize that if risks are globalized, then responsibilities have to be globalized as well."[40]

In other words, under the present, deficient system of global governance, "We get the global perils without global benefits."[41] Only a new global regulatory regime will reassure many countries that the balance has been restored between the risks and benefits of integrating with an open world economy. None of the existing political or economic institutions—the IMF, the G-7 industrialized countries, or the G-20 finance ministers—proved adequate to the task of coordinating a response to a global crisis. It is hard to imagine any major global challenge that can be effectively addressed without involving, for example, all three Asian giants: China, India, and Japan. Yet two of the three (India and Japan) are not permanent members of the UN Security Council, and two of the three (China and India) are not part of the G-7 club. The IMF has shown more skill and determination at preaching to the developing countries what they should do than at persuading industrial countries to act together, while the G-20 is more prone to blame the developed countries for its ills and ask them for handouts than to tackle the domestic governance gaps of its own membership.

A new architecture of global governance would bring together the existing G-8 (G-7 plus Russia) and the major emerging markets of Brazil, China, India, Mexico, and South Africa, as well as Saudi Arabia and/or Indonesia.[42] It is time to think about a new Bretton Woods system for the twenty-first century.

Notes

1 Robert Gilpin, *Global Political Economy* (Princeton, NJ: Princeton University Press, 2001), 388–9.
2 Randall D. Germain, "Global financial governance and the problem of inclusion," *Global Governance* 7, no. 4 (2001): 421.

3 "Collective" is an adjective that means "group-based." This modifier may imply universal or global participation (for example, the UN as a collective security organization), but it may imply much less participation (for example, NATO is a collective defense organization for 16 member states). See Arnold Wolfers, *Discord and Collaboration in a New Europe* (Lanham, Md.: University Press of America, 1994).

4 See James N. Rosenau and Ernst-Otto Czempiel, eds., *Governance without Government: Order and Change in World Politics* (Cambridge: Cambridge University Press, 1992). Also see Leon Gordenker and Thomas G. Weiss, "Pluralizing Global Governance: Analytical Approaches and Dimensions," in *NGOs, the UN, and Global Governance*, ed. Leon Gordenker and Thomas G. Weiss (London: Lynne Rienner, 1996), 17–47.

5 See Anne-Marie Slaughter, *A New World Order* (Princeton, NJ: Princeton University Press, 2004).

6 Amit Bhaduri and Deepak Nayyar, *The Intelligent Person's Guide to Liberalization* (New Delhi: Penguin, 1996), 67.

7 See, for example, Paul Hirst and Grahame Thompson, *Globalization in Question: The International Economy and the Possibilities of Governance* (Cambridge: Polity Press, 1996).

8 World Commission on the Social Dimension of Globalization, *A Fair Globalization: Creating Opportunities for All* (Geneva: International Labour Organization, 2004), xi.

9 See Deepak Nayyar, ed., *Governing Globalization: Issues and Orientations* (Oxford: Oxford University Press, 2002).

10 See Jane Boulden, Ramesh Thakur, and Thomas G. Weiss, eds., *The United Nations and Nuclear Orders* (Tokyo: UN University Press, 2009).

11 See Michael G. Schechter, *United Nations Global Conferences* (London: Routledge, 2005); and Ramesh Thakur, Andrew Cooper, and John English, eds., *International Commissions and the Power of Ideas* (Tokyo: UN University Press, 2005).

12 Hedley Bull, *The Anarchical Society: A Study* (New York: Columbia University Press, 1977). A more recent treatment is Robert H. Jackson, *The Global Covenant: Human Conduct in a World of States* (Oxford: Oxford University Press, 2000).

13 For an argument on how shaming is an effective instrument in underpinning the efficacy of the European human rights regime, see Andrew Moravcsik, "Explaining International Human Rights Regimes: Liberal Theory and Western Europe," *European Journal of International Relations* 1, no. 2 (1995): 157–89. For a slightly different interpretation of the domestic impact of norms embedded in the European human rights regime, see Jeffrey T. Checkel, "International Norms and Domestic Politics: Bridging the Rationalist-Constructivist Divide," *European Journal of International Relations* 3, no. 4 (1997): 473–95. See also his "Norms, Institutions, and National Identity in Contemporary Europe," *International Studies Quarterly* 43, no.1 (1999): 83–114.

14 See Simon Chesterman, ed., *Secretary or General? The UN Secretary-General in World Politics* (Cambridge: Cambridge University Press, 2007).

15 See Ramesh Thakur and William Maley, "The Ottawa Convention on Landmines: A Landmark Humanitarian Treaty in Arms Control?" *Global Governance* 5, no. 3 (1999): 273–302. See also Don Hubert, *The Landmine Ban: A Case Study in Humanitarian Advocacy* (Providence, RI: Watson Institute, 2000), occasional paper no. 42; and Richard Price "Reversing the Gun Sights: Transnational Civil Society Targets Land Mines," *International Organization* 52, no. 3 (1998): 613–44.

16 This is addressed in greater detail in Ramesh Thakur and Thomas G. Weiss, "United Nations 'Policy': An Argument with Three Illustrations," *International Studies Perspectives* 10, no. 2 (2009): 18–35.

17 Paul Cammack, "The Mother of all Governments: The World Bank's Matrix for Global Governance," in *Global Governance: Critical Perspectives*, ed. Rorden Wilkinson and Steve Hughes (London: Routledge, 2002), 36–54.

18 James E. Dougherty and Robert L. Pfaltzgraff, Jr., *Contending Theories of International Relations: A Comprehensive Survey*, 4th ed. (New York: Longman, 1997), 422.

19 John Gerard Ruggie, "International Regimes, Transactions, and Change: Embedded Liberalism in the Postwar Economic Order," *International Organization* 36, no. 2 (1982): 196.

20 Robert O. Keohane, "A Functional Theory of Regimes," in *International Politics: Enduring Concepts and Contemporary Issues*, 5th ed., ed. Robert J. Art and Robert Jervis (New York: Longman, 2000), 135.

21 *Report of the Panel on United Nations Peace Operations* (UN document A/55/305-S/2000/809), 21 August 2000. For an early assessment, see David M. Malone and Ramesh Thakur, "UN Peacekeeping: Lessons Learned?" *Global Governance* 7, no. 1 (2001): 11–17.

22 See Edel Hughes, William A. Schabas and Ramesh Thakur, eds., *Atrocities and International Accountability: Beyond Transitional Justice* (Tokyo: UN University Press, 2007).

23 See Chiyuki Aoi, Cedric de Coning, and Ramesh Thakur, eds., *Unintended Consequences of Peacekeeping Operations* (Tokyo: UN University Press, 2007).

24 Kofi A. Annan, *"We the Peoples": The Role of the United Nations in the 21st Century* (New York: UN, 2000), 57–8.

25 UNDP, *Human Development Report 2007/2008. Fighting Climate Change: Human Solidarity in a Divided World* (New York: Palgrave Macmillan, 2007). Available at http://hdr.undp.org/en/reports/global/hdr2007-8/.

26 Nicholas Stern, *The Economics of Climate Change: The Stern Review* (2006); www.hm-treasury.gov.uk/stern_review_report.htm.

27 Seung-soo Han, "The Global Challenge of Climate Change," *Global Asia* 2, no. 3 (2007): 11.

28 UNDP, *Human Development Report 2007/2008*, 13.

29 Bruce Tonn, "The Intergovernmental Panel on Climate Change: A Global Scale Transformative Initiative," *Futures* 39 (2007): 614–18.

30 Mukul Sanwal, "Evolution of Global Environmental Governance and the United Nations," *Global Environmental Politics* 7, no. 3 (2007): 1–13.

31 Nils Meyer-Ohlendorf, "Would a United Nations Environment Organization Help to Achieve the Millennium Development Goals?" *Review of European Community & International Environmental Law* 15, no. 1 (2006): 26.

32 See David A. Sonnenfeld and Arthur P. J. Mol, "Globalization and the Transformation of Environmental Governance," *American Behavioral Scientist* 45, no. 9 (2002): 1318–39.

33 Vlasis Oikonomou, Martin Patel, and Ernst Worrell, "Climate Policy: Bucket or Drainer?" *Energy Policy* 34 (2006): 3656.

34 Quoted in Maria Ivanova, David Gordon, and Jennifer Roy, "Towards Institutional Symbiosis: Business and the United Nations in Environmental Governance," *Review of European Community & International Environmental Law* 16, no. 2 (2007): 123.

35 See Barry G. Rabe, "Beyond Kyoto: Climate Change Policy in Multilevel Governance Systems," *Governance: An International Journal of Policy, Administration, and Institutions* 20, no. 3 (2007): 423–44; Alter Christer Christiansen, "Convergence or Divergence? Status and Prospects for US Climate Strategy,' *Climate Policy* 3 (2003): 343–58; and Henrik Selin and Stacy D. VanDeveer, "Political Science and Prediction: What's Next for US Climate Change Policy?" *Review of Policy Research* 24, no. 1 (2007): 1–27.

36 See Guri Bang, Camilla Bretteville Froyn, Jon Hovi, and Fredric C. Menz, "The United States and International Climate Cooperation: International 'Pull' versus Domestic 'Push,'" *Energy Policy* 35 (2007): 1282–91.

37 Kofi Annan, "Problems Without Passports," *Foreign Policy* 132 (September-October 2002): 30–1.

38 Emily Kaiser, "World Looks For New Leaders as Crisis Outgrows G7," Reuters, 12 October 2008. Available at: www.reuters.com/article/idUSTRE49B3H220081012.

39 Gordon Brown, "Out of the Ashes," *Washington Post*, 17 October 2008.

40 Doug Saunders, "'The man who saved the world banking system,'" *Globe and Mail* (Toronto), 15 October 2008.

41 Gerald F. Seib, "We get the global perils without global benefits," *Wall Street Journal*, 13 October 2008.

42 See Andrew F. Cooper, John English, and Ramesh Thakur, eds., *Reforming from the Top: A Leaders' 20 Summit* (Tokyo: UN University Press, 2005); and Peter C. Heap, *Globalization and Summit Reform: An Experiment in International Governance* (Heidelberg: Springer, 2008).

9

GOVERNANCE, GOOD GOVERNANCE, AND GLOBAL GOVERNANCE

Conceptual and actual challenges

"Governance" is now fashionable, but the concept is as old as human history.[1] This essay concentrates on the intellectual debates of the 1980s and 1990s, essentially since the term became widespread in development circles and prominent in the international public policy lexicon. Many academics and international practitioners employ "governance" to connote a complex set of structures and processes, both public and private, while more popular writers tend to use it synonymously with "government."

Governance for the latter refers to characteristics that generally are associated with a system of national administration. *The New Webster's International Dictionary* defines the term in much the same way as journalists from the *New York Times* or *The Economist*: "act, manner, office, or power of governing; government," "state of being governed," or "method of government or regulation." As Morten Bøås has shown, before being studied at the global level, governance was employed generically in academic discourse.[2] It was, for instance, widely used in relationship to business literature about the micro-behavior of firms.[3] Goran Hyden has argued that it refers mainly to running governments and other public agencies or private ones with social purposes.[4]

Analysts of international relations and international civil servants, in contrast, now use the term almost exclusively to describe phenomena that go beyond a synonym for "government" and the legal authority with which such polities are vested. For instance, the Commission on Global Governance defines "governance" as "the sum of the many ways individuals and institutions, public and private, manage their common affairs. It is the continuing process through which conflicting or diverse interests may be accommodated and co-operative action may be taken."[5] James Rosenau is the American academic most closely associated with the term. And for him, whether at the grassroots or global levels, it "encompasses the activities of governments, but it also includes the many other channels through which 'commands' flow in the form of goals framed, directives issued, and policies pursued."[6]

Something of an intellectual cottage industry has arisen around the term over the last two decades. Since the early 1980s, "governance" and increasingly "good governance" have permeated development discourse and especially research agendas and other activities funded by public and private banks and bilateral donors. Moreover, publications by scholars and eminent commissions have extensively used the term for contemporary global problem-solving.[7]

The emergence of governance can be traced at the country level to a disgruntlement with the state-dominated models of economic and social development so prevalent throughout the socialist bloc and much of the Third World in the 1950s, 1960s, and 1970s. At the international level, "global governance" can be traced to a growing dissatisfaction among students of international relations with the realist and liberal-institutionalist theories that had dominated the study of international organization in the 1970s and 1980s. In particular, they failed to capture adequately the vast increase, in both numbers and influence, of non-state actors and the implications of technology in an age of globalization.

This article takes seriously the proposition that ideas and concepts, both good and bad, have an impact. In pointing to the role of policy and academic "scribblers," John Maynard Keynes wrote in 1936 that "the ideas of economists and political philosophers, both when they are right and when they are wrong, are more powerful than is commonly understood."[8] This essay thus seeks to correct the fact that ideas, whether economic or otherwise, have until recently been ignored by students of international relations.[9] It situates the emergence of governance, good governance, and global governance as well as the role of the United Nations in the conceptual process.

Governance and good governance

The world organization was built on the basis of unquestioned national sovereignty. In spite of Article 2(7) of the UN Charter, sovereignty and noninterference in the internal affairs of states have come under fire. As former secretary-general Boutros-Ghali wrote, "The time of absolute and exclusive sovereignty, however, has passed."[10] Sovereignty's status and relevance are contested increasingly within international organizations and forums. Moreover, the climate for governance has changed immensely since the UN's founding. Indeed, definitions of governance vary substantially as is evident from the attached box.

The emphasis is on the last two decades even though there is a rich history of such earlier UN-related ideas as decolonization, localization, and human rights against which more recent thinking has been played out. What is important to note here is the dramatic quantitative and qualitative shift in the political ambience at the United Nations since the late 1950s and early 1960s. During the Cold War, governmental representatives of newly independent countries were successfully on the defensive within UN and related international forums; they remained

VIEWS ON GOVERNANCE

World Bank: Governance is defined as the manner in which power is exercised in the management of a country's economic and social resources. The World Bank has identified three distinct aspects of governance: (i) the form of political regime; (ii) the process by which authority is exercised in the management of a country's economic and social resources for development; and (iii) the capacity of governments to design, formulate, and implement policies and discharge functions.[11]

UNDP: Governance is viewed as the exercise of economic, political, and administrative authority to manage a country's affairs at all levels. It comprises mechanisms, processes, and institutions through which citizens and groups articulate their interests, exercise their legal rights, meet their obligations, and mediate their differences.[12]

OECD: The concept of governance denotes the use of political authority and exercise of control in a society in relation to the management of its resources for social and economic development. This broad definition encompasses the role of public authorities in establishing the environment in which economic operators function and in determining the distribution of benefits as well as the nature of the relationship between the ruler and the ruled.[13]

Institute of Governance, Ottawa: Governance comprises the institutions, processes, and conventions in a society which determine how power is exercised, how important decisions affecting society are made, and how various interests are accorded a place in such decisions.[14]

Commission on Global Governance: Governance is the sum of the many ways individuals and institutions, public and private, manage their common affairs. It is a continuing process through which conflicting or diverse interests may be accommodated and cooperative action may be taken. It includes formal institutions and regimes empowered to enforce compliance, as well as informal arrangements that people and institutions either have agreed to or perceive to be in their interest.[15]

UN Secretary-General Kofi Annan: Good governance is ensuring respect for human rights and the rule of law; strengthening democracy; promoting transparency and capacity in public administration.[16]

International Institute of Administrative Sciences: Governance refers to the process whereby elements in society wield power and authority, and influence and enact policies and decisions concerning public life, and economic and social development. Governance is a broader notion than government. Governance involves interaction between these formal institutions and those of civil society.[17]

Tokyo Institute of Technology: The concept of governance refers to the complex set of values, norms, processes, and institutions by which society manages its development and resolves conflict, formally and informally. It involves the state, but also the civil society (economic and social actors, community-based institutions and unstructured groups, the media, etc.) at the local, national, regional, and global levels.[18]

largely untouched by the rich scholarly debate about the "new political economy,"[19] "social capital,"[20] and "public goods."[21] They interpreted virtually any serious scrutiny of their economic and social choices as a threat to their newborn and weak states. And they remained impervious to the international political economy literature of the 1970s and 1980s that emphasized public choice theory, rent-seeking behavior, directly unproductive profit-seeking activities, and the new institutional economics.[22]

By playing off East versus West, moreover, developing countries deflected many criticisms by donors and investors if they hinted at shortcomings in economic and political management. Suggestions about what was wrong with economic and social policies in developing and socialist bloc countries were viewed as siding with the "enemy" in the East-West struggle. And the "other" side could be persuaded to be less critical, and even financially supportive, as part of worldwide competition.

The result was an unquestioning, and at times almost obsequious, acceptance of the status quo. Francis M. Deng and Terrence Lyons have summarized the situation in Africa, but their comment has greater resonance:

> Rather than promote good governance by awarding sovereign rights to those regimes that effectively or responsibly administered a given territory, African diplomatic principles, epitomized by the Organization of African Unity (OAU), accepted whatever regime occupied the presidential palace, regardless of who (or even whether) the regime governed.[23]

Ironically, the Organization of the Petroleum Exporting Countries' ability to increase oil prices in 1973–74 and again in 1979 strengthened the collective bargaining strength of the Group of 77 and produced foreign exchange shortages and unsustainable indebtedness that, in turn, forced many non–oil-exporting developing countries to accept intrusive structural adjustment. Outside interference in economic policy was the *quid pro quo* for desperately needed international finance, especially from the International Monetary Fund (IMF) as the lender of last resort or the seal of approval required by other funders.[24]

As the twin pillars of the postwar economic system, the World Bank and the IMF had emphasized domestic policies for sometime.[25] But the UN system had a different orientation and profile. The preponderance of developing countries in the membership made debates distinct from those in Washington where weighted voting privileged the voices of powerful donors. However with the arrival of the Kohl, Thatcher, and Reagan administrations, Western rhetoric had a substantial impact on New York as well as Washington.

The refrain to emphasize domestic priorities assumed more weight and was increasingly pertinent after the September 1981 World Bank report from Elliot Berg.[26] Later in the decade, the Bank issued a more holistic sequel that emphasized political and institutional change as prerequisites for effective economic reform.[27]

Within the UN system too, the new orthodoxy of more aid and investment in exchange for economic liberalization eroded the reluctance to intrude in domestic policies, what two analysts had described as "the global Keynesian social pact suggested by the Brandt Commission."[28]

Such external economic factors as commodity prices and interest rates could not be set aside totally as explanations for poverty and poor economic performance. But it became untenable to attribute all of the woes of developing countries to outside forces beyond their control. This was particularly the case after Mikhail Gorbachev's ascension to power in 1985 and the onset of "new thinking" in Moscow. There was no longer a geopolitical counterweight in the East to Western demands for economic liberalization and political democratization.

Domestic policies and priorities were central to the dire problems faced by both developing countries and members of the socialist bloc. And it became politically more correct in international forums to say so and thereby begin a conversation about how state and society were structured. As Goran Hyden has written: "Getting politics right is different from getting policy right in that it calls for a restructuring of the polity itself. The structural adjustment programs that are associated with getting policy right have been and could be pursued by an autocratic government as well as a democratic one."[29] A discussion about the quality of a country's political and economic governance system became acceptable within international public policy forums for four reasons.

First, there was the glaring illegitimacy of regimes headed by such international pariahs as Uganda's Idi Amin, Kampuchea's Pol Pot, Haiti's Jean-Claude Duvalier, or the Central African Empire's Jean-Bédel Bokassa. After having successfully lobbied the so-called international community to consider as genuinely "international" the domestic policies of white-minority governments in Rhodesia and South Africa, it was illogical for developing countries to maintain that their own domestic behavior was out-of-bounds. Moreover, the end of the Cold War suddenly removed both the willingness to turn a blind-eye toward outlandish regimes as well as incentives for the West to support authoritarian rule.

Second, Samuel Huntington correctly characterized the "third wave"[30] of democratic rule. Both the Third World and the former Soviet bloc were engulfed by a tidal wave of political reforms especially when the collapse of the Berlin Wall was so closely followed by the implosion of Moscow's empire. Widespread democratization, including United Nations monitoring of elections in such former dictatorships as El Salvador and Haiti, brought squarely into focus the character and quality of local governance. Regimes in the Third World and Eastern Europe adopted civilian rule, elections, and multiparty democracy. They understood that the form, if not always the spirit and content, of elections were prerequisites to legitimize their rule and to attract Western financing. Investors and aid agencies insisted, and most potential recipients—with notable exceptions like China, North Korea, Cuba, Libya, and Iraq—accepted this approach.

Third, the proliferation of non-state actors changed the political landscape in most countries. In addition to the organizations of the UN system and the

Washington-based financial institutions, such international nongovernmental organizations (NGOs) as Human Rights Watch and CARE, such transnational corporations as Shell and Citibank, and such global media as BBC and CNN penetrated what had formerly been something of a governmental *chasse guardée*. They exerted a growing influence on what once had been almost exclusively matters of state policy. Within developing and socialist bloc countries, civil society burgeoned after decades of repression. In particular, the growth of NGOs is a striking dimension of contemporary international relations whose implications for global governance and social policy in the UN system are not fully understood or appreciated.[31] In short, economic and social policy is no longer the exclusive preserve of governments. Human rights advocates, gender activists, developmentalists, and groups of indigenous peoples have invaded the territory of states, literally and figuratively.

Fourth, the 1990s witnessed a phenomenal transformation of the widespread view that the "Charter is a Westphalian document *par excellence*."[32] Although the UN's constitution prohibits actions dealing with the domestic policies of member states, nonetheless humanitarian interventions have encouraged the insertion of responsibility as a necessary additional component of national sovereignty, in addition to the three traditional characteristics (territory, people, and authority). Leading the human rights charge were none other than the last two UN secretaries-general, Boutros Boutros-Ghali and Kofi Annan, who painstakingly put forward the contingent character of sovereignty.[33] Francis Deng, their special representative on internally displaced persons, labeled this approach "sovereignty as responsibility."[34] The acute suffering of such failed states as Somalia, the former Yugoslavia, and Rwanda opened the door to scrutinizing domestic policies that had led to mass displacement and even genocide. Given the need for the international system to pick up the costly humanitarian bill for such tragedies, the prevention of future disasters lent additional weight to the argument to examine governance patterns in as-yet un-failed states.[35]

As a result of these four developments, probing domestic policies and priorities became the norm; and efforts to come to grips with the term can be interpreted as part of an intellectual struggle to capture the various units of governance that are not instruments of the state. At the national level, the work of Morten Bøås is particularly instructive because governance is embedded in and interwoven with state–civil society interactions. It is the part of the public realm that encompasses both. Essential to governance is the civic realm, which is maintained by political actors from both the state and society, and in which "access to participation in the public realm is built on respected and legitimate rules." Therefore, "governance is concerned with the regime which constitutes the set of fundamental rules for the organization of the public realm, and not with government. . . . Governance clearly embraces government institutions, but it also subsumes informal, non-governmental institutions operating within the public realm."[36] By conceptualizing governance in terms that transcend traditional notions of domestic politics, Bøås' treatment of the subject clarifies how national governance involves nongovernmental actors exercising authority legitimately in the public realm.

Although Rosenau focuses on the dynamics of the international system, his analytical lenses are helpful in pointing out that all governance "refers to mechanisms for steering social systems toward their goals."[37] As such, agency is important. At the national level then, we need to conceptualize governance in terms that include but also transcend the formal government apparatus. However, and in spite of the explosive growth in profit and not-for-profit groups in civil society, governments remain the primary agents. The provision of public goods as well as incentive structures for corporations' and voluntary agencies' contributing to social problem-solving are largely determined by government policy.

In short, actions to foster *good* governance concentrate on attenuating two undesirable characteristics that had been prevalent earlier, the unrepresentative character of governments and the inefficiency of non-market systems. As governance is the sum of the ways that individuals and institutions, in both public and private spheres, manage their affairs, the systems of governance in much of the Third World and Eastern Europe had to change. As Bøås has written, "the World Bank operationalised 'bad governance' as personalisation of power, lack of human rights, endemic corruption and un-elected and unaccountable governments." And so, "good governance must be the natural opposite."[38] Since good governance has become an important component of the international agenda, discourse about good governance was linked to new policies in those countries receiving development assistance or investments from international lending agencies. Good governance has become a political and economic conditionality that is inseparable from debates about appropriate bilateral and multilateral financing for developing and formerly socialist bloc countries. International efforts, in recent decades, have thus supported political democratization (including elections, accountability, and human rights) and economic liberalization.

Recent experience with good governance has led to criticism from the UN system, which seeks to balance assessments about costs and benefits as well as to confront the political and economic conditionality viewed by many recipient countries as unwelcome intrusions. Good governance definitely is on the international agenda. But three types of substantive UN commentary have applied the brakes and slowed the momentum of the Washington consensus.

The first is the need to capture the complex reality of governance, which encompasses all the structures and processes for determining the use of available resources for the public good within a country. Although debate continues about its precise components, good governance is more than multiparty elections, a judiciary, and a parliament, which have been emphasized as the primary symbols of Western-style democracy. The list of other attributes, with the necessary resources and culture to accompany them, is formidable: universal protection of human rights; nondiscriminatory laws; efficient, impartial, and rapid judicial processes; transparent public agencies; accountability for decisions by public officials;

devolution of resources and decision making to local levels from the capital; and meaningful participation by citizens in debating public policies and choices.

The United Nations Development Programme leads in defining the characteristics of a population that lives within a society in which governance is good. The annual *Human Development Report* provides as close to an authoritative snap-shot as we have. Following ten years of structural adjustment loans, the effort began in 1990 under the leadership of Mahbub ul Haq and continued after 1996 under Richard Jolly. The UNDP has sought to shed light systematically on the actual lives of people, especially those on the bottom of the income scale.[39] In many ways, the decade's collection of the annual *Human Development Report*—which now are available on a single compact disc—was a prelude to and a prolongation of the 1995 Social Summit in Copenhagen. Without denying the benefits of growth, these reports and the Copenhagen conference insist on cataloging: the aggravation of poverty and the growing divides between rich and poor, within societies and well as among them; increasing unemployment; a disintegrating social fabric and exclusion; and environmental damage.

The value of the Human Development Index (HDI) is the modification of what constitutes an acceptable way to measure a society with good governance. Economic well-being and human progress are not synonymous. Countries with the same per capita income can have quite different HDIs, and countries with the same levels of income can also have similar HDIs. The clear message is that the content of domestic policies and priorities is crucial.

The United Nations Children's Fund (UNICEF) has, since 1987, issued annual reports on the lives of vulnerable children and women;[40] this coincided with the pioneering earlier efforts by the organization to put social problems at the center of the debate about the impact of adjustment.[41] The UN High Commissioner for Refugees (UNHCR) has published a bi-annual overview of the beleaguered status of war victims since 1993.[42] One consequence of these analytical efforts is that the World Bank's informationally rich annual *World Development Report* has gradually become more attuned to measuring the "softer" side of living conditions within countries.[43]

The second substantive criticism from the UN system is the need to strike a balance between the public and private sectors. Again, analyses have sought to go beyond democratic symbols and portray the necessary elements of public welfare. The composite view of the UN system amounts to something of a *reprise* of Keynesianism by pointing to the ineluctable importance of state decisions to determine the management of both supply and demand.[44]

In attempting to correct the euphoria that had surrounded the Washington consensus of the early 1990s, arguments have consistently counterbalanced the stereotypical conservative approaches in vogue since the beginning of the Reagan and Thatcher administrations—namely, that anything the government can do, the private sector can do better; and that more open markets, free trade, and capital flows are necessarily beneficial. In many ways, an attentive reader of UN documents of the 1990s would not have been surprised by the disruptions in Seattle of the

World Trade Organization's Third Ministerial Summit in December 1999 or in Washington of the annual sessions of the World Bank and the IMF in April 2000.

An unquestioned faith in the normative principles of neoliberalism had become so widespread among Western and transnational elites that seemingly the only acceptable and common-sensical prescriptions about how to structure political and economic life were those of the Washington consensus. The intellectual climate had changed so much that for a decade between the mid-1980s and mid-1990s, it was almost heretical to argue that an efficient, thriving market economy and civil society require an effective and strong government. Antonio Gramsci would have found an apt illustration of his argument that ideologies can have the "same energy as material force."[45]

But an artificial dichotomy had been created between "state" and "market." The UN's incipient heresy against this conventional wisdom was perhaps best exemplified by analyses of the former Soviet bloc, where "shrinking" but not "rolling back" the state was the policy recommendation. A report from UNDP's Regional Bureau for Europe and the Commonwealth of Independent States emphasized the prerequisites for equity, legitimacy, and efficiency:

> A legitimately strong government can be described as one that commands sufficient confidence in its legitimacy to allow for a strong civil society, and for a network of non-governmental institutions and regulations that ensure the development of a well-functioning economic system, the strengthening of democratic procedures, and a widespread participation by people in public life.[46]

In a departure from previous orthodoxy and as a sign of the pendulum's swing, the World Bank's *World Development Report 1997* emphasized that the state is capable, and indeed should perform the role, of producing welfare-enhancing outcomes. As the text itself argues: "And there is a growing recognition that some needed public goods and services can only be secured through international cooperation. Thus, building state capacity will mean building more effective partnerships and institutions internationally as well as at home."[47] The report's subtitle, *The State in a Changing World*, was indicative of a reversal led by Joseph Stiglitz, until December 1999 the much-discussed chief economist and senior vice-president.[48] The controversy surrounding Stiglitz's tenure in Washington reflected the fact that, in comparison with most other officials in the World Bank and the IMF, he appeared more sympathetic toward striking a balance between market and state and more agnostic about the potential for unfettered market forces.

Thus, the UN's conceptual contribution has altered the emphasis in the "good governance" debate of the mid-1980s to mid-1990s. Rescuing the baby from the discarded bath water, today's debate about good governance has moved away from a visceral dismantling of the state. In contrast with narrower economic liberalization programs in vogue earlier, political liberalization programs of the late 1990s (with greater emphasis on leadership and management as well as democracy, human rights, rule of law, access to justice, and basic freedoms) have weakened the force of arguments by proponents of a "minimalist state." Whereas the original debate about good governance was cast as the antithesis of state-dominated economic and social development of previous decades, today's is less about jettisoning state institutions than improving and reforming the functioning of democratic institutions, including the "deepening" of democracy and exploring more active and creative roles for non-state actors. Leaders are being held to higher standards of accountability, and they have to contend with the forces of globalization. But there is less faith in a blanket prescription to roll-back the state.

The World Bank's published stance presupposes what is "good" and what is "not good" governance.[49] In working to remove "politics" from the debate (its charter supposedly precludes directly addressing political issues), the Bank's position on governance is pre-occupied with public sector management, the reduction of transaction costs, and contract enforcement. These issues are certainly linked to sustainable human development but are not framed as central to a conception of and strategy for governance that as a priority seeks to maximize local participation in addressing the most pressing needs in a given community. In contrast, the UNDP's and the UN system's evolving human development approach to governance exhibits relatively greater support for empowerment—that is, providing the tools of democracy and freedom that are integral to the political and civic dimensions of governance. The Bank may not be averse to these issues but treats them as second order concerns, or "tag on's," that are not valuable in and of themselves but rather desirable insofar as they contribute to efficiency and growth. Under the new political economy of the 1970s and 1980s, political rationality by policymakers was stressed as a variation on the neoclassical theme of economic rationality. This theme greatly influenced the crafting of the international financial institutions' governance priorities of the 1980s and 1990s aimed at increasing economic efficiency and growth.

Since the early 1990s, the UNDP has begun shifting away from traditional public sector management (particularly civil service reform) and modest decentralization programs to addressing such sensitive governance areas as human rights, legislative support, judicial reform, and corruption. Responding to the growth in transitional democracies, the UNDP's emphasis on electoral assistance has provided an entry point to dealing with this "new generation" of governance projects. With resources to pursue this agenda, other factors also contributed to UNDP's growing involvement: fewer ideological tensions since the end of the Cold War; a growing consensus about the need for such political reforms; better information flows; and dissatisfaction with, and continual decreases in, traditional development assistance.[50]

The new frontiers of governance policy and support for institution building require trust and a perceived neutral position in a target country. Capacity-building for civil society and the private sector meant that the UN system has a comparative advantage in many developing countries in relationship to the IFIs. The UNDP's approach to governance will continue to differ from Bretton Woods institutions' as long as they view "good governance" in terms of strict political and economic conditionality. Given the UNDP's role as the lead UN agency in the field and as a prominent contributor to UN policy debates, it is likely that the rest of the UN system will gradually adopt UNDP's brand of governance. This argument has particular salience after the 1999 establishment of a Governance Division along with the enthusiasm for this topic from the new administrator, Mark Malloch Brown.

We are moving toward common ground that good governance does not necessarily mean less but sometimes more appropriate government. There is no need to resurrect the folly of the stereotypical hyper-active state of the 1960s and 1970s. However, we require processes or rules of decision making that are more likely to result in actions that are truly in the public interest, rather than favoring the private exploitation of the public interest. There is need to balance the role of government and other political and economic institutions with functioning markets. More than occasionally, a countervailing power to market externalities is required. And the only candidate is the state. The central challenge is not to halt the expansion of the market but to establish proper rules and institutions so that the benefits of growth are more widely beneficial.

The third and final substantive criticism from the United Nations is the need to introduce subtlety into the infatuation with democracy and democratization as surrogates for good governance. The argument that individual political rights and democratization go hand-in-hand with good governance is not wrong. But it has been expanded to reflect economic and social rights as part of a comprehensive "package."[51]

In short, the initial debate over good governance was concerned less with improving the political leadership of democracy and integrating economic and social goals (e.g., through the initiation of more active and creative roles for non-state actors) than with reversing decades of state-dominated economic and social development. Now that the state's role has come into question, the emphasis in UN circles has changed. Going beyond the largely empty Cold War clash between "first" (political and civil right) and "second generation" (economic and social) rights, UN high commissioner for human rights and former Irish president Mary Robinson continually stresses integration of economic and social welfare into the bundle of goods that any well governed society must have.[52] As such, good governance can also entail improvements in governmental institutions and sound development management. As Bøås writes, "State and civil society are constituted through iterated interaction, and the governance produced (bad or good) is an outcome of this process."[53] Mahbub ul Haq went further still toward the end of his life. Maintaining that "the concept of good governance has so far failed to match the radicalism of the notion of human development,"[54] researchers at his center in Islamabad launched an inclusive and ambitious idea, "humane governance." This definition includes good political, economic, *and* civic governance.

Humane governance involves those structures and processes that support the creation of a participatory, responsive, and accountable polity (that is, good political governance) embedded in a competitive, nondiscriminatory, yet equitable economy (that is, good economic governance). This requires the resources contributed by people to be plowed back to serve their own basic human needs, which will in turn expand the opportunities open to them; people must be given the ability to self-organize (that is, good civic governance). Bounded together by such principles as "ownership," "decency," and "accountability," the components of humane governance are inextricably linked.

The host of definitions earlier in this essay suggest the importance of ideas. Governance and its prescriptive partner of good governance have elicited not only commentary by scholars and development practitioners but also policy changes by national governments and international funding agencies. The forces of demo-cratization and globalization are pressuring "good governance" proponents to re-orient their priorities from the exigencies of economic growth and efficiency to those governance policies and institutions that best promote greater freedom, genuine participation, and sustainable human development. It is on this fundamental point that thinking at the United Nations currently is ahead of the curve, compared to the conventional wisdom in the corridors of the Washington-based IFIs. Ironically, the UN probably would not have moved so quickly without the sea change in world politics after the end of the Cold War and without pressure from donors.

The conceptual and operational battles about governance and good govern-ance are a few decades old, but the journey to explore global governance has just begun. It is hardly surprising then that the debate is more inchoate than the one about governance within countries. Thus far, the commentary from academics and practitioners has led to more heat than light—there is no consensus about desirable changes in policy or discourse. The intellectual trek is, however, important to have started. It is to this story that we now turn.

Global governance

At the same time that most of Europe adopts the euro and moves toward a common defense and security policy, how can the former Yugoslavia implode? Rosenau invented the term "fragmegration"[55] to capture the confusion in the simultaneous integration and fragmentation of societal interactions and authority patterns. Moreover, burgeoning information, communication, market, finance, networking, and business activities are producing a world in which patterns are extremely difficult to discern.

This has not slowed publications and speculations. One analyst has gone so far as to quip that "we say 'governance' because we don't really know what to call what is going on."[56] The rubric of "global governance" is akin to "post–Cold War," which signifies that one period has ended but that we do not as yet have an accurate short-hand to depict the essential dynamics of the new epoch. Analysts are under-standably uncomfortable with the traditional frameworks and vocabulary used to describe international relations; today's conceptual tools are elementary.

In spite of vagueness in ongoing scholarly and policy debates, the application of the notion of governance to the globe was the natural result of mounting evidence that the international system was no longer composed simply of states, but rather that the world was undergoing fundamental change. Although such actors as the Catholic Church, General Motors, and the International Committee of the Red Cross (ICRC) are hardly new to the Westphalian system, the proliferation of non-state actors and their growing importance and power is a distinctive feature of contemporary world affairs.[57]

Global governance invokes shifting the location of authority in the context of integration and fragmentation. Rosenau describes the process as "a pervasive tendency . . . in which major shifts in the location of authority and the site of control mechanisms are under way on every continent, shifts that are as pronounced in economic and social systems as they are in political systems."[58] The essential challenge for international cooperation jumps from the title of his edited volume, *Governance Without Government*. Mobilizing support from the bottom-up involves increasing the skills and capacities of individuals and altering the horizons of identification in patterns of global life. Elsewhere, Rosenau characterizes global governance as "systems of rule at all levels of human activity—from the family to the international organization—in which the pursuit of goals through the exercise of control has transnational repercussions."[59] Oran Young has argued that the value of the concept is that identifiable social practices can be envisaged and sometimes undertaken to improve economic, social, and environmental performance even without the formal institutions capable of authoritatively taking action.[60]

The phenomenal economic expansion and technological progress of the 1990s have not benefited equally the world's citizens. The unevenness of the economic playing field and the power of players on it is evident. Using the three essential components of the human development idea—equality of opportunity, sustainability, and empowerment of people—a bleaker picture emerges from the UNDP and other UN reports than from conventional wisdom. For instance, income per capita and average purchasing power in some 100 countries was lower in 1994 than in the 1980s; in 70 it was actually lower than in the 1970s, and in 35 lower than in the 1960s.[61] If information technologies are driving growth or are a prerequisite for it, the increasing concentration of income, resources, and wealth among people, corporations, and countries does not bode well. The richest 20 percent of the world's population living in the wealthiest countries account for over 93 percent of internet users while the bottom 20 percent only 0.2 percent.[62]

Globalization is neither uniform nor homogeneous, but it is indisputably accelerating the pace and intensity of economic and social interactions at all levels. Although globalization has a long history,[63] its present manifestation is fundamentally different in scale, intensity, and form from what preceded. As David Held and others have put it, "Contemporary globalization represents the beginning of a new epoch in human affairs . . . as profound an impact as the Industrial Revolution and the global empires of the nineteenth century."[64] Students and professors, policy analysts and practitioners should not feel uncomfortable about admitting their uneasiness and ignorance about understanding the details of the contemporary political economy, and especially not about the best way to address a bewildering array of global problems.

As such, the logical link between the patterns of governance at the national and global levels lies in solving the collective action puzzle to provide public goods. "In both modern domestic political systems and the modern international system, the state has been the key structural arena within which collective action has been situated and undertaken," observes Philip Cerny. And as a result of a multiplicity of interactions, "the authority, legitimacy, policymaking capacity, and policy-implementing effectiveness of the state will be eroded and undermined both within and without."[65] Globalization has profound consequences for the nature of collective action in both domestic and international politics. Cerny argues that, as market activity intensifies and economic organization becomes increasingly complex, the institutional scale of political structures is no longer capable of providing a suitable range of public goods. In effect, economic globalization is undermining the effectiveness of state-based collective action, which was extremely weak in the first place. Although the state remains a cultural force, its effectiveness as a civil association has declined. The result may be a crisis of legitimacy. State-based collective action has not reached its end, but it is significantly different from the past.

Although realists and idealists who analyze international organizations disagree about many issues, they agree that the state system is "anarchic." Whatever the framers of the UN Charter had in mind and whatever Keynes and his colleagues imagined at Bretton Woods, nothing like an overarching authority for either the high politics of international peace and security or the low politics of economic and social development has emerged.

In one essential aspect then, "global governance" is quite distinct from good or bad governance at the national level. A "good" (that is, accountable, efficient, lawful, representative, and transparent) government usually leads to good governance, while bad governance is closely correlated with a conspicuously bad government. Prescriptions to improve policymaking flow naturally, albeit controversially, from adjusting both the potential contribution of the state as agent and the rules of the economic and social game so that more contributions to the public good can be teased from non-state actors. The merits of more or less interventionist stances can be debated, but there is at least a primary and identifiable sovereign agent at the helm.

There is no such actor for the planet. Although the glass clearly is less full than we would like, Mark Zacher reminds us that the modest order in today's international economic system results from international efforts: "In short, without these and other regimes and public goods generated by the UN system, it would truly be 'a jungle out there.'"[66] At the same time, the conceptual and operational challenges of global governance are formidable.

We require a term to signify the reality that there has never been a world government, and there undoubtedly will never be one. Thus, at both the country and global levels, governance encompasses more than government. But as there is no government at the global level, of what utility is the notion? Is it, as Brian Urquhart once quipped, like the grinning but body-less Cheshire cat in *Alice in Wonderland*, an agreeable notion because it is without substance?

Global governance perhaps should be seen as a heuristic device to capture and describe the confusing and seemingly ever-accelerating transformation of the international system. States are central but their authority is eroding in important ways. Their creations, intergovernmental organizations, are no more in control than they ever were. Local and international NGOs are proliferating and gaining authority and resources. And technological developments are increasing the wherewithal of corporations and criminal groups. Within this context, collective action problems associated with the provision of global public goods have become even more of a challenge, conceptual and practical, than is their provision in the national setting.

Purposeful activity for the planet necessitates a conceptual framework to capture the reality that supranational control or even countervailing power are not operational concepts for the time being. Ironically we are not even closer than we were in 1945. One prominent group of economists has observed that "international institutions have weakened precisely at a time when global interdependence has increased."[67] Canadian economist Gerry Helleiner asked the Second Committee of the General Assembly, "Who plays the role of the development-oriented state in the global economy?" "Today's global financial world," he asserted, "is utterly different from that facing the original architects of the Bretton Woods system in 1944."[68]

It is humbling to realize that even a relatively powerful institution like the IMF is not the global monetary manager that it was supposed to be. It is a pale imitation of the institution for which Keynes was such a passionate advocate. Instead of reserves equal to half of world imports, the IMF's liquidity equals less than 2 percent of global imports.

In such a world, proponents and theorists of global governance face enormous difficulties in making hard-hitting policy prescriptions. In the face of anarchy, what mechanisms should be primarily responsible for global governance? Is there a way to structure a reasonable measure of coordination and cooperation among governments, intergovernmental organizations, nongovernmental organizations, and the private sector that would constitute meaningful, or at least improved, patterns of global governance? If it is the product of purposeful decisions and goal-oriented behavior, how can global governance exist in the absence of a clear consensus about goals? To what extent does global governance depend on shared values and norms?

One common reaction, especially among representatives of governments, is to fall back on familiar ways of thought by attempting to recapture the "good old days" of state-centric authority. Russian and Chinese reactions in the Security Council join those of developing countries there and in the General Assembly in trying to emphasize the centrality of the state and forestall erosions of its prerogatives. The American reliance upon exceptionalism and unilateralism within the multilateral system is another illustration of related rearguard impulses.[69]

Sovereignty is not dead, but it is hardly as sacrosanct as it once was. In attempting to protest too much, governmental representatives are highlighting daily in international forums the extent to which contemporary authority patterns are in flux and quite different from those of the past. The visceral resistance to change among governments and intergovernmental secretariats contrasts markedly with the greater agility of most businesses and NGOs. There is no philosophical justification or constitutional specification that assigns the highest form of authority to states, but representatives from national governments act as if there were.

Other analysts seek to recapture the naïveté of the period just before and after the end of World War II when intergovernmental organizations were panaceas that would make the world safe from both war and economic recession. Larry Finkelstein, for instance, sees global governance as "doing internationally what governments do at home."[70] But his formulation fails to specify the agents that are supposed to accomplish globally the numerous tasks that governments do nationally.

Neither our understanding nor our problem-solving efforts are any longer served, as Rosenau cautions, "by clinging to the notion that states and national governments are the essential underpinnings of the world's organization."[71] With an increasing diffusion of authority and a corresponding loss of control, states and the intergovernmental organizations created by them are no longer always the only or even the most important players on the world stage. Depending on the issue, member states retain many attributes of sovereignty, but they are past their prime and share the spotlight with numerous other actors.

Interestingly enough, the Commission on Global Governance was composed of 28 commissioners whose professional experiences were almost exclusively within governments and intergovernmental secretariats. They were clear about not advocating a world government or even world federalism. In light of their backgrounds, it is noteworthy that global governance for the members of the commission does not mean a single model, nor even a single structure or set of structures. Instead, "it is a broad, dynamic, complex process of interactive decision-making that is constantly evolving and responding to changing circumstances."[72] Global governance implies a wide and seemingly ever-growing range of actors in every domain. Global economic and social affairs have traditionally been viewed as embracing primarily intergovernmental relationships, but increasingly they must be framed in comprehensive enough terms to embrace local and international NGOs, grassroots and citizens' movements, multinational corporations, and the global capital market.

There is one notable similarity to democratization at the national level because more inclusive and participatory—hence, truly "democratic"—mechanisms for consultations and ultimately governance must be created at the global level as well. They should be malleable enough to respond to an ever-changing environment. There is a crucial similarity in the reasoning of both theorists like Rosenau and practitioners such as the members of the Commission on Global Governance to distinguish "governance" from "government." At the global level there can be no single model or form, nor even a single structure or set of structures.

For the moment, we are unable even to describe accurately all of the dimensions of international economic and social interactions—what Rosenau has aptly described as causal chains that "follow crazy-quilt patterns."[73] The proverbial bottom line is: there is no clear-cut equivalent at the global level to the national prescriptions of democratization and economic liberalization as the constituent components of humane governance.

Conclusion

In light of its universality and scope, the United Nations will have a special role, albeit not a monopoly, on future leadership for global governance. One group of UN watchers was supportive of the world organization's involvement. They "saw global governance—both in terms of the playing field and the players—as lagging behind globalization, and there was broad consensus that the United Nations should have a significant, but as yet undefined, role in 'bridging the gap.'"[74] If this is to be the case, the UN system should do better than in the past in swimming against the powerful currents of orthodoxy. As Amartya Sen, the 1998 Nobel laureate in economics, who has played a major intellectual role within and from his positions outside the United Nations, prods us to recall at the dawn of the twenty-first century: "The need for critical scrutiny of standard preconceptions and political-economic attitudes has never been stronger."[75]

Within this context, intergovernmental organizations, both universal and regional, should be strengthened. This is the most constant refrain throughout over half a century of the UN's stewardship over economic and social ideas. There is of course more than a dollop of institutional self-interest behind this conviction. But more important is the dramatic reality that some countervailing power is required to off-set the excesses of a decentralized system of states pursuing their national interests in combination with the private sector pursuing individual gains.

The need for a more cohesive and effective multilateral system is logical and evident. At the same time that a longing for a monolithic and top-down view of governance is comprehensible, it seems misplaced in an increasingly decentralized world. At a historical juncture when both problems and solutions transcend national borders and there is no likelihood of a central sovereign, the decibel level of calls from internationalists to strengthen intergovernmental institutions is understandably loud but ultimately wistful. We should think creatively about ways to pool the collective strengths and avoid the collective weaknesses of governments, intergovernmental organizations, NGOs, and global civil society.

This irony is behind the UN's convening of the Millennium Assembly in September 2000[76] and the growing emphases on the private sector and NGOs by the last two secretaries-general.[77] Paradoxically, this is the conceptual and operational challenge for proponents of global governance and of the United Nations in light of a changing world political economy.[78]

Notes

1 I am grateful to Kevin Ozgercin and Richard Ponzio for their assistance in researching this essay. Parts of the argument appear in Louis Emmerij, Richard Jolly, and Thomas G. Weiss, *Ahead of the Curve? UN Ideas and Global Challenges* (Bloomington: Indiana University Press, 2001).

2 Morten Bøås, "Governance as Multilateral Bank Policy: The Cases of the African Development Bank and the Asian Development Bank," *European Journal of Development Research* 10, no. 2 (1998): 117–34.

3 See, for example, Dan Bawley, *Corporate Governance and Accountability: What Role for the Regulator, Director, and Auditor?* (Westport, Conn.: Quorum, 1999); OECD, *Corporate Governance: Improving Competitiveness and Access to Capital in Global Markets: A Report to the OECD* (Paris: OECD, 1998); Fred J. Weston, *Takeovers, Restructuring, and Corporate Governance* (Upper Saddle River, NJ: Prentice Hall, 1998); Donald H. Chew, *Studies in International Corporate Finance and Governance Systems: A Comparison of the U.S., Japan, and Europe* (New York: Oxford University Press, 1997); Margaret M. Blair, *Ownership and Control: Rethinking Corporate Governance for the Twenty-First Century* (Washington, DC: Brookings Institute, 1995); United States Congress, *Corporate Governance: Hearing Before the Subcommittee on Telecommunications and Finance of the Committee on Energy and Commerce, House of Representatives, 103rd Congress, First Session, April 21, 1993* (Washington, DC: US Government Printing Office, 1994).

4 See Goran Hyden, "Governance and the Study of Politics," in *Governance and Politics in Africa*, ed. Göran Hyden and Michael Bratton (Boulder, Colo.: Lynne Rienner Publishers, 1992), 1–26.

5 Commission on Global Governance, *Our Global Neighbourhood* (Oxford: Oxford University Press, 1995), 2.

6 James N. Rosenau, "Governance in the Twenty-First Century," *Global Governance* 1, no. 1 (1995): 14.

7 Since 1995 Lynne Rienner Publishers has, in cooperation with the Academic Council on the United Nations System and the UN University, published the journal *Global Governance*. The first issue contained contributions by then secretary-general Boutros Boutros-Ghali and his special representative on internally displaced persons, Francis M. Deng, as well as articles by Rosenau and three younger academics. The Commission on Global Governance was chaired by Sonny Ramphal and Ingmar Carlsson and published the views of the eminent practitioners on it (see note 1) in 1995. In addition, see James N. Rosenau and Ernst-Otto Czempiel, eds., *Governance without Government: Order and Change in World Politics* (Cambridge: Cambride University Press, 1992); Jan Kooiman, ed., *Modern Governance: New Government-Society Interactions* (London: Sage, 1993); Mihaly Simai, *The Future of Global Governance: Managing Risk and Change in the International System* (Washington, DC: US Institute of Peace, 1994); Meghnad Desai and Paul Redfern, eds., *Global Governance: Ethics and Economics of the World Order* (London: Pinter, 1995); Richard Falk, *On Humane Governance* (University Park: Penn State Press, 1995); Paul F. Diehl, ed., *The Politics of Global Governance: International Organizations in an Interdependent World* (Boulder, Colo.: Lynne Rienner, 1997); Martin Hewson and Timothy J. Sinclair, eds., *Approaches to Global Governance Theory* (Albany: State University of New York, 1999); and Errol E. Harris and James A. Yunker, eds., *Toward Genuine Global Governance: Critical Reflection to Our Global Neighbourhood* (Westport, Conn.: Praeger, 1999). In addition, numerous publications from international agencies have used the concept in their titles and analyses. See, for example, World Bank, *Governance and Development* (Washington, DC: World Bank, 1992); and UN Development Programme, *The Shrinking State: Governance and Human Development in Eastern Europe and the Commonwealth of Independent States* (New York: UNDP, 1997).

8 John Maynard Keynes, *The General Theory of Employment, Interest and Money* (London: Macmillan, 1936), 383.

9 For an important contemporary investigation of the role of ideas, see Judith Goldstein and Robert O. Keohane, eds., *Ideas and Foreign Policy: Beliefs, Institutions, and Political Change* (Ithaca, NY: Cornell University Press, 1993). See also Ngaire Woods, "Economic Ideas and International Relations: Beyond Rational Neglect, *International Studies Quarterly* 39 (1995): 161–80.

10 Boutros Boutros-Ghali, *An Agenda for Peace* (New York: United Nations, 1992), para. 17.

11 World Bank, *Governance, The World Bank's Experience* (Washington, DC: The World Bank, 1994), xiv.

12 UNDP, *Governance for Sustainable Human Development* (New York: UNDP, 1997), 2–3.

13 OECD, *Participatory Development and Good Governance* (Paris: OECD, 1995), 14.

14 See: http://infoweb.magi.com/~igvn.

15 Commission on Global Governance, *Our Global Neighbourhood* (New York: Oxford University Press, 1995), 2.

16 See: www.soc.titech.ac.jp/uem/governance.html.

17 See: www.britcoun.org/governance/ukpgov.html.

18 See: www.soc.titech.ac.jp/uem/governance.html.

19 See, for example, Jagdish Bhagwati, "Directly Unproductive, Profit Seeking (DUP) Activities," *Journal of Political Economy* 90, no. 5 (1982): 988–1002; J.M. Buchanan, R.D. Tollison, and G. Tullock, eds., *Toward a Theory of the Rent-Seeking Society* (College Station: Texas A&M University Press, 1980); Anthony Downs, *An Economic Theory of Democracy* (New York: Harper and Row, 1957); Douglas North, *Structure and Change in Economic History* (New York: Norton, 1981) and *Institutions, Institutional Change, and Economic Performance* (New York: Cambridge University Press, 1990); Gustav Ranis and T. Paul Schultz, eds., *The State of Development Economics* (Oxford: Basil Blackwell, 1982); and S. Wellisz and R. Findlay, "The State and the Invisible Hand," *World Bank Research Observer* 3, no. 1 (1988): 59–80.

20 See, for example, Francis Fukuyama, *Trust: The Social Virtues and the Creation of Prosperity* (New York: Free Press, 1995); and Robert Putnam with Robert Leonardi and Raffaella Nanetti, *Making Democracy Work: Civic Traditions in Modern Italy* (Princeton, NJ: Princeton University Press, 1993).

21 See, for example, Inge Kaul, Isabelle Grunberg, and Marc Stern, *Global Public Goods: International Cooperation in the 21st Century* (New York: Oxford University Press, 1999); Ruben Mendez, *International Public Finance* (New York: Oxford University Press, 1992); and Mancur Olson, *The Logic of Collective Choice* (Cambridge, Mass.: Harvard University Press, 1965) and *The Rise and Decline of Nations: Economic Growth Stagflation, and Social Rigidities* (New Haven, Conn.: Yale University Press, 1982).

22 This summary was adapted from Ronald Findlay, "The New Political Economy: Its Explanatory Power for LDCs," in *Politics and Policy Making in Developing Countries*, ed. Gerald M. Meier (San Francisco: ICS Press, 1991), 13.

23 Francis M. Deng and Terrence Lyons, "Promoting Responsible Sovereignty in Africa," in *African Reckoning: A Quest for Good Governance*, ed. Francis M. Deng and Terrence Lyons (Washington, DC: Brookings Institution, 1998), 1.

24 See Nassau Adams, *Worlds Apart: The North-South Divide and the International System* (London: Zed Books, 1997).

25 See Eric Helleiner, *States and the Re-emergence of Global Finance: From Bretton Woods to the 1990s* (Ithaca, NY: Cornell University Press, 1994). For a discussion of the importance of international institutions in transmitting ideas that in part sustain the dominant order, see Robert W. Cox with Timothy Sinclair, *Approaches to World Order* (Cambridge: Cambridge University Press, 1996).

26 World Bank, *Accelerated Development in Sub-Saharan Africa: An Agenda for Action* (Washington, DC: World Bank, 1981).

27 World Bank, *Sub-Saharan Africa: From Crisis to Sustainable Growth* (Washington, DC: World Bank, 1989). For African responses, see Goran Hyden, Dele Oluwu, and Hastings Oketh Ogendo, *African Perspectives on Governance* (Trenton, NJ: Africa World Press, 2000).

28 Enrico Augelli and Craig Murphy, *America's Quest for Supremacy and the Third World* (London: Pinter, 1988), 184.

29 Goran Hyden, "Sovereignty, Responsibility, and Accountability: Challenges at the National Level in Africa," in *African Reckoning*, ed. Francis M. Deng and Terrence Lyons (Washington, DC: Brookings Institution, 1998), 38.

30 Samuel P. Huntington, *The Third Wave: Democratization in the Late Twentieth Century* (Oklahoma City: University of Oklahoma Press, 1991).

31 See Thomas G. Weiss, *International NGOs, Global Governance, and Social Policy in the UN System*, GASPP Occasional Paper No. 3 (Helsinki: Stakes, March 1999), and Thomas G. Weiss and Leon Gordenker, eds., *NGOs, the UN, and Global Governance* (Boulder, Colo.: Lynne Rienner, 1996), originally published as a special issue of *Third World Quarterly* 16, no. 3 (1995). There is an ever-growing literature in the last decade, and readers may wish to consult a few key pieces from that time, see Bertrand Schneider, *The Barefoot Revolution: A Report to the Club of Rome* (London: IT Publications, 1988); David Korten, *Getting to the 21st Century: Voluntary Action and the Global Agenda* (West Hartford, Conn.: Kumarian, 1990); Paul Wapner, *Environmental Activism and World Civic Politics* (New York: State University of New York Press, 1996); Peter Willetts, ed., *"The Conscience of the World": The Influence of Non-Governmental Organisations in the U.N. System* (London: Hurst, 1996); Steve Charnowitz, "Two Centuries of Participation: NGOs and International Governance," *Michigan Journal of International Law* 18, no. 2 (1997): 183–286; and John Boli and George M. Thomas, eds., *Constructing World Culture: International Nongovernmental Organizations since 1875* (Stanford, Calif.: Stanford University Press, 1999). See also UN Non-Governmental Liaison Service, *The United Nations, NGOs and Global Governance: Challenges for the 21st Century* (Geneva: NGLS, 1996).

32 Kalevi J. Holsti, *The State, War, and the State of War* (Cambridge: Cambridge University Press, 1996), 189.

33 For a discussion, see Thomas G. Weiss, "The Politics of Humanitarian Ideas," *Security Dialogue* 31, no. 1 (2000): 11–23.

34 Francis M. Deng, *Protecting the Dispossessed: A Challenge for the International Community* (Washington, DC: Brookings Institution, 1993); Francis M. Deng, Sadikiel Kimaro, Terrence Lyons, Donald Rothchild, and I. William Zartman, *Sovereignty as Responsibility* (Washington, DC: Brookings Institution, 1995); and Francis M. Deng, "Frontiers of Sovereignty," *Leiden Journal of International Law* 8, no. 2 (1995): 249–86. For more recent analyses and case studies, see Roberta Cohen and Frances M. Deng, *Masses in Flight: The Global Crisis in Displacement* (Washington, DC: Brookings Institution, 1998), and Roberta Cohen and Frances M. Deng, eds., *The Forsaken People: Case Studies of the Internally Displaced* (Washington, DC: Brookings Institution, 1998).

35 See, for example, Carnegie Commission on the Prevention of Deadly Conflict, *Preventing Deadly Conflict* (New York: Carnegie Corporation, 1997).

36 Bøås, "Governance as Multilateral Bank Policy," 120. Morten Bøås and Desmond McNeill are directing a research project at the University of Oslo that is seeking to trace the influence of good governance and three other ideas within selected intergovernmental organizations.

37 James N. Rosenau, "Toward an Ontology for Global Governance," in Hewson and Sinclair, eds., *Approaches to Global Govenance Theory*, 296.

38 Bøås, "Governance," 119.

39 United Nations Development Programme, *Human Development Report 1990* (New York: Oxford University Press, 1990), and the subsequent yearly reports. Mahbub ul Haq's own account of this effort is found in *Reflections on Human Development* (New York: Oxford University Press, 1995).

40 See UNICEF, *The State of the World's Children 1987* (New York: Oxford University Press, 1987) and the subsequent yearly reports.

41 Giovanni Andrea Cornia, Richard Jolly, and Frances E. Stewart, *Adjustment with a Human Face* (Oxford: Oxford University Press, 1987).

42 See UNHCR, *The State of the World's Refugees 1993: The Challenge of Protection* (Oxford: Oxford University Press, 1993); *The State of the World's Refugees 1995: In Search of Solutions* (Oxford: Oxford University Press, 1995); and *The State of the World's Refugees 1997–98: A Humanitarian Agenda* (Oxford: Oxford University Press, 1997).

43 See, for example, the expositions on poverty and health, respectively in World Bank, *World Development Report 1990* (New York: Oxford University Press, 1990) and *World Development Report 1993* (New York: Oxford University Press, 1993).

44 See Stephen Marglin and J. Schor, *The Golden Age of Capitalism: Reinterpreting the Post-War Experience* (Oxford: Clarendon Press, 1990).

45 Antonio Gramsci, *Selections from the Prison Notebooks* (London: Lawrence and Wishart, 1971), 377.

46 UN Development Programme, *The Shrinking State*, 1.

47 World Bank, *World Development Report 1997: The State in a Changing World* (New York: Oxford University Press, 1997), 131.

48 See, for example, Joseph Stiglitz, "Redefining the Role of the State: What Should It Do? How Should It Do It? And How Should These *Decisions Be Made?*" www.world bank.org.

49 See especially, *World Bank, World Development Report 1997* and *World Development Report 1992* (New York: Oxford University Press, 1992).

50 Remarks by Thomas Carothers, from the Carnegie Endowment on International Peace, at UNDP's Global Resident Representatives Meeting, 29 February 2000.

51 UNDP, *Human Development Report 2000* (New York: Oxford University Press, 2000).

52 See, for example, *Report of the United Nations High Commissioner for Human Rights*, UN document A/54/36, 23 September 1999.

53 Bøås, "Governance," 129.

54 The Mahbub ul Haq Human Development Centre, *Human Development in South Asia 1999: The Crisis of Governance* (Oxford: Oxford University Press, 1999), 28.

55 James N. Rosenau, "'Fragmegrative' Challenges to National Security," in *Understanding US Strategy: A Reader*, ed. Terry Hens (Washington, DC: National Defense University, 1983), 65–82.

56 Lawrence S. Finkelstein, "What Is Global Governance?" *Global Governance* 1, no. 3 (1995): 368.

57 For a persuasive discussion, see David Held, Anthony McGrew, David Goldblatt, and Jonathan Perraton, *Global Transformations: Politics, Economics, and Culture* (Stanford, Calif.: Stanford University Press, 1999).

58 Rosenau, "Governance in the Twenty-First Century," 18.

59 Rosenau, 13.

60 Oran Young, *International Governance: Protecting the Environment in a Stateless Society* (Ithaca, NY: Cornell University Press, 1994).

61 UNDP, *Human Development Report 1996* (Oxford: Oxford University Press, 1996), 3.

62 UNDP, *Human Development Report 1999* (Oxford: Oxford University Press, 1999), 2.

63 Emma Rothschild, "Globalization and the Return of History," *Foreign Policy*, no. 115 (Summer 1999): 106–16.

64 David Held, Anthony McGrew, David Goldblatt, Jonathan Perraton, "Globalization," *Global Governance* 5, no. 4 (1999): 494. See also Simai, *The Future of Global Governance*, 349–54.

65 Philip G. Cerny, "Globalization and the Changing Logic of Collective Action," *International Organization* 49, no. 4 (1995): 595 and 621.

66 Mark W. Zacher, *The United Nations and Global Commerce* (New York: UN, 1999), 5.

67 Mahbub ul Haq, Richard Jolly, Paul Streeten, and Khadija Haq, eds., *The UN and the Bretton Woods Institutions* (London: Macmillan, 1995), 13.

68 Gerry Helleiner, "A New Framework for Global Economic Governance," speech to the Second Committee of the General Assembly, 15 October 1999, 2.
69 Edward C. Luck, *Mixed Messages: American Politics and International Organization 1919–1999* (Washington, DC: Brookings Institution, 1999).
70 Finkelstein, "What Is Global Governance?" 369.
71 Rosenau, "Toward an Ontology," 287. See also James N. Rosenau, *The United Nations in a Turbulent World* (Boulder, Colo.: Lynne Rienner, 1992).
72 Commission on Global Governance, *Our Global Neighbourhood*, 4.
73 Rosenau, "Toward an Ontology," 293.
74 Stanley Foundation, *Global Governance: Defining the United Nations' Leadership Role* (Muscatine, Iowa: Stanley Foundation, 1999), report of the United Nations of the Next Decade Conference, Adare Manor, 13–18 June 1999, 15.
75 Amartya Sen, *Development As Freedom* (New York: Knopf, 1999), 112.
76 Kofi A. Annan, *"We the Peoples": The Role of the United Nations in the 21st Century* (New York: UN, 2000).
77 For example, see Boutros Boutros-Ghali, "Foreword," in *NGOs, the UN, and Global Governance*, ed. Thomas G. Weiss and Leon Gordenker (Boulder, Colo.: Lynne Rienner, 1995), 7–12; and Kofi Annan, *Renewing the United Nations: A Programme for Reform* (New York: United Nations, July 1997).
78 Thomas G. Weiss, David P. Forsythe, Roger A. Coate, and Kelly-Kate Pease, *The United Nations and Changing World Politics* (Boulder, Colo.: Westview, 2010), 6th ed., especially chapter 11.

10

PLURALIZING GLOBAL GOVERNANCE

Analytical approaches and dimensions

With Leon Gordenker

Nongovernmental organizations (NGOs) have in increasing numbers injected unexpected voices into international discourse about numerous problems of global scope. Especially since the 1970s, human rights advocates, gender activists, developmentalists, groups of indigenous peoples, and representatives of other defined interests have become active in political work once reserved for representatives of states. Their numbers have enlarged the venerable, but hardly numerous, ranks of transnational organizations built around churches, labor unions, and humanitarian aims.

The United Nations system provides a convenient, accessible vantage point to observe some of the most active, persuasive NGOs in the world. During the last 50 years, various UN organizations have felt the direct and indirect impact of NGOs. According to the Union of International Associations, the NGO universe includes well over 15,000 recognizable NGOs that operate in three or more countries and draw their finances from sources in more than one country; this number is growing all the time.[1] In their own ways, NGOs and intergovernmental organizations (IGOs) grope, sometimes cooperatively, sometimes competitively, sometimes in parallel toward a modicum of "global governance." We define global governance as efforts to bring more orderly and reliable responses to social and political issues that go beyond capacities of states to address individually. Like the NGO universe, global governance implies an absence of central authority, and the need for collaboration or cooperation among governments and others who seek to encourage common practices and goals in addressing global issues. The means to achieve global governance also include activities of the United Nations and other intergovernmental organizations and standing cooperative arrangements among states.

This essay generally discusses the NGO phenomenon. It proposes a definition of NGOs to serve for the purpose of this issue, although much controversy remains about the concept and individual authors may offer refinements. It also provides a general backdrop of historical, legal, and political factors for the study. It offers some analytical detail needed for deeper understanding of the phenomenon, and outlines a set of fundamental factors for studying NGOs. It does not assume that NGOs always or even usually succeed in reaching their goals or, if they do, that the result is beneficial for peace, social or personal welfare, or human rights.

The United Nations is a central and reasonably transparent point of observation that has legal and historical underpinnings, and branching activities that reach to the social grass roots. Moreover, NGOs are omnipresent in many aspects of international relations, and they may have become crucial to the UN's future. It is significant that in its essay, "Reforming the United Nations," the Commission on Global Governance—whose members are virtually all former governmental officials or international civil servants—examined NGOs and observed that "in their wide variety they bring expertise, commitment, and grassroots perceptions that should be mobilized in the interests of better governance."[2] NGOs assume center stage for activities that once "were irrelevant to the overall plot."[3] The case studies, each written by an author who has directly observed or experienced NGO activities, examine NGO work on human rights, complex humanitarian emergencies, the United Nations relationship, the global environment, AIDS, the international women's movement, scaling up and scaling down, operational coalitions, and state relations. The final essay draws on the specific studies to reach conclusions about the nature, function, and prospects for NGOs in relation to the UN system.

The phenomenon

In spite of the growth of the NGO phenomenon, confusion or ignorance persists as to the definition of the participants and the nature of their relationships to the UN system and to one another. Theoretical explorations have tended to be few in number and specific to a particular sector of activity, especially aspects of economic and social development and of the environment. A considerable body of writing has a primarily legal character, which overlooks or understates the richness of NGO activity and politics. Definitional clarity connects closely with concepts of structure, organization, and institutionalization.

The very site of NGO activity under examination here suggests paradoxes. IGOs join with governments in common undertakings. By definition, NGOs have no formal standing in this realm. Yet they have become exponentially more visible precisely in connection with governments. IGOs were intended to serve governments and to assist in cooperatively reaching goals on which both generally agree. Yet NGOs have now become an integral part of the process of setting agendas for cooperation and in carrying the results not only to governments but to other NGOs and individuals. This study seeks to analyze this process, which requires examining both broad and deep interorganizational relationships.

The term "nongovernmental organization" itself is challenged by a host of alternative usages. These include officials, independent sector, volunteer sector, civic society, grassroots organizations, private voluntary organizations, transnational social movement organizations, social change organizations, and non-state actors. Some of these refer to highly specialized varieties and many are synonyms for each other. There seems no quarrel, however, with the notion that these organizations consist of durable, bounded, voluntary relationships among individuals to produce a particular product, using specific techniques. Like-minded organizations may analogously develop lasting relationships to one another and thus form meta-organizations.

Although the term "non-state actors" may more closely resemble our inclusion of several varieties of meta-organizations that are engaged in transnational relationships, we maintain the term "nongovernmental organizations" because of its common currency and because this is the term that appears in Article 71 of the UN Charter. At the same time, "non-state actors," according to a Lexis-Nexis search, connotes a host of transnational entities that we deliberately exclude from our inquiry. These include profit-making corporations and banks, criminal elements (both organized crime and terrorists), insurgents, churches in their strictly religious function, transnational political parties, and the mass communication media.

A metaphor suggested by Marc Nerfin provides a starting point for locating NGOs in the political realm: the prince represents governmental power and the maintenance of public order; the merchant symbolizes economic power and the production of goods and services; and the citizen stands for people's power.[4] As such, the growth of NGOs arises from demands by citizens for accountability from the prince and the merchant. In this perspective, NGOs compete and cooperate with the prince and the merchant for guidance in aspects of social life. They function to "serve undeserved or neglected populations, to expand the freedom of or to empower people, to engage in advocacy for social change, and to provide services."[5]

Such an approach contains much that is subjective. Citizens may believe themselves underserved by, or deprived of, rightful power, or they may seek more freedom and advocate change. Doing so implies reform or drastic changes in existing societies. Yet it is equally conceivable that citizens could demand preservation of the status quo as part of the accountability of merchants and princes. The objective point of such approaches, however, lies in the identification of organization and activity beyond the conventional categories of state and business.

Questions can be raised about the accuracy of this metaphor. Although recognizing the legitimacy of each sector of society, it tends to glorify NGOs at the expense of states and markets. NGO "citizens" are portrayed as vanguards of the just society, as "princes" and "merchants" strive to dominate or to make profits. In a study of environmental NGOs in world politics, two authors concluded that the crucial function of NGOs was to create transnational links between state and non-state. NGOs, in this model, politicize the previously unpoliticized and connect the local and the global.[6]

Some NGOs do, in fact, politicize issues otherwise regarded by some as part of the nonpolitical realm, AIDS being a recent case in point. They also bring local experience to bear on international decision-making. This may be the most important contribution NGOs have made to global governance. Once again, however, generalization is dangerous because some NGOs continue to lead a more marginal existence, without links to international bodies. Most NGOs have not managed to break out of the local setting and become engaged in transnational activities.

If NGOs exist and operate above and beneath the level of government, they parallel the pattern of IGOs, particularly those of the UN system. These entities, too, are intended to operate to some degree beyond the states that form them. IGOs do not govern; they attempt to cope with and help manage complex inter-relationships and global political, economic, and social changes by arranging cooperation of other actors, especially governments. In doing so, they have also extended their operations below the classical boundaries of governmental autonomy.

Distinctions between IGOs and NGOs rest on legal grounds and tend to exaggerate the boundary between the two categories. In reality, there are great variations within, and unclear borderlines between, the two categories. The sheer number of different types of NGOs, ranging from community-based self-help groups to international NGOs with staff and budgets surpassing those of many IGOs, calls for conceptual differentiation and clarification.

Students of international relations have proposed alternative terminologies to conceptualize transnational relations. James Rosenau, for instance, distinguishes between sovereignty-bound and sovereignty-free actors.[7] While sociological rather than legal, this dichotomy can also be misleading insofar as organizations composed of governments are automatically assumed to be sovereignty-bound and other actors sovereignty-free. Perhaps it would make more sense to speak of sovereignty-bound and sovereignty-free behavior.[8] Regardless of their legal status, organizations may engage in behavior that is guided by, or pays heed to, state sovereignty to varying degrees. Loyalties do not always follow state borders, and secretariats of IGOs are not necessarily more dominated than secretariats of big NGOs.

This essay retains the traditional IGO–NGO distinction for lack of better alternatives, while remaining attentive to sovereignty-bound and sovereignty-free behavior by IGOs and NGOs alike. The important puzzle is what specific roles NGOs may play in transnational networks as intermediary organizations that provide links between state and market, between local and global levels.

The challenges to sovereignty, according to a recent analytical study, include four categories of interdependence—trade and finance, security, technology, and ecological problems—and "the emergence of new social movements with both local and transnational consciousness."[9] Both NGOs and IGOs, then, busy themselves with the paradox of global economic and technological integration with local fragmentation of identities.

Apart from the function of representing people acting of their own volition, rather than by some institutional fiat, NGOs have other defining characteristics. They are formal organizations that are intended to continue in existence; they are thus not ad hoc entities. They are or aspire to be self-governing on the basis of their own constitutional arrangements. They are private in that they are separate from governments and have no ability to direct societies or to require support from them. They are not in the business of making or distributing profits. The NGOs of interest here have transnational goals, operations or connections, and have active contacts with the UN system.

Not every organization that claims to be an NGO exactly fits this definition of a private citizens' organization, separate from government but active on social issues, not profit making, and with transnational scope. At least three significant deviations from these specifications can be identified. The first of these is a GONGO—government-organized nongovernmental organization. They achieved notoriety during the Cold War because many so-called NGOs owed their very existence and entire financial support to communist governments in the Soviet bloc or authoritarian ones in the Third World. There were also a few such "NGOs" in the West, particularly in the United States, where they were often a front for administration activities. Although the Western species may have been more nongovernmental than their Soviet or Third World counterparts, they were not created for the classic purposes of NGOs. Thus, GONGOS can be treated as only tangential to our examination.

The second special type of NGO is QUANGOS (quasi-nongovernmental organizations). For example, many Nordic and Canadian NGOs, a handful of US ones, and the International Committee of the Red Cross (ICRC) receive the bulk of their resources from public coffers. The staffs of such organizations usually assert that as long as their financial support is without strings attached and their own priorities rather than those of donor governments dominate, there is no genuine problem. This is clearly a subjective judgment, but most of these NGOs are relevant for our discussion. Their services aim at internationally-endorsed objectives and their operations are distinct from those of governments, even if their funding is public.

We are at an early stage in understanding how NGOs adapt to changing external and internal environments. In examining recent trends at the domestic level in the United States and Britain, one analyst has gone so far as to call into question voluntary agencies as a "shadow state."[10] With more governmental and inter-governmental resources being channelled through international NGOs, the issue of independence—or a willingness to bite the hand that feeds in order to make autonomous programmatic decisions in spite of donor pressures—assumes greater salience. "One of the real issues for NGOs is how much money can they take from the government while still carrying out advocacy activities that may involve criticizing the source of those funds."[11]

The third mutant type—the donor-organized NGO (DONGO)—is also distinguished by its source of funds. "As donors become more interested in NGOs, they also find themselves tempted to create NGOs suited to their perceived needs."[12] Both governments and the UN system have "their" NGOs for particular operations and purposes. The United Nations Development Programme (UNDP) has been involved in fostering their growth for a decade. The UN itself created local NGOs that contributed to mobilizing the population for elections in Cambodia[13] and to de-mining in Afghanistan.[14]

QUANGOS and DONGOS fit well enough in the general definition to warrant inclusion in this study. They aim at internationally endorsed purposes and have a private status, even if their funding is public. They offer services that clearly fall within the usual range of NGO operations.

Relationship to the UN

A conventional, legally-based way of describing NGOs and their relationship to the United Nations begins with the formal structure that derives from UN Charter Article 71.[15] It empowers the Economic and Social Council (ECOSOC) to "make suitable arrangements for consultation with nongovernmental organizations which are concerned with matters within its competence." It is the only mention of NGOs in the Charter, largely an afterthought stimulated by the Soviet Union's attempt to put a GONGO on a par with the International Labour Organization (ILO), another IGO dating to the formation of the League of Nations that constitution- ally included representation of labor and management in its governing structure.[16] Early attempts to give meaning to Article 71 were heavily colored by Cold War maneuvers, but a growing list of organizations with consultative status developed around fairly restricted practices laid down by ECOSOC.[17] Historically speak- ing, the UN Charter formalizes the relationship between NGOs and the world organization in a significantly different way from the previous experience with inter- national organization. For example, NGOs were completely excluded from the Hague Conferences in 1899 and 1907. At the League of Nations, NGOs achieved only an informal consultative arrangement that had some effect, however, on proceedings there.[18]

The present legal framework dates from 1968 in the form of the elaborate ECOSOC resolution 1296. It is now undergoing reexamination in a stately process whose diplomatic tone is heavily colored by NGO participation. Resolution 1296 retains but refines the earlier UN principle that any international organization not established by intergovernmental agreement falls into the NGO category. In 11 paragraphs of principles, the text emphasizes that NGOs that seek consultative status must have goals within the UN economic and social ambit. These NGOs must also have a representative and international character, and authorization to speak for members who are supposed to participate in a democratic fashion. The text requires submission of data from organizations on their budgets and the sources of their financing. It also promotes a vague hierarchy by encouraging the forma- tion of umbrella organizations composed of organizations with similar purposes that pool their advice to the council and transmit results of consultations from national organizations. The process of admission to consultative status is super- vised by the Committee on Non-Governmental Organizations, elected each year by ECOSOC from among its member governments, 19 of which provide the actual personnel.

Consultations remain largely under ECOSOC control, in contrast to the fuller rights of participation available to IGOs in the UN system. NGOs can be granted status in one of three categories, designated as "I," "II," and "the roster." Those in category I are supposed to have broad economic and social interests and geographical scope; those in category II have more specialized interests. The remainder of accepted applicants are listed in a roster for organizations that may make occasional contributions. Category I organizations have the broadest access to the council. They may propose ECOSOC agenda items to the Committee on Non-Governmental Organizations, which in turn can ask the Secretary-General to include their suggestions on the provisional list. This is far from a right to submit agenda items. Like category II NGOs, category I organizations may send observers to all meetings and may submit brief written statements on their subject matter. The council has the right to ask for written statements from any of the consultative NGOs, and it may invite category I and II organizations to hearings, which, in fact, are rare. Other rules set out limitations on NGOs in dealing with ECOSOC subsidiaries and international conferences summoned by it.

The UN Department of Public Information (DPI) simultaneously developed a parallel set of relationships with NGOs under its own legislative authority.[19] This emphasizes the information-disseminating function of NGOs, rather than any input in policy formation. It includes briefings, mailings, access to documentation, and an NGO Resources Center in New York.[20]

Both of these consultative arrangements gave birth to meta-organizations representing NGOs. Some of those in contact with ECOSOC soon formed a Conference of Non-Governmental Organizations in Consultative Status, which adopted the acronym CONGO. It takes no substantive positions, but concentrates on procedural matters and the promotion of better understanding of the ECOSOC agenda. For the organizations in the public information orbit, an NGO/ DPI Executive Committee serves as liaison.[21]

These consultative arrangements signal the presence of two trends. One of them indicates the almost unprecedented establishment of "formal relations between 'interest' groups and an intergovernmental body."[22] Even though this relationship was conditioned by the Cold War, both in the formation of the list of accredited organizations and the attention given them by the largely diplomatic ECOSOC, it offered some access to the UN system by NGOs. The fact that this access was seen as worthwhile by NGOs may be inferred from the growth in category I listings from seven in 1948 to 41 in 1991, and in category II organizations from 32 to 354 during the same period, while an even faster expansion took place on the roster.[23]

The other trend looks toward the vast broadening of scope and reach of the programs reviewed in ECOSOC. Although this organ by itself has never achieved the influence implied by its place in the UN Charter,[24] reports submitted from elsewhere in the system make it a central source of documentation and information. Senior officers of other IGOs also appear as authors, and those related to ECOSOC in the UN system make statements. The subject matter covers not only old-style international cooperation, but also takes in new subjects such as the environment, an enlarged operation to succor refugees and disaster victims, and a variegated web of economic and social development projects.[25]

Furthermore, the ECOSOC machinery and the international secretariats that serve it are intimately involved in the organization of large-scale international conferences on special themes, such as population, the status of women, and the environment. Such gatherings, in which governments are represented by senior officials, attract heavy NGO interest. The UN Conference on the Environment and Development in Rio de Janeiro in 1992, for example, registered 1,400 NGO representatives who formally participated in a Global Forum and informally did their best as lobbyists. Only a minority of these NGOs had official consultative status with ECOSOC.

Consequently, over the years ever more officials and members of NGOs have come into contact with UN affairs or see some reason to seek such connections. In addition, the formation of NGO alliances and coalitions among them—the UN has picked up social science jargon and calls them "networks"—has become a routine response to activities in the UN system.[26]

A salient phenomenon

Evidence of an NGO presence around the IGOs of the UN system alone hardly demonstrates what the Club of Rome has called "the barefoot revolution" and the Worldwatch Institute has called "people power."[27] Instead, both external and internal factors can be cited in what has become a salient phenomenon in international policymaking and execution.

The first and perhaps most important explanation of NGO expansion is the end of the Cold War. With the breakdown of ideological and social orthodoxy, the reluctance of many, perhaps most, diplomats and UN practitioners to interact with nongovernmental staff evaporated. This has opened new possibilities of communication and cooperation within decision-making processes. With the waning of East-West tensions, the United Nations has become a better forum for the reconciliation of views among governments on the old geopolitical compass of North-South-East-West. The UN also has become an obvious forum for discussions between governments and NGOs. "Before it was not possible to have any contact with nongovernmental organizations in the Soviet Union, for example, because this would be seen as neo-imperialist intervention," said UN secretary-general Boutros Boutros-Ghali. "On the other side, it was called communist intervention."[28]

The explanation goes beyond procedures. Issues recognized in the revealing light of the post–Cold War world as extending beyond and below state borders also needed and demanded the strengths of NGOs. As part of a major reappraisal of the role of the state and of alternative ways to solve problems, NGOs are emerging as a special set of organizations that are private in their form but public in their purpose.[29] The environment, grassroots development, more equitable trade relations, human rights, and women's issues had been on NGO agendas throughout the last two or three decades. But now they have assumed new vitality. Additional pressures for NGO involvement grew around such new issues as investment needs of the erstwhile socialist bloc and ethno-nationalism, with its accompanying flood of refugees and internally displaced persons. These issues simply could not be addressed solely through intergovernmental operations and recommendations characteristic of the United Nations.[30]

Moreover, when high politics and security, particularly over nuclear issues, dominated the international agenda, NGOs were at a comparative disadvantage. They obviously had no weapons and only limited access to people wielding decision-making power. As low politics rose on the international agenda, NGOs that had promoted relevant policies and actions energetically exploited or expanded direct access to policymakers. For example, NGOs not only have a capacity for direct action but they may also bring advanced knowledge to bear on such issues as gender, the environment, AIDS, relief assistance, human rights, and community development.

Technological developments represent a second explanation for the increasing salience of NGOs in UN activity. "[New] technologies increasingly render information barriers either ineffective or economically infeasible."[31] Governments that are hostile to NGOs fail in their sometimes zealous efforts to prevent information flows, interaction and networking through the Internet and fax communications. Electronic means have literally made it possible to ignore borders and to create the kinds of communities based on common values and objectives that were once almost the exclusive prerogative of nationalism.[32]

Modern communications technology is independent of territory. "By providing institutional homes in the same way that states have accommodated nationalism," one observer suggests, "NGOs are the inevitable beneficiaries of the emergence of the new global communities."[33] Consequently, global social change organizations (GSCOs), another study claims, "may represent a unique social invention of the postmodern, postindustrial, ie information-rich and service-focused, globally-linked world system."[34]

A third explanatory factor can be found in the growing resources and professionalism of NGOs. Both indigenous and transnational NGOs have recently attracted additional resources from individual donors, governments, and the UN system. In 1994 over 10 percent of public development aid ($8 billion) was channelled through NGOs, surpassing the volume of the combined UN system ($6 billion) without the Washington-based financial institutions. About 25 percent of US assistance is channelled through NGOs; at the Social Summit in Copenhagen, Vice-President Al Gore committed Washington to increasing this figure to 50 percent by the turn of the century.[35] Western governments have increasingly turned toward NGO projects on the basis of a reputation for cost-effectiveness.

This trend fits well with the progressively declining funds for foreign assistance and generally with domestic pressures in donor countries to cut back on overseas commitments. In fact, two prominent analysts have recently written: "The increase of donor-funded NGO relief operations and Western disengagement from poor countries are two sides of the same coin."[36]

Interorganizational relations in the NGO realm

Networking is perhaps a cliché in the lexicon of transnational organization, but it aptly points to a key function of many NGOs: the process of creating bonds, sometimes formal but primarily informal, among like-minded individuals and groups across state boundaries. New communications technologies are helping to foster the kinds of interaction and relationships that were once unthinkable except through expensive air travel. Scaling up certain kinds of transnational efforts from neighborhoods and regions to the global level and scaling down to involve grassroots organizations are no longer logistic impossibilities, but may be treated as institutional imperatives.

Claims about NGOs eclipsing the role of the state are exaggerated, but significant change is nonetheless taking place regarding their weight in world politics. NGOs may "create conditions that facilitate the formation of international institutions" and "reinforce the norms promoted by these institutions through public education as well as through organized attempts to hold states accountable to these, and enhance institutional effectiveness by reducing the implementation costs associated with international institutions." Moreover, the potential for enhanced networking increases the "capacity to monitor states' compliance with international agreements, promote institutional adaptation and innovation, and challenge failed institutions."[37]

NGOs that have relations with IGOs go far beyond the officially sanctioned diplomatic networks and the narrowly defined contacts implied by a legalistic approach. NGOs are based upon interpersonal ties and relationships among people with similar convictions, goals, and interests. The result is a web of personal connections that do not fit within a formal, legal framework.

NGOs employ a variety of devices to increase the persuasiveness and efficiency of their work in conjunction with IGOs. Some of these have formal structures, while others rely primarily on interpersonal relationships. Some are constructed for service with only one UN organization, while others have a more general scope across the UN system. Four types of interorganizational devices that involve NGOs—formal bridging groups, federations, UN coordinating bureaus, and connections to governments—can be identified. Aside from these fairly defined structures, many NGOs coordinate their activities with others for a specific issue or within a particular geographical area. These occurrences may be formal but are probably usually informal and may last only briefly. There is a variety of mechanisms for NGOs to relate collectively to the UN system. Probably the best known coordination mechanisms are represented by the World Bank within its own investment or aid projects, or by the United Nations Development Programme within a country-wide framework. Many NGOs coordinate their own activities for a specific issue or within a particular geographical area through formal coalitions and these, too, should be considered in understanding NGOs and the United Nations.

Some NGOs have a long institutional history or are part of federations of the organizations that they represent. Others get together only for particular issues for short periods. In either form, NGO coalitions seek to represent the views of their constituent members and to pursue shared goals. Examples would be the International Council of Voluntary Agencies (ICVA) in Geneva, originally for European NGOs but now composed primarily of Third World ones; InterAction in Washington, DC, for US-based NGOs; or a gathering of the various Oxfams or country chapters of Médecins Sans Frontières (MSF). Within a recipient country where UN organizations operate, there sometimes exist umbrella groups for indigenous NGOs—for example, Coordinación in Guatemala facilitates contacts between external donors and local groups working with uprooted populations. Within a region there can also exist a similar pooling of efforts—for example, Concertación links development NGOs in five Central American countries.

A main function of formal coalitions of NGOs is to develop as far as possible or to harmonize common positions for issues. Some examples are the lobbying efforts within the United States for the extension of Public Law 480, the source of foodstuffs for relief and development; or the search for a common stance by women's groups for international conferences on human rights in Vienna and on population in Cairo. Concrete examples include an invitation to ICVA to address the Executive Committee of the UN High Commissioner for Refugees (UNHCR), and a request to EarthAction (one of the largest global NGO networks with over 700 member associations in about 125 countries) to put forward views to the Commission on Global Governance.

These formal coalitions may attempt headquarters-level coordination of activities within a certain region or in relationship to a specific crisis, as for example, Somalia and Rwanda. Member NGOs of formal groups are not, however, bound by organizational decisions, and dissenters are free to follow their own counsel or take individual positions on policies of IGOs.

"Bridging organizations," created for service in developing countries, seek on one hand to create both horizontal links across economic and social sectors and vertical links between grassroots organizations and governments. On the other hand, they try to form similar links to external donors, whether governmental, intergovernmental, or nongovernmental.

Constituent NGOs working in different sectors can interact in these bridging organizations that furnish what otherwise would be absent—a forum for discussion and cooperation. As a consequence, grassroots groups get a voice and attempt to influence policymaking. Bridging organizations function as a conduit for ideas and innovations, a source of information, a broker of resources, a negotiator of deals, a conceptualizer of strategies, and a mediator of conflicts. Such organization, it is argued, helps lead to sustainable development.[38] Examples of such bridging organizations include the Asian NGO Coalition for Agrarian Reform and Rural Development (ANGOC Asia), the Society for Participatory Research in Asia (PRIA), Savings Development Movement (SDM, Zimbabwe), and the Urban Popular Movement and the Coalition of Earthquake Victims (MUP and CUD, Mexico City).

Relief operations, and to a lesser extent development efforts, have drawn together in-country consortia of local and international NGOs with the support of donors. These groupings are often shaped to accommodate a division of labor for a geographical region or for a function like transport.[39] The Khartoum-based Emergency Relief Desk, for example, was backed by a number of European religious NGOs and then reorganized and adapted to help crossborder operations into Eritrea and Tigray.[40] In the southern Sudan, the combined Agency Relief Team was established in the mid-1980s as a relief transport consortium.[41]

Save the Children, Oxfam, Amnesty International, MSF, the International Federation of Red Cross and Red Crescent Societies (IFRC), and CARE are examples of large NGOs with a global scope and autonomous chapters in individual countries. Organizational members of a federation share an overall image and ideology. For example, Oxfam's ideology sets out a grassroots development orientation that all its national affiliates employ. But the national groups are responsible for their own fundraising and projects. Although members of such federations meet periodically at both the management and working levels to discuss common problems, each national member maintains autonomy.

Federations of NGOs try to, and frequently do, present a united front on the policies that they advocate in IGOs and in their field operations. Yet this is not always possible because of differences in view and leadership styles, and the needs in respective country branch offices and headquarters. Federations differ in how much control they can exert over their branches and how much branch activity can be coordinated with worldwide partners as well as how they finance administrative costs for common activities.

For example, Save the Children US has limited coordination with its European partners, and there is little consensus about how to address this rift. Save the Children UK does not necessarily wish to increase coordination, but the US headquarters seeks to increase interaction to improve cost-effectiveness. Also, some Save the Children branches and projects have different emphases and agendas. For example, Save the Children Sweden acts as a sort of Amnesty International for children, focusing on child abuse and child advocacy to a greater extent than other chapters do.

Large federations with headquarters and many branches face the tension of accountability versus autonomy and independent action by their many satellites. Friction rises when branch offices stray from a supposedly common vision of a federation or engage in controversial or unprofessional activities. These could have negative repercussions for other chapters. At the same time, imposing constraints on branch offices may be impossible and may risk sacrificing independent and innovative thinking and acting.

In contrast to the conventional Roman wisdom of divide and conquer, UN officials concerned about the proliferation of nongovernmental entities have responded with the attitude: "If you can't beat 'em, organize 'em." The efforts by the World Bank, the UNHCR, and the UNDP to structure project relationships are probably the best known.[42] UN organizations vary not only in how they coordinate their activities with NGOs but also in the extent to which they work with NGOs in the first place. When no formal structures for coordination exist, cooperation often proceeds on a case-by-case basis. Even with the existence of formal mechanisms, coordination is often ad hoc, based on individual relationships. Especially in crises, coordination may occur spontaneously. Nevertheless, NGOs are notorious for their independence; coordinating NGOs is "like herding cats," according to one UN official.

Cooperation is not cost-free for NGOs. From a logical management perspective, for example, the current systems for development cooperation or humanitarian action have too many moving parts.[43] Greater collaboration among the various agencies would appear at first glance to be helpful in limiting random activity, overlap, and duplication. Yet, assuming it could be arranged, even improved coordination may involve significant opportunity costs for NGOs in terms of use of personnel and resources or even diminished credibility because of their association with the United Nations. There is no guarantee of greater effectiveness or savings. As James Ingram, the former executive director of the World Food Programme (WFP), has written: "The appearance of improved coordination at the center is not necessarily a factor in more effective and timely interventions in the field."[44] Hence, formal UN-led efforts at coordination, comprehensive or not, are not viewed by NGO leaders as always desirable.

Such coordinating bodies in fact have a mixed record for viability and effectiveness. They have often struggled to find funding, a task that is more than a mere forum for endless NGO meetings.[45] If the main concern is effectiveness, then both formal and informal coordinating should be able to increase contact and collaboration among NGOs (exchange ideas and information); provide genuine services to members; improve liaison with governments and the UN system; and increase resources available for NGOs.

An intriguing question arises as to why certain operational IGOs—observers point to UNICEF and the UNHCR—cooperate easily with NGOs while others experience considerably more difficulty. The structures, charters, and goals of these UN organizations play a part, but more intangible elements such as organizational culture are among the plausible explanations.

A significant number of staff in both UNICEF and the UNHCR have themselves worked in NGOs and appreciate their strengths and weaknesses. The rough-and-ready, roll-up-the-sleeves approach to disasters also makes cooperation seem more necessary and sensible than in other contexts, where the lack of an emergency permits more time and leisure for turf battles.

On a more political level, one possible explanation for easy cooperation is complementary tasks. For example, in election monitoring within UN-orchestrated operations in El Salvador and Cambodia, NGOs could more easily make public pronouncements about irregularities than could the civilian or military staff of the UN Observer Mission in El Salvador and the UN Transition Authority in Cambodia. In such circumstances, rather than rivalry, a sensible division of labor appeared between NGOs and IGOs. For some of the same reasons, discernible complementarity has developed between Amnesty International or Human Rights Watch and the United Nations. Because NGOs can push harder and more openly for more drastic changes, which can then be codified over time by the UN, a "symbiotic" relationship has developed in the context of establishing new human rights standards and implementing existing ones.[46]

Some participants view the coordination effort launched in the early 1990s by the UNHCR and ICVA as promising. It is titled PARinAC (Partners in Action) and is intended to "enhance dialogue and understanding between UNHCR; to facilitate closer collaboration and increase the combined capacity to respond to the global refugee problem and . . . the problem of internal displacement." PARinAC aims to "enhance and improve future NGO/UNHCR collaboration," and is motivated by the UNHCR'S belief that NGOs have a "community-based approach [that] is an asset in bridging the gap between relief and development."[47] Behind the official language lies the intense field experience of Bosnia and elsewhere in the former Yugoslavia and northern Iraq as well as the belief among some leading participants that earlier contact mechanisms delivered less than was hoped.

The relationships between governments and NGOs take several forms. Some of these are adversarial, as certain NGOs criticize and hope to change governmental policies. Other relationships are cooperative and businesslike. Host governments regulate activities by NGOs through domestic legislation and activities of international NGOs by administrative procedures (for example, visas and foreign exchange procedures). Donor governments hire NGOs to implement projects and sign contracts subject to national legislation. NGOs may lobby governments for altruistic reasons, such as new international agreements and policies, and for more self-serving reasons, such as increased budgetary allocations for their own work. In the process, they must abide by national regulations governing such activity. In some extraordinary situations, NGOs have provided services to citizens that are normally expected from governments. For example, the primary education system in the north of Sri Lanka was coordinated largely by NGOs after the government system collapsed following the onset of civil war in 1987; and the Bangladesh Rural Action Committee is responsible for 35,000 schools.

In general, throughout much of the Third and former Second World, the decline of oppressive regimes and the rise of democracy mainly since the end of the Cold War has tempered the former automatic hostility by governments toward the activities of local and international NGOs. Previously, NGO-government relationships were often ones of benign neglect at best, or of suspicion and outright hostility at worst.

One noteworthy international experiment in combining intergovernmental and nongovernmental action in a coordinated policy and resource mobilization for refugees and internally displaced populations took place in the early 1990s when the International Conference on Refugees in Central America (CIREFCA) brought together UN organizations and the NGO community.[48] With the UNHCR in the lead, such organizations as the UNDP and the WFP were brought into greater contact with external and local NGOs.

Actual and potential beneficiaries were involved from the outset in project design, implementation, and monitoring. The process induced governmental, intergovernmental, and nongovernmental organizations to forge new relationships with one another as well as with dissident and insurgent groups outside internationally recognized governments. This wider orchestration also took into consideration the activities of the various UN peacekeeping and peacemaking operations.

Finances, size, and independence

The relationship between governments and NGOs includes many complexities and rapid changes that sometimes run parallel to the pluralism permitted by governments. Most governments that decide to do so have little difficulty in crippling NGO activities or favoring those that increase governmental capacity either to do harm or to provide popular benefits. Foreign-based NGOs may be particularly vulnerable to host government pressure since they need permission to bring in personnel and goods, such as automobiles and communications equipment. Relief NGOs that must import large quantities of supplies, as was repeatedly demonstrated in the Horn of Africa during the two decades beginning in the 1970s, can encounter direct limitations emanating from political authorities, either in the host government or in insurgent territory.

At the same time, some NGOs operating outside of their base countries have reached formidable proportions. Agencies such as CARE or Oxfam have enough prestige not to be easily or silently dismissed with the wave of an authoritative hand. Some have programs that, once begun, burrow deep into the social fabric. To liquidate such activities can cost a government popularity and even stimulate resistance. Moreover, development NGOs may have close working relationships and direct support from IGOs, thereby raising the potential that a local incident of interference can become a matter of unpleasant discussion in an international forum. In addition, other NGOs have impressive bases of popular support. Repressive governments, for instance, intensely dislike the activities of human rights monitoring groups and try to inhibit them. Yet such interference is also restrained by the sure knowledge that these groups have developed the ability to persuade powerful governments in Western countries. Thus, a government or an insurgent group that acts in an unrestrained manner against human rights monitors may soon be faced with formal protests and action through bilateral or intergovernmental channels.

The vigor of NGO activities may ultimately be determined by the levels and sources of their finances. Some of the largest NGOs, such as the International Committee of the Red Cross and CARE, rely on contributions from governments of rich countries for most of their operating funds. As much as 90 percent of financing emanates from governments. The World Bank has entered into numerous partnerships with DONGOS that execute projects financed by the International Bank for Reconstruction and Development. In 1993, for example, 30 percent of World Bank projects had provisions for NGO participation.[49] The UNDP has changed policy over the last decade so that local NGOs are receiving allocations in the indicative planning figures that used to be exclusively reserved for governments. The depth of such relationships, however, may vary from formal to close collaboration in phases from planning to execution.

Many organizations of the UN system routinely rely upon both international and indigenous NGOs for the delivery of relief and development assistance. For instance, in northern Iraq since the April 1991 Kurdish crisis, NGOs (including the Red Cross) have been responsible for 40 percent of refugees, whereas the UN system has been responsible for about 30 percent.[50]

Putting an exact dollar value on these resources is not easy. It would be hard to prove the contention that "[i]n net terms, NGOs now collectively transfer more resources to the South than the World Bank."[51] Over time, however, shifts of a significant magnitude have taken place. During the last two decades, private grants from the 21 Western countries of the Development Assistance Committee (DAC) to DAC-country NGOs for use in developing countries have grown dramatically. NGO activities represent well over 10 percent (perhaps even 13 percent) of official development assistance (ODA) in comparison with only 0.2 percent in 1970.[52] Particularly over the last decade, when ODA has stagnated, NGOs have positioned themselves for a greater proportional share of total resources. Moreover, the visibility and credibility of such efforts have increased dramatically.

From another direction, private foundations have increasingly stimulated the growth of NGOs and added to the knowledge base for their work.[53] Favorable tax laws and a tradition of voluntarism have made this influence particularly important in the United States, where the family names of Ford, Rockefeller, MacArthur, and Pew are familiar philanthropic entities. In fact, 5,500 independent foundations, not including those from corporations, have assets in excess of $2 million or give grants of at least $200,000 per year.[54] Such institutions as the Volkswagen Foundation attest to the significance of this type of source in other parts of the Western world as well. Although the exact numbers are difficult to gauge, many directly finance operational activities, institution building, and research by NGOs at home and in connection with partners in other countries.

All NGOs and foundation donors operate under some governmental, donor-imposed or doctrinal restrictions. Especially in the United States, foundations owe their prosperity to provisions of tax laws that could be changed. They are also forbidden to act in electoral and other political spheres, and may not lobby in the way that special interest groups do. As for NGOs receiving outside governmental or IGO financing, these set out in program proposals their plans for using funds. Proposals for programs that ran counter to donor policies would hardly be likely to succeed.

Conversely, NGOs dispose of some persuasiveness in relations with donors, whether official or private. No donor would wish to invest in a program that was foredoomed to failure. NGOs can thus signal their estimate of the practicality of policies. Moreover, once embarked on the execution of an agreed project, the NGO is in a good position to suggest policy and methodological changes, if only because the donors prefer their funds to be used in ways that can be defended against criticism.

Theories of international cooperation

Despite the rapidly rising curve of NGO numbers and activity in the context of the UN system, a firm consensus about their nature and function remains elusive. Consequently, some generalizing about NGOs that operate in the international environment is necessary for a better understanding of NGO roles, but it is larded with uncertainty. The rest of this essay takes up some of the theoretical approaches that pertain to NGOs and sets out a set of dimensions that may be useful in drawing conclusions.

In general, theoretical approaches to explain international cooperation provide little specific insight into the nature and function of NGOs. Most are based on the state as the only noteworthy entity in international cooperation, and provide no category for considering the possibility that NGOs are significant actors in their own right.

The dominant approaches employed by governmental representatives, international officials, and academic scholars to transnational cooperation emphasize states as the basic units of analysis.[55] Officials usually leave this assumption in implicit form, although international civil servants constantly underline the role of member states in their organizations. Academic scholars of this persuasion quite explicitly use the state as the basic counter, although biodiversity is increasingly obvious for a category that cannot be captured by narrow nations.[56]

Since the state stands by definition, not to speak of ideology, as an autonomous organization in a universe where only consensual limits to action are accepted as binding, an explanation is needed as to why they sometimes cooperate. Two main possibilities, both based on promotion of national interest, emerge.

The first is that cooperation among states is actually induced by the use of persuasion or coercion by one state over another.[57] This line of argument accords with analyses that set out mainly military power as the final arbiter of international relations. No state finds it in its interest to be expunged or defeated militarily, and therefore it eventually bows to superior force, whether it is latent or applied. Thus, a hierarchy based on military calculation in fact reigns among nominally equal states. This approach, incidentally, accords with much of the rhetoric of diplomats and foreign policy specialists.

The second explanation relies implicitly or explicitly on a market rather than a military calculation.[58] States cooperate in the search for material advantages. Thus, they reckon whether there is more to gain from cooperation than from withdrawal or conflict. If they do not cooperate, in all but a few instances coercion to do so is absent.

This line of reasoning is the basis for the extensive academic theorizing about international regimes.[59] These institutions for international governance, based on the voluntary acceptance of rules of state conduct in regard to specific issues, do not require explicit international organizations or even formal international accords, but they continue over extended periods of time as the actual guides to state policy. Thus, international regimes do not necessarily always have much relationship to the organizations of the UN system, even though their concerns may overlap.

Paralleling these approaches is the conventional legal approach to NGOs.[60] This depends on the exercise of authority by states, on the consent of states as the basis of application of rules, and on the notion of some type of self-interest as the underlying reason for acceding to cooperative arrangements. International organizations are treated ultimately as creatures of national self-interest, however, and by whomever that is defined. NGOs fit into this scheme of thinking as entities whose activities have to be regulated to conform to the broader undertakings of states.

Even if it is accepted that the state is the primary unit of international relations, the political and legal explanations based on self-interest leave little room for autonomous NGO activity. If such theoretical approaches are made more sophisticated by incorporating considerations of domestic political processes as the determinant of national interest, a focus on transnational NGO activity in shaping decisions is usually left distant or obscured. Moreover, the national self-interest approaches imply a crisp consensus within governments as to the degree of international cooperation and its desired outcome. Whether this can be demonstrated empirically is subject to doubt. Finally, the implicit emphasis of rational decision-making on the basis of national interest draws attention away from the social bases of the state. The state is an abstraction. Governments, not states, actually make decisions to cooperate or not. Governments consist of people, a point that NGOs obviously do not neglect.

A different and less widely accepted approach to international cooperation emphasizes the social bases of politics.[61] It begins with the proposition that governments are social organs made up of people who have complex relationships with other parts of their own and other societies. It is presumed that these relationships may have a bearing on the decisions taken by governments as the vital representation of states to involve themselves in international cooperation.

Among such approaches, organization theory has general application but has been infrequently used as the basis for research on international cooperation.[62] This theory abandons the traditional view of organizations as formal and self-contained units. It is concerned with relations between formally autonomous organizations with diffuse accountability and division of responsibility, whether in the national or international arenas. Such relations typically involve interorganizational bargaining where informal organization is of the essence.

Organization theory posits that organizations are made up of people who work together to produce a particular product by means of a relevant technique. From this base, propositions can be developed to analyze at least subgovernmental units, if not governments as a whole, as well as international agencies and NGOs. It asks what people are involved, what joint work they perform, what methods they use, and what emerges from their work. Such analyses can also trace changes taking place in organizations and their products.

Organizations, moreover, can be bound together to form new organizations, or what could be termed meta-organizations. International organizations such as the UN system, for instance, can be viewed as such meta-organizations, as can federations of NGOs. This notion necessarily involves interorganizational relationships that have great importance at the international level and in particular in connection with NGOs. But these relationships are carried on by people, rather than by abstractions, just as is the case within organizations made up only of individuals.

A commonplace of organizational analysis holds that informal links among organizational participants congeal alongside formal structures. This is a phenomenon that every diplomat and political leader acknowledges by seeking personal contacts with people who have ability to persuade within their own circles. Informal links often prove to be essential to organizational work, adaptation to changing conditions, and continued existence. In transnational organizational relationships, which include those formed by NGOs, it is natural that a web of informal links develops to confront issues defined in the formal structures.

This points in the direction of network analysis, which focuses on the links between interdependent actors. Formal organizations—private and public, national and international—form the foundation of transnational networks. However, participants in networks are not organizations in their entirety but certain individuals in the constituent organizations. The interface between organizations consists primarily of boundary-role occupants. As "activist brokers" between their organization and its environment, boundary-role occupants must represent the organization to its environment, and also represent the environment to their constituents.[63]

Students of networks have pointed to the centrality of so-called linking-pin organizations, which occupy central positions in terms of being reachable from and being able to reach most other organizations in the network. Serving as brokers and communication channels between organizations in the networks, linking-pin organizations are the "nodes through which a network is loosely joined."[64] One research question is to what extent NGOs have been able to assume linking-pin positions in transnational networks.

The sophisticated conceptual device of the social network has found little use in research on international cooperation. What exactly are the durable sets of relationships among individuals who are in a position to exchange information, resources, and prestige? Individuals in this position in interorganizational relationships can usually be described as occupying boundary roles. In that role, they can easily be engaged in the activities characterized as a social network, which affect their own organizations as well. Thus, a transnational social network would depend on persons from different countries and organizations who engage in their relationships over a considerable period. The network, then, is defined by what it does, not by an organizational form, defined structure, or material appurtenances.

In brief, networks represent flat or horizontal organizational forms in contrast to vertical ones based on hierarchical authority. Networks, in other words, rest on the coexistence of autonomy and interdependence. Whereas hierarchy is the natural organizing principle of states, and markets are the natural organizing principle of business organizations, networks are readily associated with NGOs.[65] By positioning themselves centrally in informal networks, NGOs can exert an influence above and beyond their weak formal status. In the international arena, these possibilities are enhanced because effective cooperation among states operating in an anarchic environment often implies precisely the kind of informality and network building that work well for NGOs. Although network analysis requires the assembly of detailed data and sometimes lengthy observation, it would seem a most promising technique for analyzing the function of transnational NGOs.

Another socially-oriented analytical concept that has been applied to international cooperation is that of the epistemic community.[66] This notion seeks to explain changes in the programs and doctrines of international organizations through the operation of transnational sets of experts. Their common vision on the proper outlook on a set of issues—protection of the environment has featured most prominently—underlies their efforts to capture existing organizations and redirect their work. Their persuasiveness derives from consensual knowledge growing from advanced technological competence. It eventually convinces other leaders and organizational managers. This concept, too, would appear to be relevant to a better understanding of NGOs, although its emphasis on technological expertness may limit its appropriateness to a narrow range of issues.

An even less formally organized type of participant in international policy and administrative processes is composed of prominent persons who, by dint of expertise, experience, office, or other distinguishing characteristic, earn deference. They may be asked to serve on honorific official commissions and as highly expert technical consultants on defined issues. Many have high visibility and credibility from their previous tenure in senior positions in governments and parliaments, or from their reputations as insightful intellectuals. Some work on their own accounts, others for governments, corporations, universities, and specialist firms. Some of the assignments are ongoing, some are for a fixed period. Their tasks are sometimes performed for immediate consumption by UN organizations but also with an eye on other consumers in a broader public. Examples are the members of the UN Advisory Committee on the Peaceful Uses of Atomic Energy (appointed by Dag Hammarskjöld) or Max van der Stoel, former foreign minister of the Netherlands, who was appointed by the Commission on Human Rights as rapporteur on human rights in Iraq. Such "influentials," with or without official appointments, are often consulted informally by opinion leaders and national and international officials.

An increasingly common practice has been to ask such prominent individuals to serve as members of high-visibility ad hoc commissions—those headed by Willy Brandt, Olaf Palme, Gro Harlem-Brundtland, Sadruddin Aga Khan, Julius Nyerere and, most recently, by Ingmar Carlsson and Sonny Ramphal are perhaps the best known.[67] They constitute visible groups that come together for short-term specialized advisory assignments. Their work has much in common with the efforts of educational NGOs. Other groups of less prominent professionals—not just Médecins Sans Frontières but also, for instance, architects and physicists without borders—attempt to make their collective views known in international policy circles and among broader publics. Parliamentarians for Global Action is one such pooling of politicians who have a primary interest in global problem-solving and in the United Nations.

Broad roles for NGOs

These theoretical approaches to international cooperation could aid in analyzing NGO activity and in reaching conclusions, but none of them appears fully apt for an investigation that emphasizes concrete activities and observation born of participation. Rather, it might be better to base such an examination on a close scrutiny of goals, relationships among various organizations, and operating methods. This may eventually lead to more general conclusions about the weight and scope of NGO participation in international cooperation. An initial sorting sets out two general roles that reflect both goals and operating methods. Few if any NGOs are likely at all times to set out goals and use methods that are confined exclusively to these discrete categories, but this broad typology can help point out their main thrust.

At least part of the activities of most NGOs falls into the category of operations. Operational NGOs are the most numerous and have the easiest fund-raising task. They are more and more central to international responses in the post–Cold War world. Most NGOs provide some services, if only to their members, while others concentrate on providing them to other organizations and individuals. The delivery of services is the mainstay of most NGO budgets and the basis for enthusiastic support from a wide range of donors. Such services include intangible technical advice as well as more tangible resources for relief, development, and other purposes. Many NGOs operate development programs; they have become increasingly active in migration and disaster relief, which may now be their most important operational or advisory activities in total financial terms.

Bilateral and multilateral government organizations are relying upon NGOs more and more as project subcontractors. Some of these contractors, known as DONGOS, could be dedicated organizations and even disappear after the conclusion of a project. Others have long histories as contractors. NGOs recover their staff costs and overheads in addition to the direct costs of the products that they deliver but, unlike private contractors, they do not make a profit to redistribute since there are no shareholders. Some NGO managers are delighted with this trend since it expands the scope of their activities with increased resources. Others, however, are troubled about being exploited by governments or intergovernmental organizations rather than remaining institutions with their own unique purposes and independent wherewithal.

Such contractual relationships on the one hand offer opportunities to NGOs to persuade donors to adopt their approaches; but on the other hand they include powerful incentives in the form of financial support to accede to the views of donor organizations. The key to operational integrity is being a partner and not simply a contractor. The former term connotes authentic collaboration and mutual respect, and it accepts the autonomy and pluralism of NGOs. Such relationships are rare, more an aspiration than a reality.[68] It is difficult to imagine NGOs enjoying authentic collaboration and genuine partnership with large and powerful agencies. However, in certain circumstances and as mentioned earlier, there seems to be a greater possibility with more sympathetic funders such as UNICEF and the UNHCR.[69]

The targets of operational NGOs are beneficiaries (or victims in emergencies), whereas those for educational and advocacy NGOs are their own contributors, the public, and decision makers. Educational NGOs seek primarily to influence citizens, whose voices are then registered through public opinion and bear fruit in the form of additional resources for their activities as well as new policies, better decisions, and enhanced international regimes. They often play a leading role in promoting the various dedication of "days," "years," and "decades" that the UN system regularly proclaims. NGOs can help to reinforce various norms promoted by intergovernmental organizations through public education campaigns. This heightened awareness among public audiences can then help hold states accountable for their international commitments.[70]

Western operational NGOs are under growing pressure from their Third World partners to educate contributors and Western publics about the root causes of poverty and violence. This logic is driving some organizations to adapt to such harsh criticism as the following: "Conventional NGO project activities are manifestly 'finger-in-the-dike' responses to problems that require nothing short of worldwide and whole-hearted governmental commitment to combat."[71] Hand-in-hand with operational activities is the need to educate populations and mobilize public opinion about the requirements for fundamental alterations in the global order.

Educational NGOs direct activities toward a broad public or toward specifically differentiated publics in order to persuade them to voice opinions on governmental policies in international organizations. The primary tool of the educational and advocacy NGO is collecting and disseminating information, which sometimes incorporates a high degree of expertness and sometimes consists of mainly emotional appeals.

Educational as well as other varieties of NGOs can be distinguished from social movements,[72] even if the aims and methods are sometimes similar. The former are organizations with visible structures, are generally tolerated as parts of the polity and can make sure that their interests are represented in decision processes.

Social movements, in contrast, have loose or skimpy structures to give effect to a rather spontaneous coming together of people who seek to achieve a social goal that may include changing or preserving aspects of society. One or more NGOs may be associated with social movements but do not define or direct them.

Linked to education are the related concerns of NGOs working primarily in the corridors of governments and intergovernmental organizations. Using a distinctive venue for advocacy, these organizations aim at contributing to international agenda-setting, the design of programs, and overall supervision of international organization activities. They do so by seeking discussions with national delegates and staff members of international secretariats. Under some circumstances they can make formal statements before UN deliberative organs, and they frequently submit documentation for use by government representatives. In the corridors of UN organizations, they offer expertise, research, drafting, and even mediation to governmental representatives and organizational staff. In doing so, the NGO representatives hope to promote acceptance of their positions, which involve adjustment or change of policies.

These advocates pursue discussions with national delegates and staff members of international secretariats in order to influence international public policy. Calling this activity "lobbying" is perhaps an accurate image but an inaccurate description according to dictionary definitions. In seeking to alter the policies of governments as well as of governmental, intergovernmental, and nongovernmental agencies, these NGOs seek to influence all policymakers, not only legislators.

Rather than aiming at beneficiaries or the general public, as is the case for the operational and educational types, advocacy NGOs target key decision makers in parliaments as well as in governments and intergovernmental secretariats. Because they have a direct impact on international responses, advocacy NGOs have the most difficulty raising funds.

NGO advocacy may be generally described as unofficial participation by internal and external modes.[73] Internal modes can be observed in capitals and domestic arenas. They include such things as pressure on a government to participate in a treaty-making effort; formation of domestic coalitions and the mobilization of public opinion to influence the positions a state takes during treaty negotiations; public pressure on a government to sign a treaty; and using the strengths and weaknesses of a country's domestic system to challenge governments, companies, and others to comply.

External modes consist of urging the United Nations or one of its associated agencies to add an issue to the agenda; gathering data to help frame or define a problem or a threat in ways that influence the work of official UN-sanctioned conferences; and contributing to the implementation of treaties by assisting countries without expertise to meet their obligations. Through formal statements in UN forums and through informal negotiations with international civil servants and members of national delegations, advocacy NGOs seek to ensure that their positions, and those of their constituencies, find their way into international texts and decisions. They sometimes offer their research and drafting skills, and they provide scientific or polling data to support their positions.[74] Also, first-hand reports and testimony from field staff can be powerful tools before parliamentary committees.

External functions generally require mobilization across state boundaries. Independent researchers and scholars, usually as part of transnational networks, contribute theoretical arguments or empirical evidence in favor of a particular response. This information is used by NGOs and helps build coalitions of individuals and groups that otherwise would not join forces.

A great deal of past NGO advocacy has been directed against government and UN policy. An important evolution is that a growing number of NGOs are eager to institutionalize a "full-fledged partnership with the governmental members of the United Nations."[75] Historically NGOs have had some responsibility for treaty implementation, but they may aspire to a more direct involvement in treaty making. Some NGOs have contributed substantially to international agenda setting, as at the San Francisco conference in April 1945, where NGOs played a pivotal role in securing the inclusion of human rights language in the final draft of the UN Charter. In fact, they have spurred action since the middle of the nineteenth century at each stage in the evolution of international protection for human rights.[76]

As with the venerable debate over the impact of the media on foreign policy, there is disagreement about NGO influence on governmental responses. However, NGOs that seek government policy change can be crucial for the timing and nature of international responses, even in such controversial arenas as civil wars. NGOs in the United States, for example, failed to get the Clinton administration to acknowledge genocide and to take action in Rwanda in April and May 1994, but eventually they were more successful in getting the Pentagon to help in Zaire and Tanzania. For three years, many US NGOs encouraged a robust enough military invasion to restore the elected government of Jean-Bertrand Aristide in Haiti. In France, NGOs have been successful in launching and sustaining an activist humanitarian policy, *le droit d'ingérence*, which became the official policy of the Mitterrand government and its visible Minister Bernard Kouchner, and which survives both of their departures.[77]

NGOs that focus exclusively on education or advocacy in their own countries without overseas activities are not numerous, but they exist. For example, the Refugee Policy Group, Refugees International, and the US Committee for Refugees all focus on research with a view toward informing the public and altering public policy on people displaced by war. However, many of the most effective educators and advocates are those with the credibility, knowledge, and convictions resulting from substantial operational activities.

Many NGOs that started their work at a project level mitigating the symptoms of problems have moved into attacking the structural roots of those problems. As such, they draw away from an exclusive concern with projects and move toward preventing the need for assistance in the first place. Projects alone cannot promote structural change and prevention. The logic of the shift toward educating the public about the necessity for systemic change moves away from a preoccupation with relief, and is summed up by two observers:

> Many of the causes of underdevelopment lie in the political and economic structures of an unequal world ... and in the misguided policies of governments and the multilateral institutions (such as the World Bank and IMF) which they control. It is extremely difficult, if not impossible, to address these issues in the context of the traditional NGO project.[78]

In these efforts to target officials within governmental and intergovernmental institutions, NGOs can be loud and theatrical, like Médecins Sans Frontières and Greenpeace, or discreet and more subtle, like the International Committee of the Red Cross.

Advocacy is an essential and growing activity. As such, the debate about possible modifications of consultative status in UN forums is important at least for some NGOs. Consultative status provides additional access to and enhanced authority in the eyes of many governments and UN officials.

Political levels and constraints

A complementary or alternative approach to NGO roles depends on identifying relationships among them and their governmental levels of activity.[79] Primary associations are those serving members at the community level; these may be called people's organizations. As their base, scope of operations, and methods are circumscribed, they can be excluded from the group of transnational NGOs with direct relevance to the UN system. Secondary organizations include public-serving groups that operate at the community level as well as federations of member-serving primary associations. Tertiary organizations are those that do not operate at the community level and also comprise federations of secondary organizations. Thus, only public-serving organizations and meta-organizations that they form may be considered as NGOs with transnational significance.

Further distinctions can be drawn between organizations that work at the community level and those that do not. National NGOs that work only within the boundaries of one developing country can be distinguished from international NGOs that are based in developed countries. Refining classificatory factors include constituency, primary functions and activities, ideology/philosophy, scale and coverage, or organizational structure.

NGO interactions may be constrained or facilitated according to the consensus surrounding the issues that they address. Environmental NGOs, for instance, work within an overall and seemingly expanding agreement about protecting the biosphere. Development NGOs, in contrast, are partly sustained by a consensus about the necessity for growth, even though they often encounter significant discord when they begin to threaten elites. Human rights NGOs, however, pursue agendas in which governments, intergovernmental organizations, and NGOs disagree profoundly about goals, ideas, the nature of violations, and appropriate forms of redress. Therefore, NGOs working on the front lines where ethnic cleansing takes place, lobbying for human rights changes, or doing education and advocacy work face different constraints from NGOs struggling to save rain forests or to advance development.

Separate microsystems of issues have their own attributes and exigencies that condition the existence of NGOs. Within each microsystem, the potential for collaboration or conflict by NGOs and the UN is distinct.[80] Moreover, the varied aims and methods of NGOs range from constructive dialogue, that is incrementalism or reform from within, to shouting from the sidelines for revolution, rejection, and nihilism.

Dimensions for analyzing NGOs

An exploration of NGO identities suggests four sets of dimensions: organization, governance, strategies, and output. These dimensions are displayed in Table 10.1 and are discussed in the succeeding paragraphs.

The dimensions are divided into four categories. The first two, organization and governance, have special relevance to locating the site of activities within governing structures and understanding the structures and aims of NGOs. The second two, strategic and output, have to do with the techniques and products of NGOs.

Organizational dimensions

These dimensions are intended to make clear two aspects of NGO existence and operation. The first is where they fit in an organizational framework that extends from the village to the globe, and who supports them. The second aspect concerns their internal arrangements and participation, their resource bases, and their legal status. Membership and financial information make possible comparisons relating to the size of NGOs. Since the legal dimensions of NGOs have had a great deal of attention, they are touched on only briefly in the case studies.

Governance dimensions comprise information about the instruments of governmental policy and program administration with which NGOs come into contact. The subcategory, "Range of Concern," helps distinguish among the characters of the arrangements for governance in which NGOs may participate. For example, a substantial difference in governance may be presumed between a situation in which an NGO simply works as a contractor for a regional intergovernmental agency from one that is involved in the discussion of a new global law-making treaty.

Strategic dimensions set out what NGOs hope to achieve within the organizational and governance dimensions. The emphasis here is on relationships directed inward, i.e., how NGOs choose to relate to IGOs and governments on policy issues and design of projects. They include both the normative basis for action and, under tactical modes, the methods employed for reaching the goals. A wide range of data can be expected by searching out the effects of these dimensions. Along their lines, NGOs differentiate themselves from each other and reinforce their support bases. The tactical modes, however, have primary significance in their relation to the UN system.

TABLE 10.1 NGO dimensions

Organizational dimensions	*Governance dimensions*	*Strategic dimensions*	*Output dimensions*
Geographic range	*Governmental contact*	*Goal definition*	Information
Community	Intergovernmental	Single issue	Expert advice
Subnational	International	Multisectoral	Financing
National	conferences	Broad social	Material goods and
Regional	Regional	Church related	services
Transnational	National	Social ideology	Support for policies
	Subnational	Revolutionary/	Mobilization of
	Community	rejectionist	opinion (leaders
	Informal transnational		and followers)
			Maintenance of
			interorganizational
			relations
			Political feedback
			among govern-
			mental units
			Encouragement of
			networks
			Education of specific
			publics
Support base	*Range of concern*	*Tactical modes*	
Personal memberships	Norm setting	Monitoring	
Other organizations	Policy setting	Advocacy/lobbying	
Quasi-governmental	Policy execution	Mass propaganda	
Mixture of above	Contractor	Mass demonstration	
	Mediation between		
	levels		
Personnel			
Managerial			
Basic research			
Expert and professional			
(applied)			
Undifferentiated			
(popular,			
voluntary)			
Financing			
Membership dues			
Contributions			
Endowment income			
Compensation			
Legal relationships			
General rules			
Regulations			
Ad hoc guidelines			

Output dimensions are framed to make evident the results of NGO activity within the framework of the UN system. They are highly significant in determining whether NGOs can reach their goals. They include a set of products of organizational work that bear on how the UN system reacts and also on how NGOs maintain relationships with one another in reaching their goals. The outputs relate to services delivered to organizational membership as well as to external persons and organizations.

Conclusion

NGOs are omnipresent in the policy and administrative process of UN organizations; the extent of their participation has progressively deepened. The turbulent pluralism of the NGO realm has clearly brought new and unanticipated groups into the process. Without attributing either a positive or negative value to NGO activity, it can nevertheless be recognized as a factor in global governance. Yet this phenomenon, contrary to the conventional assumptions about the virtually exclusive role of governments in international politics, has not been fully described nor adequately encompassed in theoretical approaches.

Defining categories of NGO tasks, their transnational relationships, and the impact of their efforts marks an initial step toward understanding the variety of nongovernmental interactions with the UN system. They form part of a larger set of analytical challenges as the international community gropes and copes with changing world politics and trends toward the decentralization and democratization of global governance. These include a vast variety of cooperative structures and practices that have emerged in and around the United Nations and its associated organizations.

There is an obvious hypothesis: NGOs have been essential in this evolution. Because NGOs, both local and international, increasingly affect world politics, theoretical and practical understandings of NGO activities are intrinsically important. Moreover, they are crucial for comprehending the problems and prospects of the UN system more generally.

Notes

1 *Yearbook of International Associations* (Brussels: Union of International Associations, 1993/94). The actual figure is 16,142, but it is increasing constantly. In fact, the figure more than doubled from 1991. The *OECD Directory of NGOs* (Paris: Organisation for Economic Cooperation and Development, 1991) estimates some 2,500 INGOs in OECD countries in 1990, up from 1,600 a decade earlier. They also estimate some 20,000 local NGOs in developing countries, although the UNDP's *Human Development Report 1994* (New York: Oxford University Press, 1994) estimates that the number is considerably higher, at about 50,000.
2 Commission on Global Governance, *Our Global Neighbourhood* (Oxford: Oxford University Press, 1995), 254.
3 John Clark, *Democratizing Development: The Role of Voluntary Organizations* (Hartford, Conn.: Kumarian Press, 1991), 3.

4 Marc Nerfin, "Neither Prince Nor Merchant: Citizen—an introduction to the third system," *IFDA Dossier* 56 (November/December 1986): 3–29. See also David C. Korten, *Getting to the 21st Century: Voluntary Action and The Global Agenda* (Hartford, Conn.: Kumarian Press, 1990), 95–112.

5 Kathleen D. McCarthy, Virginia Hodgkinson, and Russy Sumariwalla, *The Nonprofit Sector in the United States* (San Francisco: Jossey-Bass, 1992), 3.

6 Thomas Princen and Matthias Finger, *Environmental NGOs in World Politics* (London: Routledge, 1994).

7 James N. Rosenau, *Turbulence in World Politics: A Theory of Continuity and Change* (Princeton, NJ: Princeton University Press, 1990), and *The United Nations in a Turbulent World* (Boulder, Colo.: Lynne Rienner, 1992).

8 The authors are grateful to Christer Jönsson and Peter Söderholm for their formulations.

9 Joseph A Camilleri and Jim Falk, *The End of Sovereignty? The Politics of a Shrinking and Fragmenting World* (Aldershot, UK: Edward Elgar, 1992), 3.

10 Jennifer Wolch, *The Shadow State: Government and Voluntary Sector in Transition* (New York: The Foundation Center, 1990).

11 Brad Smith, President of the Inter-American Foundation, quoted by Mary Morgan, "Stretching the development dollar: the potential for scaling-up," *Grassroots Development* 14, no. 1 (1990): 7.

12 David L Brown and David Korten, *Understanding Voluntary Organizations: Guidelines for Donors*, Working Papers no. 258 (Washington, DC: Country Economics Department, World Bank, September 1989), 22.

13 *UNIFEM Annual Report 1993* (New York: United Nations Development Fund for Women, 1993), 9. See also Stephen P. Marks, "Forgetting the Policies and Practices of the Past: Impunity in Cambodia," *The Fletcher Forum of World Affairs* 18, no. 2 (1994): 17–43; and Jarat Chopra, *United Nations Authority in Cambodia*, Occasional Paper no. 15 (Providence, RI: Watson Institute, 1994).

14 Antonio Donini, "Missions impossibles," *Le Monde des Débats*, July–August 1994, 4.

15 For a useful discussion of the literature about NGOs in the context of teaching international relations, international law, and international organization, see Lawrence T. Woods, "Nongovernmental Organizations and the United Nations System: Reflecting upon the Earth Summit Experience," *Research Note* 18, no. 1 (1993): 9–15.

16 Leland M. Goodrich, Edvard Hambro, and Anne Patricia Simons, *Charter of the United Nations* (New York: Columbia University Press, 1969), 443–6.

17 See United Nations, Economic and Social Council resolutions 3 (II) (1946) and 288 B (X) (1950).

18 Chiang Pei-Heng, *Non-Governmental Organizations at the United Nations: Identity, Role and Function* (New York: Praeger, 1981), 19–57. For historical discussions, see also J. Joseph Lador-Lederer, *International Non-governmental Organizations and Economic Entities: A Study in Autonomous Organization and Ius Gentium* (Leiden: Sythoff, 1963); Borko Stosic, *Les Organisations non Gouvernementales et les Nations Unies* (Geneva: Librarie Droz, 1964); and Lyman C. White, *International Non-Governmental Organizations: Their Purposes, Methods, and Accomplishments* (New Brunswick, NJ: Rutgers University Press, 1951).

19 UN General Assembly resolution 13 (1), Annex I (1946); and ECOSOC resolution 1297 (XLIV).

20 UN, Economic and Social Council, Open-Ended Group on the Review of Arrangements for Consultations with Non-Governmental Organizations, "General Review of Arrangements for Consultations with Non-governmental Organizations," UN document E/AC.70/1994/5, 26 May 1994, 18. Hereafter cited by document number. The ILO tri-partite structure was an earlier precedent.

21 Ibid., 17–18.

22 Ibid., 11.

23 Ibid., 17.

24 Johan Kaufmann and Nico Schrijver, *Changing Global Needs: Expanding Roles of the United Nations System* (Hanover, NH: Academic Council on the United Nations System, 1990), 40–5.

25 See Francesco Mezzalama and Siegfried Schumm, *Working with NGOs: Operational Activities of the United Nations System with Non-governmental Organizations and Governments at the Grassroots and National Levels* (Geneva: Joint Inspection Unit, 1993), document Jiu/REP/93/1.

26 UN document E/AC.70/1994/5, 8.

27 Bertrand Schneider, *The Barefoot Revolution* (London: IT Publishers, 1988); and Alan Durning, "People power and development," *Foreign Policy* 76 (Fall 1989): 66–82.

28 Barbara Crossette, "UN Leader to Call for Changes in Peacekeeping," *New York Times*, 3 January 1995.

29 For a theoretical and empirical investigation, see Lester M. Salamon and Helmut K. Anheier, *The Emerging Sector: An Overview* (Baltimore, Md.: Johns Hopkins University Institute for Policy Studies, 1994).

30 See Jackie Smith, Ron Pagnucco, and Winnie Romeril, "Transnational Social Movement Organizations in the Global Political Arena," *Voluntas* 5, no. 2 (1994): 121–54.

31 Maria Garner, "Transnational Alignment of Nongovernmental Organizations for Global Environmental Action," *Vanderbilt Journal of Transnational Law* 23, no. 5 (1991): 1077.

32 See Benedict Anderson, *Imagined Communities: Reflections on the Origins and Spread of Nationalism* (London: Verso, 1991).

33 Peter Spiro, "New Global Communities: Nongovernmental Organizations in International Decision Making Institutions," *Washington Quarterly* 18, no. 1 (1995): 48.

34 David Cooperrider and William Pasmore, "The Organization Dimension of Global Change," *Human Relations* 44, no. 8 (1991): 764.

35 "NGOs and Conflict: Three Views," *Humanitarian Monitor* 2 (February 1995): 32–3.

36 Rakiya Omaar and Alex de Waal, *Humanitarianism Unbound? Discussion Paper no. 5* (London: African Rights, November 1994), 6.

37 Janie Leatherman, Ron Pagnucco, and Jackie Smith, *International Institutions and Transnational Social Movement Organizations: Challenging the State in a Three-level Game of Global Transformation*, Working Paper Series (South Bend, Ind.: Kroc Institute, October 1993), 4.

38 L. David Brown, "Bridging Organizations and Sustainable Development," *Human Relations* 44, no. 8 (1991): 807–31. On page 825 Brown argues that "development sustainability depends in part on institutional factors—effective local organizations, horizontal linkages that enable intersectoral cooperation, and vertical linkages that enable grassroots influence on policy-making—that can be influenced by bridging organizations."

39 See Mark Duffield, "Sudan at the Cross Roads: From Emergency Preparedness to Social Security," IDS Discussion Paper no. 275 (Brighton, UK: Institute for Development Studies, 1990).

40 Barbara Hendrie, "Cross Border Operations in Eritrea and Tigray," *Disasters* 13, no. 4 (1990): 351–60.

41 R. Graham and J. Borton, *A Preliminary Review of the Combined Agencies Relief Team (CART), Juba 1986–1991* (London: Overseas Development Institute, 1992).

42 UN document E/AC.70/1994/5, 67–71.

43 For a discussion in relationship to the UN, see Erskine Childers with Brian Urquhart, *Renewing the United Nations System* (Uppsala, Sweden: Dag Hammarskjöld Foundation, 1994).

44 James O. Ingram, "The Future Architecture for International Humanitarian Assistance," in *Humanitarianism Across Borders: Sustaining Civilians in Times of War*, ed. Thomas G. Weiss and Larry Minear (Boulder, Colo.: Lynne Rienner, 1993), 181.

45 Carolyn Stremlau, "NGO Coordinating Bodies in Africa, Asia and Latin America," *World Development* 15, Supplement (1987): 213–25.

46 Ramesh Thakur, "Human rights: Amnesty International and the United Nations," *Journal of Peace Research* 31, no. 2 (1994): 143–60.

47 Sadako Ogata, UNHCR High Commissioner, "Opening statement to the 44th Session of the Executive Committee of the High Commissioner's Programme," PARinAC Information Note and Update no. 1 (Geneva: UNHCR and ICVA, 1993), 1.

48 See Adolpho Aguilar Zinzer, *CIREFCA: The Promises and Reality of the International Conference on Central American Refugees* (Washington, DC: CIPRA, 1991); and Cristina Eguizábal, David Lewis, Larry Minear, Peter Sollis, and Thomas G. Weiss, *Humanitarian Challenges in Central America: Learning the Lessons of Recent Armed Conflicts*, Occasional Paper no. 14 (Providence, RI: Watson Institute, 1993).

49 World Bank, *Cooperation Between the World Bank and NGOs: 1993 Progress Report* (Washington, DC: World Bank, 1993), 7. Some NGOs would contest that "participation" is not as meaningful as these statistics might imply.

50 Judith Randel, "Aid, the Military and Humanitarian Assistance: An Attempt to Identify Recent Trends," *Journal of International Development* 6, no. 3 (1994): 336.

51 Mark Duffield, "NGOs, Disaster Relief and Asset Transfer in the Horn: Political Survival in a Permanent Emergency," *Development and Change* 24 (1993): 140.

52 UN document E/AC.70/1994/5, Annexes IV and V.

53 See James G. McGann, *The Competition for Dollars, Scholars and Influence in the Public Policy Research Industry* (Lanham, Md.: University Press of America, 1995).

54 Margaret M Feczko, ed., *The Foundation Directory* (New York: The Foundation Center, 1984), vii.

55 See, for example, Hans J. Morgenthau, *Politics Among Nations* (New York: Knopf, 1973); and Kenneth N. Waltz, *Theory of International Politics* (Reading, Mass.: Addison-Wesley, 1979). See also Robert O. Keohane, *Neorealism and Its Critics* (New York: Columbia University Press, 1986).

56 See Stephen J. Del Rosso, Jr., "The Insecure State: Reflections on 'the State' and 'Security' in a Changing World," *Daedulus* 124, no. 2 (1995): 175–204.

57 Robert Gilpin, *The Political Economy of International Relations* (Princeton, NJ: Princeton University Press, 1987).

58 See, for example, Joseph S. Nye, Jr., *Bound To Lead: The Changing Nature of American Power* (New York: Basic Books, 1990), which makes a case for the validity of "soft power." See also Hedley Bull, *The Anarchical Society* (New York: Oxford University Press, 1977).

59 See, for example, Stephen D. Krasner, ed., *International Regimes* (Ithaca, NY: Cornell University Press, 1983); and Robert O. Keohane, *After Hegemony: Cooperation and Discord in the World Political Economy* (Princeton, NJ: Princeton University Press, 1984).

60 See Henry G. Schermers, *International Institutional Law* (Alphen aan den Rijn, Netherlands: Sijthoff and Noordhoff, 1980), 15–18, 164–75. Much legal commentary relates to specific subject matter: for example, the UN Conventions on Human Rights, the UN Convention on the Status of Refugees, and a host of other legal documents in force or in the developmental stage.

61 An overview of this approach is found in Leon Gordenker, Christer Jönsson, Roger A. Coate, and Peter Söderholm, *International Responses to AIDS* (London: Pinter, 1995).

62 Gail D. Ness and Steven B. Brachin, "Bridging the Gap: International Organizations as Organizations," *International Organization* 42, no. 2 (1988): 245–74.

63 Dennis W. Organ, "Linking Pins between Organizations and Environment," *Business Horizons* 14 (1971): 73–80.

64 Howard Aldrich and David A. Whetten, "Organization-sets, Action-sets, and Networks: Making the Most of Simplicity," in *Handbook of Organizational Design*, vol. 1, ed. Paul C. Nystrom and William H. Starbuck (New York: Oxford University Press, 1981).

65 Grahame Thompson, Jennifer Frances, Rosalind Levacic, and Jeremy Mitchell, eds., *Markets, Hierarchies and Networks: The Coordination of Social Life* (London: Sage, 1991).

66 Ernst B. Haas, *When Knowledge Is Power: Three Models of Change in International Organizations* (Berkeley: University of California Press, 1990); and Peter M. Haas,

"Introduction: Epistemic Communities and International Policy Coordination," *International Organization* 46, no. 1 (1992): 1–35, and "Do Regimes Matter? Epistemic Communities and Mediterranean Pollution Control," *International Organization* 43, no. 3 (1989): 377–403.

67 Independent Commission on International Development Issues, *North-South: A Programme for Survival* (London: Pan, 1980); Independent Commission on Disarmament and Security Issues, *Common Security: A Blueprint for Survival* (New York: Touchstone, 1982); World Commission on Environment and Development, *Our Common Future* (New York: Oxford University Press, 1987); Independent Commission on International Humanitarian Issues, *Winning the Human Race?* (London: Zed Books, 1988); South Commission, *The Challenge to the South* (Oxford: Oxford University Press, 1990); and Commission on Global Governance, *Our Global Neighbourhood* (Oxford: Oxford University Press, 1995).

68 See International Council of Voluntary Agencies, NGO Working Group on the World Bank, "Brief History of the NGO Working Group on the World Bank," informal document dated December 1993.

69 Part of the explanation may be that many UN staff members in these institutions have actually worked in NGOs or are at least very sympathetic toward their goals and styles of operation. For example, see the UNHCR's special issue of *Refugees*, vol. 97 (March 1994), entitled "Focus: NGOs & UNHCR."

70 See Leatherman, Pagnucco, and Smith, *International Institutions*.

71 John Clark "Policy Influence, Lobbying and Advocacy," in *Making a Difference: NGOs and Development in a Changing World*, ed. Michael Edwards and David Hulme (London: Earthscan, 1992), 199.

72 Dennis R. Young, "The Structural Imperatives of International Advocacy Association," *Human Relations* 44, no. 9 (1991): 925. See also M.N. Zald and J.D. McCarthy, eds., *Social Movements in an Organizational Society* (New Brunswick, NJ: Transaction Books, 1987).

73 Lawrence Susskind, *Environmental Diplomacy: Negotiating More Effective Global Agreements* (New York: Oxford University Press, 1994), 50.

74 For discussions, see Cynthia Price Cohen, "The Role of Nongovernmental Organizations in the Drafting of the Convention on the Rights of the Child," *Human Rights Quarterly* 12, no. 1 (1990), 137–47; Thakur, "Human rights"; and Princen and Finger, *Environmental NGOs in World Politics*.

75 Susskind, *Environmental Diplomacy*, 51.

76 See David P. Forsythe, *Human Rights and World Politics* (Lincoln: University of Nebraska Press, 1989), 83–101, 127–59.

77 See Bernard Kouchner and Mario Bettati, *Le devoir d'ingérence* (Paris: Denoël, 1987); Bernard Kouchner, *Le malheur des autres* (Paris: Odile Jacob, 1991); and Mario Bettati, "Intervention, ingérence ou assistance?" *Revue Trimestrielle des Droits de l'Homme*, 19 July 1994, 308–58.

78 Edwards and Hulme, eds., *Making a Difference*, 20.

79 The authors are grateful to Marty Chen for suggesting these categories.

80 The authors are grateful to Charles MacCormack for having helped develop ideas along these lines during the July 1994 summer workshop organized by the Academic Council on the United Nations System.

PART III

Humanitarian action in a turbulent world

11

POLITICAL INNOVATIONS AND THE RESPONSIBILITY TO PROTECT

With the possible exception of the prevention of genocide after World War II, no idea has moved faster or further in the international normative arena than the "responsibility to protect," commonly called R2P, the title of the 2001 report from the International Commission on Intervention and State Sovereignty (ICISS).[1] This chapter, like others in the volume, contains a strong dose of ethics, but its main purpose is to explore political innovations that could make "never again" an actuality instead of an aspiration. As Princeton University's Gary Bass puts it in his history of early efforts to halt mass atrocities, "We are all atrocitarians now—but so far only in words, and not yet in deeds."[2] Or as David Rieff writes, "there is considerable evidence of changing norms, though not, of course, changing facts on the ground."[3] More specifically still, the title of a 2008 Stanley Foundation report put it another way: "actualizing the responsibility to protect."[4] In other words, we require additional measures and the mobilization of political will to ensure the provision of the global public good of protecting and assisting forced migrants.

The UN Security Council's inability to address the woes of the Democratic Republic of the Congo (DRC), and especially its painful dithering since early 2003 over massive murder and displacement in Darfur, demonstrate the dramatic disconnect between multilateral rhetoric and the reality of protecting and aiding the displaced.[5] As Roméo Dallaire, the Canadian general in charge of the feeble United Nations force during the 1994 slaughter in Rwanda, lamented, "Having called what is happening in Darfur genocide and having vowed to stop it, it is time for the West to keep its word."[6] Normative change often is a necessary but insufficient condition for mobilizing the political will to act.

The "responsibility to protect" is a more politically acceptable reformulation of the more familiar "humanitarian intervention."[7] At the outset, it suffices to say that R2P redefines sovereignty as contingent rather than absolute, and R2P locates responsibility for human rights in the first instance with the state. But it also argues that if a state is unwilling or unable to honor its responsibility, or itself becomes the perpetrator of atrocities, then the residual responsibility to protect the victims of mass atrocity crimes shifts upward to the international community of states, ideally acting through the Security Council.

The most reliable indicator of suffering in war zones traditionally has been the number of refugees, who are, in the vernacular or according to the text of the 1951 UN Convention Relating to the Status of Refugees, exiles who flee across the borders of their country of origin. Physical displacement is prima facie evidence of vulnerability, because people who are deprived of their homes and communities and means of livelihood are unable to resort to traditional coping capacities. When such people are forced migrants within their own countries, especially as a result of war, however, they may be even more vulnerable.

Whatever one's views about legal niceties or political necessities, the ratio of refugees to internally displaced persons (IDPs) has reversed dramatically over the past two decades. The number of refugees at the beginning of the twenty-first century is fewer than 10 million while the number of IDPs is considerably higher —depending on who is counting, certainly as many as 26 million people have been internally displaced by wars in some 50 countries (13 million in Africa, 3 million in Asia, 2.5 million in Europe, 3.5 million in the Middle East, and 4 million in the Americas), and similar or even greater numbers were displaced by natural disasters and development projects.[8] When IDP data were first gathered in 1982, there was one IDP for every 10 refugees; at present the ratio is approximately 2.5:1.

Whereas international law entitles refugees to physical security and human rights protection in addition to assistance to offset their other vulnerabilities, no such legal guarantees exist for those who participate in an "exodus within borders."[9] Agencies seeking to come to the rescue of persons who have not crossed a border often require permission from the very political authorities responsible for the displacement and abuse.

While the origins of the responsibility to protect emerged from work by Francis Deng and Roberta Cohen, who pursued the cause of IDPs, analytical and practical distinctions between refugees and internally displaced persons increasingly seem insignificant.[10] At the same time, David Hollenbach correctly points out that "humanitarian concern with the protection of internally displaced people has been one of the stimuli for a serious reconsideration of the meaning and implications of the sovereignty of the nation-state."[11] The slavish respect for the sovereign prerogatives of states was undermined by efforts on behalf of IDPs, whose assistance and protection were viewed as especially subversive because outsiders were seeking ways to succor and protect victims of human rights abuse within a state. So the concept of "sovereignty as responsibility" was one way to square the circle, maintaining the fiction of state sovereignty and its corollary of nonintervention but in fact making room for international action in the face of mass atrocities. Although not so attributed, the opening lines of the ICISS report sound as if they had come from the word processor of Deng and his Brookings colleagues: "State sovereignty implies responsibility."[12]

A dramatic illustration of the potential mass appeal of R2P appeared in Pope Benedict XVI's April 2008 address to the General Assembly. In his words, "The principle of 'responsibility to protect' was considered by the ancient *ius gentium* as the foundation of every action taken by those in government with regard to the governed." While R2P "has only recently been defined . . . it was always present implicitly at the origins of the United Nations, and is now increasingly characteristic of its activity."[13] Normally, the Vatican takes far more time to weigh in so clearly in favor of an emerging norm, but this declaration came only a few years after the 2005 World Summit session of the UN General Assembly endorsed R2P. The impact of the pope's support on the foreign policies of Latin American countries, for example, may be substantial. It reinforces the earlier judgment about R2P by former *New York Times* columnist Anthony Lewis, who sees R2P as "the international state of mind," and by one of its harshest opponents, Mohammed Ayoob, who admits its "considerable moral force."[14]

Occasionally, my generic optimism is rewarded, for instance by the results of the November 2008 US presidential elections and, before that, the civic engagement during the primaries. But such domestic progress is rarely matched for the global challenges of war and peace or human rights. It is certainly difficult for anyone exploring the history of genocide and mass atrocities to remain optimistic. We can easily recall crimes committed by governments against their own citizens and evils allowed by other governments unwilling or unable to stop them. The "never again" moments since the Holocaust include Cambodia, Rwanda, and Srebrenica. Every time, collectively we ask in horror and shame how we could have let it happen once again.

However, I firmly believe that we have had an ethical breakthrough of sorts: R2P qualifies as emerging customary law after centuries of more or less passive and mindless acceptance of the proposition that state sovereignty was a license to kill. In the interest of full disclosure, I was the ICISS research director and the Ralph Bunche Institute at The City University of New York Graduate Center, which I direct, houses the Global Centre for the Responsibility to Protect.

This chapter has three parts. The first provides the historical backdrop of human rights. The second examines more specifically the evolution of the R2P norm and actual efforts to protect civilians in the 1990s. The third part proposes five political innovations that could reduce the disparities between rhetoric and reality.

The human rights "grapevine"

The history of diplomacy and international law shows that states accept limits on their conduct.[15] In a speech at the United Nations in 1948, Eleanor Roosevelt presciently predicted that "a curious grapevine" would spread human rights ideas.[16] More specifically for our purposes, the Universal Declaration of Human Rights requires that states protect individual and social rights; the Geneva Conventions and various treaties and covenants prohibiting torture, trafficking in persons, or nuclear proliferation similarly restrict the behavior of states. Moreover, there has been a shift in the understanding of sovereignty, spurred not only by globalization and technological advances but also by a growing sensitivity to human rights and by a reaction to atrocities perpetrated upon citizens by their own leaders. Sovereignty is increasingly defined not only as a license to control those within one's borders but also as a set of obligations toward citizens. Kofi Annan spoke of the sovereignty of the individual as well as of the state.[17] Francis Deng, now the special representative on the prevention of genocide and the former representative of the UN secretary-general on internally displaced persons, developed the concept of "sovereignty as responsibility."[18] Chief among those responsibilities, he and others argued, is the responsibility to protect citizens from the most atrocious forms of abuse. In terms of values, and simply put, people should come before sovereigns.

Our collective lack of historical perspective and institutional memory can make it hard to recall the extent to which human rights were so much more marginal to geopolitics and everyday politics not only at the UN's founding in 1945 but also, for instance, when Amnesty International took form in the 1960s and Human Rights Watch in the 1970s. If we fast forward to the September 2005 World Summit in New York on the occasion of the UN's sixtieth anniversary, human rights were the third pillar of the world organization's architecture, along with security and development.[19] More specifically, the largest-ever gathering of heads of state and government agreed unanimously to protect people from four extreme forms of abuse: genocide, war crimes, ethnic cleansing, and crimes against humanity.

During the first half of the 1990s, twice as many resolutions were passed as during the UN's first 45 years. Many of these contained repeated references, in the context of Chapter VII enforcement actions, to humanitarian and human rights crises amounting to threats to international peace and security, and they repeated demands for parties to respect the principles of international humanitarian law. The unanimous 1992 decision in Security Council resolution 794 to authorize the US-led intervention in Somalia, for example, set a modern multilateral record for redundancy by mentioning "humanitarian" 18 times. In short, today's normative and political landscape for humanitarian intervention is substantially different from that dominating international relations during the Cold War.

Is there a downside? The International Council on Human Rights Policy answers, "As their standing and influence have increased, human rights have also been more actively contested."[20] The transformation of the Soviet Union, the differences in North-South perspectives on universality of rights, and the importance of economic and social versus political rights, and more recently the global war on terror have caused many governments to revisit, restrict, or reverse the application of human rights.

This is the ambiguous and sometimes contradictory context within which to situate the highly volatile topic of outside intrusions, including military intervention, on human rights and humanitarian grounds. On the one hand, the responsibility to protect is not new; on the other hand, it reframes and reaffirms the primary and continuing responsibilities of states to protect their populations within the contemporary, contested climate. With the advent of R2P, the larger international community of states accepted for the first time the collective responsibility to act should states fail to protect citizens from genocide, ethnic cleansing, war crimes, and crimes against humanity. R2P thus imposes two obligations—the first upon each state individually, the second on the international community of states collectively. Skeptics and foes remain, to be sure, but the long debate over whether to act has become, instead, a discussion about how and when to act. The new activism also explains why the humanitarian field is asking many questions about its orientation and operations.[21]

Evolution of the R2P norm

The historical trajectory captured by the snapshot found in paragraphs 138–9 of the 2005 *World Summit Outcome Document* is breathtaking—moving from the early 1990s with Frances Deng and Roberta Cohen's sovereignty as responsibility to help internally displaced persons, to Secretary-General Kofi Annan's "two sovereignties," to the ICISS. At a minimum, state sovereignty seems less sacrosanct today than in 1945. Richard Haass even proposes a bumper sticker, "abuse it and lose it."[22]

The ICISS identified two threshold cases or unequivocal just causes for taking action across borders: large-scale loss of life and ethnic cleansing, under way or anticipated. Humanitarian intervention also should be subject to four precautionary conditions: right intention, last resort, proportional means, and reasonable prospects of success. Finally, the Security Council is the preferred decision maker, or just authority. That many would rightly see R2P as an adaptation of just war doctrine is easy to understand, even if the effort was purposefully not so labeled in order to avoid the political complications arising from its Western provenance.

The differences between the World Summit paragraphs and the original ICISS formulation are not trivial, but caricatures of the former's being R2P lite or providing a license for imperial intervention are exaggerations. The text agreed to by more than 150 princes, presidents, and prime ministers is woollier, wordier, and wafflier than one would like, but the World Summit's language nonetheless reflects a unanimous and historic agreement to protect citizens from mass atrocities. The core of R2P remains: state sovereignty does not include the license to commit murder and other conscience-shocking crimes.

The so-called new wars of the 1990s witnessed precedent-setting military interventions to come to the rescue of civilians in northern Iraq in 1991, Somalia in 1992, and Haiti in 1994; later in the decade, Kosovo and East Timor also were important victories for civilians.[23] Others disagree with my positive evaluation of the overall beneficial impact of many of these efforts.[24] However, the more important thought here is that the ICISS moved beyond the largely sterile political confrontations of the 1990s that accompanied the horrors of Rwanda and the Balkans when the Security Council was unable to act. The pitched battles about whether there was or was not a right to intervene were fought between partisans of humanitarian intervention like me and the defenders of unrestricted and sacrosanct state sovereignty, who saw humanitarian intervention as a Trojan horse for imperial intervention or as a destabilizing factor for international society.[25]

The Responsibility to Protect report found a way to square the circle, to put forward a more politically acceptable way to halt mass atrocity crimes. Kofi Annan was the first head of the world organization to systematically use the Secretary-General's bully pulpit almost continually to champion human rights. As a result, he was obliged to wear the equivalent of a diplomatic flak jacket at the end of the 1990s after he dared suggest that people were more important than sovereignty. Annan met with a predictable salvo of vituperative attacks in the General Assembly and elsewhere. When he received the first copy of the ICISS report, he quipped, "I wish I had thought of that."

R2P is a new normative tool to help protect the most basic human right, life itself. It makes a dent in the age-old practice of what Hugo Slim has documented as "killing civilians."[26] Robert J. Rummel's scholarly career has been spent counting how many people have been killed through wars, pogroms, genocides, and mass murder. His estimate for the twentieth century alone is 217 million.[27] And of course this figure does not include the many more uncounted who have lived diminished lives as refugees, IDPs, detainees, widows or widowers, orphans, and paupers.

As a result of the R2P norm, the notion of outside military intervention for human protection purposes is more feasible than it has ever been in the modern era, even if it remains far from palatable and certainly should not be the first policy option. Such intervention is not really a North-versus-South issue, but that is how it is often parsed in UN circles. The ICISS tried to overcome this dysfunctional fiction not only by having cochairs from the North and the South, but also by having a geographical balance among the other ten commissioners. ICISS also held ten consultations in both the Northern and Southern Hemispheres to expose the views of governments, scholars, NGOs, and journalists. The cacophony cannot be summarized except to say that what was notable, in historical perspective, is that nowhere did a substantial number of people argue that intervention to sustain humanitarian objectives was never justifiable. Rwanda's horror had a clear impact: few policymakers, pundits, or practitioners dared to exclude humanitarian intervention in principle. This change, for those of us who follow such developments, was momentous.

The R2P norm broke conceptual ground in three ways. First, the primary responsibility to protect rights resides in a sovereign state and its government. So in addition to the usual attributes of sovereignty that students encounter in undergraduate and graduate international relations and law courses and in the 1934 Montevideo Convention—people, authority, territory, and independence—there is another, namely a modicum of respect for basic human rights. In other words, the traditional emphasis on the privileges of a sovereign has made room for modest responsibilities. Moreover, when a state is unable or manifestly unwilling to protect the rights of its population—indeed, especially when it is the central perpetrator of abuse—that state temporarily loses its sovereignty, along with the accompanying right of nonintervention, and an international responsibility results to assist and protect that population.

Second, ICISS turned the language of humanitarian intervention on its head and moved away from the language of intervention, detested at least in much of the global South, which had become visible and widespread after debates in France starting in the mid-1980s. The movement away from the "right to intervene" and toward the "responsibility to protect" was accompanied by the removal of the "H" word.[28] Taking away the adjective "humanitarian" was crucial because it meant that particular situations should be analyzed and evaluated rather than simply blessed as "humanitarian." For anyone familiar with the number of sins justified by the use of that adjective during the colonial period, this change involves more than mere semantics. In particular, the language marked a dramatic shift in the focus away from the rights of outsiders to intervene and toward the rights of populations at risk to assistance and protection and the responsibility of outsiders to come to the rescue.

Third, ICISS developed a three-part framework that included the responsibility to prevent and the responsibility to rebuild before and after the responsibility to react in the eye of a storm. In conceptualizing international responsibilities, deploying international armed forces is thus neither the first nor the last step. The full spectrum of activities is integral to R2P and essential to dispel the impression that only military intervention matters.

Thus, in what Gareth Evans aptly calculates to be "a blink of the eye in the history of ideas," R2P evolved from the prose and passion of an international commission to a broadly accepted international norm.[29] It is a norm with a substantial potential to evolve further in customary international law and to contribute to the evolution of the ongoing conversations about the responsibilities of states that are expected as characteristics of legitimate sovereigns.

Normative developments and political reality are rarely in synch, however. Sometimes norm entrepreneurs scramble to keep up with events, and sometimes they are ahead of them.[30] In this case the humanitarian interventions in northern Iraq in 1991 and Somalia in 1992 were actually endorsed by the United Nations before there was any significant discussion of conditioning state sovereignty on human rights. Plotting the growing normative consensus about R2P on a graph would reflect a steady growth since the early 1990s, whereas the actual operational capacity and political will to engage in humanitarian intervention during the same period—like the transformed humanitarian system—has witnessed peaks and troughs.[31] Hence, the 2005 World Summit marked the zenith of international normative consensus about R2P. But the blowback from September 11, 2001, and the war in Iraq, along with the absence of substantial military capacity in the West besides the American one, which is tied down in Afghanistan and Iraq, explains the current decline in actual humanitarian intervention in spite of the horrors in Darfur, the DRC, Somalia, Burma—and the list goes on. This is another manifestation of what I called "collective spinelessness" in the Balkans.[32]

It is worth spending a moment on the war in Iraq, which sometimes is a bit of a conversation stopper for R2P.[33] The blowback from Iraq means that military intervention for human protection purposes is no longer on the side of the angels. Many fear Washington will manipulate it and strengthen the rationale for pre-emptive strikes against so-called rogue states and terrorists. The emerging norm of the responsibility to protect has been contaminated by association with the Bush administration's spurious humanitarian justifications for invading Iraq after the supposed links to al-Qaeda and the possession of weapons of mass destruction were exposed as vacuous. The position of the United Kingdom may have been even more damaging. In March 2004 Tony Blair offered a most worrisome example of abusing R2P when he applied it retroactively to Iraq. "We surely have a duty and a right to prevent this threat materializing," Blair announced, "and we surely have a responsibility to act when a nation's people are subjected to a regime such as Saddam's."[34]

In spite of incantations by numerous actors—including the ICISS, the Secretary-General's High-level Panel on Threats, Challenges and Change; secretaries-general Kofi Annan and Ban Ki-moon; and the World Summit—the responsibility to protect is oftentimes a harder sell these days than earlier because a Bush-like administration might manipulate any imprimatur. A rigorous application of R2P would not lend itself to becoming a veiled pretext to intervene for preemptive purposes, especially if the Security Council's authorization were a sine qua non for an authorization.[35] But this is scarce consolation for those who see Washington's and London's loose application of humanitarian rhetoric to Iraq ex post facto. In brief, it is hard to dismiss out of hand the fiercest claims that R2P conceals an imperial agenda.

The notion that the rights of human beings trump state sovereignty, while radiating briefly across the international political horizon, is now overshadowed as the US military is tied down in Afghanistan and Iraq, with the latter morphing into a vague humanitarian intervention. Because the United States cannot commit significant political and military resources to human protection, political will and the operational capacity for humanitarian intervention have evaporated. Yet the cosmopolitan logic underpinning R2P is uniquely compelling for international relations, "given the fact that sovereignty is one of the few principles that has universal appeal among national elites and mass publics."[36]

The current moment's diplomatic atmosphere could be described as toxic in UN diplomatic circles, which may not bode well for advancing the responsibility to protect norm in the immediate term. Beginning with the fall 2007 General Assembly debates concerning the appointment of the special representative on the prevention of genocide and the special adviser with a focus on R2P, the most backward-looking states have again been sharpening their swords and are attempting to skewer proponents of R2P by arguing in public forums everything ranging from "the summit rejected R2P" to "R2P exists only in the minds of Western imperialists." In essence, the responsibility to protect flies in the face of strongly held views by states, especially younger ones in the global South, about the sacrosanct nature of state sovereignty. The 1965 General Assembly resolution 2131 on the "Inadmissibility of Intervention" asserted: "No state has the right to intervene, directly, or indirectly, for any reason whatsoever, in the internal or external affairs of any other state." The animus in North-South relations today, in my view, is akin to that of the mid-1970s in the heyday of confrontation over the establishment of the New International Economic Order.

That does not make political innovation for R2P easy. Innovation never is. "The crisis in Iraq has revived more traditional interpretations of state sovereignty," United Nations high commissioner for refugees António Guterres notes. "But a reinvigorated global consensus on the R2P has to be forged nonetheless."[37]

Five political innovations

It is tempting to compose a short paragraph recommending a radical international political innovation, namely, that states actually implement the international agreements that they have signed and even ratified. While awaiting that unlikely development, however, my road map for innovations that would help R2P has something for everyone: for analysts, conceptual clarity; for civil society, a long-term strategy; for UN reformers, a consolidated relief agency; for the military, more robust and numerous forces in Europe; and for weak, fragile countries, enhanced state capacities. Progress here would help move us along what Ramesh Thakur and I call the "unfinished journey" toward better global governance.[38]

Conceptual clarity

The lengthy 2005 *World Summit Outcome Document* was agreed by consensus; but like most diplomatic compromises, the agreement on the responsibility to protect meant that differences were papered over and that the usual suspects were not really on board. As a UK House of Commons document put it, "It also is somewhat ironic that in trying to use language to take heat out of the policy debate, R2P has become an amorphous concept meaning vastly different things to different people."[39]

My first political innovation may be dismissed because it reflects the scholar's penchant for more research, but it nonetheless is essential to push forward the conceptual understanding of R2P. To be sure, practical actors must seek new structures and processes, both national and international, to ensure that timely and adequate preventive and reactive responses are forthcoming. We also need to build political bases so that when a new atrocity takes place (e.g., Darfur) or a potential one is looming (e.g., DRC, Iraq, or Kenya), the actual response is predictable. But if ridding the world of mass atrocities is to become more feasible, we also must get the concepts right, which is a comparative advantage of people like the contributors to this volume. We need to frame the issues correctly and to embed moral instincts so that there are fewer stumbling blocks to a global effort to protect civilian populations at risk.

There are two kinds of challenges to the Goldilocks problem of getting the R2P porridge just right. To date, we have not been clear enough about describing exactly what the responsibility to protect is about, to what kinds of situations it applies, and what kinds of policies are essential at different stages in the evolution of crises that threaten to degenerate into mass atrocities. This has permitted second-guessing among governments that are genuinely confused or skeptical. While engaging the spoilers is not a priority, having more precise concepts for honest skeptics is.

The first conceptual challenge is to ensure that R2P not be seen too narrowly. It is not, and this cannot be said too frequently, only about the use of military force. R2P is not a synonym for humanitarian intervention. As mentioned above, this task is especially pertinent after the rhetoric in Washington and London morphed into a humanitarian justification for the war in Iraq when weapons of mass destruction (WMDs) and links to al-Qaeda proved to be nonexistent.

Also as specified earlier, R2P is above all about taking effective preventive action. It is about identifying situations that are capable of deteriorating into mass atrocities and bringing to bear all appropriate preventive political, diplomatic, legal, or economic responses. Paragraphs 138–9 of the *World Summit Outcome Document* stress that the responsibility to prevent is very much of the state itself, and part of the outside or international prevention responsibility is to help countries to help themselves. And if prevention fails, reaction becomes necessary. But here too we need to develop an entire tool kit of nonmilitary measures that go from persuasive to intrusive, from less to more coercive, which is true of military measures as well. We require action long before the only option remaining is the US Army's 82nd Airborne Division, and we also require a commitment after deploying outside military forces. R2P prevention and R2P peace building have to be distinct from the normal panoply of preventive and postconflict measures, or there is no value added for the responsibility to protect label.

This feeds into, ironically, the second conceptual challenge at the opposite end of the spectrum: R2P is not about the protection of everyone from everything. While broadening the perspective from reaction to include prevention and peace building was a conceptual step forward, the downside has been opening the floodgates to appeals to address too many problems under this rubric. For example, part of the support at the World Summit reflected a desire to mobilize more support for root-cause prevention, or investments in economic and social development. As bureaucrats invariably seek justifications for what they are doing or new pet projects, we run the risk that there is nothing that may not figure on the R2P agenda. It is emotionally and perhaps politically tempting to say that we have a responsibility to protect people from HIV/AIDS and small arms, or the Inuit from global warming.

But such pleas are counterproductive; it is not sensible to make the responsibility to protect overlap with the full scope of human security. The uncomfortable truth is that R2P is irrelevant for many types of forced migration—both the push and the pull of armed conflict and economic opportunity—unless they involve mass atrocities. Displacement, actual or anticipated, has to be truly horrific before R2P comes into play. In brief, if it means everything, it means nothing. The responsibility to protect has to be focused because we do not wish to lose the sharp agenda that can energize political will and action at least in the worst cases. The value of R2P is as a rallying cry for visceral international reactions in the face of such conscience-shocking crises as mass murder and ethnic cleansing.

Long-term strategy

It is important to develop a longer-term strategy, one that takes the best from the original ICISS report and the *World Summit Outcome Document* but is not constrained by either.[40] There are a number of challenges if we are to consolidate and advance the R2P norm. Among them is the confusion about R2P that persists even among its most ardent proponents, so that the norm is being characterized inappropriately. In the aftermath of the World Summit, diplomatic opponents of R2P have become more adept than proponents in making their case, with the result that the claims of hard-line opponents sometimes go unchallenged. The overall debate on the responsibility to protect within the United Nations often is skewed because of the diplomatic skills and power of a few key Third World states and because the Secretary-General's job description and the current incumbent's disposition mean that addressing and satisfying the concerns of the most determined opponents assumes pride of place. The strength of the opposition has often been compounded because proponents do not have sufficiently coherent strategies to get R2P to a point where it will galvanize timely action to save lives.

Civil society's norm entrepreneurs can make a difference. R2P supporters need to advocate for an alternative vision that is intellectually and doctrinally coherent and clearly expressed. The long-term goal is protecting the essence of the R2P norm such that it triggers effective action to save lives from mass atrocities. The more immediate goal is ensuring that R2P supporters influence the purpose and tenor of any debate on R2P in the General Assembly so that the 2005 agreement is not weakened. The secretary-general's promising July 2008 speech in Berlin was followed by a disappointing laundry list instead of a strategy in a document to the General Assembly early in 2009.[41] A debate followed within the assembly in July 2009, the first time since the adoption by the World Summit. As one independent assessment summarized, "What emerged was a clear commitment from the vast majority of member states to the prevention and halting of atrocity crimes. Indeed, only four countries sought to roll back what heads of state had embraced."[42]

The R2P notion is complex and multifaceted. Earlier, in discussing the need for conceptual clarity, we saw that some observers hope that the responsibility to protect can be a springboard for all international responses to prevent and resolve armed conflicts, while others see it as a framework for international efforts to protect civilians. Still others see it as a basis for military intervention. Whatever else it may be, R2P is fundamentally about overriding sovereignty when mass atrocities occur; and so the concept will always be fraught. Diplomacy to keep all countries happy all of the time is a fool's errand.

Civil society should mobilize around a narrow notion of R2P for those situations that require highly intrusive and rapid outside military and civilian responses. The strategy should not take seriously the disingenuous and convoluted arguments from those, such as the 2008 Non-Aligned Movement leadership of Cuba, Malaysia, and Egypt, who will never be mollified by conceptual arguments. At the same time, the strategy should avoid the all-embracing approaches (something for everyone) usually favored by coalition builders in civil society as well as in the UN Secretariat. Anything other than a narrow focus on the responsibility to protect civilians from mass atrocities will needlessly politicize international work on human rights, conflict prevention, and the protection of civilians.

An agency for war victims

For frustrated humanitarian institutional reformers, I return to a long-standing yet orphaned innovation, namely, to set aside perennial institutional rivalries and create a consolidated UN agency to assist and protect war victims. This would entail pulling together the current capacities for assisting and protecting refugees and others in refugee-like situations (mainly IDPs) located in the Office of the UN High Commissioner for Refugees (UNHCR) and the major humanitarian operational capacities of the World Food Programme (WFP), UNICEF, and the UN Development Programme (UNDP), along with the UN Secretariat's Office for the Coordination of Humanitarian Affairs (OCHA). Such a consolidation would have the advantage not only of addressing squarely the problems of IDPs, who have no legal or institutional home, but also of reducing the legendary waste and turf battles within the UN system. Such a reform would involve the consolidation of parts of the United Nations organization proper; it would thus not require constitutional changes.

Ironically, it almost came about in 1997, shortly after Kofi Annan took over from Boutros Boutros-Ghali as Secretary-General. Annan ordered a systemwide review of the world organization with especial attention to humanitarian and human rights operations. He put in charge Maurice Strong, the Canadian businessman and old UN hand who had first made his mark as secretary-general of the 1972 Stockholm Conference on the Human Environment. Strong's penultimate draft of proposals for reform recommended handing responsibility for internally displaced persons over to the UNHCR, and an appendix even fleshed out the possibility of creating over the longer run a consolidated UN humanitarian agency along the lines that I have indicated.

Other UN agencies—especially UNICEF and the WFP—as well as NGOs in the guise of their US consortium, InterAction, sensed a threat to their territory. They feared that the UNHCR would come to loom over them in size and authority, and that their increasingly important, in budgetary and personnel terms, humanitarian capacities would dwindle and even be subsumed in a new consolidated agency. Annan backed off in light of the fierce opposition led by donors who preached coherence and consolidation but had their own agendas as well— including protecting the territory and budget allocations of their favorite intergovernmental and nongovernmental organizations in quintessential patron-client relationships. The final version of his 1997 reorganization was largely a repackaging of the former Department of Humanitarian Affairs as OCHA.[43] The quintessential old-wine-in-a-new-bottle routine meant that largely meaningless cooperation was reaffirmed as the UN's mechanism of choice for dealing with crises of forced displacement. Ironically, the final group of eminent persons organized during the Annan era was the High-level Panel on UN System-wide Coherence on Development, Humanitarian Assistance, and the Environment. Its recommendations for consolidation, or "delivering as one," have met the same inglorious fate as earlier calls, including Robert Jackson's 1969 *Capacity Study*—namely, no action.[44] The UN's default setting is more coordination, the mere mention of which makes eyes glaze over because there is no power of the purse to compel working together. The result is a low level of actual collaboration, which Antonio Donini dubbed "coordination by default."[45] Prospects for successful coordination for R2P or anything else depend on getting the main UN operational agencies that play a role for refugees and internally displaced persons (UNHCR, UNICEF, UNDP, and WFP) and those outside the UN framework (the International Committee of the Red Cross, the International Organization for Migration, and the largest international NGOs) to pull together. Wherever the United Nations orchestrates an overall humanitarian response, there is no structural explanation for well-coordinated efforts when they happen; rather, they depend on good faith, luck, and personalities.

The IDP situation is especially problematic, not only because no agency is responsible, but also because no legal statute guides state or agency behavior. Susan Martin has argued in favor of a new agency for IDPs because "accountability is the bottom-line. And no one is accountable."[46] Starting in 2005 the Inter-agency Standing Committee initiated the so-called cluster approach as the latest experiment in coordination, first to address the needs of IDPs but then expanding more generally to other chronic and sudden-onset emergencies. The most generous and positive assessment to date was written by independent consultants for OCHA. Its conclusion is underwhelming: "the weight of evidence points to the conclusion that the costs and drawbacks of the new approach are exceeded by its benefits."[47]

Not one of the bevy of organizations that flock to emergencies has the ability to meet the needs of IDPs. But my argument here is that decentralization hardly serves refugees either, so yet another UN agency for IDPs is not the answer. Coordination lite works on occasion because of serendipity. As numerous NGO and UN officials lament, "Everyone is for coordination but nobody wants to be coordinated." It is time, certainly within the context of an international responsibility to protect civilians from mass atrocities, to consolidate the various moving parts of the core UN system rather than just hoping that the current provider of last resort will manage to provide what are essential services.

Non-US military capacity

Downsizing the armed forces over the last twenty years has meant an insufficient supply of equipment and manpower to meet the demands for military intervention for human protection purposes. There are bottlenecks in the US logistics chain— especially in airlift capacity—that make improbable a rapid international response to a fast-moving, Rwanda-like genocide.[48] Using the conventional military logic that it takes four units to sustain one in the field, about half of the US Army is tied down in Afghanistan and Iraq and a quarter of its reserves overseas, while about a third of the National Guard is committed to the "war on terror."[49] Questions are being raised even about the capacity to respond to a serious national security threat or a natural disaster like Hurricane Katrina, let alone minor distractions like Haiti or major ones like the Democratic Republic of the Congo. Moreover, too little doctrinal rethinking about R2P has taken place within Western militaries.[50]

Nonetheless, the change in the normative approach should not be minimized and is one on which the new Barack Obama administration could and should build, starting with a report from a bipartisan Genocide Prevention Task Force led by Madeleine Albright and William Cohen.[51] We have witnessed a values break-through of sorts: the responsibility to protect qualifies as emerging customary law after centuries of more or less passive and mindless acceptance of the proposition that state sovereignty was a license to kill.[52] And Susan Rice, having been part of the lamentable Clinton administration's decision that kept the United States out of Rwanda, has expressed clearly the need for Washington not to repeat that mistake and to take the lead in conscience-shocking situations. Along with Hillary Clinton and James Jones, there is what could be called a dream team to prevent genocide, according to John Prendergast of the "Enough" project.[53]

Mass starvation, rape, and suffering will continue in the post-9/11 world, and we will know about them rapidly. For at least some conscience-shocking cases of mass suffering, there simply will be no viable alternative to military coercion for human protection purposes. There is some flexibility for action in minor crises. For instance, the prediction that major powers other than the United States would not respond at all with military force to a new humanitarian emergency after 9/11 proved too pessimistic. France's leading of a European Union (EU) force into Ituri in the Democratic Republic of the Congo in the summer of 2003 temporarily halted an upsurge of ethnic violence and demonstrated to Washington that the EU could act outside of the continent independently of the North Atlantic Treaty Organization (NATO). This possibility was strengthened by Europe's takeover from NATO of the Bosnia operation in December 2004 as well as ongoing efforts in Chad and the possibilities for a European addition to the UN force deployed in the eastern DRC.

While there is little evidence that European or Canadian populations or governments are willing to invest more public resources in their militaries, a faint hope remains that at least an EU security identity could underpin a more operational responsibility to protect in modest crises. *A Secure Europe in a Better World*, formulated in 2003, lacks the crispness of US national security strategies.[54] While spending on hardware falls considerably short of targets, nonetheless the number of European troops deployed abroad has doubled over the last decade and approaches the so-called Headline Goals, which set targets for the European Union in terms of military and civilian crisis management. As two Europeans have noted, "This incremental approach may move some way further yet, but it will come up against budgetary ceilings, against the unwillingness of some governments to invest in the weapon and support systems needed, and against the resistance of uninformed national publics."[55]

Europeans should share the burden of boots on the ground better even if US airlift capacity, military muscle, and technology are required for larger and longer-duration deployments. For better or worse, the United States in the Security Council and elsewhere is what former US secretary of state Dean Rusk called the fat boy in the canoe: "When we roll, everyone rolls with us."[56] With Washington's focus elsewhere, the danger is not too much but rather too little military intervention for human protection purposes. Unless European and other populations support higher expenditures on the military, there is little alternative to the overworked global policeman.

Rebuilding state capacity

Unlike humanitarian intervention, the responsibility to protect seeks to place less emphasis on reaction (that is, coercion under Chapter VII) and more on less intrusive policy measures, what some have called "upstream R2P."[57] The importance of preventive measures was very much in evidence in the reactions to forestall Kenya's postelection violence from becoming even more horrific. Both former secretary-general Kofi Annan, who was the chief mediator, and current secretary-general Ban Ki-moon have described the collective efforts in early 2008 as an effective application of R2P prevention logic.[58]

As indicated earlier, one political innovation of the responsibility to protect is to help potential failed states to build capacity to protect their citizens. One of the major changes in emphasis is on rebuilding states. What is described as the "second pillar" of the World Summit's agreement on R2P is the international commitment to help states to help themselves. The United Nations and its intergovernmental and nongovernmental partners should seek to help states succeed, and not simply react once weak ones have failed to meet their prevention and protection requirements or actually have been responsible for mass atrocities.

The innovation here is to identify the value that is added by looking through an R2P lens in order to help identify additional efforts and potential synergies among the host of ongoing projects and programs of the UN system and international NGOs. Efforts, so often frustrated in the past, to encourage interagency collaboration and cross-sectoral efforts could and should receive additional impetus with the motivation to avoid R2P situations. More broadly, the wide-ranging efforts to rebuild and reconstruct countries like Burundi and Sierra Leone—the first pilot projects of the Peacebuilding Commission that began operations in 2006—are helped by referring to R2P. Such efforts are valuable in and of themselves, but also they can be justified because they reduce the risk of a recurrence of armed conflict and boost a state's resilience to face future crises. Part of the innovation required here is within the UN system itself, to ensure better collaboration between New York and the field.

Conclusion

While the political innovations just described are the central purpose of this essay, it is important in conclusion to indicate the three ways that the ICISS's work on R2P pushed the ethical and normative envelope so that vocabulary and values have changed at UN headquarters in New York as well as in other settings. The first is in the report's opening sentences, which insist that sovereignty encompasses a state's responsibility to protect populations within its borders. That is, sovereignty entails responsibilities and not merely privileges. An important spillover from the R2P norm is that even committed advocates of human rights and robust intervention now see state authority as elementary to enduring peace and reconciliation, and they recommend fortifying failed or fragile states. This realization does not reflect nostalgia for any national security state of the past, but a realistic appraisal of a new bottom line: it is neither NGOs nor UN human rights monitors, as important as they are, but rather reconstituted, functioning, and responsible states that will guarantee human rights.

The second ICISS ethical and normative contribution consists of moving away from the rights of outsiders to intervene toward a framing that spotlights the rights of those suffering from war and violence to assistance and protection. Abandoning the picturesque vocabulary of the French Doctors Movement shifts the fulcrum away from the rights of interveners toward the rights of affected populations and the responsibilities (if not legal obligations) of outsiders to come to the rescue. The new perspective thus prioritizes the rights of those suffering from murder, starvation, or systematic rape and the duty of states and international institutions to respond. Rather than looking for a legalistic trigger to authorize states to inter- vene—that is, legal hairsplitting about whether there is really genocide according to the 1948 convention—R2P specifies that it is shameful to do nothing when conscience-shocking events cry out for action.[59] The norm thus attempts to mobilize responsibility based on embarrassment in front of peers, but not yet on a sense of legal obligation.

The third ethical and normative contribution is a straightforward recognition that the responsibility to halt mass atrocities may be too much too late. The responsibility to react is preceded by responsibility to prevent. Indeed, ICISS said "prevention is the single most important dimension of the responsibility to protect," a sentiment reinforced by the World Summit.[60] This cannot be said too frequently, because a limited number of Third World spoilers frequently get substantial diplomatic resonance from claiming that humanitarian intervention is a synonym for Western imperialism.

The R2P norm has moved quickly, but the concept is in its infancy. The secretary-general's special adviser, Edward Luck, provides a note of caution: "Like most infants, R2P will need to walk before it can run."[61] Nonetheless, many victims will suffer and die if R2P's adolescence is postponed. Vigilance is required to keep up the pressure to better provide this public good for displaced populations. The early 2009 report by the Secretary-General was discussed by the General Assembly in July, which afforded civil society and supportive governments the occasion to push skeptical countries and the UN bureaucracy to take seriously Secretary-General Ban Ki-moon's earlier words: "R2P speaks to the things that are most noble and most enduring in the human condition. We will not always succeed in this cardinal enterprise, and we are taking but the first steps in a long journey. But our first responsibility is to try."[62]

R2P is an idea, and we should remind ourselves that ideas matter, for good and for ill. Political theorist Daniel Philpott's study of revolutions in sovereignty demonstrates that they are driven primarily by the power of ideas, and we are in the midst of a revolution in which state sovereignty is becoming more contingent on upholding basic human rights values.[63] Gareth Evans encourages us in his new book on the subject: "And for all the difficulties of acceptance and application that lie ahead, there are—I have come optimistically, but firmly, to believe—not many ideas that have the potential to matter more for good, not only in theory but in practice, than that of the responsibility to protect."[64]

Patience may be a virtue, but so too is impatience in that the normative and operational potential of R2P is enormous and the political bar is not impossibly high. We are, after all, speaking of halting mass atrocities. The ICISS triggers for an international responsibility were massive loss of life and ethnic cleansing. And the World Summit identified genocide, war crimes, ethnic cleansing, and crimes against humanity as triggers. We are thus starting with the morally, legally, and politically easy cases. We are not talking about dampening the 75 smoldering conflicts that the International Crisis Group is monitoring this month that could turn deadly, we are not trying to establish peace on earth, and we are not attempting to rid the planet of all human rights abuses. Surely it's not quixotic to say no more Holocausts, Cambodias, and Rwandas—and to mean it.

Notes

1 International Commission on Intervention and State Sovereignty, *The Responsibility to Protect* (Ottawa: International Development Research Centre, 2001). See also Thomas G. Weiss and Don Hubert, *The Responsibility to Protect: Research, Bibliography, Background* (Ottawa: International Development Research Centre, 2001). For the interpretations of one of the cochairs, see Gareth Evans, *The Responsibility to Protect: Ending Mass Atrocity Crimes Once and for All* (Washington, DC: Brookings Institution Press, 2008). For the perspective of one of the commissioners, Ramesh Thakur, see *The United Nations, Peace, and Security: From Collective Security to the Responsibility to Protect* (Cambridge: Cambridge

University Press, 2006). The author's own version of this itinerary can be found in Thomas G. Weiss, *Humanitarian Intervention: Ideas in Action* (Cambridge: Polity Press, 2007). See also Alex J. Bellamy, *Responsibility to Protect: The Global Effort to End Mass Atrocities* (Cambridge: Polity Press, 2009).

2 Gary J. Bass, *Freedoms Battle: The Origins of Humanitarian Intervention* (New York: Knopf, 2008), 382.

3 David Rieff, "A False Compatibility: Humanitarian Action and Human Rights," *Humanitarian Stakes Number 1*, MSF Switzerland, September 2008, 41.

4 Stanley Foundation, *Actualizing the Responsibility to Protect* (Muscatine, Iowa: Stanley Foundation, 2008).

5 Hugo Slim, "Dithering over Darfur? A Preliminary Review of the International Response," *International Affairs* 80, no. 5 (2004): 811–33. See also Cheryl O. Igiri and Princeton N. Lyman, *Giving Meaning to "Never Again": Seeking an Effective Response to the Crisis in Darfur and Beyond* (New York: Council on Foreign Relations, 2004), CFR no. 5.

6 Roméo Dallaire, "Looking at Darfur, Seeing Rwanda," *New York Times*, 4 October 2004. See also Roméo Dallaire, *Shake Hands with the Devil: The Failure of Humanity in Rwanda* (Toronto: Brent Beardsley, 2004).

7 See Ramesh Thakur, "Humanitarian Intervention," in *The Oxford Handbook of the United Nations*, ed. Thomas G. Weiss and Sam Daws (Oxford: Oxford University Press, 2007), 387–403. For other views, see Christopher Bickerton, Philip Cunliffe, and Alexander Gourevitch, eds., *Politics without Sovereignty* (New York: Routledge, 2007); Simon Chesterman, *Just War? Just Peace? Humanitarian Intervention and International Law* (Oxford: Oxford University Press, 2001); Martha Finnemore, *The Purpose of Intervention: Changing Beliefs about the Use of Force* (Ithaca, NY: Cornell University Press, 2003); and Fernando Tesón, *Humanitarian Intervention: An Inquiry into Law and Morality*, 3rd ed. (Ardsley, NY: Transaction Publishers, 2005).

8 Norwegian Refugee Council, *Internal Displacement: Global Overview of Trends and Developments in 2007* (Geneva: Internal Displacement Monitoring Centre, 2008), 6–21. This is not to say that existing statistics are uncontested because of disputes as to who counts. These statistics reflect the usual practice of referring only to persons uprooted by conflict, but some observers press for much broader notions to encompass millions more uprooted by natural disasters and development. Moreover, there is also no consensus about when displacement ends, thereby inflating figures in some cases. For a discussion, see Erin D. Mooney, "The Concept of Internal Displacement and the Case for IDPs as a Category of Concern," *Refugee Survey Quarterly* 24, no. 3 (2005): 9–26; the title of the entire issue is "Internally Displaced Persons: The Challenges of International Protection," and its sections are titled "Articles," "Documents," and "Literature Survey."

9 See David A. Korn, *Exodus within Borders* (Washington, DC: Brookings Institution, 1999).

10 This story is told by Thomas G. Weiss and David A. Korn, *Internal Displacement: Conceptualization and Its Consequences* (London: Routledge, 2006).

11 David Hollenbach, "Internally Displaced People, Sovereignty, and the Responsibility to Protect," in *Refugee Rights: Ethics, Advocacy, and Africa*, ed. David Hollenbach (Washington, DC: Georgetown University Press, 2008), 179.

12 ICISS, *Responsibility to Protect*, xi.

13 Pope Benedict XVI, "Address to the General Assembly of the United Nations" (Vatican City: Holy See Press Office, 18 April 2008).

14 Anthony Lewis, "The Challenge of Global Justice Now," *Dædalus* 132, no. 1 (2003): 8; and Mohammed Ayoob, "Humanitarian Intervention and International Society," *International Journal of Human Rights* 6, no. 1 (2002): 84. For the context that drives Ayoob's skepticism, see Simon Chesterman, Michael Ignatieff, and Ramesh Thakur, eds., *State Failure and the Crisis of Governance: Making States Work* (Tokyo: UN University Press, 2005).

15 See Bertrand G. Ramcharan, *Contemporary Human Rights Ideas* (London: Routledge, 2008); Julie A. Mertus, *The United Nations and Human Rights*, 2nd ed. (London: Routledge, 2009); and Roger Normand and Sarah Zaidi, *Human Rights at the UN: The Political History of Universal Justice* (Bloomington: Indiana University Press, 2007).

16 Quoted by William Korey, *NGOs and the Universal Declaration of Human Rights: "A Curious Grapevine"* (New York: St. Martin's Press, 1998), 9.

17 Kofi A. Annan, *The Question of Intervention: Statements by the Secretary-General* (New York: UN, 1999).

18 See, for example, Frances M. Deng, Sadikiel Kimaro, Terrence Lyons, Donald Rothchild, and I. William Zartman, *Sovereignty as Responsibility: Conflict Management in Africa* (Washington, DC: Brookings Institution Press, 1996); Francis M. Deng, "Frontiers of Sovereignty," *Leiden Journal of International Law* 8, no. 2 (1995): 249–86; Roberta Cohen and Francis M. Deng, *Masses in Flight: The Global Crisis of Internal Displacement* (Washington, DC: Brookings Institution Press, 1998); Roberta Cohen and Francis M. Deng, eds., *The Forsaken People: Case Studies of the Internally Displaced* (Washington, DC: Brookings Institution Press, 1998); Francis M. Deng, *Protecting the Dispossessed: A Challenge for the International Community* (Washington, DC: Brookings Institution Press, 1993); and Francis M. Deng, "Dealing with the Displaced: A Challenge to the International Community," *Global Governance* 1, no. 1 (1995): 45–57.

19 2005 *World Summit Outcome*, UN document A/60/1, October 24, 2005. Paragraphs 138–40 concern the R2P but human rights also are sprinkled throughout the text and are especially prominent in "Section IV. Human Rights and the Rule of Law," paras. 119–45.

20 International Council on Human Rights Policy, *Catching the Wind—Human Rights* (Geneva: International Council on Human Rights Policy, 2007), 7.

21 See Michael Barnett and Thomas G. Weiss, eds., *Humanitarianism in Question: Politics, Power, Ethics* (Ithaca, NY: Cornell University Press, 2008).

22 Richard N. Haass, *The Opportunity: America's Moment to Alter History's Course* (New York: Public Affairs, 2005), 41.

23 See Mary Kaldor, *New and Old Wars: Organized Violence in a Global Era* (Stanford, Calif.: Stanford University Press, 1999). For a discussion of the nature of humanitarian action in these armed conflicts, see Peter J. Hoffman and Thomas G. Weiss, *Sword & Salve: Confronting New Wars and Humanitarian Crises* (Lanham, Md.: Rowman & Littlefield, 2006); and David Keen, *Complex Emergencies* (Cambridge: Polity Press, 2008).

24 Thomas G. Weiss, *Military-Civilian Interactions: Humanitarian Crises and the Responsibility to Protect*, 2nd ed. (Lanham, Md.: Rowman & Littlefield, 2005).

25 See, for example, Mohammed Ayoob, "Humanitarian Intervention and International Society," *Global Governance* 7, no. 3 (2001): 225–30; and Robert Jackson, *The Global Covenant: Human Conduct in a World of States* (Oxford: Oxford University Press, 2000).

26 Hugo Slim, *Killing Civilians: Method, Madness, and Morality in War* (New York: Columbia University Press, 2008).

27 Robert J. Rummel, *Death by Government* (New Brunswick, NJ: Transaction Publishers, 1994), chapter 1.

28 Mario Bettati and Bernard Kouchner, eds., *Le Devoir d'ingérence: Peut-on les laisser mourir?* (Paris: Denoël, 1987); and Mario Bettati, *Le Droit d'ingérence: Mutation de l'ordre international* (Paris: Odile Jacob, 1987).

29 Evans, *Responsibility to Protect*, 28.

30 Martha Finnemore and Kathryn Sikkink, "International Norm Dynamics and Political Change," *International Organization* 52, no. 4 (1998): 887–917.

31 Michael Barnett, "Humanitarianism Transformed," *Perspectives on Politics* 3, no. 4 (2005): 723–40.

32 Thomas G. Weiss, "Collective Spinelessness: U.N. Actions in the Former Yugoslavia," in *The World and Yugoslavia's Wars*, ed. Richard H. Ullman (New York: Council on Foreign Relations, 1996), 59–96.

33 Thomas G. Weiss, "The Sunset of Humanitarian Intervention? The Responsibility to Protect in a Unipolar World," *Security Dialogue* 35, no. 2 (2004): 135–53.

34 "Speech Given by the Prime Minister in Sedgefield, Justifying Military Action in Iraq and Warning of the Continued Threat of Global Terrorism," 5 March 2004, www.guardian.co.uk/politics/2004/mar/05/iraq.iraq.

35 See, for example, Gareth Evans, "Uneasy Bedfellows: 'The Responsibility to Protect' and Feinstein-Slaughter's 'Duty to Prevent,'" speech at the American Society of International Law Conference, Washington, DC, 1 April 2004, www.gevans.org/speeches/speech104.html.

36 J. Martin Rochester, *Between Peril and Promise: The Politics of International Law* (Washington, DC: CQ Press, 2006), 95.

37 António Guterres, "Millions Uprooted: Saving Refugees and the Displaced," *Foreign Affairs* 87, no. 5 (2008): 93.

38 Thomas G. Weiss and Ramesh Thakur, *Global Governance and the UN: An Unfinished Journey* (Bloomington: Indiana University Press, 2010), especially 308–40.

39 Adele Brown, *Reinventing Humanitarian Intervention: Two Cheers for the Responsibility to Protect?* (London: House of Commons Library, 2008), 18.

40 I acknowledge here insights from Don Hubert's private paper developed for the Global Centre for the Responsibility to Protect, August 2008.

41 Ban Ki-moon, *Implementing the Responsibility to Protect, A Report from the Secretary-General* (New York: UN, 2009).

42 Global Centre for the Responsibility to Protect, *The 2009 General Assembly Debate: An Assessment* (New York: GCR2P, 2009), 1. The four states were the usual suspects: Venezuela, Cuba, Sudan, and Nicaragua.

43 Kofi A. Annan, *Renewing the United Nations: A Programme for Reform* (New York: UN, 1997). For the details of this story, see Thomas G. Weiss, "Humanitarian Shell Games: Whither UN Reform?" *Security Dialogue* 29, no.1 (1998): 9–23.

44 High-level Panel on UN System-wide Coherence on Development, Humanitarian Assistance, and the Environment, *Delivering as One* (New York: UN, 2006); and United Nations, *A Capacity Study of the United Nations Development System*, 2 vols. (Geneva: UN, 1969), document DP/5. The importance of changing the excessively decentralized UN system is a major theme in Thomas G. Weiss, *What's Wrong with the United Nations and How to Fix It* (Cambridge: Polity Press, 2009), 72–106, 173–90.

45 See, for example, Antonio Donini, *The Policies of Mercy: UN Coordination in Afghanistan, Mozambique, and Rwanda* (Providence, RI: Watson Institute, 1996), occasional paper no. 22.

46 Interview with the author, 11 October 2005.

47 Abby Stoddard, Adele Harmer, Katherinie Haver, Dirk Salomons, and Victoria Wheeler, *Cluster Approach Evaluation: Final Draft* (New York: OCHA Evaluation and Studies Section, 2007), 1.

48 See Alan J. Kuperman, *The Limits of Humanitarian Intervention: Genocide in Rwanda* (Washington, DC: Brookings Institution Press, 2001).

49 See Patrice C. McMahon and Andrew Wedeman, "Sustaining American Power in a Globalized World," in *American Foreign Policy in a Globalized World*, ed. David P. Forsythe, Patrice C. McMahon, and Andrew Wedeman (New York: Routledge, 2006), 12–14.

50 See Victoria K. Holt and Tobias C. Berkman, *The Impossible Mandate? Military Preparedness, the Responsibility to Protect, and Modern Peace Operations* (Washington, DC: Stimson Center, 2006).

51 Genocide Prevention Task Force, *Preventing Genocide: A Blueprint for U.S. Policymakers* (Washington, DC: American Academy of Diplomacy, United States Holocaust Memorial Museum, and the U.S. Institute of Peace, 2008).

52 For a brief discussion, see Thomas G. Weiss, "The Ultimate UN and Human Value: Making 'Never Again' More than a Slogan," in *The United Nations and the Evolution of*

Global Values, ed. J.J.G. van der Bruggen and Nico J. Schrijver (Cambridge: Cambridge University Press, 2009).

53 Quoted in *The Economist*, 13 December 2008, 43.

54 *A Secure Europe in a Better World*, European Security Strategy, Brussels, 12 December 2003, www.consilium.europa.eu/uedocs/cmsUpload/78367.pdf.

55 See Bastian Giegrich and William Wallace, "Not Such a Soft Power: The External Deployment of European Forces," *Survival* 46, no. 2 (2004): 163–82, quote 179.

56 Quoted by Lincoln Palmer Bloomfield, *Accidental Encounters with History (and Some Lessons Learned)* (Cohasset, Mass.: Hot House Press, 2005), 14.

57 Edward C. Luck, "The United Nations and the Responsibility to Protect," *Policy Analysis Brief* (Muscatine, Iowa: Stanley Foundation, 2008), 6.

58 Roger Cohen, "How Kofi Annan Rescued Kenya," *New York Review of Books*, 14 August 2008. See also Desmond Tutu, "Taking the Responsibility to Protect," *International Herald Tribune*, 19 February 2008.

59 See Scott Straus, "Darfur and the Genocide Debate," *Foreign Affairs* 84, no. 1 (2005): 123–33.

60 ICISS, *Responsibility to Protect*, xi.

61 Luck, "The United Nations and the Responsibility to Protect," 8.

62 Ban Ki-moon, "Secretary-General Defends, Clarifies 'Responsibility to Protect' at Berlin Event on 'Responsible Sovereignty: International Cooperation for a Changed World,'" address of the secretary-general, Berlin, 15 July 2008, UN document SG/SM/11701.

63 Daniel Philpott, *Revolutions in Sovereignty: How Ideas Shaped Modern International Relations* (Princeton, NJ: Princeton University Press, 2001).

64 Evans, *Responsibility to Protect*, 7.

12

THE FOG OF HUMANITARIANISM

Collective action problems and learning-challenged organizations

With Peter J. Hoffman

In the rush to respond to the horrors of war, humanitarians race to bring relief, but tunnel vision often leads them to overlook their own role in worsening crises and inhibits learning from past mistakes. "The fog of war" refers to an inability of those in combat to accurately perceive what is happening around them.[1] And aid workers must recognize that they are susceptible to "the fog of humanitarianism."

There is of course much in conflicts of the past 20 years, sometimes called "new wars," which is confounding. Most notably, battlefields that were once the sole domains of soldiers are now crowded with militarized non-state actors (NSAs) who ignore international humanitarian law and prey on civilians. Over this same period, the international humanitarian system has grown substantially, and its many branches have approached the crises accompanying new wars myopically and inconsistently. With each agency adapting and developing its own strategic framework, the "new humanitarianisms" result in suboptimal or even counterproductive consequences. Thus, on top of the incompetence, corruption, and war crimes within war zones that imperil populations, a second set of failures results from the aggregate efforts of agencies. Peculiar challenges surface in the wake of the new wars in combination with tensions inherent in the new humanitarianisms.

This essay discusses two structural challenges plaguing the international humanitarian system: collective action problems and learning-challenged organizations. We bring together obstacles faced in the field (the impact of war) and in headquarters (the influence of donors) to consider the mindset of agencies. Although some have begun to adapt to changed conditions, most have not. Fundamentally they lack a will as well as a way—culturally they are not inclined to spend scarce financial and human resources on research that would foster more effective adaptation.

Until humanitarians analyze and adapt to environments, the fog of humanitarianism will be more opaque than need be, costing lives and tarnishing the credibility of the enterprise. Consequently, tensions in post-conflict state-building will be exacerbated. A critical first step to alter this state of affairs would be to devote funds and personnel to information gathering, policy analysis, and strategic planning —in short, to develop a humanitarian equivalent of military science. Learning, not spurning, lessons is urgent.

Violent inputs: new wars

Our analytic focus is on flaws of the international humanitarian system, but the mechanics of war and their impact on suffering is a necessary starting point. There has always been an intimate relation between them. Wars trigger humanitarian crises and elicit responses, and humanitarianism inspires norms and alters outcomes. For example, life-threatening violence may limit agency access to victims, but humanitarian principles also mitigate the worst practices of combatants. Indeed, that the "laws of war" and "international humanitarian law" are synonyms recognizes the link. However, war usually exercises greater influence on humanitarianism than vice-versa.

During the 1990s, soldiers and scholars debated the extent to which war was undergoing a fundamental shift, with some proposing that contemporary armed conflicts were such a significant departure from earlier ones to merit the moniker "new wars."[2] This is not the place to take sides in this debate. Our purpose is to highlight how recent wars have affected the ability of aid agencies to rescue victims and shape subsequent statebuilding.

We consciously use the plural form of "new wars." There is no model to encompass the nuances of every conflict so labelled, but a collection of trends with common themes. There are multiple realities to every war; armed conflicts often open the door to a variety of cleavages, including ideological, religious, tribal, and ethnic struggles. Although the greatest concern for agencies is the increased numbers and range of victims, the most outstanding feature of the so-called new wars is the pronounced presence of non-state combatants who often serve as gatekeepers for affected populations. Moreover, some who have been afflicted by war are also participants—Aristide R. Zolberg, Astri Suhrke, and Sergio Aguayo[3] use the term "refugee warriors," but we prefer "belligerent-victims" because it includes all those who make war possible (fighters, support workers, and profiteers) as well as internally displaced persons (IDPs). Thus, the nub of the new wars are actors that neither conform to established patterns nor respect the status of non-combatants, yet have become political, economic, and military fixtures.

As the Cold War ended and the United States and the Soviet Union turned their attention away from a global ideological struggle toward economic interests, international politics entered a period of uncertainty and instability. Since the mid-seventeenth century, states had dominated armed conflicts. However during the turbulent 1990s, the position of the state in international affairs and on battlefields changed profoundly, making war less centered on protecting borders with large, disciplined conventional armies and more about disputing internal spaces with small, undisciplined irregular forces.

Global security no longer hinged exclusively on the West's defense of strategic territory but expanded to encompass the viability of states as political units in strife-prone areas. In developing countries, particularly those where the government had relied on their status as Cold War proxies to receive economic and military support, state capacities dwindled and authority fragmented. Westphalian sovereignty was never absolute; there were always holes in the web of state control over illicit activities such as smuggling and piracy. However, the gap between textbook depictions and unvarnished reality became apparent in the 1990s; many Third World governments experienced shrinking resources (economically and militarily) and encountered serious challenges to their statehood. Some such as Chad were slightly weakened, some like Somalia failed altogether, while most others—sometimes called "shadow" or "quasi" states—fell in between these poles.[4]

Often the result was war, but a species that deviated from archetypes of the twentieth century. By the 1990s the geography of armed conflicts moved from frontlines of major powers' interstate wars to pockets of destabilizing civil wars in the Third World: in western and central Africa (Liberia, Sierra Leone, Ivory Coast, and Nigeria), central and south Asia (Afghanistan, the Caucuses, and Kashmir), South America (Colombia, Peru, and Bolivia), and the Pacific Rim (Indonesia, Papua/New Guinea, and the Solomon Islands). However, bloody internecine strife in the Balkans showed that such violence was not a monopoly of the global South.

With crumbling states, power shifted to non-state actors. The cast of combatants includes warlords, militias, guerrillas, mercenaries, private military companies, and other informal militarized groups. Although national military forces also participate, they do not retain a monopoly on force. NSAs project power and exercise authority. Sometimes referred to as "pseudo" states, they become vital interlocutors in the delivery of humanitarian assistance.[5] NSA gatekeepers allow "spoilers" to undermine delivery and protection.

These developments are troubling. Non-state actors are not signatories to international humanitarian law and often do not abide by it. While the populations whom they represent have suffered from violence, they may also have been, or are, combatants. The duality of belligerent-victims challenges agencies trying to determine who to help and how without sustaining violence.

Like all armed conflicts, new wars have economic underpinnings. In fact often in these conflicts, political domination appears hollow relative to economic agendas. Historically, states dominated economic activity within their jurisdictions and harnessed their energies for national military expenditures. Domestic taxes and customs on foreign goods paid for border defenses and underwrote counter-insurgency. The corrosive effects of economic interests dictating military decisions prompted Dwight D. Eisenhower in 1961 to warn of the "military-industrial complex" that pushes war for profits. In new wars where states are less significant or nonexistent, NSAs wield substantial economic power. Their interests comprise a differently layered but nonetheless structured war economy.

Where such war economies drive armed conflicts, livelihoods revolve around plunder and price-fixing (natural resources), extortion (commercial security), and aid (manipulating assistance). Agricultural and mineral commodities—diamonds, cobalt, gold, oil, and hardwoods—are often exploited by NSAs to fund political projects and military endeavors or for purely personal gain.[6] While natural resources used to be considered a blessing, they may also be a curse because the World Bank indicates that the chances of war in countries with "lootable resources" are four times greater than less endowed states.[7]

Another aspect of war economies are "guns for hire." Local militias are enriched through protection "taxes." Mercenaries are unqualifiedly drawn to insecure environments for pay. Private military companies (PMCs) provide security under public and private sector contracts.[8] Trade in commodities and markets for coercion are only part of the economic activity in new wars because profit-minded NSAs, like governments, manipulate "aid economies" to improve their standing.[9] The most notorious, recent instance of aid feeding a war economy was when Hutu militants skewed aid in refugee camps in eastern Zaire.

The shift away from regular armies is also reflected in targets and victims, and the overarching consequence of new wars is the massive toll on civilians. The numbers, while approximations and often contested, nonetheless are chilling.[10] When front lines were meaningful in the trench warfare of World War I, soldiers accounted for around 90 percent of all combat fatalities. During World War II, national militaries brought civilians into the fray—the Holocaust, Japanese atrocities, and Allied firebombing of German cities as well as the nuclear devices used against Hiroshima and Nagasaki. Nonetheless, military to civilian casualties were only 1:2.5. In the new wars of the 1990s, however, fatalities of combatants to non–combatants were thought to be 1:9. While later contested, this proportion of civilian-to-soldier battlefield fatalities was widespread and guided policymakers. This dynamic was found in virtually all conflicts in the decade.[11]

This is not to suggest that "ethnic cleansing" or deliberate attacks on civilians are unprecedented—Sherman's 1864 march on Atlanta or the 1915 Armenian genocide remind us otherwise—but to indicate how truly unexceptional they have become. As a 2001 report by the UN Secretary-General states, "Affected civilians tend not to be the incidental victims of new irregular forces; they are their principal object."[12]

A final note about civilian victims concerns the nature of forced displacement, an additional hurdle for humanitarians and state builders. Earlier, victims normally fled war-torn countries to become refugees. However, in the new wars many victims do not cross borders, or cross them and return. Although similar to refugees, IDPs do not benefit from the same international law and institutional mechanisms—in fact, they usually are the worst off.[13] When the first data were collected in the early 1980s, there were a million IDPs and some 10 million refugees. Over the 1990s, the numbers of IDPs soared between 20- and 30-fold while refugees in 2006 fell below 10 million.[14] The case of IDPs is a microcosm of the fog of humanitarianism. The fastest growing category of war-affected populations still has no institutional sponsor or formal legal framework while diminishing refugee populations continue to benefit from well-developed institutional and legal efforts by the UN High Commissioner for Refugees (UNHCR).

The literature on new wars arose from the armed conflicts in Africa and the Balkans in the 1990s, but the twenty-first century species in Afghanistan and Iraq are extreme examples of the trends identified earlier. Although beginning as inter-state conflicts, they quickly degenerated into exaggerated variants of the proto-typical new war. For instance, after central governments were defeated, powerful NSAs emerged to dictate the course of, and in many cases to spoil, humanitarian operations. The resort to PMCs reached unheard-of dimensions—in Iraq in 2006 the 25,000 military contractors outnumber the second highest contingent, the United Kingdom's, over 3-to-1.

If these conflicts are not aberrations but have become the new standard, three other points should be made about the distinctive attributes of Afghanistan and Iraq. First, the politics of terrorism place humanitarianism in the limelight on a big stage. The September 2001 attacks by al-Qaeda made state failure and the accompanying humanitarian disaster in Afghanistan vital global security issues. By this logic, humanitarian action is an extension of the global war on terrorism. Second, al-Qaeda is an especially noxious spoiler. Supporters of extremist Muslim organizations contribute to these wars and take aim at aid workers and journalists. Third, each country has a unique and volatile war economy. Post-Taliban Afghan-istan derives much of its wealth from the production of opium (accounting for about 90 percent of world supply). These warlords who allow humanitarian action rely on drug-trafficking for their livelihoods. The economics of oil in Iraq make it unlike any other theater. Not only are the sums of money staggering, but the network of economic actors with an agenda for Iraqi oil is extensive.

In short, the new wars present an amalgam of actors and agendas that are a far cry from past routines. Potent militarized NSAs are now featured as belligerents while civilians constitute the bulk of the surge in victims. While one can critique how "new" some of the civil wars of the 1990s were, Afghanistan and Iraq clearly represent distinctly new challenges for humanitarians and state builders.

Mixed reactions: new humanitarianisms

Twenty years of daunting challenges have compelled the members of the interna-tional humanitarian system to re-examine who they are, what they do, and how they do it. Questions that were once essentially answered, or were asked rhetorically with ready-made replies, are now open for debate. Perhaps the most gutwrenching one is whether outside assistance actually helps or hinders. Good intentions are no longer enough—if they ever were. The recognition that well-intentioned humanitarian action can lead to negative consequences—what David Kennedy dubbed "the dark sides of virtue"[15]—has forced humanitarian organizations to rethink their effectiveness. Such exercises require contemplating not only the values that motivate actions but also consequences. "Accountability" has become a buzzword, and Janice Stein demonstrates that we need better data and thinking because it is not easy to answer "why, to whom, for what, and how?"[16]

With traditional responses failing, some agencies explored new humanitarianisms that strayed from the mainstays of neutrality, impartiality, and consent in order to gain access through NSAs, limit aid manipulation, and protect civilians. Mark Duffield notes:

> Towards the end of the 1990s, a new or political humanitarianism emerged . . . on a consequentialist framework. Assistance is conditional on assumptions regarding future outcomes: especially, it should do no harm, nor should it entrench violence while attempting to ameliorate its effects.[17]

Furthermore, the international humanitarian system expanded considerably during this period, and more agencies had more funds than ever before. Again, we use the plural form of "new humanitarianisms" to underline the multiple changes in humanitarian action and the sprawling number of agencies with independent perspectives and practices.

Prior to discussing controversies surrounding strategies for gaining access (the establishment of humanitarian space through force when necessary) and minimizing an unintended skewing of relief (do-no-harm guidelines), two prefatory comments are warranted. First, there are important historical antecedents that must be acknowledged. There is a timeless element to debates. The international humanitarian system was born of a compromise between states as belligerents —agencies remain neutral and states permit access. At times this arrangement failed to protect the vulnerable. For example, during World War II, the International Committee of the Red Cross (ICRC) was criticized for neutrality and not denouncing Nazi atrocities.[18] In the late 1960s as Biafra sought to secede from Nigeria, ICRC orthodoxy provoked some staff to break away and in 1971 establish Médecins Sans Frontières (MSF), which abandoned discretion in favor of bearing witness.[19] The "classicist" approach of the ICRC was never the sole form of humanitarianism; other more politicized agencies took sides and skewed aid distributions.[20] Falling into this category would be other groups and organizations that are not humanitarian in mission and have more parochial aims, but send relief (such as diasporas). New humanitarianisms emerged in the 1990s, but the principal debates that spawned the mainstreaming of these strategies are perennial.

Second, the overall expansion of the international humanitarian system gives greater importance to philosophical differences. Throughout the 1990s, despite some mid-decade ebbing to the flow, the amount of resources dedicated to humanitarian assistance has exploded over ten-fold from its 1989 total of $800 million.[21] In 1991 $4.5 billion was channelled through agencies, though only $3.8 billion in 1997, but climbed again reaching $5.8 billion by 2000 and soaring to approximately $10 billion in 2004.[22]

In the late 1980s, the international humanitarian system developed rapidly to address crises of statelessness. Large populations of victims without legally recognized authorities to serve as interlocutors posed a new problem. Previously, the humanitarian enterprise was not well positioned, although international humanitarian law had taken some strides with the 1977 Additional Protocols to the 1949 Geneva Conventions that required belligerents in non-international wars to respect rights and prohibitions. However, civilian protection was still mostly neglected. Aside from legal architecture, international organizations were also slow to protect civilians. In the 1970s and 1980s, the Cold War froze the Security Council and inhibited acting in areas where either the United States or Soviet Union had clashing interests.[23]

Two humanitarian crises in the transition years bridged the bipolar and post–Cold War eras and hastened the rise of the new humanitarianisms, Sudan in 1989 and northern Iraq in 1991. The UN recognized in Operation Lifeline Sudan that obtaining access to victims would require engaging both the central government in Khartoum and the rebel Sudanese Liberation Army. Consequently, a new space for humanitarian action appeared, "corridors of tranquility," where victims could find protection and agencies operate. A few years later when major powers had much at stake in oil-rich Iraq and following the dismantling of central authority in Baghdad, the Security Council declared the crisis to the north in the Kurdish region a threat to international peace and security and sanctioned the establishment of "safe havens." The General Assembly also furthered the principle of agencies' rights to access in resolution 182/46 (1991). Later in the decade, other disasters led to organizing "safe areas" in Bosnia and "secure humanitarian areas" in Rwanda.

However, formal political negotiations and international statements were often not enough to secure access in new wars. Genocide in Rwanda and ethnic cleansing in the Balkans changed the thinking and operational guidelines of humanitarian agencies. Such crises required more than relief, they necessitated protection for victims. By the close of the decade, the proponents of the new humanitarianisms had melded humanitarian and security concerns by designating humanitarian disasters as threats to international peace and security so that the Security Council could act.

Indeed, the growing calls for humanitarian intervention—the use of military force without the consent of a government to guarantee access to victims and halt widespread human rights violations—reflected new realizations by humanitarians. They called for the use of force when parties were unable or unwilling to live up to their responsibilities under international law. Such a notion was firmly on display in NATO's 1999 attack on the Federal Republic of Yugoslavia in response to Serb violence against Albanian Kosovars. The Independent International Commission on Kosovo characterized NATO's operation "illegal but legitimate,"[24] and military force to protect civilians became attractive to humanitarians and diplomats frustrated by earlier failures, particularly the paralysis during the 1994 Rwandan genocide and timidity in stopping the 1995 massacre at Srebrenica, Bosnia.

The Canadian government pulled together the International Commission on Intervention and State Sovereignty (ICISS) whose reformulation of humanitarian intervention as "the responsibility to protect" (R2P) enabled consensus building among states for what the Security Council should do when a state is unwilling or unable to protect its population from mass murder or ethnic cleansing.[25] R2P implies that ensuring humanitarian action may require regime change. This document represents a seismic shift away from consent and neutrality and is indicative of the movement of many agencies into the new humanitarianisms' camp, a development that may be fostered by the 2005 World Summit's blessing of R2P.

Another innovation is the introduction of do-no-harm criteria, which reflects Mary Anderson's[26] and others' concerns to interject the Hippocratic ethos— treatments should never worsen the condition of patients—into humanitarian action. This part of the new humanitarianisms responds to fears of aid going to feed or nurture belligerents or other spoilers. In addition to tackling short-term concerns about the manipulation of assistance and other unintended consequences, do-no-harm practices also address longer-term worries that aid may cultivate dependency and undermine subsequent state building.

The new humanitarianisms cope with the challenges of new wars by incorp-orating new tactics for operational arrangements—including pragmatic agreements with interlocutors and a willingness to withdraw. However, expanding agency practices moves the goalposts of humanitarian action from emergency to human rights protection, peace building, economic development, and security sector reform.[27] Analysts have begun to examine the pluses and minuses of new humanitarianisms, particularly in relationship to Afghanistan and Iraq.

Incoherent outputs: humanitarianism as a collective action problem

We have already seen that international assistance in war zones grew rapidly and substantially in the 1990s, which was a mixed blessing in that an already dizzy-ing and decentralized system was endowed with even more moving parts. The use of military force felled certain barriers to entry in war zones—until the end of the Cold War, the ICRC had enjoyed a virtual monopoly. The openness of the aid marketplace meant that increasing funds and the number of agencies yielded greater relief as well as fiercer competition—"NGO scramble" was how two analysts portrayed the situation,[28] and a similar label would apply to intergovernmental agencies. "System" has always been a euphemism for the totality of humanitarian action. "Atomization" is more accurate.

Humanitarian action can best be understood as a collective action problem involving simultaneous but differentiated assistance activities by a host of aid organizations. Wars blind combatants through a haze of violence and uncertainty, and humanitarians also confront baffling conditions—some of which derive from the nature of contemporary wars, and some from the singularities of the contem-porary international humanitarian system.

Individual agencies usually lack information about both belligerents and other humanitarian institutions, and they are unable to acknowledge perverse incentive structures. The collective action problem is at the center of the dynamics unleashed by the new humanitarianisms. Struggling to find language for the challenges of the new wars, humanitarians invented "complex political emergency"—a

> humanitarian crisis in a country, region or society where there is a total or considerable breakdown of authority resulting from internal or external conflict and which requires an international response that goes beyond the mandate or capacity of any single agency and/or the ongoing UN country programme.[29]

The very nature of needs requires a multiplicity of agencies, but as one observer pointed out, "the need for a concerted approach . . . contradicts the current independence of each responding agency and organization in an international response."[30] To summarize, effective humanitarian responses in areas with limited or no authorities demand pooling the capacities of many agencies, yet individualized goals and financing make this highly unlikely if not impossible.

In terms of addressing shortcomings in humanitarian efforts, three approaches to collective action should be distinguished—cooperation, centralized coordination, and consolidation. Cooperation is an informal and often ad hoc arrangement, which allows each agency to develop its own approaches to complement whatever willing partners exist. Cooperation is exemplified for NGOs by such groups as InterAction, the International Council of Voluntary Agencies, and the Emergency Committee for Humanitarian Response, and for the UN by the Inter-Agency Standing Committee (IASC) and the Office for the Coordination of Humanitarian Affairs (OCHA). Cooperation does not ensure coordination when interests do not coincide or personalities clash.

Centralized coordination is a more structured variation of cooperation, but similarly cannot assure compliance. Under this format, the more open-ended and non-committal form of cooperation is replaced with a single hub for operational decisions and appeals. Earlier the UN system relied upon a "lead agency," but at present OCHA plays this role for UN agencies through several mechanisms—most notably the Consolidated Appeals Process (CAP). However, OCHA acts more as a meeting convener than a decision maker. There is no clear line responsibility or power of the purse to enforce so-called decisions. After the debacle in Rwanda, integrative practices became more common as evidenced by the 1998 Strategic Framework for Afghanistan.[31] Although humanitarians are quick to see the utility of being on the same page in crises, getting and keeping them there was and is not easy.

Consolidation, an integration of efforts and collective action at a different level, would be a dramatic break from the operating style used throughout the history of humanitarianism. Every so often there are attempts to fuse parts of the UN system. In 1997 it was discussed but never materialized;[32] and a similar discussion about consolidated pillars began but went nowhere in 2006 when the secretary-general appointed his High-level Panel on System-wide Coherence in the Areas of Development, Humanitarian Aid and the Environment,[33] whose recommendations amount to "more of the same."

Greater coherence requires a greater commitment by individual agencies to at least abide by agreements among themselves. But four primary constraints hinder collective humanitarian action.

The value of independent operations

Many agencies put a premium on independence and thus opt out of coordination or give lip-service while continuing on their own. Traditionally the diversity of the system was seen as a strength—different and overlapping operations saw to it that no needy victims were excluded. Moreover, independence ensures that values, not political machinations, dominate. The ICRC refuse to participate in coordination schemes, and MSF tend to keep their distance from efforts that determine to whom they may send assistance. For them, aid is the right of victims, not a reward to be meted out by aid workers. In this view coordination is not a method for improving effectiveness but for subjecting humanitarianism to politicized agendas.

Divergent perceptions of needs, sequence, and tactics

Some humanitarians object to the substance of policies being coordinated. Their opposition reflects their perceptions of victims' needs, the sequence of international responses, and specific tactics. New wars are extremely uneven; the conditions are unlikely to be similar throughout a conflict and also will differ from one area to another. Therefore, agencies may genuinely differ about how best to proceed. For instance, many envision a clear "relief-to-development continuum" in which there are logical steps from an emergency to peace. But needs and the sequence of responses to address them are hardly obvious because many differently conceived and implemented operations are underway. If there is more a "simultanuum" than a continuum, disagreements may arise over what sorts of aid is needed and in what order, which present incentives to defect from coordination exercises. Even when agencies have achieved a degree of consensus regarding aid, they may differ about which victims should receive priority treatment.

Institutional rivalries

Economic competition among aid organizations also short-circuits coordination. Agencies require resources, and a distinctive mode of operation may well appeal to donors. David Rieff points to the preoccupation of individual agencies with "market share" as driving behavior to engage in practices (including withdrawing from coordinating bodies) to raise their media profile and receive funding, no matter what the impact on agreed divisions of labor.[34] Although rivalries are counterproductive to humanitarian outcomes, as Alexander Cooley and James Ron show, "dysfunctional organization behaviour is likely to be a rational response to systematic and predictable institutional pressures."[35] Finding interlocutors and forging access is another front for competition. With reference to the destabilizing consequences of aid agency negotiations with the Revolutionary United Front in Sierra Leone, the Security Council remarked that "common ground rules would help make access negotiations more predictable and effective, and reduce the risk of mistakes or of agencies being played off against each other by warring parties."[36] In short, the need for resources, grandstanding for attention, and turf wars lead many humanitarian organizations to downplay or reject binding coordination.

The blowback from insecurity

Insecurity can lead agencies to defect from collective efforts. Collaborating with other aid agencies or military forces may incite the wrath of belligerents. Although humanitarians traditionally have worked to maintain neutrality, extreme polarization has made such a posture implausible in many theaters—at least in the eyes of belligerents. Indeed, aid workers are sometimes intentionally targeted by combatants in order to send political messages. In the 1990s, the UN's pursuit of Mohammed Aideed in Somalia and actions to deter Serb militias in Bosnia heightened security threats against aid workers.[37] In Afghanistan and Iraq, agencies that have been perceived as contributing to the US occupation have been attacked—for example, the August 2003 attack on UN headquarters in Baghdad and on the ICRC in October.[38] Consequently, some agencies have pulled out of partnerships so that they are not associated with the Western coalition.

The incoherent outcomes of the 1990s led to a clarion call for agencies to better coordinate their efforts. Yet despite the drumbeat of pleas and some retooling of the international humanitarian system—for instance, the creation of the Department of Humanitarian Affairs (DHA) in 1992 and its conversion into OCHA in 1998— the alleged system remains atomized. New wars have altered the inputs (a torrent of civilian victims and new untrustworthy combatants) while new humanitarianisms have changed relief organizations (increasing funds for and functions of humanitarianisms). In brief, more crises with more interlocutors combined with more agencies with more capabilities have increased incoherence and undercut the collective effort. There is no consensus on what humanitarianism means or who a humanitarian is, and thus it is no surprise that how to work together to achieve humanitarian outcomes remains enigmatic and elusive.

Lessons lost: the dearth of learning and strategy

Although external factors have certainly contributed to counterproductive humanitarianism, aid agencies themselves are loath to share in the blame, searching for scapegoats. As Kennedy declares: "When things do go wrong, rather than facing the consequences of humanitarian work, we too often redouble our efforts and intensify our condemnation of whatever other forces we can find to hold responsible."[39] Agencies are not adjusting to difficult environments and reckoning with poor performance—as Larry Minear argues: "Humanitarian organizations' adaptation to the new realities has been for the most part lethargic and phlegmatic. Institutional reform among humanitarian actors has not kept pace with the changing political-military landscape."[40] Unable to muster more than the token UN forces assigned to prevent what became the 1994 genocide in Rwanda, Roméo Dallaire lambasted the actions of the international humanitarian system in the 1990s as "a decade of adhocracy."[41]

At the root of the problem is that humanitarian agencies are learning-disabled— they do not possess and are unwilling to invest in the capabilities to process information, correct errors, and devise alternative strategies and tactics. While they are consumed with providing life-saving relief to victims, good intentions are inadequate and can be self-defeating. We review some key instances of agencies attempting to learn from their experiences, which lead to some thoughts about how they might overcome learning impediments by emulating the institutionalized learning practices of top-notch militaries.

Evaluation and policy analysis have never been priorities for humanitarians. Although data on the intentions of belligerents and the performance of humanitarians are a prerequisite for retooling new strategies and adopting better tactics, the visceral reaction of most humanitarians is to spend virtually every euro on succor. Nonetheless, four cases illustrate a growing realization about the importance of investing in learning.

The ICRC offers perhaps the best illustration of an agency inclined to spend significant time and resources to reflect upon its own efforts in the unsettling 1990s. The Avenir ("future" in French) process of 1996–97 meant that senior staff and outside consultants hammered out revisions in mandates, strategy, and structure.[42] The final report concludes that the agency has much work to do in adjusting to circumstances while maintaining its special character: "[the ICRC] will have to reinforce the overall coherence of its activity and adapt to change, without, however, losing its identity."[43] Avenir demonstrates recognition of the need to learn and reformulate practices. But it would be foolish to underestimate the difficulties in modifying 150 years of conservative institutional culture.

A second example is the Sphere Project spearheaded by the International Federation of Red Cross and Red Crescent Societies.[44] In 1999 Sphere Minimum Standards were promulgated to improve the accountability of over 400 organizations, but data are inconclusive about the extent to which collective guidelines are making a difference. Moreover, there is also some concern that a draconian enforcement of standards might steer donors away from smaller agencies that do not have the resources to meet all criteria and others that run risks or otherwise deviate from the charter.

Another promising illustration is the Active Learning for Accountability and Performance in Humanitarian Action (ALNAP). Started in 1997, this group has generated some 5,000 performance evaluations and an annual *Review of Humanitarian Action*. Discerning and disseminating lessons are invaluable and necessary but by themselves are insufficient first steps. Substantive learning only occurs when agencies actually make use of information to change strategy, policies, and tactics.

Piecemeal or unproductive learning in the UN is typified by the UNHCR, ironically one of the most dedicated and effective of intergovernmental institutions. Several analyses of the organization have zeroed in on its conservative culture.[45] Despite having a budget of some $1 billion in the late 1990s, for instance, only one half of a statistician was budgeted to amass and analyze data on refugees. The biannual analytical report of the organization, *The State of the World's Refugees*, was discontinued when Ruud Lubbers replaced Sadako Ogata—although it will be revived. As a staff member affirms: "We're CNNish. We respond; we don't do long-term strategic planning." Ergo, this study states, the "lack of planning and reflection have an impact on outcomes and ability to learn from experience."[46] Furthermore, another analysis points out that the UNHCR has resisted assisting IDPs because "operational decision making is uncertain, inconsistent, and unpredictable."[47] The airing of grievances against the UNHCR is a good sign—criticism offers building blocks for learning—but its seeming minor impact divulges a deeper anti-learning pathology that undoubtedly is prevalent throughout the UN system.

Perhaps the most dramatic gauge of institutional foot-dragging results from the most traumatic crisis for humanitarians in the 1990s, the genocide in Rwanda. Following the recriminations that poured forth in its aftermath, many countries and agencies vowed to rethink responses. Denmark sponsored the Joint Evaluation of Emergency Assistance to Rwanda that produced a five volume study in March 1996. For the tenth anniversary of the tragedy, the Danish International Development Agency hired the two consultants who had produced the previous evaluation to gauge its effect. They noted that it "had a wide reach in the research and policy communities . . . [and] improvements in the areas of professionalism, standards, and accountability mechanisms since 1996 . . . as the area where the Joint Evaluation has had the greatest impact."[48] Nevertheless, agencies have often gone through the motions of building knowledge but without a commitment to change. In judging responses to the December 2004 tsunami, David Rieff is closer to the mark and questions whether agencies have taken seriously the need to implement lessons.

Confronted with all this hard work, thought, and scruple, it might be reasonable to assume that the most egregious errors would have become a thing of the past. What the tsunami has demonstrated is that, for all the conferences, internal reviews, pledges of accountability and transparency, codes of conduct, and the like, the humanitarian circus is alive and well.[49]

With so many lives at stake, why do agencies not invest more in self-criticism? Why after analysis does policy change lag? We identify five main impediments:

- Despite obvious shifts in war and politics, many agencies are locked into old orientations. Whether it is in the hopes that today's conflicts can be tended to with yesterday's programming or denial as to the significance of changes, standardized operating procedures often dictate current practices. Rigid bureaucracies do not experiment until incentives change.

- When information is gathered and analyzed, management often fails to get the data to decision makers. Outdated and incompatible informational technologies may derail communication and exchange—within agencies but certainly among them.[50]
- In many ways humanitarians behave more like firefighters than as strategists or tacticians. Agencies fear "paralysis by analysis" and are more geared to responding to current emergencies than revisiting past actions. They value speed —racing from one emergency to the next—while devaluing the time and resources spent on reflection.
- Reviewing failures is not only painful, it can also sour perceptions. Humanitarians are reticent to advertise mistakes for fear of donor retaliation.
- Resources play a big role in the lack of learning; few agencies consider the investment in analytic capabilities and strategic planning important. Research is viewed as a luxury; it is the last item to be funded in flush times and the first to be cut during downturns. As Koenraad Van Brabant insists: "The short funding cycles of humanitarian action, even in chronic crises, are, however, a serious disincentive to more strategic thinking."[51] Moreover, learning requires that staff take time to document and digest experiences, which may draw limited and skilled personnel away from pressing operations.

These impediments often compound to stymie timely information gathering, evaluation, and strategic planning. Thus, Alex de Waal laments that the international humanitarian system has an "extraordinary capacity to absorb criticism, not reform itself, and yet emerge strengthened."[52] When data is not collected, processed, or disseminated, lessons are not learned. They are lost.

By now it is abundantly clear that more needs to be known to address collective action problems. We wholeheartedly endorse Ian Smillie and Larry Minear's plea for "a more holistic approach . . . that puts learning at centre stage."[53] To borrow from Ernst Haas, humanitarian agencies should not settle for "muddling through" but become "learning institutions."[54] While they may resist the idea, there is a model that humanitarians could look at: national militaries.

Conclusion

The criticism that military strategists are behind the curve in understanding threats—preparing for the last war and thus ill-equipped to confront current challenges—has stirred many professional armed forces to appreciate that knowledge is an essential weapon in a modern arsenal. War fighting has become a vastly complex endeavor requiring an immense orchestration of materiel and manpower. War's reputation for chaos contrasts with the measured behavior of professional military forces—sophisticated militaries prepare, synchronize, and execute operations with a remarkable degree of creativity and self-criticism. The timeless adages coined by Sun Tzu "know thy self" and "know thy enemy" mean that military victory is not guaranteed by a mindless dispatch of force but rather by grasping intentions, positions, strengths, and weaknesses. To that end, the organizational arrangements and cultural traditions of upper echelon militaries reward institutional memory, stress continual learning, and promote adaptive practices. Knowledge production is part and parcel of daily procedures, career development, and long-term strategizing.

Two aspects of military organizations are instructive: a culture that values learning, and an institutional infrastructure to assemble and act on lessons. Military academies epitomize how this works; previous and on-going operations are analyzed, new procedures are tried and tested, and student-soldiers are educated about best practices and adapting tactics to field specifics. Career development and promotions require regular time-off for study and reflection before new assignments. Ongoing operations have historians attached to them. While critics could undoubtedly dismiss these orientations as a result of institutional "fat" and overly generous budget allocations, we see them as an essential cultural difference that should be replicated by humanitarians.

A useful illustration of militaries as learning organizations regards instances of "friendly fire." Following such errors, an incident is reviewed, procedures are updated, and soldiers are drilled on new protocols. The parallels with do-no-harm principles are obvious—inadvertent acts undermine capabilities and incur casualties. While militaries are often rightly condemned for their obsessive secrecy and unbending hierarchies, they also exemplify the merits of strategic doctrines that can be adapted by creative and flexible agents who are expected to gather and analyze data.

In sum, the role of and resources dedicated to information, analysis, and planning in military organizations are edifying for humanitarians. Military science and career development prepare soldiers to make decisions about how to win wars. What is needed is a "humanitarian science" to make agendas and actors in war, as well as their consequences, intelligible. Humanitarians require boot camps and academic settings where information is processed into lessons and staff can become better informed about the interrelated mechanics of war and humanitarianism. Personnel require time for reflection and recycling before they return to the field.

Humanitarians have made some progress in the past 15 years to improve performance and institutional memory, but they are still fundamentally unaccomplished in distilling and disseminating lessons. While reflection does not guarantee better results, refraining from it certainly hurts performance. Learning organizations capable of strategic planning cannot completely dissipate the fog of humanitarianism; nothing can do that. But investments in learning can illuminate a beacon for humanitarians to get their bearings amid collective action problems and avoid running aground the shoals represented by intransigent spoilers.

Paradoxically, the "can-do" culture of humanitarians works against investing in the necessary measures to stimulate an analytical culture in which reflection is valued as much as reaction. Most aid workers are initially attracted to the work because of its active rather than analytical orientation, and many move on (burnout is common). The fog of humanitarianism has always been present, but it has grown denser in recent years. Until agencies take steps to apprehend the disorder in humanitarian action, it will be impossible to bridge noble objectives and optimal outcomes; and ultimately prospective state building will be endangered. Agencies now face a choice: drift passively and ignorantly or develop the determination and means to find their way and avoid being lost in the fog.

Notes

1 Carl von Clausewitz, *On War* ("Vom Krieg," trans. J. J. Graham) (New York: Penguin, 1968).
2 Mary Kaldor, *New and Old Wars: Organized Violence in a Global Era* (Stanford, Calif.: Stanford University Press, 1999); and Mark Duffield, *Global Governance and the New Wars: The Merging of Development and Security* (London: Zed, 2001).
3 Aristide R. Zolberg, Astri Suhrke, and Sergio Aguayo, eds., *Escape From Violence: Conflict and the Refugee Crisis in the Developing World* (New York: Oxford University Press, 1989).
4 Gerald B. Helman and Steven R. Ratner, "Saving Failed States," *Foreign Policy* 89 (Winter 1992–93): 3–20; William Reno, "Shadow States and the Political Economy of Civil War," in *Greed and Grievance: Economic Agenda in Civil Wars*, ed. Mats R. Berdal and David M. Malone (Boulder, Colo.: Lynne Rienner, 2000), 43–68; and Robert Jackson, *Quasi-states: Sovereignty, International Relations, and the Third World* (Cambridge: Cambridge University Press, 1990).
5 Stephen J. Stedman and Fred Tanner, eds., *Refugee Manipulation: War, Politics, and the Abuse of Human Suffering* (Washington, DC: Brookings, 2003).
6 David Keen, "Incentives and Disincentives for Violence," in *Greed and Grievance: Economic Agenda in Civil Wars*, ed. Mats R. Berdal and David M. Malone (Boulder, Colo.: Lynne Rienner, 2000), 19–41; and Michael T. Klare, *Resource Wars: The New Landscape of Global Conflict* (New York: Henry Holt, 2002).
7 Paul Collier, *Economic Causes of Conflict and Their Implications for Policy* (Washington, DC: World Bank, 2000); and Indra de Soysa, "Resource Curse: Are Civil Wars Driven by Rapacity or Paucity?" in *Greed and Grievance: Economic Agenda in Civil Wars*, ed. Mats R. Berdal and David M. Malone (Boulder, Colo.: Lynne Rienner, 2000), 113–35.
8 Peter W. Singer, *Corporate Warriors: The Rise of the Privatized Military Industry* (Ithaca, NY: Cornell University Press, 2003); and Robert Mandel, *Armies without States: The Privatization of Security* (Boulder, Colo.: Lynne Rienner, 2002).
9 Stedman and Tanner, eds., *Refugee Manipulation*.
10 Carnegie Commission, Carnegie Commission on Preventing Deadly Conflict, *Preventing Deadly Conflict: Final Report* (Washington, DC: Carnegie Commission on Preventing Deadly Conflict, 1998), 11; and Kaldor, *New and Old Wars: Organized Violence in a Global Era*, 100.
11 Peter Wallensteen and Margareta Sollenberg, "Armed Conflict, 1989–2000," *Journal of Peace Research* 38, no. 5 (2001): 629–44, quote at 632.
12 Kofi A. Annan, "Report of the Secretary-General to the Security Council on the Protection of Civilians in Armed Conflict," UN document S/2001/331, 30 March 2001, para. 3.
13 Thomas G. Weiss and David A. Korn, *Internal Displacement: Conceptualization and Its Consequences* (London: Routledge, 2006).
14 Norwegian Refugee Council, *Internal Displacement: Global Overview of Trends and Developments in 2005* (Geneva: Global IDP Project, 2005), 9–10; and US Committee on Refugees and Immigrants, *World Refugee Survey 2006* (Washington, DC: USCR, 2006), 11.

15 David Kennedy, *The Dark Sides of Virtue: Reassessing International Humanitarianism* (Princeton, NJ: Princeton University Press, 2004).

16 Janice G. Stein, "Humanitarian Organizations: Accountable—Why, to Whom, for What, and How?" in *Humanitarianism in Question: Politics, Power, Ethics*, ed. Michael Barnett and Thomas G. Weiss (Ithaca, NY: Cornell University Press, 2008), 124–42.

17 Duffield, *Global Governance and the New Wars*, 75.

18 David P. Forsythe, *The Humanitarians: The International Committee of the Red Cross* (Cambridge: Cambridge University Press, 2005).

19 Fabrice Weissman, ed., *In the Shadow of "Just Wars": Violence, Politics, and Humanitarian Action* (Ithaca, NY: Cornell University Press, 2004).

20 Thomas G. Weiss, "Principles, Politics, and Humanitarian Action," *Ethics & International Affairs* 13, no. 1 (1999): 1–22; and Michael Barnett, "Humanitarianism Transformed," *Perspectives in Politics* 3, no. 4 (2005): 723–40.

21 OECD, Development Assistance Committee, *Development Cooperation Report 2000* (Paris: Organisation for Economic Co-operation and Development, 2001), 180–1.

22 Judith Randel and Tony German, "Trends in Financing of Humanitarian Assistance," in *The New Humanitarianisms: A Review of Trends in Global Humanitarian Action*, Humanitarian Practice Group, Report 11, ed. Joanna Macrae (London: Overseas Development Institute, 2002), 20, www.odi.org.uk/resources/download/243.pdf; and Ian Smillie and Larry Minear, *The Charity of Nations: Humanitarian Action in a Calculating World* (West Bloomfield, Conn.: Kumarian, 2004), 8.

23 David Malone, ed., *The UN Security Council: From the Cold War to the 21st Century* (Boulder, Colo.: Lynne Rienner, 2004).

24 Independent International Commission on Kosovo, *Kosovo Report: Conflict, International Response, Lessons Learned* (Oxford: Oxford University Press, 2000), 4.

25 International Commission on Intervention and State Sovereignty (ICISS), *The Responsibility to Protect* (Ottawa: International Development Research Centre, 2001); and Thomas G. Weiss and Don Hubert, *The Responsibility to Protect: Research, Bibliography, Background* (Ottawa: International Development Research Centre, 2001).

26 Mary Anderson, *Do No Harm: How Aid Can Support Peace—Or War* (Boulder, Colo.: Lynne Rienner, 2002).

27 Barnett, "Humanitarianism Transformed."

28 Alexander Cooley and James Ron, "The NGO Scramble: Organizational Insecurity and the Political Economy of Transnational Action," *International Security* 27, no. 1 (2002): 5–39.

29 Inter-Agency Standing Committee (ISAC), "Working Paper on the Definition of Complex Emergency" (New York: UN, December 1994).

30 John Mackinlay, "Globalisation and Insurgency," Adelphi Paper 352 (Oxford: Oxford University Press, 2002), 100.

31 Antonio Donini, "An Elusive Quest: Integration in the Response to the Afghan Crisis," *Ethics & International Affairs* 18, no. 2 (2004): 21–7.

32 Thomas G. Weiss, "Humanitarian Shell Games: Whither UN Reform?" *Security Dialogue* 29, no. 1 (1998): 9–24.

33 United Nations, *Delivering as One*, Report of the Secretary-General's High-level Panel on System-wide Coherence in the Areas of Development, Humanitarian Aid and the Environment (New York: UN, 2006).

34 David Rieff, *A Bed for the Night: Humanitarianism in Crisis* (New York: Simon and Schuster, 2002), 228.

35 Cooley and Ron, "The NGO Scramble," 6.

36 Max Glaser, "Humanitarian Engagement with Non-State Armed Actors," *The Parameters of Negotiated Access*, Humanitarian Practice Network, Paper 51 (London: Overseas Development Institute, 2005), 17.

37 Susan F. Martin, Patricia Weiss Fagen, Kari Jorgensen, Lydia Mann–Bondat, and Andrew Schoenholtz, *The Uprooted: Improving Humanitarian Responses to Forced Migration* (Lanham, Md.: Lexington Books, 2005), 198.

38 Nicolas de Torrente, "Humanitarianism Sacrificed: Integration's False Promise," *Ethics & International Affairs* 18, no. 2 (2004): 3–4.

39 Kennedy, *The Dark Sides of Virtue*, 327.

40 Larry Minear, *The Humanitarian Enterprise: Dilemmas and Discoveries* (West Bloomfield, Conn.: Kumarian, 2002), 7.

41 Roméo Dallaire, "Keynote Address," conference organized by CARE Canada and the Humanitarianism and War Project, Parliament Hill, Ottawa, 24 April 2001.

42 Forsythe, *The Humanitarians*, 310.

43 International Committee of the Red Cross (ICRC), "Initial Conclusion of the ICRC Avenir Project," press release, 16 December 1997, www.icrc.org/Web/Eng/siteeng0.nsf/htmlall/57JNW5.

44 Sphere Project, *Humanitarian Charter and Minimum Standards in Disaster Response* (Geneva: International Federation of Red Cross and Red Crescent Societies, 1996); and Lola Gostelow, "The Sphere Project: The Implications of Making Humanitarian Principles and Codes Work," *Disasters* 23, no. 4 (1999): 316–25.

45 Gil Loescher, *The UNHCR and World Politics: A Perilous Path* (Oxford: Oxford University Press, 2001); and Barb Wigley, *The State of UNHCR's Organizational Culture*, United Nations High Commissioner for Refugees Evaluation and Policy Analysis Unit, UNHCR document EPAU/2005/08, May 2005.

46 Wigley, *The State of UNHCR's Organizational Culture*, 5.

47 Vanessa Mattar and Paul White, *Consistent and Predictable Responses to IDPS: A Review of UNHCR's Decision-Making Processes*, United Nations High Commissioner for Refugees Evaluation and Policy Analysis Unit, UNHCR document EPAU/2005/2, March 2005.

48 John Borton and John Eriksson, *Lessons from Rwanda—Lessons for Today: Assessment of the Impact and Influence of the Joint Evaluation of Emergency Assistance to Rwanda* (Copenhagen: Ministry of Foreign Affairs, 2004), 11, 16, www.um.dk/Publikationer/Danida/English/Evaluations/Rwanda/rwanda.pdf.

49 David Rieff, "Tsunamis, Accountability and the Humanitarian Circus," The Humanitarian Practice Network at ODI, *Humanitarian Exchange Magazine* 29 (March 2004): 49–50.

50 Stanley Foundation, *The UN on the Ground* (Muscatine, Iowa: Stanley Foundation, 2004), 7–12.

51 Koenraad Van Brabant, "Organisational and Institutional Learning," in *The Charitable Impulse: NGOs and Development in East and North-East Africa*, ed. Ondine Barrow and Michael Jennings (West Bloomfield, Conn.: Kumarian, 2001), 183–99, quote at 193.

52 Alex de Waal, *Famine Crimes: Politics & the Disaster Relief Industry in Africa* (Oxford: James Currey, 1997), xvi.

53 Smillie and Minear, *The Charity of Nations*, 224.

54 Ernst B. Haas, *When Knowledge is Power: Three Models of Change in International Organizations* (Berkeley: University of California Press, 1990).

13

THE HUMANITARIAN IMPULSE

Humanitarian values have become central to foreign and military policies since the outset of the 1990s. Humanitarians often lament that national interests are obstacles to realizing their objectives. In truth, calculations about vital interests by governmental decision-makers explain intervention, which is unlikely to succeed unless there is a demonstrated willingness to take casualties and stay the course. This chapter focuses on the trends that have emerged since the 1990s that may circumscribe the chances for a more consistent respect for humanitarian values over the next ten years.

The end of the Cold War made possible UN decisions about international security that had not been feasible for some 40 years. A key explanation for the sheer expansion in activity by the Security Council in the 1990s was the humanitarian "impulse," the understandable human desire to help those in life-threatening distress resulting from armed conflict.[1] Invariably, this urge translates into a limited political momentum and a sliding scale of commitments. This impulse does not necessarily imply efforts that are "impulsive," which are more likely to be "emotionally-charged and based on incomplete or biased media coverage."[2] Rather it reflects the stark reality of international politics that permits action to come to the rescue of some, but not all, war victims. This momentum, for instance, has made coalitions of the willing an episodic phenomenon in world politics. When humanitarian and strategic interests coincide, a window of opportunity opens for those seeking to act on the humanitarian impulse in the Security Council.

The title of this essay is not slanted to the humanitarian "imperative," the preference of those who believe that humanitarian values must be universal to be meaningful and who are dismayed by the uneven quality of Security Council decisions. The humanitarian imperative entails an obligation to treat victims similarly and react to crises consistently—in effect, to deny the relevance of politics, which consists of drawing lines and weighing effectiveness and available resources.

Humanitarian action is desirable but not obligatory. The humanitarian impulse is permissive. The humanitarian imperative would be peremptory.

The humanitarian impulse is the maximum to which the community of states can aspire. It was respected more often in the 1990s than earlier, and it may be respected more systematically still. Lest the ideal become the enemy of the good, international action in some cases is better than in none.

The dramatic evolution in attitudes toward the limits of sovereignty affects the ability of humanitarian organizations to come to the rescue. The post–Cold War years underscore the expectations to respect fundamental human rights placed on sovereign political authorities. The growth in the weight of humanitarian values to sustain diplomatic and military action is clear to seasoned observers—although David Rieff would now contest whether this development has been productive.[3] "In the 1990s," summarizes Adam Roberts, "humanitarian issues . . . played a historically unprecedented role in international politics."[4]

S. Neil MacFarlane notes that "normatively based challenges to the sovereign rights of states are hardly new in international history," but still the Security Council was largely missing in action regarding humanitarian matters during the Cold War.[5] There was virtually a humanitarian tabula rasa at the outset of the 1990s. No resolution mentioned the humanitarian aspects of any conflict from 1945 until the Six Day War of 1967, and the first mention of the International Committee of the Red Cross (ICRC) was not until 1978.[6] In the 1970s and 1980s, "the Security Council gave humanitarian aspects of armed conflict limited priority . . . but the early nineteen-nineties can be seen as a watershed."[7] During the first half of the decade, twice as many resolutions were passed as during the first 45 years of UN history. They contained repeated references to humanitarian crises amounting to threats to international peace and security, and they repeated demands for parties to respect international humanitarian law.

Whether one takes issue with Edward Luttwak's disparaging remarks about "Kofi's rule . . . whereby human rights outrank sovereignty," humanitarian intervention undoubtedly was among the most controversial topics within UN circles in the 1990s.[8] The secretary-general's own speeches were widely debated.[9] "The age of humanitarian emergencies" led to policies of "saving strangers."[10] An academic cottage industry grew,[11] and governments sponsored a host of policy initiatives and published reports on the topic: the Canadian-inspired International Commission on Intervention and State Sovereignty (ICISS) published *The Responsibility to Protect*;[12] a Swedish initiative, the Independent International Commission on Kosovo, published the *Kosovo Report*;[13] the US government published an overview of humanitarian programs and a report on humanitarian intervention;[14] and the Dutch and Danish governments published major inquiries into the legal authority for intervention.[15]

"Intervention" here only refers to three categories of threatened or actual coercion against the expressed wishes (or without the genuine consent) of a target state or group of political authorities: sanctions and embargoes, international criminal prosecution, and military force. The Security Council approved all varieties of coercion in unprecedented numbers during the 1990s. Sanctions are a vast and heated topic; much has already been written about their negative humanitarian impact, particularly in reference to Iraq.[16] International criminal prosecution, even of heads of state, assumed new vitality with the arrest of Manuel Noriega in 1989 but assumed even greater importance with legal actions against Slobodan Milosevic and Biljana Plavsic at The Hague.[17] The council's decisions in the 1990s proved highly innovative in shaping norms and stimulated legal developments, including the international tribunals for the former Yugoslavia in 1993 and Rwanda in 1994 and the creation of the International Criminal Court in 1998. And the most severe and intense kind of intervention, the use of deadly force by outside militaries, constituted a most notable story of the 1990s.

This essay focuses on the Security Council's demonstrated concerns with the plight of the civilian victims of armed conflicts, particularly of internal wars. Extreme suffering consistently led to intense scrutiny but selective responses, especially with respect to Chapter VII military operations. A minority of international lawyers suggested that there was emerging customary law on humanitarian intervention.[18] Others disputed the extent to which custom could actually take precedence over treaty and viewed Kosovo as an unfortunate departure that threatened the Charter regime.[19]

Legal interpretations notwithstanding, state behavior and expectations certainly changed over the decade. Exceptions to the principle of nonintervention became less exceptional. Post-1991 practice demonstrates support or tolerance for respecting the humanitarian impulse, often against the will of local authorities. UN-authorized actions with an expressed humanitarian purpose were manifest (northern Iraq, Somalia, Haiti, the former Yugoslavia, Rwanda, Albania, and East Timor) along with non-UN authorized actions that were seen by many states as legitimate (the North Atlantic Treaty Organization [NATO] in Kosovo) or that were endorsed ex post facto (the Economic Community of West African States [ECOWAS] in Liberia).

Significant institutional innovations in the international handling of humanitarian challenges usually occur after wars have ended, when new kinds of horrors shock consciences and expose the inadequacies of existing organizations and their standard operating procedures. The founding of the modern humanitarian system is usually dated to 1864, when Henri Dunant, appalled by the slaughter wrought by a fierce battle between French and Austrian forces in Solferino, Italy, in the wake of the War of Italian Unification, established the ICRC. Immediately after World War I and the Russian Revolution, two sisters, Eglantyne Jebb and Dorothy Buxton, founded Save the Children. Albert Einstein and other refugees founded the International Rescue Committee (IRC) during the 1930s as Nazism reared its ugly head. World War II and its immediate aftermath led to the founding of a host of agencies—Oxfam, Catholic Relief Services (CRS), World Vision, and CARE along with the United Nations family, including the UN Children's Fund (UNICEF) and the UN High Commissioner for Refugees (UNHCR). The French Doctors Movement—beginning with Médecins sans Frontières—emerged when dissident staff within the ICRC revolted against institutional orthodoxy in the Biafran War.

The sea changes in world politics in the 1990s led to no next generation of humanitarian institutions, nor to a transformation of existing institutional machinery—except the establishment of the largely powerless Department of Humanitarian Affairs in 1992 (and its successor, the Office for the Coordination of Humanitarian Affairs, in 1997).[20] Whether September 11, 2001, has altered the terrain sufficiently to foster more significant change is a proposition worth examining, but it appears unlikely.

The end of the Cold War led to new conflicts and crises, along with the eruption of long-simmering ones held in check by East-West tensions. Moreover, the budgets of humanitarian organizations expanded from US$2 billion at the beginning of the decade to US$6 billion in 2000.[21] In an unprecedented fashion the numbers and activities of intergovernmental and nongovernmental organizations grew, and "humanitarian" became a household word.

The implications of changes in the nature and scope of Security Council decisions resulting from the humanitarian impulse since 1991 are examined here from three angles: ethical, rhetorical, and military. The different perspectives applied to recent humanitarian trends nonetheless overlap. The difficulties in separating them mirror the increased connections between the formerly more discrete members of the international humanitarian enterprise.[22]

Ethical landscape

In the 1990s, lively debates unfolded about the right of the community of states to intervene in internal affairs to protect civilians, with some observers contending that there even exists a duty to do so.[23] The proper conduct of military and civilian personnel in humanitarian operations also was the subject of controversy. ICISS's reframing of the central moral issue is noteworthy—replacing the rights of outsiders to intervene with the rights of affected populations to assistance and protection and the obligations of outsiders to come to the rescue. Moving away from the picturesque vocabulary of the French Doctors Movement alters the debate in fundamental ways. The new framework not only requires an evaluation from the perspective of intervening capitals, but it also means emphasizing those in need and the duty of others to aid and protect them.

Whatever one's views on the feasibility, desirability, or likely impact of vigorous military efforts on behalf of war-affected populations, the dominant moral discourse about humanitarian action has changed. This can be illustrated by reviewing a scholarly journal devoted to the study of the impact of values on international politics, *Ethics & International Affairs*. At the outset of the post–Cold War era, humanitarian action was central in only about 10 percent of articles, whereas in the mid-1990s it reached almost a third and, by the end of the decade, comprised nearly half of the journal's main articles.

Greater moral attention from policymakers will not bring peace on earth, but it can help protect and improve the fragile character of norms that protect the vulnerable. In the United States and elsewhere, some cynics even claim that there was no policy in the 1990s except this soft-hearted and soft-headed approach, which was distracting attention from more central security threats.

Since September 11, there has been an adjustment between narrowly defined national interests and moral impulses. Washington's response in Afghanistan resembles interventions in the 1970s undertaken by India, Tanzania, and Vietnam. Self-defense and regime change were immediate justifications, but humanitarian benefits were an important byproduct of what Michael Walzer calls "the most successful interventions in the last thirty years."[24]

They generated substantial humanitarian benefits but were not even partially justified by the interveners in such terms. At the time, international order was grounded unquestionably on the inviolability of state sovereignty, and states were far less attuned to humanitarianism than vital interests. India's invasion of East Pakistan in 1971 and, later in the decade, Tanzania's invasion of Uganda and Vietnam's invasion of Kampuchea were unilateral efforts geared to overthrow menacing and destabilizing regimes in contiguous countries, and all were explicitly justified as self-defense. None was approved by the Security Council—and Vietnam's was actually condemned. Yet they now are frequently cited as evidence of an emerging right to humanitarian intervention.

The US intervention in Afghanistan is a mixture of the 1970s and 1990s. What began as essentially a US operation, albeit in concert with other nations and the Northern Alliance, was recognized by the Security Council as a legitimate act of self-defense, thereby making moot Article 51's call for possible ongoing scrutiny by the council. Operation Enduring Freedom is unique to date, but it is perhaps a harbinger by combining legitimate self-defense and the humanitarian impulse. The *casus belli* in Afghanistan was an attack on US soil. However, a humanitarian rationale and rhetorical flourishes accompanied defense of US territory. Ex post facto, Washington pointed to favorable and indisputable humanitarian consequences —liberation of women and girls, an end to malnutrition, and reconstruction. That the military baton has been partially passed to NATO strengthens this argument.

To return to the 1990s, many Security Council decisions had an ethical grounding. Resolution 794, which approved the US-led military effort in Somalia in December 1992, set a new standard for "humanitarian" hype—the word was mentioned no fewer than 18 times. The debate in October 1993 led to the publication of Presidential Decision Directive 25 and reticence about the desirability of humanitarian intervention in the midst of the Rwandan genocide.[25] Nonetheless, humanitarian concerns remained central to US and Western responses. Joseph Nye's remark about Kosovo merits repeating: "Policy experts may deplore such sympathies, but they are a democratic reality."[26]

What happens to the centrality of national interests and power maximization at the beginning of a new century? If the distance between ethical and interest perspectives has shrunk since September 11, is the way open for new thinking about the intersection of values and interests?

Michael Ignatieff has noted that places leading to moral pleas for humanitarian intervention are "bad neighborhoods" in which groups such as al-Qaeda can flourish. This argument seemed far-fetched when attacks took place against US embassies in East Africa and the USS *Cole*. It is less so now. "Our current debate about humanitarian intervention continues to construe intervening as an act of conscience," Ignatieff writes, "when in fact, since the 1990s began, intervening has also become an urgent state interest: to rebuild failed states so that they cease to be national security threats."[2]

Newly discovered "harder" interests join the "softer" line of argument from those who state that vital interests should also include wider international stability, respect for multilateral decisions, and compliance with such norms as international human rights and humanitarian law. Hence, humanitarian intervention not only can be morally legitimate but also can be justified on security grounds.

The humanitarian impulse has permeated foreign and defense policy establishments as well as transformed conceptions of interests and parameters of policy. The belief that democratic states have a long-term national interest as well as moral responsibility to promote human rights was dubbed "good international citizenship" by Australian foreign minister Gareth Evans.[28] Lloyd Axworthy's conviction about the link between basic rights and international security sustained Canada's human security agenda, which was continued by Sadako Ogata and Amartya Sen as chairs of the Commission on Human Security.[29]

The wake of the war on terrorism represents clear dangers for humanitarians and civil libertarians. Less obvious is the possibility that appropriately framed vital interests can also coincide with the humanitarian impulse. In a less interconnected world, collapsing states and humanitarian disasters could be isolated and kept at arm's length. Responses, if any, were mainly driven by moral imperatives because there were few genuine implications for security. Now failed states and human catastrophes pose problems not only to the denizens of war zones and their immediate neighbors but also to peoples worldwide. Robust responses, including military ones, "are thus strategic and moral imperatives."[30]

An accurate scorecard for intervention is required. Keeping the "humanitarian" in "humanitarian intervention" requires a just war focus on means and ends. This is not a trivial semantic distinction designed to score debating points but rather to ensure that informed discussions occur about the reality of the humanitarian impulse when vital interests are present. Even when there is a requirement to address extreme cases of suffering, one can never set aside the possibility of abuse or selective application. After September 11 the temptation to "take off the gloves" and set aside the laws of war in the pursuit against terrorism must be resisted.[31]

The dynamics of state failure and the challenge of non-state actors enter into this discussion. States are not created equal—neither strong nor failed ones. With 191 UN member states and growing, it is hardly surprising that some are crumbling or have collapsed. But not all weak states actually fail (Chad), and some failed states make a comeback (Lebanon). Viable indicators are required for thresholds that could justify both humanitarian and strategic responses, either reactive or preventive, in weak states. The rise of non-state actors presents still other problems for fulfilling the promise of the humanitarian impulse in contemporary wars. Despite the predilection to exercise the humanitarian option, the UN's capacity to respond adequately remains a question mark.[32]

Rhetorical landscape

At the beginning of the 1990s, many observers resented the Security Council's powers of self-definition about what constituted a "threat to international peace and security," which supposedly reflected mainly the diabolical wishes of the great powers. In the middle of the decade the Commission on Global Governance supported decisions motivated by the humanitarian impulse but found the stretched definition ill-advised. It recommended "an appropriate Charter amendment permitting such intervention but restricting it to cases that constitute a violation of the security of people so gross and extreme that it requires an international response on humanitarian grounds."[33]

Factors seen as legitimate by the Security Council included a range of humanitarian disasters, especially those involving large exoduses by internally and internationally displaced persons. Civil wars became the standard bill of fare, but rights trumped sovereignty in enough decisions that it was no longer fatuous to hope for what Francis M. Deng, the special representative of the secretary-general for internally displaced persons, had dared to call "sovereignty as responsibility."[34]

Endorsed by ICISS in its opening sentence, state sovereignty is not challenged but reinforced. However, if a state is unwilling or unable to protect the rights of its own citizens, it temporarily forfeits a moral claim to be treated as legitimate. Its sovereignty, as well as its right to nonintervention, are suspended, and a residual responsibility necessitates vigorous action by outsiders to protect populations at risk. In brief, the three traditional characteristics of a state in the Westphalian system—territory, authority, and population—are supplemented by a fourth: respect for human rights.

Vituperative reactions to Kofi Annan's speeches sought to parse the issue as pitting a North enthusiastic about humanitarian intervention against a reluctant South. Historically, the invocation by powerful states against weaker ones made that caricature politically attractive, at least on the surface. In addition, diplomats as well as officials of the UN and nongovernmental organizations seem unable to imagine organizing discussions except across a North-South divide.

However, regional consultations by ICISS and by the Fund for Peace and the Council on Foreign Relations suggest that such simplistic generalizations—if they ever made sense—no longer apply.[35] For example, many Africans tend to see the necessity for more, not less, humanitarian intervention. Rwanda was a sufficient enough trauma that the founding document of the newly christened African Union contains objectives that are diametrically opposed to those of its predecessor, the Organization of African Unity. Article 4 of the Constitutive Act stipulates "the right of the Union to intervene in a Member State pursuant to a decision of the Assembly in respect of grave circumstances, namely: war crimes, genocide and crimes against humanity."[36] Although the motivations are anything except humanitarian, powerful states that routinely spouted anti-intervention stances (China, India, and Russia) have become more openly supportive—in their cases, against armed fundamentalists with separatist agendas in Muslim areas.[37]

Recent initiatives reflect changes in the moral and strategic landscape. Humanitarian intervention becomes more plausible while motives become more clouded. When there is sufficient operational capacity and political will, legal objections have little consequence. Article 2 of the UN Charter, stipulating the principle of nonintervention, is one thing. But sovereignty is "organized hypocrisy," as Stephen Krasner reminds us.[38]

Moreover, humanitarian issues are only the tip of the increasingly visible iceberg of human security. By the end of the decade, AIDS was recognized in Security Council resolution 1308 as a threat to international peace and security. A Charter amendment for humanitarian intervention was hardly necessary when, increasingly, states accept the legitimate purview of the Security Council to define "threats to international peace and *human* security."

The broadening of the acceptable basis for Security Council decisions, as well as an opening of minds and perspectives about North-South divisions, has implications for multilateral diplomacy. The energy spent and the ink spilled on Security Council reform have been poor investments. Rather than any official constitutional changes, the broadened scope of activities and the gradual evolution in working procedures hold more potential for substantial change than proposals for altering the council's composition, eliminating the veto, or using emergency sessions of the General Assembly.[39]

The resilience of long-standing shibboleths among many nonpermanent members of the council suggests a need for more pragmatic and less predictable positions. Is rapid and complete localization the best strategy (i.e., the Afghan model), or a more massive external presence with longer-term trusteeship (i.e., the model in the Balkans and East Timor)? Are the recommendations to strengthen the UN's military oversight as recommended by the Brahimi report not better seen as desperately needed by countries torn by conflict rather than as a possible invasion of sovereignty and a drain on development funds? What would be the operational and resource implications of implementing the doctrine of responsible sovereignty?

Political correctness has long been the bane of the UN's existence. It does not serve the individual or collective interests of the vulnerable and weak states in the global South.

Military landscape

The extent to which the Security Council has adopted decisions under Chapter VII was without precedent, but so too was the UN's demonstrated inability to conduct enforcement operations. The unwillingness by major powers to spend money was matched by an unwillingness to run risks. Whether or not the council adequately anticipated and appreciated the difficulties is open to question, but too many UN-mandated or UN-controlled military activities encountered significant resistance and loss of life. Decisions were not matched by resources (e.g., in the so-called safe areas in Bosnia, probably the least safe havens in the Balkans). And after forces were deployed, they failed to generate consent in the field. Worst of all, in the face of casualties, the world organization cut and ran in Somalia and Rwanda and thereby made a mockery of the humanitarian impulse.

Moreover, moral and realpolitik consequentialists alike argued that the unintended negative effects (rewards for ethnic cleansers in Bosnia, mass flight from Kosovo once bombing began) meant that bad consequences often outweighed good intentions.[40] Others saw the use of force as undermining international order or obfuscating neocolonial projects.[41]

By the end of the 1990s, the United Nations itself was effectively out of the business of serious military action. The ambitions of Secretary-General Boutros Boutros-Ghali in his 1992 *Agenda for Peace* were considerably subdued by 1995 in his *Supplement to an Agenda for Peace*.[42] The world organization's comparative advantage was in peacekeeping. Acting on the humanitarian impulse, let alone peace enforcement, required not consent and impartiality but the personnel of a major-league military.

The dominant military trend over the 1990s was "subcontracting" by the Security Council.[43] The devolution of responsibility for the enforcement of Chapter VII decisions, virtually all of which had a substantial humanitarian rationale, went to "coalitions of the willing." Instead of being the "doer" envisaged by the Charter, the Security Council often became the "approver" of operations conducted by others. What began as an experiment in the Gulf War and northern Iraq ended up being the standard operating procedure in Somalia, the Balkans, Haiti, and East Timor. The disparity between demand and supply—along with inadequate financing and diminished confidence—meant that the world organization increasingly relied on regional organizations and ad hoc coalitions to ensure compliance with enforcement decisions.

In brief, not everyone can act on the humanitarian impulse. The nature of violence in contemporary war zones means that only the militaries of major powers, and not neutrals or smaller powers, need apply. Military clout is far more important than moral clout, as evidenced by "humanitarian bombing." Furthermore, certain kinds of heavy airlift capacity are absolutely essential for many humanitarian efforts. Yet such technology and airlift capacity are available only from NATO and the United States.

Over the course of the 1990s, the Security Council adopted new roles in acting upon the humanitarian impulse. Sometimes the world organization handed over responsibilities entirely, sometimes it was in the backseat (instead of the driver's seat), and sometimes it worked in tandem with an array of regional institutions. For these eventualities, there are at least three conceptual challenges to military doctrine.

The most critical is to fill a doctrinal void in operationalizing the humanitarian impulse. A number of specific challenges are distinct from those of either peacekeeping or war fighting, the well-understood endpoints on a spectrum of international military action. What about challenges in-between? How can protection be afforded to populations at risk? How can those who prey upon them be deterred?

Over the course of the 1990s, operations in the middle of the spectrum were common. Two related but distinct sets of objectives exist within the category of enforcement decisions—namely, compelling compliance and providing protection.[44] The former, commonly referred to as "peace enforcement," requires vast military resources and political will. It involves the search for comprehensive political settlements leading to sustainable peace. It contains traditional peacekeeping tasks such as monitoring ceasefires, but it also encompasses complex tasks whose ultimate success requires deadly force. Examples include the Implementation Force and the Stabilization Force organized by NATO in Bosnia, the US-led Multinational Force in Haiti, and the UN Mission in Sierra Leone. A variant is the application of deadly force to compel parties to the negotiating table. NATO air strikes preceding the signing of the Dayton Accords are one example. Another is the early phase of intervention in Liberia where ECOWAS deployed its monitoring group (ECOMOG).

Another form of enforcement action, "coercive protection," is directly pertinent for the humanitarian impulse, but it has a variety of forms that are rarely specified. The most common are maintaining humanitarian corridors, disarming refugees, protecting aid convoys, and creating safe havens or protected areas. Prominent examples include the no-fly zone in northern Iraq and the so-called safe areas in Bosnia.

A particularly important dimension of this kind of operation is the force posture of intervening troops. Coercive protection is distinct from other operations, which have military forces oriented in relation to other military forces. Peacekeeping involves the monitoring of military ceasefires or the interposition of forces between armed parties to the conflict; compelling compliance involves the potential use of force against conflicting parties or spoilers; and war fighting involves combat against designated opponents. In contrast, the provision of coercive protection requires the interposition of forces between potential attackers (armies, militias, and gangs) and civilians.

Buried in the "gray area" of the responsibility to protect civilians are numerous tasks that are not favored by militaries around the world: the forcible disarmament of belligerents (especially in refugee camps like those in the mid-1990s in eastern Zaire); the meaningful protection of safe areas (the gruesome counterexample of Srebrenica comes immediately to mind); and the protection of humanitarian workers (as expatriates like Fred Cuny and local officials alike would testify, if they were alive).

There has been little success in meeting the challenges of coercive protection since the end of the Cold War. There seems to be a lack of institutional adjustment, at least as is indicated by military doctrines that, to date, have failed to specify ways to meet the needs for coercive protection of civilians, the challenge of the responsibility to protect.[45]

The second challenge results from the necessity to ensure more than a modicum of international accountability for operations that are approved by the United Nations but fall totally under another institution's operational control. In only a few conflicts—Georgia and West Africa—has the world organization monitored the activities of the regional organizations acting as subcontractors for an internationally approved operation. If the UN's imprimatur for a coalition of the willing is to be meaningful, more accountability and transparency are necessary for future subcontractors. What kinds of monitors in which situations with which types of mandates would be helpful? What kinds of independent reports should go back to the Security Council before an ongoing mandate is renewed? Can international finance be used to secure, as a quid pro quo, independent international monitoring?

Finally, military establishments have become interested in humanitarian tasks that were until recently seen as peripheral. No longer are politicians and humanitarians chasing a uniformly reluctant military and pleading for help. Military budgets, operational training, and officers' career paths are benefiting from humanitarian tasks. "Military humanitarianism" was once viewed as an oxymoron—indeed, some humanitarians still refuse to put the two words together—but it is an accurate depiction of a central aspect of contemporary preparations by armed forces. What was once feared as "mission creep" is not necessarily unwelcome. Although National Security Adviser Condoleezza Rice quipped that the 82nd Airborne Division's comparative advantage was not in escorting schoolchildren, there are other tasks in operations motivated by humanitarianism that require first-rate militaries.

Conclusion

The prominence of the humanitarian impulse altered the ethical, rhetorical, and military landscapes of Security Council decision making in the 1990s. The nature and scope of enforcement decisions have amounted, on occasion, to a fundamental increase in the relevance of humanitarian values in relationship to narrowly defined vital interests. After September 11, the distinction between the moral and the self-interested has become less pronounced—or, perhaps better stated, the threat of terrorism has added salience to issues that transcend previously humanitarian dimensions. The beat of war drums for Iraq and the war itself had nothing to do with humanitarian action, but that justification eventually emerged after others fell flat. Indeed, the initial aftermath had all the makings of a major humanitarian crisis. In any event, the experience of the 1990s is clear: potential victims and perpetrators of genocide and ethnic cleansing may find that neighbors, ad hoc coalitions, or even single states have two reasons, moral and geostrategic, to intervene.

At the end of the day, however, predictions are not sensible. As any military historian anxious to avoid fighting the last war knows, lessons are difficult enough to identify in the first place because political, temporal, military, strategic, and geographic translations from one situation to another are methodologically arduous and operationally problematic. Everything is not sui generis, but there are severe limits to comparisons across cases. In thinking merely of temporal dimensions, for instance, making use of cases of intervention during the Cold War has little contemporary significance. And trying to apply lessons from cases between 1990 and the events in October 1993 in Mogadishu is of limited utility when attempting to gauge the willingness of Washington and others to run risks in the Congo even after Rwanda's genocide. The ultimate impact of wars in Afghanistan and Iraq is anyone's guess.

Three stages of individual and organizational learning are commonplace in the business literature but too rarely penetrate analyses of humanitarian intervention: identification, when problems are observed and data are collected; diagnosis, when information is analyzed and underlying beliefs are questioned; and implementation, when revised policies and procedures are actually institutionalized and public and bureaucratic support is mobilized on behalf of changes. Scholars and practitioners who are members of the international conference circuit frequently employ the conventional vocabulary of "lessons learned," but decision makers and bureaucrats rarely take steps to correct their courses. Have governments and agencies really learned from efforts in Bosnia that halfhearted or symbolic military action may be as bad as or worse than no action at all? Have they actually learned that humanitarian gestures cannot replace substantial commitments?

Why is there a gap between lessons compiled and lessons actually learned, between rhetoric and reality? Some suggest that evaluations defuse pressure for change rather than stimulate it. Cynics simply point to hypocrisy and leave it at that. Sometimes they are right, but often there are other reasons. Governments and agencies are not monoliths. Those who conduct evaluations, draft resolutions, and make statements have not always secured political backing. Competing interests dominate bureaucratic decision-making. Even when lessons appear to have been agreed in headquarters, it can prove extremely difficult to translate them into practice on the ground.

To the extent that lessons remain relegated to file drawers, coffee tables, or book jackets, the concept of learning is perverted. It would be more accurate to speak of "lessons spurned." Alex de Waal points to a puzzling contemporary paradox— the international system "appears to have an extraordinary capacity to absorb criticism, not reform itself, and yet emerge strengthened."[46] Academic and policy analysts should be struck about how little the international humanitarian system has changed over the 1990s.[47] A greater-than-usual degree of modesty is in order.

Policy analysis tends to extrapolate from recent headlines—an acute version of Andrew Hurrell's criticism of social scientists as being mired in a "relentless presentism."[48] In the aftermath of the intervention on behalf of the Kurds, there was nothing that humanitarians could not do; the end of the Cold War signaled not only a UN renaissance but also the birth of a new world order. Virtually to the day only three years later, in April 1994, apparently nothing could be done in the face of Rwanda's genocide. In 1999, depending on one's point of view, the humanitarian intervention vintage was either an *annus mirabilis* or an *annus horribilis* because of Kosovo and East Timor.

The tragic attacks of September 11 riveted the world's attention upon an international response to terrorism, and the war in Iraq then became the obsession. But in spite of the distractions, diplomats and scholars are forced to revisit thorny humanitarian issues. In the wake of military action against the Taliban and a spreading war on terrorism, dilemmas of humanitarian intervention once again found the spotlight, and the aftermath of the war in Iraq brought back to center stage the familiar challenges of access to, as well as assistance and protection of, civilians trapped in hapless countries. So too is the cast of characters, humanitarian agencies, and outside military forces. Furthermore, "it is only a matter of time before reports emerge again from somewhere of massacres, mass starvation, rape, and ethnic cleansing," write Gareth Evans and Mohamed Sahnoun. "And then the question will arise again in the Security Council, in political capitals, and in the media: What do we do?"[49]

Undoubtedly the attacks against New York and Washington, and the Bush administration's vendetta against Saddam Hussein, have increased pressures on the armed forces, especially in the United States, to focus on fighting wars and avoid the "distractions" of humanitarian work. However, there have been substantial humanitarian dimensions to the effort—including the liberation of the female half of the Afghan population. Indeed, the effort has partially been sold in such terms, and satisfying humanitarian needs is crucial to the mission's ultimate success. One analyst somewhat optimistically speculates that "it may be that mobilization on this scale, although its first aim is self-defense, will galvanize the Western allies to a more activist concern for misery across the globe."[50] Another argues in a more instrumental way that "if America and the West are to achieve safety for themselves in the coming years, they will have to show that they care about more than just their own suffering."[51]

Even when conscience-shocking events occur in faraway places that do not directly threaten vital interests, publics often clamor that "something be done." If interests and humanitarian concerns overlap—if there is sufficient symmetry between the humanitarian impulse and strategic stakes—perhaps publics will demand more robust action to protect civilians from the ravages of war and thugs posing as political leaders. If previous experience in Afghanistan and the ongoing efforts on the ground in Iraq are any indication, and as the ever-widening war against terrorism in such places as Indonesia makes clear, the challenges of fragmentation and humanitarian action are certainly not unique to the 1990s. The humanitarian impulse remains vital.

Notes

1 Such an impulse also appears in the face of natural disasters, but the politics of helping are totally different when acting upon request rather than against the will or stated wishes of local political authorities.

2 Matthew S. Parry, "Pyrrhic Victories and the Collapse of Humanitarian Principles," *Journal of Humanitarian Assistance* (October 2002): 4, www. jha.ac/articles/a094.htm.

3 David Rieff, *A Bed for the Night: Humanitarianism in Crisis* (New York: Simon and Schuster, 2002).

4 Adam Roberts, "The Role of Humanitarian Issues in International Politics in the 1990s," *International Review of the Red Cross* 81, no. 833 (1999): 19. See also Michael Ignatieff, "Human Rights: The Midlife Crisis," *New York Review of Books* 46, no. 9 (1999): 58–62.

5 See S. Neil MacFarlane, *Intervention in Contemporary World Politics*, Adelphi Paper no. 350 (Oxford: Oxford University Press, 2002), 79. He cites, among others, the struggles between Protestants and Catholics in fifteenth- and sixteenth-century Europe, the interventionist tendencies of the French Revolution, and the position of the Holy Alliance in the nineteenth century; humanitarian intervention is also a theme.

6 Christine Bourloyannis, "The Security Council of the United Nations and the Implementation of International Humanitarian Law," *Denver Journal of International Law and Policy* 20, no. 3 (1993): 43.

7 Th. A. van Baarda, "The Involvement of the Security Council in Maintaining International Law," *Netherlands Quarterly of Human Rights* 12, no. 1 (1994): 140.

8 Edward Luttwak, "Kofi's Rule: Humanitarian Intervention and Neocolonialism," *National Interest*, no. 58 (Winter 1999–2000): 60.

9 Kofi A. Annan, *The Question of Intervention* (New York: United Nations, 1999).

10 See Raimo Väyrynen, *The Age of Humanitarian Emergencies*, Research for Action no. 25 (Helsinki: World Institute for Development Economics Research, 1996); and Nicholas J. Wheeler, *Saving Strangers: Humanitarian Intervention in International Society* (Oxford: Oxford University Press, 2000).

11 For example, see the 2,200 entries essentially in English from the 1990s in the key-worded bibliography of Thomas G. Weiss and Don Hubert, *The Responsibility to Protect: Research, Bibliography, and Background*, supplementary volume of the International Commission on Intervention and State Sovereignty (Ottawa: International Development Research Centre, 2001), 225–336, www.iciss-ciise.gc.ca.

12 International Commission on Intervention and State Sovereignty, *The Responsibility to Protect* (Ottawa: International Development Research Centre, 2001).

13 Independent International Commission on Kosovo, *Kosovo Report* (Oxford: Oxford University Press, 2000).

14 *Interagency Review of U.S. Government Civilian Humanitarian and Transition Programs*, document dated 12 July 2000; and Alton Frye, ed., *Humanitarian Intervention: Crafting a Workable Doctrine* (New York: Council on Foreign Relations, 2000).

15 Advisory Council on International Affairs and Advisory Committee on Issues of Public International Law, *Humanitarian Intervention* (The Hague: AIV and CAVV, 2000); and Danish Institute of International Affairs, *Humanitarian Intervention: Legal and Political Aspects* (Copenhagen: Danish Institute of International Affairs, 1999).

16 For overviews, see David Cortright and George A. Lopez, eds., *The Sanctions Decade: Assessing UN Strategies in the 1990s* (Boulder, Colo.: Lynne Rienner, 2000); and Thomas G. Weiss, David Cortright, George A. Lopez, and Larry Minear, eds., *Political Gain and Civilian Pain: Humanitarian Impacts of Economic Sanctions* (Lanham, Md.: Rowman Littlefield, 1997).

17 For overviews, see Michael J. Perry, *The Idea of Human Rights: Four Inquiries* (New York: Oxford University Press, 1998); and Thomas Risse, Stephen C. Ropp, and Kathryn Sikkink, eds., *The Power of Human Rights: International Norms and Domestic Change* (Cambridge: Cambridge University Press, 1999).

18 Christopher Greenwood, *Humanitarian Intervention: Law and Policy* (Oxford: Oxford University Press, 2001).

19 See Simon Chesterman, *Just War or Just Peace? Humanitarian Intervention and International Law* (Oxford: Oxford University Press, 2001); and Michael Byers and Simon Chesterman, "Changing Rules About Rules? Unilateral Humanitarian Intervention and the Future

of International Law," in *Humanitarian Intervention: Ethical, Legal, and Political Dilemmas*, ed. J. F. Holzgrefe and Robert O. Keohane (Cambridge: Cambridge University Press, 2003), 177–203.

20 For a discussion, see Thomas G. Weiss, "Humanitarian Shell Games: Whither UN Reform?" *Security Dialogue* 29, no. 1 (March 1998): 9–24.

21 See Joanna Macrae, ed., *The New Humanitarianisms: A Review of Trends in Global Humanitarian Action*, HPG Report no. 11 (London: Overseas Development Institute, 2002).

22 See, for example, Larry Minear, *The Humanitarian Enterprise: Dilemmas and Discoveries* (Bloomfield, Conn.: Kumarian, 2002); Marc Lindenberg and Coralie Bryant, *Going Global: Transforming Relief and Development NGOs* (Bloomfield, Conn.: Kumarian, 2001), esp. 65–99; and Thomas G. Weiss, *Military-Civilian Interactions*, 2nd ed. (Lanham, Md.: Rowman Littlefield, 2004).

23 See Mario Bettati and Bernard Kouchner, *Le devoir d'ingérence* (Paris: Denoël, 1987); and Mario Bettati, *Le droit d'ingérence: Mutation de l' ordre international* (Paris: Odile Jacob, 1996).

24 Michael Walzer, "The Argument About Humanitarian Intervention," *Dissent* (Winter 2002): 29.

25 See Samantha Powers, *"A Problem from Hell": America and the Age of Genocide* (New York: Basic Books, 2002).

26 Joseph P. Nye Jr., "Redefining the National Interest," *Foreign Affairs* 78, no. 4 (1999): 30.

27 Michael Ignatieff, "Intervention and State Failure," *Dissent* (Winter 2002): 115.

28 See Nicholas J. Wheeler and Tim Dunne, "Good International Citizenship: A Third Way for British Foreign Policy," *International Affairs* 74, no. 4 (1998): 847–70.

29 Lloyd Axworthy, "Human Security and Global Governance: Putting People First," *Global Governance* 7, no. 1 (2001): 19–23; and Rob McRae and Don Hubert, eds., *Human Security and the New Diplomacy* (Montreal: McGill-Queen's University Press, 2001).

30 See Robert I. Rotberg, "Failed States in a World of Terror," *Foreign Affairs* 81, no. 4 (2002): 127.

31 See Michael Ignatieff, "Human Rights, the Laws of War, and Terrorism," Dankwart Rustow Memorial Lecture, The CUNY Graduate Center, 10 October 2002.

32 The role of non-state actors is discussed in Thomas G. Weiss and Peter J. Hoffman, "Making Humanitarianism Work," in *Making States Work: State Failure and the Crisis of Governance*, ed. Simon Chesterman, Michael Ignatieff, and Ramesh Thakur (Tokyo: UN University, 2005), 296–317.

33 Commission on Global Governance, *Our Global Neighbourhood* (Oxford: Oxford University Press, 1995), 90.

34 Francis M. Deng, "Frontiers of Sovereignty," *Leiden Journal of International Law* 8, no. 2 (1995): 249–86; and Frances M. Deng, Sadikiel Kimaro, Terrence Lyons, Donald Rothchild, and I. William Zartman, *Sovereignty as Responsibility: Conflict Management in Africa* (Washington, DC: Brookings Institution Press, 1996).

35 For a summary of ICISS consultations, see Weiss and Hubert, *The Responsibility to Protect*, 349–98. See the Fund for Peace website, www.fund-forpeace.org, regarding perspectives from Africa and the Americas.

36 See www.africa-union.org/root/au/Aboutau/Constitutive_Act_en.htm.

37 Giandomenico Picco, "New Entente After September 11th? U.S., Russia, China, and India," *Global Governance* 9, no. 1 (2003): 15–21.

38 Stephen D. Krasner, *Sovereignty: Organized Hypocrisy* (Princeton, NJ: Princeton University Press, 1999).

39 Thomas G. Weiss, "The Illusion of UN Security Council Reform," *Washington Quarterly* 26, no. 4 (2003): 141–67.

40 A vast array of humanitarian agencies supported this stance, joining forces with Henry Kissinger following his book *Does America Need a Foreign Policy? Toward a Diplomacy for the Twenty-First Century* (New York: Simon and Schuster, 2001).

41 See Robert Jackson, *The Global Covenant: Human Conduct in a World of States* (Oxford: Oxford University Press, 2000); and Mohammed Ayoob, "Humanitarian Intervention and State Sovereignty," *International Journal of Human Rights* 6, no. 1 (2002): 81–102.

42 Boutros Boutros-Ghali, *An Agenda for Peace* (New York: United Nations, 1995).

43 See Thomas G. Weiss, ed., *Beyond UN Subcontracting: Task-Sharing with Regional Security Arrangements and Service-Providing NGOs* (London: Macmillan, 1998).

44 This is spelled out in detail in Weiss and Hubert, *The Responsibility to Protect*, 177–206.

45 John Mackinlay has analyzed the doctrinal need to define accurately types of insurgents in order to avoid a "one fix approach and craft different force postures and counter-strategies." The same argument applies to the protection of civilians. See John Mackinlay, *Globalisation and Insurgency*, Adelphi Paper no. 352 (Oxford: Oxford University Press, 2002), 12.

46 Alex de Waal, *Famine Crimes: Politics and the Disaster Relief Industry in Africa* (Oxford: James Currey, 1997), vi.

47 For a discussion of the failures to change as a result of analyses, see Nicola Reindorp and Peter Wiles, *Humanitarian Coordination: Lessons from Recent Experience* (London: Overseas Development Institute, 2001); and A. Wood, R. Apthorpe, and J. Borton, eds., *Evaluating International Humanitarian Action: Reflections from Practitioners* (London: Zed Books, 2001).

48 Andrew Hurrell, foreword to Hedley Bull, *The Anarchical Society: A Study of Order in World Politics*, 3rd ed. (New York: Columbia University Press, 2002), xiii.

49 Gareth Evans and Mohamed Sahnoun, "The Responsibility to Protect," *Foreign Affairs* 81, no. 6 (2002): 100.

50 Dana H. Allin, *NATO's Balkan Interventions,* Adelphi Paper no. 347 (Oxford: Oxford University Press, 2002), 98.

51 Nicolaus Mills and Kira Brunner, preface to Nicolaus Mills and Kira Brunner, eds., *The New Killing Fields: Massacre and the Politics of Intervention* (New York: Basic Books, 2002), ix–x.

14

THE SUNSET OF HUMANITARIAN INTERVENTION?

The responsibility to protect in a unipolar era

The notion that human beings matter more than sovereignty radiated brightly, albeit briefly, across the international political horizon of the 1990s. The wars on terrorism and in Iraq—the current obsession both in the United Nations and in the United States[1]—suggest that the political will for humanitarian intervention has evaporated at the outset of the new millennium. The United States is the preponderant power, but its inclination to commit significant political and military resources for human protection has waned.

Nonetheless, and before we close the door on humanitarian intervention, we should remind ourselves to avoid Andrew Hurrell's "relentless presentism,"[2] which reared its head on 11 September 2001. The use of military force to protect human life had been an international priority, but the al-Qaeda attacks were a political earthquake—changing the strategic landscape, intellectual discourse, and international agenda. And when the dust from the World Trade Center and the Pentagon settled, humanitarian intervention became a tertiary issue.

As purse strings are often attached to heart strings, the pages of *Ethics & International Affairs* provide a useful illustration of the changing fortunes of humanitarian intervention.[3] The topic was central to only about 10 percent of articles at the outset of the 1990s, whereas in the middle years it reached almost a third and by the end of the decade comprised nearly half of the journal's main articles. Then, after 11 September 2001, the moral shifted dramatically from fad to fade. The new focus became rules of the game for preemptive war and fighting terrorism.

Hence, a longer historical perspective is instructive in thinking about future possibilities for military rescue of human beings under extreme duress in war zones. While "normatively based challenges to the sovereign rights of states are hardly new in international history,"[4] nonetheless with respect to humanitarian affairs the Security Council was missing in action during the Cold War. No resolution mentioned the humanitarian dimensions of any conflict from 1945 until the Six

Day War of 1967, and the first mention of the International Committee of the Red Cross (ICRC) was not until 1978. In the 1970s and 1980s, "the Security Council gave humanitarian aspects of armed conflict limited priority . . . but the early nineteen-nineties can be seen as a watershed."[5] The Security Council had a virtual humanitarian *tabula rasa* when, suddenly from 1990 to 1994, twice as many resolutions were passed as during the first 45 years of UN history. Through repeated references, in the context of Chapter VII, to humanitarian crises as threats to international peace and security, the council's broader approach took shape.

For Adam Roberts the decade was one during which "humanitarian issues have played a historically unprecedented role in international politics."[6] Some dispute Edward Luttwak's characterization of "Kofi's rule . . . whereby human rights outrank sovereignty,"[7] but humanitarian intervention was a most controversial topic within UN circles. The secretary-general's own speeches[8] were widely debated because "the age of humanitarian emergencies" had led to policies of "saving strangers."[9] An academic cottage industry grew, and governments sponsored a host of policy initiatives: a Swedish initiative, the Independent Commission on Kosovo;[10] the Clinton administration's overview by the Policy Planning Staff and a report from the Council on Foreign Relations;[11] and major inquiries into the legal authority for intervention by the Dutch and Danish governments.[12]

Future policy debates and actions will be framed by the International Commission on Intervention and State Sovereignty (ICISS), whose *The Responsibility to Protect* and an accompanying research volume were published in December 2001.[13] A host of largely positive reviews have appeared.[14] While some were cool about the principles, even one of the concept's harshest opponents, Mohammed Ayoob, admits its "considerable moral force."[15]

Humanitarian issues have temporarily been downgraded on the public policy agenda, but as ICISS cochairs Gareth Evans and Mohamed Sahnoun remind readers of *Foreign Affairs*: "It is only a matter of time before reports emerge again from somewhere of massacres, mass starvation, rape, and ethnic cleansing."[16] Military responses to complex humanitarian emergencies remain uncomfortable challenges for the state system; but when another "military intervention for human protection purposes" is required, *The Responsibility to Protect* provides an essential framework.

Because I take the document seriously, this essay focuses on a number of shortcomings with the ICISS approach. First, the report is not as forward-looking as the commissioners thought or as many opponents feared. Second, the concerns of the most vehement critics, especially developing countries, are misplaced, because the problem is too little humanitarian intervention, not too much. Third, the purported danger that the concept of the responsibility to protect might become a Trojan horse to be used by the great powers to intervene is fundamentally incorrect; rather, intervention by the United States in its preemptive or preventive war mode is *the* most pressing concern. Fourth, the notion of reforming the UN Security Council is an illusion; the real challenge is to identify crises where Washington's tactical multilateralism kicks in.

The responsibility to protect: ahead or behind the curve?

ICISS identified only two threshold cases: large-scale loss of life and ethnic cleansing, underway or anticipated. Humanitarian intervention should be subject to four precautionary conditions: right intention, last resort, proportional means, and reasonable prospects of success. And finally, the Security Council is the preferred decision maker.[17]

ICISS pushed out the normative envelope in two ways. The first is in the report's opening sentences:

> State sovereignty implies responsibility, and the primary responsibility for the protection of its people lies with the state itself. Where a population is suffering serious harm, as a result of internal war, insurgency, repression or state failure, and the state in question is unwilling or unable to halt or avert it, the principle of non-intervention yields to the international responsibility to protect.[18]

The report affirmed the notion of sovereignty but insisted that it also encompassed a state's responsibility to protect populations within its borders. For those who chart changes in international discourse, the evolution toward reinforcing state capacity is key. This is not nostalgia for the repressive national security state of the past, but recognition, even among committed advocates of human rights and robust intervention, that state authority is elementary to enduring peace and reconciliation. Human rights can really only be defended by democratic states with the authority and the monopoly of force to sustain such norms. The remedy thus is not to rely on international trusteeships and transnational NGOs, but rather to fortify, reconstitute, or build viable states from failed, collapsed, or weak ones.

Sovereignty "is not just a protection for the state against coercion by other states," writes one set of analysts. "It is also the means of locating responsibility for the protection of people and property and for the exercise of governance in a territory."[19] There is a growing awareness not only of the international legal bases of the contemporary state system but also of the practical reality that domestic authorities are best positioned to protect fundamental rights. In brief, the three recognized characteristics of a sovereign state since the Peace of Westphalia (territory, authority, population) are supplemented by a fourth (respect for human rights).

The second contribution of ICISS consists of shifting the burden away from the rights of outsiders to intervene toward a framing that spotlights those suffering from war and violence. Moving away from the picturesque vocabulary of the French Doctors Movement[20] shifts the fulcrum of debate away from the rights of interveners and toward the rights of affected populations and the responsibilities (if not obligations) of outsiders to protect. The new perspective prioritizes those suffering from starvation or being raped and the duty of international institutions to respond.

For all of its inherent value in moving the idea from scholarly journals to the policy mainstream, the concept is not as innovative as ICISS thought. For example, the work of special representative of the secretary-general on IDPs Francis Deng on "sovereignty as responsibility" appeared throughout the 1990s.[21] Former *New York Times* columnist Anthony Lewis describes the consensus and the report as capturing "the international state of mind."[22]

Were the commissioners more timid than they could and should have been? They set the bar for humanitarian intervention very high:

> Large-scale loss of life, actual or apprehended, with genocidal intent or not, which is the product either of deliberate state action, or state neglect or inability to act, or a failed state situation; or large-scale "ethnic cleansing," actual or apprehended, whether carried out by killing, forced expulsion, acts of terror or rape.[23]

This double-barreled justification addresses two conscience-shocking triggers, but the "just cause threshold" is higher than many would have hoped. For instance, these recommendations fall short of the 1998 Statute of the International Criminal Court (ICC), whose "crimes against humanity" mentions everything from murder and slavery to imprisonment and "other inhumane acts of a similar character intentionally causing great suffering."

The value of a shopping list is debatable, but there were at least two other obvious candidates for inclusion in ICISS's threshold conditions: the overthrow of democratically elected regimes (especially favored by states and regional institutions in Africa as well as in parts of Latin America) and massive abuses of human rights (favored by many in the West). The insertion of "actual *or* apprehended" opens the door, but compromise among enthusiastic and skeptical commissioners required a lower common denominator.

The height of the bar is puzzling in that the Security Council–approved and US-led effort in Haiti in 1994 had already set the precedent of outside pressure—including the threat of the 82nd Airborne Division—to restore an elected government; and the UN, the Economic Community of West African States (ECOWAS), and the Organization of African Unity condemned the overthrow of the government in Sierra Leone in 1997, which led to the Nigeria-led ECOWAS intervention subsequently sanctioned by the council. Moreover, the ICISS thresholds do not include systematic racial discrimination and massive human rights abuse, *jus cogens* norms for most international lawyers. Indeed, the new charter of the African Union codifies lower thresholds for humanitarian intervention than those of ICISS. As one specialist observed, "the ICISS thresholds for intervention are apparently more conservative than those of African states, but perhaps not more so than those of Asian and Latin American states, which historically are among the staunchest subscribers to the international law principles of nonintervention and state sovereignty."[24]

Thus, the ICISS report is neither forerunner nor pacesetter. It usefully stakes out a helpful middle ground.

11 September and US strategic priorities

ICISS finalized its report in mid-August 2001, and the chairs reconvened the group in late September of that year. To their credit, the commissioners did not try to repackage their report with the flavor of that tragic month: "The Commission's report was largely completed before the appalling attacks of 11 September 2001 on New York and Washington DC, and was not conceived as addressing the kind of challenge posed by such attacks."[25] However, they added a passage stating that the special challenges of fighting the scourge of terrorism demand adherence to the commission's precautionary principles.

Though ICISS met with Hubert Védrine, they failed to appreciate adequately the implications of what the French foreign minister dubbed the *hyper-puissance*. Bipolarity had given way to what was supposed to be US primacy, but the military prowess in Afghanistan and Iraq makes "primacy" a vast understatement. Scholars speculate about the nuances of economic and cultural leverage resulting from US soft power,[26] but the hard currency of international politics undoubtedly remains military might. Before the war on Iraq, Washington was already spending more on its military than the next 15–25 countries (depending on who was counting); with an additional appropriation of almost $90 billion for the war on Iraq, the United States now spends more than the rest of the world's militaries combined.[27]

Security Council efforts to control US actions are beginning to resemble the Roman Senate's attempts to control the emperor. Diplomats along First Avenue in New York almost unanimously describe the debate surrounding the resolution withdrawn on the eve of the war in Iraq as "a referendum not on the means of disarming Iraq but on the American use of power."[28] The notion of "empire" is inaccurate and, as John Ikenberry aptly notes, "misses the distinctive aspects of the global political order that has developed around U.S. power. . . . there are limits on American imperial pretensions even in a unipolar era."[29]

Today, there are two world "organizations': the United Nations—global in membership—and the United States—global in reach and power. Critics of US hegemony—and several members of ICISS are among them—argue that the exercise of military power should be based on UN authority instead of US capacity.[30] But the two are inseparable. As its coercive capacity is always on loan, UN-led or UN-approved operations with substantial military requirements take place only when Washington approves or at least acquiesces. Although small battalions of British and French soldiers had demonstration effects in toning up UN operations in Sierra Leone in 2000 and the eastern Congo in 2003, US air-lift capacity and military muscle and technology are required for larger and longer-duration deployments. For enforcement (as opposed to traditional peacekeeping), the value added by other militaries is political, not operational.

This reality will not change unless Europeans have an independent military capacity, and to date neither populations nor parliaments have demonstrated any willingness to spend more on defense. Rhetoric on ESDP (European Security and Defence Policy) far outpaces spending. Andrew Moravcsik argues for a division of labor between US enforcement and European peacekeeping.[31] But the next Kosovo will almost surely take place outside of the continent, and Europe's failure to develop an independent capacity—indeed, its military capabilities continue to decline vis-à-vis those of the United States—imposes a binding constraint on UN activities, especially humanitarian intervention.

With Washington's focus elsewhere, the danger is not too much but rather too little humanitarian intervention. US and UN dawdling as Liberia came apart in mid-2003 provides a more likely future scenario than any abuse of the responsibility to protect. ICISS was originally established in response to the Security Council's failure to address dire humanitarian crises in Rwanda and Kosovo. In 1994, intervention was too little and too late to halt or even slow the murder of what may have been as many as 800,000 people in the Great Lakes region of Africa. In 1999, the formidable North Atlantic Treaty Organization (NATO) finessed the council and waged war for the first time in Kosovo. But many observers saw the 78-day bombing effort as being too much and too early, perhaps creating as much human suffering as it relieved. In both cases, the Security Council was unable to authorize the use of deadly force to protect vulnerable populations.

However, the lack of reaction in Rwanda represents a far more serious threat to international order and justice than the Security Council's paralysis in Kosovo. Not all claims to justice are equally valid, and NATO's was greater than Serbia's or Russia's. At least in the Balkans a regional organization took a unanimous decision to enable human protection. Justified criticism arose about timidity: Washington's domestic politics meant that military action remained at an altitude of 15,000 feet when ground troops would have prevented the mass exodus. Nonetheless, past or potential victims would undoubtedly agree with NATO's decision. The only survey to date of victims in war zones reports that fully two-thirds of civilians under siege who were interviewed in 12 war-torn societies by the ICRC want more intervention, and only 10 percent want none.[32]

Is humanitarian intervention a smokescreen for bullies?

If there is a genuine concern to prevent future Rwandas, what explains the fear that the concept might become hostage to great powers and be manipulated as an excuse for intervention? Using the "H" word—for "humanitarian," though it may also be used facetiously for "hurrah" or bitterly for "hypocritical"—stakes out prematurely the moral high ground. Thucydides put it starkly in his *History of the Peloponnesian War*: When the citizens of Melos refused to bow to Athens, the sentiment that the strong do what they will and the weak suffer what they must was etched into the template for international order. Stephen Krasner was briefer, "organized hypocrisy."[33]

History counsels caution to anyone even vaguely familiar with so-called humanitarian interventions of the colonial period—or more recently by Washington on behalf of the contras in Nicaragua or by Moscow on behalf of comrades in Budapest and Prague. Concerns about the degradation of sovereignty come often from countries whose borders have been breached by many countries that now champion protecting human beings and ignoring borders. Hence, an honest debate about motivations and likely costs and benefits is required, not visceral accolades because of a qualifying adjective. Such a discussion has become particularly relevant because outside assistance can do more harm than good or can become entangled in a local political economy that favors war.[34]

US rhetoric and the invocation of humanitarian values in Afghanistan and Iraq suggest the heightened need for analysis. Jennifer Welsh notes three ways in which the responsibility to protect and the war against terrorism connect. First, ICISS principles should govern any use of force in international society. Second, September 11 leads one to ask what the community of states could and should have done to prevent massive human rights violations by the Taliban. Third, the issue of selectivity may ebb because the situation in Afghanistan underlined the consequences of state failure anywhere in the world.[35]

Simon Chesterman raises the possibility that ICISS recommendations could directly advocate the application of the principle of the responsibility to protect to Afghanistan and Iraq. "If more had been done to induce or compel the Taliban regime to protect the Afghan population, Afghanistan might have proved a less inviting haven for al Qaeda," he writes. "And, once the United States successfully removed that regime from power, it imposed a special responsibility (with the assistance of the United Nations and other countries) to leave Afghanistan a better place than they found it."[36]

The National Security Strategy of the United States of America,[37] unveiled by President George W. Bush in September 2002, is bound to circumscribe future discussions about using force. Many regard the new doctrine itself as such a threat that it requires renewing the principle of nonintervention rather than downgrading sovereign prerogatives. The Bush doctrine "has had the effect of reinforcing fears both of US dominance and of the chaos that could ensue if what is sauce for the US goose were to become sauce for many other would-be interventionist ganders," according to Adam Roberts.

> One probable result of the enunciation of interventionist doctrines by the United States will be to make states even more circumspect than before about accepting any doctrine, including on humanitarian intervention or on the responsibility to protect, that could be seen as opening the door to a general pattern of interventionism.[38]

Indeed, the worst fears of observers are exemplified in an article by Lee Feinstein and Anne-Marie Slaughter in *Foreign Affairs* early in 2004. The authors use the responsibility to protect as a springboard to developing a corollary principle of "a duty to prevent" the acquisition of weapons of mass destruction (WMDs). Their proposal "extrapolates from recent developments in the law of intervention for humanitarian purposes."[39] Meanwhile, Allan Buchanan and Robert Keohane are calling for the "cosmopolitan" use of preventive military force.[40]

A special issue of *The Nation* in July 2003 was billed as "Humanitarian Intervention: A Forum" but had nothing to do with the billed topic. Instead, it covered the slippery slope of facilitating actions by the Bush administration. The concern by its dozen commentators (including ICISS member Ramesh Thakur) was captured by Richard Falk: "After September 11, the American approach to humanitarian intervention morphed into post hoc rationalizations for uses of force otherwise difficult to reconcile with international law."[41] The hostile reaction to Canadian prime minister Jean Chrétien's and British prime minister Tony Blair's efforts at the mid-July 2003 Progressive Governance Summit to insert the idea of the responsibility to protect into the final communiqué reflects a new hostility among countries that earlier might have supported the concept.

To situate the new reluctance, it is important to distinguish Afghanistan and Iraq and explore how US actions are akin to three interventions of the 1970s that were justified as self-defense but had substantial humanitarian benefits: East Pakistan in 1971, Cambodia in 1978, and Uganda in 1979. At the time, the notion of humanitarian intervention simply was too far from the mainstream to be used successfully as a justification for state actions. International order was firmly grounded on the inviolability of sovereignty, and humanitarian considerations were beside the point. Specifically, India's invasion of East Pakistan, Tanzania's in Uganda, and Vietnam's in Kampuchea were unilateral efforts to overthrow menacing, destabilizing regimes. In retrospect, these operations are sometimes invoked as evidence of an emerging norm of humanitarian intervention, but they were conducted by single states interested in regime change for their own self-defense. Moreover, none was approved by the Security Council—and Vietnam's was condemned.

The parallels with Afghanistan (Security Council resolution 1368 recognizes legitimate self-defense) and Iraq (the United States also makes the claim) become clear. The human rights situations have improved, but the rationale in both cases was self-defense not humanitarian. In Afghanistan, the quick overthrow of the regime led to continuing insecurity but no Osama bin Laden; and Washington's claims shifted away from the destruction of al-Qaeda to the importance of liberating Afghans from Taliban brutalities. The slippery humanitarian logic reached an extreme in Iraq, as argued by Human Rights Watch's executive director.[42] With no evidence uncovered to date, the prewar justifications of the Iraqi threat (WMDs and links to al-Qaeda) gave way to embellishing the rationale of freeing subjected Iraqi populations from Saddam Hussein's thuggery.

Rigorous application of the tenets of the responsibility to protect does not permit their being used as a pretext for preemption. But Washington's broad and loose application of humanitarian rhetoric to Afghanistan and Iraq ex post facto suggests why care should be given to parsing ICISS's criteria.

Right authority and the distraction of Security Council reform

Secretary-General Kofi Annan's opening statement to the General Assembly in September 2003 returned to a tired theme, Security Council reform, which is a priority for his High-level Panel on Threats, Challenges and Change. ICISS too recommended that changing the council was of "paramount importance"[43] to address its uneven performance, double standards, veto, and unrepresentative character.

The reservations of many states toward humanitarian intervention are summarized by Algerian president Abdelazia Bouteflika:

> We do not deny that the United Nations has the right and the duty to help suffering humanity, but we remain extremely sensitive to any undermining of our sovereignty, not only because sovereignty is our last defense against the rules of an unequal world, but because we are not taking part in the decision-making process of the Security Council.[44]

The history of efforts to make the Security Council more reflective of growing UN membership and of changing world politics suggests slim prospects for change.[45] The veto was an essential component of the original 1945 deal with the permanent five (P-5), who have resisted change from the outset.[46] The only significant reform of the Security Council came in 1965—enlarging it from 11 to 15 members and the required majority from 7 to 9 votes—but the P-5's veto power was left intact. The change reflected the dramatic growth in the number of member states, all from the South, whose voices were inadequately represented in UN decision making.

The current calls for reform reflect a similar concern with representation—important for humanitarian intervention and especially critical after Iraq. Most governments support the call for increasing membership and eliminating the veto. True, the council does not reflect the actual distribution of twenty-first century power, but reform proposals from diplomats and analysts do not address the true discrepancy between having a Security Council seat and a finger on the trigger of a powerful arsenal. It would be easier to take proposals for reform more seriously if candidature—either continued or new, with or without a veto—were to entail an obligation to contribute troops or finance as part of membership qualifications.

The issue resurfaced, paradoxically, as a byproduct of the Security Council's initial successes in the early post–Cold War era and Secretary-General Boutros Boutros-Ghali's bullish *An Agenda for Peace*.[47] Was it not high time to restructure the Security Council's composition and revise its anachronistic procedures so that matters of might would take second place to matters of right? So went conventional wisdom and proposals from the 38th floor and elsewhere.[48]

A Security Council of 21 or 25 members would hardly improve effectiveness—a "rump" General Assembly certainly would facilitate what one observer called the Sitzkrieg for Iraq.[49] The group would be too large to conduct serious negotiations, and still too small to represent the UN membership as a whole. Vague, rhetorical agreement about expansion to accommodate the underrepresented "global South" does not translate into consensus about how. Every option opens another Pandora's box. How does Argentina or Mexico feel about Brazil's candidacy? Pakistan about India's? South Africa or Egypt about Nigeria's? If dominance by the industrialized countries is the problem, why are Germany and Japan obvious candidates? Would Italy not be more or less in the same league? Would it not make more sense for the European Union to be represented collectively rather than Paris, London, Berlin, and Rome individually? How do such traditional UN stalwarts as Canada and the Nordic countries feel about a plan that would leave them on the sidelines but elevate larger developing countries, some of which represent threats to international peace and security?

The logic of "if it ain't broke, don't fix it" should find more resonance. Practical effectiveness should trump grumblings about representation, especially as humanitarian intervention would be even less likely with a reformed council. This reality was present before what Charles Krauthammer called "the unipolar moment."[50] As this moment is likely to last for some time, continued jostling about Charter reform is at best a distraction. As Robert Kagan writes, "Hopes that a multi-polar regime might emerge have faded since the 1990s. Almost everyone concedes today that U.S. power will be nearly impossible to match for decades."[51] If military intervention to protect human beings is desirable, the critical task is to engage the United States in multilateral efforts.

Rather than wasting energy on Security Council reform, concerned diplomats, scholars, and activists should try to understand when Washington's instrumental multilateralism, and hence when the humanitarian impulse, kicks in. The roller coaster of humanitarian intervention in the 1990s suggests that US participation often is essential and helpful. Kosovo and Afghanistan demonstrated the superiority of both US firepower and collective action. Edward Luck notes: "In the end, other states and international secretariats will largely determine whether US policy-makers and legislators find international bodies to be places where America's exceptional potential is welcomed and embraced or is resented and restrained."[52]

Hubris about the value of "going it alone" seems to be fading somewhat in Washington. The return to the Security Council in October 2003 in pursuit of a blue-tinged resolution 1511 was followed by a request for UN assistance in helping to spell out the necessary steps toward returning Iraqi sovereignty. The administration's "strategy is one of partnerships that strongly affirms the vital role of NATO and other U.S. alliances—including the UN," according to Secretary of State Colin Powell. Although it is hard to take this assertion at face value, the occupation of Iraq seems to have had a sobering impact. As Theodore Sorensen writes, "What is more unrealistic than to believe that this country can unilaterally decide the fate of others, without a decent respect for the opinions of mankind, or for the judgment of world institutions and our traditional allies?"[53] Perhaps a differing perception of multilateralism is emerging. "There may be times when the United States must act alone," write Lee Hamilton and Hans Binnendijk, "but these instances should remain the exception."[54]

The Security Council is not a road Washington always, or never, takes. Clearly, no US administration will permit the council to stand in the way of pursuing perceived national security interests. At the same time, the council often serves vital interests and gives the United States cause to proceed cautiously and with international acquiescence, if not jubilant support. Depending on the issue, the stakes, the positions of potential allies, and the plausibility of collective military action, Washington has the power to act unilaterally or multilaterally.[55] However, the Bush administration is discovering that "even imperfectly legitimated power is likely to be much more effective than crude coercion."[56]

Conclusion

In spite of normative progress, we hardly are able to rescue all war victims. With the possible exception of genocide, there is no legal and certainly no political obligation to act, but a moral one.[57] Security Council decisions in the 1990s reflected the humanitarian "impulse," the laudable desire to help fellow human beings threatened by armed conflict.[58] Invariably, this urge translates into a limited political momentum and a sliding scale of commitments, reflecting the stark international political reality that we rescue some, but not all war-affected populations. When humanitarian and strategic interests coincide, a window of opportunity opens for coalitions of the willing to act on the humanitarian impulse in the Security Council, or elsewhere.

Recent experience provides evidence of this impulse but not of an "imperative," the preference of those who are dismayed by the unevenness of Security Council decisions and international efforts to succor war victims. The humanitarian imperative would entail an obligation to treat all victims similarly and react to all crises consistently—in effect, to deny the relevance of politics, which proceeds on a case-by-case basis by evaluating interests and options, weighing costs, and mustering necessary resources. The humanitarian impulse is permissive, the humanitarian imperative would be peremptory.

The Responsibility to Protect contains normative ideas for which many people in the multilateral and humanitarian communities have been waiting. As Jack Donnelly put it in his revised textbook on human rights, "the December 2001 report of the International Commission on Intervention and State Sovereignty to the General Assembly promises to be a watershed event in international discussions of humanitarian intervention."[59] Expectations to respect rights are increasingly placed on political authorities.

The report provides an accurate snapshot of mainstream views about sovereignty as responsibility. It is too tame for some and beyond the pale for others. But it does not open the floodgates to justifications of non-humanitarian intervention dressed in humanitarian garb. Those familiar with colonial history and uneasy about US actions in Iraq are understandably cautious, but a rigorous application of the criteria spelled out in *The Responsibility to Protect* should prevent abuse.

One analyst describes the US's international liberalism as "hegemony on the cheap."[60] And so as the US presidential election approaches, the UN will become more appealing.[61] As well as pursuing elections, weapons inspections, and a host of other tasks in Iraq, other obvious examples where US interests would be fostered more through cooperation than "going it alone" include fighting terrorism (intelligence-sharing and anti-money laundering efforts), confronting the global specter of infectious diseases, monitoring of human rights, and criminal tribunals. And, of course, humanitarian intervention is a quintessentially multilateral task.

For all of these undertakings, more than lip service to the interests of other countries must be paid. Multilateralism is not an end in itself, but working through the UN can help achieve crucial US objectives. Joseph Nye points to the "paradox of American power," or the inability of the world's strongest state to secure some of its major goals alone. Unless Washington is prepared to bend on occasion, governments are unlikely to sign on when their helping hands are necessary for US priorities. The present administration's approach is thus hard to fathom for Nye because "the United States may find others increasingly reluctant to put tools into the toolbox. One day the box might even be bare."[62] It is this reality that provides some leverage even with Washington, and humanitarian intervention is an important tool for everyone.

If reluctant states and skeptical diplomats solicit US participation and make compromises to facilitate humanitarian intervention, would we begin to slide down that slippery slope and teeter on the brink of justifying unjustifiable actions like the decision to go to war against Iraq? The answer is no if ICISS counsel is followed. The just cause threshold could have been invoked earlier and the humanitarian rationale satisfied—given Saddam Hussein's record as a bona fide war criminal. At the same time, the four other criteria would not have been satisfied: right intention, last resort, proportional means, and reasonable prospects.

Moreover, even if the five previous criteria had been met, which clearly they were not, ICISS emphasizes just authority, which essentially means an overwhelming show of international support, preferably from the Security Council or at least from a regional organization. Dissent about the war in Iraq within the council, and indeed around the globe, was far more visible and substantial than in Kosovo—an apt contrast because that particular intervention was "illegal" (that is, without council approval) but "legitimate" (or at least "justifiable") in humanitarian terms.[63] The resolution to authorize military force against Iraq in March 2003 was withdrawn because Washington and London were not even assured a simple majority and were confronting three vetoes. In Kosovo, there were three negative votes (two with veto weight) in the offing. Moreover, there was not unanimous approval for the Iraq campaign from a 19-member regional body—in fact, both NATO and the European Union were split. And all of the regional organizations in the geographic area covered by the crisis were categorically against the war. In short, the "coalition" in Iraq was not truly multilateral in any meaningful way, nor was the decision to wage war. Widespread international backing, let alone right authority, was conspicuously absent.

Iraq involved nothing more than a humanitarian veneer applied after no evidence was found of either the purported WMDs or links to al-Qaeda. John Ikenberry points out the irony: "The worst unilateral impulses coming out of the Bush administration are so harshly criticized around the world because so many countries have accepted the multilateral vision of international order that the United States has articulated over most of the twentieth century."[64] *The Responsibility to Protect* could be one means to re-engage Washington in the world organization.

Critics and skeptics of humanitarian intervention should be less preoccupied that military action will be taken too often for insufficient humanitarian reasons, but rather more concerned that it will be taken too rarely for the right ones. The case of Congo, where since 1998 an estimated 3.5 million people have died largely from the famine and disease accompanying armed conflict,[65] demonstrates appallingly sparse responsibility to protect and plenty of inhumanitarian noninter-vention. This fact represents as great a threat to international society and global justice as preemptive or preventive war.

The sun of humanitarian intervention has set for now. Whether US power will underpin or undermine humanitarian intervention is uncertain. But one thing is clear. It will be decisive. If the responsibility to protect is to flourish, the United States must be on board. The current moment is dark, but that is not to say that humanitarian intervention will not dawn again.

Notes

1 Jane Boulden and Thomas G. Weiss, eds, *Terrorism and the UN: Before and After September 11* (Bloomington: Indiana University Press, 2004); and Thomas G. Weiss, Margaret E. Crahan, and John Goering, eds., *Wars on Terrorism and Iraq: Human Rights, Unilateralism, and U.S. Foreign Policy* (London: Routledge, 2004).

2 Andrew Hurrell, "Foreword to the Third Edition," in Hedley Bull, *The Anarchical Society: A Study of Order in World Politics* (New York: Columbia University Press, 2002), vii–xiii, quote at xiii.

3 The annual issues of *Ethics & International Affairs* included 37 articles about the moral issues surrounding the crises and interventions of the 1990s, an average of almost 4 articles per issue: 1991, 1 of 13; 1992, 1 of 11; 1993, 2 of 12; 1994, 2 of 11; 1995, 2 of 11; 1996, 3 of 10; 1997, 10 of 18; 1998, 4 of 10; 1999, 7 of 15; 2000, 5 of 9. In fact, the journal brought out a compilation of the main essays on this topic (Anthony F. Lang, Jr., ed., *Just Intervention* [Washington, DC: Georgetown University Press, 2003]). The pattern changed dramatically following 11 September 2001. Starting with the new millennium, humanitarian intervention assumed far less importance: 2001, 3 of 18; 2002, 2 of 32; and 2003, 2 of 27. The switch to ethical issues flowing from the wars on terrorism and Iraq is almost as dramatic: 2002, 11 of 32 articles; and 6 of 27 in 2003.

4 S. Neil MacFarlane, *Intervention in Contemporary World Politics*, Adelphi Paper no. 350 (Oxford: Oxford University Press, 2002), 79.

5 Th. A. van Baarda, "The Involvement of the Security Council in Maintaining International Law," *Netherlands Quarterly of Human Rights* 12, no. 1 (2004): 140.

6 Adam Roberts, "The Role of Humanitarian Issues in International Politics in the 1990s," *International Review of the Red Cross* 8, no. 833 (1999): 19.

7 Edward Luttwak, "Kofi's Rule: Humanitarian Intervention and Neocolonialism," *The National Interest* 58 (1999/2000): 60.

8 Kofi A. Annan, *The Question of Intervention* (New York: United Nations, 1999).
9 Raimo Väyrynen, *The Age of Humanitarian Emergencies,* Research for Action no. 25 (Helsinki: World Institute for Development Economics Research, 1996); and Nicholas J. Wheeler, *Saving Strangers: Humanitarian Intervention in International Society* (Oxford: Oxford University Press, 2000).
10 Independent International Commission on Kosovo (IICK), *Kosovo Report: Conflict, International Response, Lessons Learned* (Oxford: Oxford University Press, 2000).
11 Alton Frye, ed., *Humanitarian Intervention: Crafting a Workable Doctrine* (New York: Council on Foreign Relations, 2000); and US Department of State, *Interagency Review of U.S. Government Civilian Humanitarian and Transition Programs* (Washington, DC: National Security Archive, 2000).
12 Advisory Council on International Affairs (AIV) and Advisory Committee on Issues of Public International Law, *Humanitarian Intervention* (The Hague: AIV and CAVV, 2000); and the Danish Institute of International Affairs (DUPI), *Humanitarian Intervention: Legal and Political Aspects* (Copenhagen: DUPI, 1999).
13 International Commission on Intervention and State Sovereignty (ICISS), *The Responsibility to Protect* (Ottawa: International Development Research Centre, 2001); and Thomas G. Weiss and Don Hubert, *The Responsibility to Protect: Research, Bibliography, and Background* (Ottawa: International Development Research Centre, 2001).
14 Joelle Tanguy, "Redefining Sovereignty and Intervention," *Ethics & International Affairs* 17, no. 1 (2003): 141–8; Adam Roberts, "The Price of Protection," *Survival* 44, no. 4 (2002): 157–61; Ian Williams, "Righting the Wrongs of Past Interventions: A Review of the International Commission on Intervention and State Sovereignty," *The International Journal of Human Rights* 6, no. 3 (2002): 103–13; David Ryan, "Report of the International Commission on Intervention and State Sovereignty: The Responsibility to Protect," *International Affairs* 78, no. 4 (2002): 890–1; J. Peter Burgess, "The Foundation for a New Consensus on Humanitarian Intervention," *Security Dialogue* 33, no. 3 (2002): 383–4; Jane Boulden, "Book Review: The Responsibility to Protect," *Journal of Refugee Studies* 15, no. 4 (2002): 428–9; Edward Newman, "Humanitarian Intervention, Legality and Legitimacy," *International Journal of Human Rights* 6, no. 4 (2002): 102–20; Jennifer Welsh, "Review Essay: From Right to Responsibility: Humanitarian Intervention and International Society," *Global Governance* 8, no. 4 (2002): 503–21; and Jennifer Welsh, Carolin Thielking, and S. Neil MacFarlane, "The Responsibility to Protect: Assessing the Report of the International Commission on Intervention and State Sovereignty," *International Journal* 57, no. 4 (2002): 489–512.
15 Mohammed Ayoob, "Humanitarian Intervention and International Society," *International Journal of Human Rights* 6, no. 1 (2002): 81–102.
16 Gareth Evans and Mohamed Sahnoun, "The Responsibility to Protect," *Foreign Affairs* 81, no. 6 (2002): 99–110.
17 Thomas G. Weiss, "To Intervene or Not To Intervene? A Contemporary Snap-Shot," *Canadian Foreign Policy* 9, no. 2 (2002): 141–57.
18 ICISS, *The Responsibility to Protect*, xi.
19 Kathleen Newland, Erin Patrick, and Monette Zard, *No Refuge: The Challenge of Internal Displacement* (New York and Geneva: United Nations, Office for the Coordination of Humanitarian Assistance, 2003), 36.
20 Mario Bettati and Bernard Kouchner, eds., *Le Devoir d'ingérence: peut-on les laisser mourir?* (Paris: Denoël, 1987); Mario Bettati, *Le Droit d'ingérence: mutation de l'ordre international* (Paris: Odile Jacob, 1987).
21 Francis M. Deng, Donald Rothchild, Sadikei Kimaro, I. William Zartman, and Terrence Lyons, *Sovereignty as Responsibility: Conflict Management in Africa* (Washington, DC: Brookings Institution, 1996); and Francis M. Deng, "Frontiers of Sovereignty," *Leiden Journal of International Law* 8, no. 2 (1995): 249–86.
22 Anthony Lewis, "The Challenge of Global Justice Now," *Daedalus* 132, no. 1 (2003): 8.

23 ICISS, *The Responsibility to Protect*, xii.

24 Jeremy I. Levitt, "The Responsibility to Protect: A Beaver Without a Dam?" *Michigan Journal of International Law* 25, no. 1 (2003): 153–77; and Jeremy I. Levitt, ed., *Africa: Selected Documents on Constitutive, Conflict and Security, Humanitarian, and Judicial Issues* (Ardsley, NY: Transnational, 2003).

25 ICISS, *The Responsibility to Protect*, viii.

26 See Joseph S. Nye, Jr., *The Paradox of American Power: Why the World's Only Superpower Can't Go It Alone* (Oxford: Oxford University Press, 2002).

27 Center for Defense Information, "Last of the Big Time Spenders: U.S. Military Budget Still the World's Largest, and Growing," table on "Fiscal Year 2004 Budget," based on data provided by the US Department of Defense and International Institute for Strategic Studies, Washington, DC, 19 March 2003, www.cdi.org/program/document.cfm? DocumentID = 1040&.

28 James Traub, "The *Next* Resolution," *New York Times Magazine*, 13 April 2003, 51.

29 G. John Ikenberry, "Illusions of Empire: Defining the New American Order," *Foreign Affairs* 83, no. 2 (2004): 154. See also Niall Ferguson, *Colossus: The Price of America's Empire* (New York: Penguin, 2004); Benjamin R. Barber, *Fear's Empire: War, Terrorism, and Democracy* (New York: Norton, 2003); and Michael Mann, *Incoherent Empire* (New York: Verso, 2003).

30 Rosemary Foot, S. Neil MacFarlane, and Michael Mastanduno, eds., *The United States and Multilateral Organizations* (Oxford: Oxford University Press, 2003); and Michael Byers and Georg Nolte, eds., *United States Hegemony and the Foundations of International Law* (Cambridge: Cambridge University Press, 2003).

31 Andrew Moravcsik, "Striking a New Transatlantic Bargain," *Foreign Affairs* 82, no. 4 (2003): 74–89.

32 Greenberg Research, *The People on War Report* (Geneva: ICRC, 1999).

33 Stephen Krasner, *Sovereignty: Organized Hypocrisy* (Princeton, NJ: Princeton University Press, 1999).

34 Mary Anderson, *Do No Harm: How Aid Can Support Peace—Or War* (Boulder, Colo.: Lynne Reinner, 1999); Mats Berdal and David Malone, eds., *Greed and Grievance: Economic Agendas in Civil Wars* (Boulder, Colo.: Lynne Reinner, 2000); and Mark Duffield, *Global Governance and the New Wars* (London: Zed Books, 2001).

35 Welsh, "Review Essay: From Right to Responsibility: Humanitarian Intervention and International Society," 518.

36 Simon Chesterman, "Humanitarian Intervention and Afghanistan," in *Humanitarian Intervention and International Relations*, ed. Jennifer Welsh (Oxford: Oxford University Press, 2006), 163–75.

37 US Department of State, *The National Security Strategy of the United States of America* (Washington, DC: US Department of State, 2002), http://georgewbush-whitehouse.archives.gov/nsc/nss/2002/index.html.

38 Adam Roberts, "The United Nations and Humanitarian Intervention," in *Humanitarian Intervention and International Relations*, ed. Jennifer Welsh (Oxford: Oxford University Press, 2006), 71–97.

39 Lee Feinstein and Anne-Marie Slaughter, "A Duty to Prevent," *Foreign Affairs* 83, no. 1 (2004): 136–50, quote at 149.

40 Allan Buchanan and Robert O. Keohane, "The Preventive Use of Force: A Cosmopolitan Institutional Proposal," *Ethics & International Affairs* 18, no. 1 (2004): 1–22.

41 Richard Falk, contribution to "Humanitarian Intervention: A Forum," *The Nation*, 14 July 2003, www.thenation.com/article/humanitarian-intervention-forum-0. Falk and Thakur were joined by Mary Kaldor, Carl Tham, Samantha Power, Mahmood Mamdani, David Rieff, Eric Rouleau, Zia Mian, Ronald Steel, Stephen Holmes, and Stephen Zunes.

42 Kenneth Roth, "War in Iraq: Not a Humanitarian Intervention," in *Human Rights Watch World Report 2004: Human Rights and Armed Conflict*, Human Rights Watch (New York: Human Rights Watch, 2004), 13–33.

43 ICISS, *The Responsibility to Protect*, 49.

44 Newland, Patrick, and Zard, *No Refuge: The Challenge of Internal Displacement*, 37.

45 Thomas G. Weiss, "The Illusion of Security Council Reform," *Washington Quarterly* 26, no. 4 (2003): 147–61.

46 See Ruth B. Russell, *A History of the United Nations Charter: The Role of the United States, 1940–1945* (Washington, DC: Brookings Institution, 1958), 742–9; Bruce Russett, ed., *The Once and Future Security Council* (New York: St. Martin's Press, 1997); Townsend Hoopes and Douglas Brinkley, *FDR and the Creation of the U.N.* (New Haven, Conn.: Yale University Press, 1997); and Stephen C. Schlesinger, *Act of Creation: The Founding of the United Nations* (Boulder, Colo.: Westview, 2003).

47 Boutros Boutros-Ghali, *An Agenda for Peace* (New York: United Nations, 1995). For discussion see Thomas G. Weiss, David P. Forsythe, Roger A. Coate, and Kelly-Kate Pease, *The United Nations and Changing World Politics*, 6th ed. (Boulder, Colo.: Westview, 2010).

48 Commission on Global Governance, *Our Global Neighbourhood* (Oxford: Oxford University Press, 1995); Independent Working Group on the Future of the United Nations, *The United Nations in its Second Half-Century* (New York: Ford Foundation, 1995); and Bruce Russett, Barry O'Neil, and James Sutterlin, "Breaking the Security Council Logjam," *Global Governance* 2, no. 1 (1996): 65–79.

49 David C. Hendrickson, "Preserving the Imbalance of Power," *Ethics & International Affairs* 17, no. 1 (2003): 157–62, 160.

50 Charles Krauthammer, "The Unipolar Moment," *Foreign Affairs* 70, no. 1 (1990/1991): 23–33.

51 Robert Kagan, "America's Crisis of Legitimacy," *Foreign Affairs* 83, no. 2 (2004): 71.

52 Edward C. Luck, "American Exceptionalism and International Organization: Lessons from the 1990s," in *The United States and Multilateral Organizations*, ed. Rosemary Foot, S. Neil MacFarlane, and Michael Mastanduno (Oxford: Oxford University Press, 2003), 48. See also Edward C. Luck, *Mixed Messages: American Politics and International Organization 1919–1999* (Washington, DC: Brookings Institution, 1999).

53 Theodore C. Sorensen, "JFK's Strategy of Peace," *World Policy Journal* XX, no. 3 (2003): 4.

54 Lee Hamilton and Hans Binnendijk, "Foreword," in Andre J. Pierre, *Coalitions: Building and Maintenance* (Washington, DC: Institute for the Study of Diplomacy, 2002), xi.

55 Stewart Patrick and Shepard Forman, eds., *Multilateralism and U.S. Foreign Policy: Ambivalent Engagement* (Boulder, Colo.: Lynne Rienner, 2002); Stewart Patrick, "Beyond Coalitions of the Willing: Assessing U.S. Multilateralism," *Ethics & International Affairs* 17, no. 1 (2003): 37–54; and David M. Malone and Yuen Foong Khong, eds., *Unilateralism and U.S. Foreign Policy: International Perspectives* (Boulder, Colo.: Lynne Rienner, 2003).

56 Andrew Hurrell, "International Law and the Changing Constitution of International Society," in *The Role of Law in International Politics: Essays in International Relations and International Law*, ed. Michael Byers (Oxford: Oxford University Press, 2000), 344.

57 W.R. Smyser, *The Humanitarian Conscience: Caring for Others in the Age of Terror* (New York: Palgrave, 2003).

58 Thomas G. Weiss, "The Humanitarian Impulse," in *The United Nations Security Council After the Cold War*, ed. David M. Malone (Boulder, Colo.: Lynne Rienner, 2004), 37–54.

59 Jack Donnelly, *Universal Human Rights in Theory and Practice*, 2nd ed. (Ithaca, NY: Cornell University Press, 2003), 251.

60 Colin Dueck, "Hegemony on the Cheap: Liberal Internationalism from Wilson to Bush," *World Policy Journal* XX, no. 4 (2003/2004): 1–11.

61 Mats Berdal, "The UN Security Council: Ineffective but Indispensable," *Survival* 45, no. 2 (2003): 7–30; Shashi Tharoor, "Why America Still Needs the United Nations," *Foreign Affairs* 82, no. 5 (2003): 67–80; and Madeleine K. Albright, "Think Again: United Nations," *Foreign Policy* 138 (2003): 16–24.

62 Joseph S. Nye, Jr., "U.S. Power and Strategy After Iraq," *Foreign Affairs* 82, no. 4 (2003): 68.

63 Independent International Commission on Kosovo, *Kosovo Report: Conflict, International Response, Lessons Learned*, 4.

64 John G. Ikenberry, "Is American Multilateralism in Decline?" *Perspectives on Politics* 1, no. 3 (2003): 533–50, 545.

65 International Rescue Committee (IRC), "Conflict in Congo Deadliest Since World War II, Says The IRC," 8 April 2003, www.theirc.org/news/conflict-congo-deadliest-world-war-ii-says-irc-3730.

15

THE POLITICS OF HUMANITARIAN IDEAS

Few sovereign clothes

One of the Secretary-General's ceremonial tasks is to open the United Nations General Assembly, but Kofi Annan's September 1999 speech was anything but routine. The 54th session's focus was on globalization and humanitarian intervention, and his stance on the latter touched a raw nerve. His predecessor had been indirect: "The time of absolute and exclusive sovereignty . . . has passed."[1] But Annan was straightforward: "States bent on criminal behaviour [should] know that frontiers are not the absolute defence . . . that massive and systematic violations of human rights—wherever they may take place—should not be allowed to stand."[2] These are powerful words from the bully pulpit.

Moreover, he preached the heresy that righting wrongs is more important than UN self-aggrandizement. He did not endorse bombing by the North Atlantic Treaty Organization (NATO) without Security Council authorization, but he also could not condone idleness in the face of Serb atrocities in Kosovo, a theme he outlined in June 1998 in another speech at Ditchley Park.[3] In addressing "those for whom the greatest threat to the future of international order is the use of force in the absence of a Security Council mandate," Annan astutely raised a counterfactual. If there had been states willing to act in Rwanda without a council imprimatur, "should such a coalition have stood aside and allowed the horror to unfold?" Rather than posing as a bureaucrat protecting organizational turf, his rhetorical question echoed a moral voice. At the General Assembly, as earlier at Ditchley Park, he was conscious of contradicting the stereotype of a Secretary-General, especially a national from an ex-colony, who did *not* "preach a sermon against intervention."

Controversy was predictable because national delegates listen closely to ideas emanating from the 38th floor, Annan's office. Instead of the usual handful of responses during the general debate, there were almost 50, along with four plenary sessions between 6 and 11 October.[4] The Security Council had a two-day session in late November to discuss the implications of intervention[5] and developing countries are trying to establish an open-ended working group on the topic. National attitudes toward the secretary-general's oratory as voiced in both the General Assembly's and Security Council's debates were summarized by one ambassador and one senior staff member, off-the-record, in remarkably similar ways: the West (including Central Europe) and much of sub-Saharan Africa are essentially enthusiastic; large developing countries (including Nigeria, South Africa, Egypt, India, and most of Latin America) are lukewarm, expressing support contingent upon state consent and a reformed council; and Russia, China, pariahs (Iraq, Iran, Libya, North Korea, Cuba), much of Asia and the Middle East, in particular Algeria, are hostile.

Why are Annan's sermons in favor of intervention so inflammatory? A clue lies in "postmodernism." More than a mere epithet used to dismiss the Modern Language Association, postmodernism also means problematizing state interests and identities rather than taking them for granted. In fact, so-called ideationalists and constructivists[6] have appropriated labels for themselves that describe the concerns of many analysts and practitioners.

No one is upset with what Annan labels the "most pacific" part of the intervention "continuum," the standard bill-of-fare of international relations. Indeed, Annan needlessly muddies the analytical waters by using "intervention" as a synonym for all UN activities when he is really only discussing the "most coercive" ones, i.e., military force. Annan's statements amount to arguing that "sovereignty is no longer sacrosanct,"[7] which is unsettling for diplomats because attributes of state sovereignty are not being viewed as part of a predetermined superstructure but as something which is subject to change.

The most ignored part of the UN Secretary-General's job description is intellectual leadership, which does not require financial resources but requires courage (including the willingness to deliver a speech that had not been diluted after clearance from the entire senior staff). In short, Annan did the right thing in flagging the issue in stark terms, and it will have a salutary impact. Acting as the "conscience of the world" raises hackles because there has been a revolution in the ends-justifying-the-means approach to intervention. The lowered threshold for outside military force is approaching conventional wisdom. As he has written about counterproductive UN impartiality in the Balkans, "The old rules of the game no longer held."[8]

Diplomats and the governments that employ them, are troubled by pronouncements that "do not lend themselves to easy interpretations or simple conclusions." Preferring to utter old shibboleths without blushing, they are unsettled by the weight given to humanitarian values as an acceptable justification for vigorous diplomatic and military action. "In the 1990s," writes Adam Roberts, "humanitarian issues have played a historically unprecedented role in international politics."[9] For the military campaign in Kosovo, Michael Ignatieff notes that "its legitimacy [depends] on what fifty years of human rights has done to our moral instincts, weakening the presumption in favor of state sovereignty, strengthening the presumption in favor of intervention when massacre and deportation become state policy."[10]

It was one thing for the Organization for Security and Co-operation in Europe (OSCE) to approve a new charter that proclaims local conflicts to be the legitimate concern of all European states, or for President William J. Clinton in his General Assembly address to plead "to stop outbreaks of mass killing and displacement."[11] It is quite another to hear directly from the UN Secretary-General how few sovereign clothes remain on emperors who are war criminals. The host of military interventions in the 1990s add up to a set of powerful precedents. Nonintervention, the organizing principle of international relations since Westphalia, is not what it once was.

This is particularly uncomfortable in the United Nations, "the last bastion of national sovereignty," as former UN under-secretary-general Brian Urquhart regularly quips. It may not be the last, but it certainly is one of the foremost. Egregious human rights abuse is intolerable, particularly if it occurs in a country where outside military forces can make a difference at a reasonable cost. There is a noticeable, albeit inconsistent, willingness to deploy military force in defense of international norms.

This has less to do with "globalization" and "a world transformed by geopolitical, economic, technological and environmental changes" than with normative changes and a growing recognition of minimal human rights standards. To those who think that the UN Charter shields domestic affairs from international scrutiny, Annan's speech emphasizes a "living document" because "Nothing in the Charter precludes a recognition that there are rights beyond borders." This builds on another speech two weeks into the bombing of Kosovo that argued "if we allow the United Nations to become the refuge of an 'ethnic cleanser' or mass murderer, we will betray the very ideals that inspired the founding of the United Nations."[12] In his General Assembly speech, Clinton complimented the secretary-general who "spoke for all of us . . . when he said that ethnic cleansers and mass murderers can find no refuge in the United Nations, no source of comfort or justification in its charter."

Emergency delivery and the protection of human rights require the allocation of scarce resources, which are then not available for other purposes. Decisions about resource allocation mix moral calculations along with what is seen to be in the intervening states' or leaders' interests. Decisions about humanitarian action reflect calculations by politicians in democratic societies about the immediate interests of their administrations as well as of more timeless *raisons d'état*. Governments redefine national interests through the push and pull of domestic politics.

The ultimate worth of various humanitarian interventions requires examining means and consequences, which complicates facile judgments about success and failure. Although this essay concentrates on the veritable revolution in ends, a brief aside is in order because the results of this decade's various experiments with military might on behalf of humanitarian goals have been decidedly mixed.[13]

Because humanitarian action does not address fundamentally political problems, it is ambiguous. On the one hand, it can reduce suffering and save lives. On the other hand, the three-decade Sudanese civil war or the feeding of criminals mixed among Rwandan refugees both illustrate that humanitarianism can be counterproductive by freeing resources and fuelling armed conflict. Or worse yet, humanitarian action can be an alibi that impedes more vigorous responses. The appearance of "doing something" in the face of a tragedy permits cheap moralizing but can prevent riskier political and military commitments to address the roots of a crisis. The well-fed dead in Bosnia prior to Dayton aptly illustrate that a humanitarian veneer can help make collective spinelessness more palatable than collective defense or security.[14]

Although some generalizations about the recent past are contested, the post–Cold War era has certainly been characterized by considerable flux in the search for consensus about fundamental threats and interests. Judith Goldstein and Robert Keohane have demonstrated the importance of ideas to the foreign-policy process, particularly in "periods in which power relations are fluid and interests and strategies are unclear or lack consensus."[15] To state that ideas and values are important in and of themselves does not mean that they are divorced from power and interests.

Because humanitarian ideas explain what drives much of Western foreign and defense policy, it is useful to apply to intervention and sovereignty, in four ways, insights from literature about ideas in foreign policy:[16] ideas inform the definition of what constitutes interests; ideas are important in setting priorities; ideas are crucial in forming new political and bureaucratic coalitions; and ideas become embedded in institutions.

Humanitarian ideas and impact

Looking through the prism of humanitarian coercion over the past decade shows how ends have changed and how ideas operate both causally and operationally. First, humanitarian values have influenced the composition of national interests. Kosovo is on everyone's mind, but numerous operations substantiate the same reality—military force may be employed for human rights and humanitarian purposes. Rather than examining more successful cases, perhaps the way to approach the framing of vital interests is taking the Somalia debacle and posing a stark counterfactual: what would have happened with Harry Truman instead of Bill Clinton? That which constituted US interests was not predetermined and fixed, but could have been shaped creatively by a leader. The orthodox view about troop withdrawal is that vital interests were not at stake. In the wake of the dramatic images of American soldiers dying in a distant place with no connection to core interests, the argument goes, the president had no alternative besides retreat.[17]

Yet he could have responded to both conservatives and liberals. He could have stressed that Washington's credibility was on the line and that teenage grenade-launchers from a fourth-rate African military power could not get away, literally, with the murder of 18 Rangers and hold US foreign policy hostage. He also could have emphasized respect for universal standards and international commitments, in this case the Security Council's authorization to protect humanitarian space.

Domestic criticism could have been muted and Presidential Decision Directive 25 (PDD-25)[18] could have looked very different from the document that has, since its signing in the midst of the Rwandan genocide, restricted Washington's partici-pation in peace operations as well as its approval of others' operations. Washington and the larger community of responsible states cannot have a universal humanitarian impulse; we should be asking whether, how, and why. However if we fast forward to March 1999, it would not have been necessary for Clinton to make the wholly unnecessary promise to avoid the use of ground troops in Kosovo. Rather, he could have framed American interests as sufficiently threatened by the legitimization of ethnic cleansing and a tidal wave of Kosovar refugees in order to risk troops on the ground, but instead he chose to initially make matters worse by "softening up" the Serbs from 15,000 feet. In any case, the American population is not as casualty-averse as is commonly assumed. A different pitch and framing of US interests could have given a different result. Indeed, Clinton's own address to the General Assembly suggests the waning of the "Vietmalia syndrome."

Second, ideas are crucial in helping states to set priorities among conflicting norms, and here too Annan's words have real bite. Ideas provide a road map when strategists need to choose among multiple equilibria. Specifically, humanitarian ideas are key in resolving the conflict between sovereignty and human rights. Respect for the former has traditionally been viewed as the bedrock of international order, whereas respect for the latter requires the expectation that military coercion may halt massive abuses of rights.

The definitions of sovereignty and of national interests have been dramatically expanded to include humanitarian values. As social constructs, neither definition is cast in concrete but rather changes over time in response to new circumstances and human society. It is striking, as Bryan Hehir has noted, that, "The contem-porary interest in military intervention (much to the dismay of realists) is driven by normative concerns."[19] The policy relevance of those advocating justified humanitarian intervention has increased.[20]

The rapid evolution of measures on behalf of internally displaced persons (IDPs) and the embrace of their plight by intergovernmental and nongovern-mental organizations (NGOs) result from the increasing weight of humanitarian values in state decision-making.[21] In a number of publications, the secretary-general's special representative, Francis Deng, assumes the continuing centrality of the Westphalian system and seeks pragmatically to reconcile the possibility of international intervention with traditional state sovereignty in what he has called "sovereignty as responsibility."[22] To the three characteristics usually considered to be attributes of sovereignty (territory, a people, and authority), a fourth (respect for a minimal standard of human rights) has been added. The secretary-general himself has not gone as far as French activists Bernard Kouchner (presently heading the UN operation in Kosovo) and Mario Bettati would like because he espouses no duty or obligation to override sovereignty.[23] But Annan is approaching Deng's notion of sovereignty as responsibility.

The power of this approach resides in underscoring a state's responsibilities and accountabilities to domestic *and* international constituencies. Accordingly, a state is unable to claim the prerogatives of sovereignty unless it meets internationally agreed responsibilities, which include respecting human rights and providing life-sustenance to its citizens. Failure to meet such obligations legitimizes intrusion, and even military intervention, by the international society of responsible states. "In the real world, principles often collide," as Clinton told the General Assembly, "and tough choices must be made." The language of UN resolutions and of such public policy discourse as Annan's speech are not fluff but the veritable stuff of priority setting when norms clash.

Third, humanitarian intervention has made possible new coalitions. The media and the public can demand that something be done, the military can respond, and relief agencies can ask for help because on occasion they require both the war-fighting and logistic capacities of the military. Commitments by major powers rest largely on their leaders' calculations of domestic costs, benefits, and risks. The arithmetic, in part, reflects the success of domestic and transnational constituencies in mobilizing support for humanitarian action, and in altering conceptions of interests and rewards. One example is Washington's change of tack on Haiti in 1994 after effective lobbying by Jean-Bertrand Aristide and the Congressional Black Caucus.[24]

A pertinent, more recent example is the "Ottawa process" on anti-personnel landmines. A transnational coalition successfully imbued the domestic politics of a sufficient number of states with enough humanitarian concern to redefine state interests in a way that led to the treaty.[25] Unlike most cases of transnationalism, this one touches directly on the high politics of security. It is a relatively "hard case" for which civil society would be least expected to have a determining impact on state policy.

This example suggests the importance of sub-state and transnational actors in influencing, framing, and ultimately redefining state interests. The initial impetus in the anti-landmines campaign was provided by a formidable coalition of civil society organizations. The International Campaign to Ban Land Mines, founded in 1993, grew out of private advocacy organizations whose main orientation was domestic and public (that is, oriented toward change in state behavior). Its success depended on co-opting states (and notably Canada, the Scandinavian countries, and South Africa), in "determin[ing] what states want."[26] Their support depended not only on the moral appeal of the cause but also on the consideration of domestic and international political interests and risks.

State involvement was necessary to translate social pressure into international law. The key to the outcome was to move states and alter definitions of perceived interests by persuading politicians. A basic aspect of the process was to remove landmines from the "apolitical" (that is, essentially nonpartisan) realm of military strategy and to place the issue firmly in the political realm of domestic constituencies.

Fourth, humanitarian ideas have become embedded within institutions and thus taken on a life of their own. New institutional structures in governments, intergovernmental agencies, and NGOs attest to the existence of organizational manifestations of the humanitarian priorities in the secretary-general's speech. Careers, military and civilian, are being made, and promotions given, as a result of the humanitarian business of the 1990s. This is a fact of the budget processes in Washington or London or The Hague, as well as in UN and NGO headquarters. Another indication is the extent to which funding for emergencies has replaced funding for development as a major preoccupation of donors, as is clear in publications from the UN, the Organisation for Economic Co-operation and Development (OECD), and alternative sources such as *The Reality of Aid*.

Humanitarian ideas and nonintervention

So, ideas and values related to humanitarian intervention are important in defining interests and identities, setting priorities, constituting coalitions, and adapting institutions. The weight of humanitarian values has increased in calculations about foreign and defense policies throughout the Western world in the 1990s; the decibel level surrounding their articulation has risen among advocates. Indeed, very little else seems to be motivating governmental action. The rejectionism of many developing countries coincides with negativism from such conservative American critics as Charles Krauthammer, Michael Mandelbaum, and Richard Haass.[27] They are worried that the wide-ranging demand for intervention will waste resources and distract Washington from truly important issues of national security. Ironically, many developing countries are fearful that US resources will be expended in exactly the ways that conservative American pundits fear.

Depending on perspectives, 1999 was the *annus mirabilis* or *horribilis* for intervention. Kosovo constituted a "humanitarian war." In the West, and Washington particularly, intervention for humanitarian purposes was crucial enough to risk worsened relations with both Russia and China. And in some ways, the international reaction to Timor is even more remarkable because a few years ago, only area specialists and stamp collectors could have located it on a map. But in spite of official objections from the world's fourth most populous country, enough international pressure was exerted that Jakarta "requested" the deployment of the Australian-led coalition to be followed by UN trusteeship. Comparable actions are out of the question in Chechnya, Tibet, or Kashmir, but efforts against Indonesia suggest that humanitarian intervention is an option against more than just powerless or failed states. They do not suggest, however, that UN "neocolonialism" will be fashionable.[28]

Nonintervention is affirmed in Article 2(7) of the UN Charter. "[E]ssentially within the domestic jurisdiction of any state"[29] formerly was interpreted to cover state-society relations and general welfare, including human rights. This construction is increasingly contested, but its staying power is evident from the language of Security Council resolutions, which habitually stresses the exceptional character of each UN intervention. It is also evident in the hostility of two permanent members of the Security Council, China and Russia, as well as a host of developing countries.

This orthodoxy is in profound tension with contemporary humanitarian and state practice. On the one hand, there is an extreme unevenness in the application of international coercion to deal with complex emergencies in areas where the territorial integrity of important UN member states, or their allies, is challenged. In the 1990s, on the other hand, the visceral anti-interventionist biases and structures have been overturned in favor of humanitarian values often enough that a norm about contingent sovereignty is emerging. Chapter VII action to enforce humanitarian decisions can no longer be seen as exceptional, and certainly not "unique," after international intervention in northern Iraq, Somalia, Bosnia, Rwanda, Haiti, Kosovo, and Timor. There are numerous differences among these cases, but one thing links them: the UN Charter's contradiction between sovereignty and justice has been resolved in favor of the latter because responsibility is becoming an additional attribute of statehood.

In short, the definition of national interests is evolving. It is changing with circumstances and with efforts by politicians, lobbyists, aid workers, scholars, and secretaries-general. National interests are not necessarily an "obstacle to effective action," as Annan argues, but the explanation for whatever action occurs or does not. "Common interests" are not superseding national interests, as Annan implies at one juncture in his General Assembly speech, but rather they are being redefined to include human rights. Annan is on much safer ground when speaking of a "more widely conceived definition of national interests" so that, for instance, most states acknowledge that eliminating ethnic cleansing as a policy option *is* in their vital interests. His statement is a watershed that is part of a larger trend. As Kathryn Sikkink has demonstrated, "The adoption of human rights policies represented not the neglect of national interests but a fundamental shift in the perception of long-term national interests."[30]

In closing this section, two cautionary notes are in order. First, it is premature for friends or foes of humanitarian intervention to get too excited or exercised over Annan's speech or the interventions of 1999. Too frequently today's headlines dominate analyses. In April 1991 after action in northern Iraq, many humanitarians argued ebulliently that anything was possible; three years later after Rwanda's genocide, they concluded pessimistically that doing nothing was the dominant mode. Care should be taken about extrapolation from 1999's somewhat successful, at least by historical standards, humanitarian interventions.

A second word of caution is so obvious as to appear superfluous. Humanitarian interventions inevitably involve serious problems and unintended consequences. The focus here has been on objectives because of dramatic changes in conventional wisdom articulated by the secretary-general. But numerous counterproductive cases demonstrate problems with means and consequences that should brake the impulse to intervene.

Hence, there may not be many, but there will be some, Kosovos and Timors. This likelihood has particular resonance in light of NATO's efforts in the Balkans, after earlier dithering in Bosnia.[31] Adam Roberts argues that "*Operation Applied Force* will contribute to a trend towards seeing certain humanitarian and legal norms inescapably bound up with conceptions of national interest."[32] Joseph Nye writes that Kosovo is the latest indication that, despite their shortcomings, humanitarian crises "raise moral concerns that the American people consistently include in their list of foreign policy interests. Policy experts may deplore such sympathies, but they are a democratic reality."[33]

Conclusion

The old Westphalian structure is being modified, but a new one has yet to emerge. Traditional interpretations of unlimited sovereignty are under siege. There is a growing consensus that states must be held accountable for certain intolerable kinds of behavior. There remains, however, considerable uncertainty and inconsistency as well as much debate about standards, trigger mechanisms, and compliance. Annan's call for standards that are "fairly and consistently applied, irrespective of region or nation" is a clarion call. This laudable yet unrealistic proposition is the predictable part of a secretary-general's sermon. As he knows better than most social scientists, there can be no universal imperatives. States will pick and choose.

Proposals to establish definitive criteria to govern humanitarian intervention fly in the face of political reality. Even if we could somehow determine the "can" or "should" of intervention, we still could not determine when states "will" or "must" intervene. Governments ultimately will determine what costs and benefits are worth sustaining. Using a poker analogy, it seems that we are often willing to be "in for a dime but not for a dollar." A better proposal for the secretary-general would be to up the ante to a quarter.

To reiterate, humanitarian values have not superceded traditional conceptions of vital interests but rather have become increasingly central to their definition. There is a persistent tendency in the discourse of international relations to juxtapose ideals and realpolitik. Humanitarians with hearts on their sleeves lament the pernicious influence of politics.[34] But politics explains action or inaction, and there is little that is immutable about perceived interests, particularly when survival is not at stake. Both realism and neoliberalism view state interests as exogenous instead of examining the forces behind them. Yet political interests are framed or constructed by leaders. Despite the dramatic growth in numbers and significance of transnational actors, states remain the most important actors within the international system in general, and humanitarian affairs in particular. Getting state authorities to take seriously their obligations to citizens is more sensible than searching for mythical common interests or a "space of victimhood."[35]

This essay does not challenge the fact that states act on the basis of power and interests, but rather suggests the extent to which humanitarian values have shaped how those interests are perceived. Those who ultimately determine the shape of humanitarian action are leaders who act on the basis of calculating benefits, risks, and costs. Political interest is not fixed but is continually being redefined as a result of calculations about fluid domestic and international contexts.

The secretary-general appreciates that there is no escape from moral reasoning in international politics even if, as David Rieff notes, "Our moral ambitions have been revealed as being larger than our political, military, or even cognitive means."[36] Greater attention to humanitarian values from policymakers has not brought utopia but made the world a somewhat more livable place than it would have been otherwise. It is inconceivable, for instance, that a responsible Western leader could make the same argument about Kosovo as Neville Chamberlain made about Czechoslovakia. Although vigorous action was too slow in East Timor, at least the outcry over Indonesia's military and militia atrocities was immediate; an Australian-led force was deployed and followed by a full-fledged experiment with UN trusteeship.

Humanitarian values have become central to the definition of vital interests as well as to the plotting of dictators and war criminals. Notwithstanding this decade's mixed record of humanitarian intervention, the eternal policy challenge in an eternally imperfect world is to reduce the discrepancy between idealistic rhetoric and reality. The humanitarian glass is nine-tenths empty, but someday it will be fuller.

Notes

1 Boutros Boutros-Ghali, *An Agenda for Peace* (New York; United Nations, 1992), para. 17.
2 Kofi A. Annan, "Secretary-General's Speech to the 54th Session of the General Assembly," 20 September 1999.
3 The theme of the possible need for intervention with especial reference to Kosovo was introduced in his speech on "Intervention," UN document SG/SM/6613/Rev.l, 26 June 1998.
4 Intervention was also a major theme in the annual *Report of the Secretary-General on the Work of the Organization*, UN document A/54/1, 31 August 1999.
5 See "Statement by the President of the Security Council," UN document S/PRST/1999/34, 30 November 1999.
6 See, for example, Thomas J. Biersteker and Cynthia Weber, eds., *State Sovereignty as Social Construct* (Cambridge: Cambridge University Press, 1996); Peter J. Katzenstein, ed., *The Culture of National Security: Norms and Identity in World Politics* (New York: Columbia University Press, 1996); and Alexander Wendt, *Social Theory of International Politics* (Cambridge: Cambridge University Press, 1999).
7 Jarat Chopra and Thomas G. Weiss, "Sovereignty Is No Longer Sacrosanct: Codifying Humanitarian Intervention," *Ethics & International Affairs* 6 (1992): 95–118.
8 Kofi A. Annan, *Report of the Secretary-General Pursuant to General Assembly Resolution 53/35: The Fall of Srebrenica* (also known as the Srebrenica report), UN document A/54/549, 15 November 1999, para. 493.
9 Adam Roberts, "The Role of Humanitarian Issues in International Politics in the 1990s," *International Review of the Red Cross* 81, no. 833 (1999): 19.
10 Michael Ignatieff, "Human Rights: The Midlife Crisis," *New York Review of Books* XLVI, no. 9 (1999): 58.
11 William Jefferson Clinton, "Remarks to the 54th Session of the United Nations General Assembly," 21 September 1999.
12 UN Press Release SG/SM/6848, HR/CN/8998, 6 April 1999.
13 See Thomas G. Weiss, *Military-Civilian Interactions: Intervening in Humanitarian Crises* (Lanham, Md: Rowman & Littlefield, 1999).
14 Thomas G. Weiss, "Collective Spinelessness: U.N. Actions in the Former Yugoslavia," in *The World and Yugoslavia's Wars*, ed. Richard H. Ullman (New York: Council on Foreign Relations, 1996), 59–96.

15 Judith Goldstein and Robert O. Keohane, "Ideas and Foreign Policy: An Analytical Framework," in *Ideas and Foreign Policy: Beliefs, Institutions, and Political Change*, ed. Judith Goldstein and Robert O. Keohane (Ithaca, NY: Cornell University Press, 1993), 26.

16 In addition to Goldstein and Keohane, *Ideas and Foreign Policy*, see also Martha Finnemore, *National Interests in International Society* (Ithaca, NY: Cornell University Press, 1996); and M. E. Keck and Kathryn Sikkink, *Activists Beyond Borders: Advocacy Networks in International Politics* (Ithaca, NY: Cornell University Press, 1998).

17 The argument in this chapter builds on S. Neil MacFarlane and Thomas G. Weiss, "Political Interest and Humanitarian Action," *Security Studies* 9, no. 2 (2000): 112–42.

18 US Government, "Clinton Administration Policy on Reforming Multilateral Peace Operations, Presidential Decision Directive-25," The White House, May 1994.

19 J. Bryan Hehir, "Military Intervention and National Sovereignty: Recasting the Relationship," in *Hard Choices: Moral Dilemmas in Humanitarian Intervention*, ed. Jonathan Moore (Lanham, Md: Rowman & Littlefield, 1998), 30.

20 See, for example, Laura W. Reed and Carl Kaysen, eds., *Emerging Norms of Justified Intervention* (Cambridge, Mass.: American Academy of Arts and Sciences, 1993); Stanley Hoffmann, *The Ethics and Politics of Humanitarian Intervention* (Notre Dame, IN: University of Notre Dame Press, 1996); John Harriss, ed., *The Politics of Humanitarian Intervention* (London: Pinter, 1995); Oliver Ramsbotham and Tom Woodhouse, *Humanitarian Intervention in Contemporary Conflict: A Reconceptualization* (Cambridge: Polity, 1996); Anthony McDermott, ed., *Humanitarian Force* (Oslo: International Peace Research Institute, 1997), PRIO Report 4/97; James Mayall, ed., *The New Interventionism, 1991–1994: United Nations Experience in Cambodia, Former Yugoslavia and Somalia* (Cambridge: Cambridge University Press, 1996); Jan Nederveen Pieterse, ed., *World Orders in the Making: Humanitarian Intervention and Beyond* (London: Macmillan, 1998); Tim Dunne and Nicholas J. Wheeler, eds., *Human Rights in Global Politics* (Cambridge: Cambridge University Press, 1999); and Nigel Rodley, ed., *To Loose the Bands of Wickedness: International Intervention in Defence of Human Rights* (London: Brassey's, 1992).

21 See Thomas G. Weiss, "Whither International Efforts for Internally Displaced Persons?" *Journal of Peace Research* 36, no. 3 (1999): 363–73.

22 Francis M. Deng, *Protecting the Dispossessed: A Challenge for the International Community* (Washington, DC: Brookings Institution, 1993); Francis M. Deng, Donald Rothchild, Sadikei Kimaro, I. William Zartman, and Terrence Lyons, *Sovereignty as Responsibility: Conflict Management in Africa* (Washington, DC: Brookings Institution, 1996); and Francis M. Deng, "Frontiers of Sovereignty," *Leiden Journal of International Law* 8, no. 2 (1995): 249–86. For more recent analyses and case studies, see Roberta Cohen and Francis M. Deng, *Masses in Flight: The Global Crisis in Displacement* (Washington, DC: Brookings Institution, 1998); and Roberta Cohen and Francis M. Deng, eds., *The Forsaken People: Case Studies of the Internally Displaced* (Washington, DC: Brookings Institution, 1998).

23 Bernard Kouchner and Mario Bettati, *Le devoir d'ingérence* (Paris: Denoël, 1987); and Mario Bettati, *Le droit d'ingérence: mutation de l'ordre international* (Paris: Odile Jacob, 1996).

24 David Malone, *Decision-Taking in the UN Security Council: The Case of Haiti, 1990–97* (Oxford: Oxford University Press, 1998).

25 The mindset in Washington remains for the moment impervious to the humanitarian values that have penetrated the foreign policy of almost all other countries. See Stephen D. Biddle, Julia Klare, and Jaeson Rosenfeld, *The Military Utility of Landmines: Implications for Arms Control* (Alexandria, VA: Institute for Defense Analyses, 1994).

26 Richard Price, "Reversing the Gun Sights: Transnational Civil Society Targets Land Mines," *International Organization* 52, no. 3 (1998): 617.

27 Charles Krauthammer, "The Short, Unhappy Life of Humanitarian War," *The National Interest*, no. 57 (1999): 5–8; Michael Mandelbaum, "A Perfect Failure," *Foreign Affairs* 78, no. 5 (1999): 2–8; and Richard N. Haass, "What to Do with American Primacy," *Foreign Affairs* 78, no. 5 (1999): 37–49.

28 Edward Luttwak, "Kofi's Rule: Humanitarian Intervention and Neocolonialism," *National Interest*, no. 58 (Winter 1999/2000): 57–62.

29 This article is only one of many codifications of the principle of nonintervention in both multilateral and bilateral international legal instruments. Bruno Simma provides a useful account of the evolution of the interpretation of this article as it concerns human rights in *The Charter of the United Nations: A Commentary* (Oxford: Oxford University Press, 1995), 141–54.

30 Kathryn Sikkink, "The Power of Principled Ideas: Human Rights Policies in the United States and Western Europe," in *Ideas and Foreign Policy: Beliefs, Institutions and Political Change*, ed. Judith Goldstein and Robert O. Keohane (Ithaca, NY: Cornell University Press, 1996), 140. See also Thomas Risse, Stephen C. Rapp and Kathryn Sikkink, eds., *The Power of Human Rights: International Norms and Domestic Change* (New York: Cambridge University Press, 1999).

31 See John Williams, The Ethical Basis of Humanitarian Intervention, the Security Council and Yugoslavia," *International Peacekeeping* 6, no. 2 (1999): 1–23.

32 Adam Roberts, "NATO's 'Humanitarian War' Over Kosovo," *Survival* 41, no. 3 (1999): 120.

33 Joseph P. Nye, Jr., "Redefining the National Interest," *Foreign Affairs* 78, no. 4 (1999): 22, 30. For an indication of the kinds of issues increasingly before the public, see Roy Gutman and David Rieff, eds., *Crimes of War: What the Public Should Know* (New York: Norton, 1999).

34 Thomas G. Weiss, "Principles, Politics, and Humanitarian Action," *Ethics & International Affairs* 13 (1999): 1–22.

35 François Debrix, "Deterritorialised Territories, Borderless Borders: The New Geography of International Medical Assistance," *Third World Quarterly* 19, no. 5 (1998): 827–46.

36 David Rieff, "A New Age of Liberal Imperialism?" *World Policy Journal* XVI, no. 2 (1999): 3.

16
PRINCIPLES, POLITICS, AND HUMANITARIAN ACTION

The tragedies of the past decade have shaken humanitarians to the core. The mere mention of Bosnia, Somalia, Rwanda, Liberia, Afghanistan, or Sierra Leone profoundly disturbs their composure. Traumas in these countries have become synonymous with the dilemmas of humanitarian action, that is, with international attempts to help victims through the provision of relief and the protection of their human rights.

Until recently, the two most essential humanitarian principles—neutrality (not taking sides with warring parties) and impartiality (nondiscrimination and proportionality)—have been relatively uncontroversial, as has the key operating procedure of seeking consent from belligerents.[1] However, a host of developments in the 1990s has altered this attitude toward humanitarian action. These include the complete disregard for international humanitarian law by war criminals and even by child soldiers, the direct targeting of civilians and relief personnel, the use of foreign aid to fuel conflicts and war economies, and the protracted nature of many so-called emergencies that in fact last for decades. The result has been a collective identity crisis among aid workers in war zones as well as among those who analyze such efforts.

Founded in 1864, the International Committee of the Red Cross (ICRC), through its apolitical practices and principles, has shined as the beacon of humanitarianism. In 1986 the International Court of Justice chose not even to define humanitarianism but rather to equate it with the work of the ICRC. The father of the organization's Fundamental Principles, Jean Pictet, defined each principle as "a rule, based upon judgment and experience, which is adopted by a community to guide its conduct."[2] In addition to providing life-saving ministrations, the ICRC has pushed governments to adopt the rules of war: indeed, it fulfills a unique role as the custodian of the Geneva Conventions of 1949 and the Additional Protocols of 1977. The ICRC's prominence among humanitarian agencies is suggested by its having won four Nobel Peace Prizes.

Yet in many ways, international humanitarian law seems to have been formulated mainly to deal with a different world from today's—a world populated by governments and regular armies whose interests were served by adhering to the rules of warfare. Concepts once widely respected, especially domestic jurisdiction and sovereignty, have been breached even by humanitarians; for instance, nongovernmental organizations (NGOs) at times have been among the most numerous and vociferous proponents of military intervention, a position quite inconceivable a decade ago.

In today's environment, humanitarian tragedies have become "normal." Cynics even view them as growth opportunities for aid agencies, while others see winners as well as losers in a new international political economy of war.[3] Severe criticism of the aid establishment in general and relief agencies in particular has fueled the identity crisis experienced by humanitarians and analysts and has polarized debate.[4]

Understanding the differences between two groups of humanitarians is crucial: "classicists," led by the ICRC, who believe that humanitarian action can and should be completely insulated from politics; and "political humanitarians," who believe that political and humanitarian action "could not and should not be disassociated."[5] I place myself in the latter camp.

Even classicists increasingly acknowledge the need for parallel, politically savvy action. According to ICRC president Cornelio Sommaruga, "humanitarian, political, and development actors manage crisis in a comprehensive manner."[6] Thus, in the words of the ICRC's chief medical officer, projects must be "specifically tailored to the needs [of victims] while minimizing the undesirable effects of aid."[7] This is a rhetorical step beyond earlier acknowledgments by the ICRC that its activities sometimes have political implications. The organization still maintains an apolitical veneer, however, and is unwilling publicly to admit that its principles should be adapted to political exigencies, although it has commissioned a new volume about "hard choices."[8] David Forsythe has consistently argued that the ICRC has always pursued "humanitarian politics—the struggle to implement humanitarian values as part of public policy."[9] At the same time, the organization has underestimated the impact of two other types of politics, realpolitik among states and factional politics within them.

UN high commissioner for refugees Sadako Ogata notes that "political and humanitarian actors are uncomfortable bedfellows," an apt image for this awkward reality because politics and humanitarianism are intimately intertwined.[10] As a result, classical proponents of a political humanitarianism increasingly encounter problems in relating to those political humanitarians pursuing either "minimalist" or "maximalist" objectives. Minimalists aim to "do no harm," whereas maximalists have a more ambitious agenda of employing humanitarian action as part of a comprehensive strategy to transform conflict.

Classicists have always disagreed adamantly with a third group of political humanitarians—"solidarists," who choose sides and abandon neutrality and impartiality as well as reject consent as a prerequisite for intervention. Although solidarists first appeared in the Spanish Civil War, the most visible contemporary representatives are Médecins Sans Frontières (MSF), or Doctors Without Borders, who were established as a "counter" ICRC in the midst of the Biafran civil war by a group of ICRC field staff who could no longer abide by the organization's principles. The judgment of these renegade ICRC professionals that the application of traditional principles did more harm than good for the Ibos foreshadowed the current debate.

In many contemporary conflicts, humanitarians find neutrality and impartiality problematic at best and impossible at times. They also encounter serious difficulties in seeking the consent of numerous and undisciplined belligerents whose antics often have led to coercive economic and military sanctions. Even when they attempt to be neutral and impartial, aid agencies often are *perceived* to favor one side over the other. Here, though, "political humanitarianism" refers to conscious decisions to employ humanitarian action as an integral part of an international public policy to mitigate life-threatening suffering and protect fundamental human rights in active wars.

The political spectrum of humanitarians and their attitudes toward traditional operating principles

It is useful to situate humanitarians along the analytical spectrum depicted below. The diagram locates classicists, minimalists, maximalists, and solidarists according to their degree of political involvement and their willingness to respect traditional principles. From left to right, the scale indicates low to high political involvement, from the extremes of no political ties at all to complete identification with victims by fervent proponents. Humanitarian action for each group from left to right on the diagram is respectively: warranted as long as it is charitable and self-contained, defined only by the needs of victims, and divorced from political objectives and conditionalities; worthwhile if efforts to relieve suffering do not make matters worse and can be sustained locally; defensible when coupled with steps to address the roots

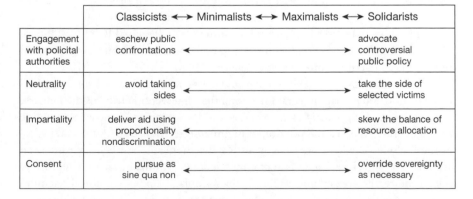

	Classicists ←→ Minimalists ←→ Maximalists ←→ Solidarists	
Engagement with policital authorities	eschew public confrontations ←————————————→	advocate controversial public policy
Neutrality	avoid taking sides ←————————————→	take the side of selected victims
Impartiality	deliver aid using proportionality nondiscrimination ←————————————→	skew the balance of resource allocation
Consent	pursue as sine qua non ←————————————→	override sovereignty as necessary

Figure 16.1 The political spectrum of humanitarians

of violence and as part of a conscious and comprehensive political strategy; and justifiable when siding with the main victims. A blurring of categories is inevitable because the four positions are not hard and fast, but are tempered by realities on the ground.

Nonetheless, these ideal types are helpful in understanding the current acrimony in international discourse, the focus of the first section of this essay. They also provide useful background for the second section, which examines why humanitarians feel such a sense of despair and defeat in the face of recent tragedies. The pros and cons of impartial versus political humanitarianism and the differing approaches by the four kinds of actors on the spectrum are the subject of the third section of the essay.

In their most straightforward form, contemporary criticisms of humanitarian practices range from moderate analyses about how to reform the international humanitarian system to fundamental questions about whether it is worthy of reform at all. Possible responses from aid agencies range from making the existing system more effective and thereby rekindling the trust of donors and recipients to revamping the conceptual basis of what it means to be "humanitarian" and making humanitarian action as relevant to problem solving and conflict management as it is to natural disasters. Representatives across the spectrum agree that substantial alterations in past practices are required: few foresee a return to the "good old days" when neutrality, impartiality, and consent were unquestioned tactics.

I situate myself to the right of center on the spectrum, but I do not believe that humanitarian action is anachronistic. Traditional principles may be helpful in one context, but in others, hard-headed and hard-hearted calculations—including triage and "tough love"—are more relevant than a formulaic recitation of the classical humanitarian mantra. Andrew Natsios has argued persuasively that "the advocates of neutrality are losing ground in the debate."[11] But within the same theater of conflict, classicist principles and the call to intervene can clash. Leading the charge is usually MSF, the most visible and vocal of the solidarists, arguing that agencies should employ humanitarian action within a political strategy on behalf of victims. The ICRC position is giving way to the notion that the two types of action—political and humanitarian—cannot and should not be dissociated. This shift was remarkably stated in a background document for the second ICRC Wolfsberg Humanitarian Forum: "It is difficult to imagine how humanitarian assistance could remain fully neutral in complex emergencies."[12]

Recent complex emergencies have given rise to a clarion call for improved collaboration and perhaps integration among the "intervention trio" of the military, the political and diplomatic elements, and the humanitarian agencies. As a guide to action, the "do no harm" position of minimalists seems hard to dismiss on logical grounds alone. Furthermore, it is plausible that humanitarian help as part of an ambitious political package, as recommended by maximalists, could ultimately relieve more life-threatening suffering than similar help in a political vacuum, however effectively it is delivered.[13] Many situations require calculations with which few are comfortable and by which many will be appalled.[14]

Cornelio Sommaruga and Adam Roberts caution that "we should not be too hasty in announcing that barbarism is back."[15] I am tempted to ask when it disappeared. David Rieff has asserted that ignoring the resurgence in grisly violence is a "humanitarian illusion" and that "disillusionment is the beginning of wisdom in the analysis of this terrible reality, this time of piety and iron."[16] A striking fact of contemporary international society is that the number of individuals and organizations fostering humanitarian norms and action has risen dramatically, along with media attention to the plight of victims. The paradox is that barbarism has kept pace. In the words of the late historian Eric Hobsbawm, there has been a "return to what our nineteenth-century ancestors would have called the standards of barbarism."[17]

Traditional humanitarian principles are now under siege. The extent to which they can be applied depends on the context. Classicists are becoming aware of the unacceptable results of applying neutrality, impartiality, and consent when dealing with unprincipled actors in a variety of armed conflicts. Humanitarian action has never been easy, but abiding strictly by traditional principles used to be a better tactical guide to sustaining the vast majority of impulses to rescue war victims than it is today. Although this approach led to dissension in ICRC ranks and the creation of MSF, in the late 1960s it was possible for classicists to view the Biafran civil war as anomalous and to dismiss the claims of dissenters. But in the post–Cold War period, Biafras have become routine, and classicists are obliged to engage in a conversation with representatives from most of the spectrum of political humanitarians.

In many war zones, context is as important as principles because the latter often clash. Thoughtful reflection thus has come to assume a growing role relative to visceral reaction. At the beginning of the 1990s and in the face of new challenges in Kurdistan and Bosnia, Larry Minear and I spelled out an alternative to the ICRC's practices, the Providence Principles, which are more flexible than the classical ones.[18] This approach was a step toward modifying established rules to guide the conduct of humanitarians in a new and troubled period. The ICRC's own Fundamental Principles are not immutable, although this is frequently over-looked. Last modified in 1965 during "an orgy of rule-making," these principles may be adapted when necessary to reflect the changing nature of war, humanitarian agencies, and donor policies.[19]

Operational principles thus are not moral absolutes. Whether from the ICRC or other agencies, they are norms toward which to strive, but without the illusion that their application is possible in every situation or that their success is guaranteed. They are means to achieve ends but not ends in themselves. Differences exist in the interpretation given to principles by various individuals and agencies, in the importance of some relative to others, and in the extent to which a given principle or set of principles will prevail in particular circumstances. The need for case-by-case judgments has been reinforced by recent experience. From sustaining vulnerable groups in the African Great Lakes region while feeding thugs and fueling the war to moving threatened populations in Bosnia while facilitating ethnic cleansing, operational situations in the 1990s have been tortuous—for victims as well as their humanitarian benefactors.

Because morally wrenching contexts are now the rule rather than the exception, it is increasingly difficult for humanitarians to occupy unequivocally the moral high ground. For those few on pedestals, it is a precarious perch. Michael Ignatieff anguishes that "almost everyone who tries . . . has a bad conscience; no one is quite sure whether our engagement makes things better or worse."[20] Bill Maynes recommends "ethical realpolitik" as an alternative for American foreign policy.[21] Mark Duffield calls for a "new ethics of working in political crises . . . [where] 'good guys' no longer exist."[22] Joanna Macrae states, "The idea that it is easy to distinguish the bad guy from the good woman and child is no longer sustainable."[23] Evoking Dante's *Inferno,* where the hottest room was reserved for those who vacillated, a Norwegian research group confronts the distinct possibility that "neutrality is a form of moral bankruptcy."[24]

To date, responses to these critics have often been semantic gymnastics, stretching concepts to such a degree that they become meaningless. For example, Secretary-General Kofi Annan and others utilize the oxymoron "induced consent,"[25] while Hugo Slim calls for a "robust form of impartiality which allows them [NGOs and UN forces] not just to dish out relief in proportion to needs, but also to dish out criticism (advocacy) or military bombardment in proportion to human rights wrong doing."[26]

What is the value of principles if problems are not uniform across war zones, and if neutrality, impartiality, and consent may be more or less pertinent depending on the type and phase of an armed conflict? The clear articulation of principles provides an emergency brake on the slippery slope of shameless opportunism. When principles bump into one another, compromise and tough trade-offs are inevitable; but those who deviate from principles should be aware of the costs. Humanitarians who are clear about the costs of departing from principles undoubtedly will be more successful in helping and protecting victims than those who have none or who are inflexible. The only absolute principle is the respect for human life. Other principles are standard operating procedures reflecting empirical judgments about experience. They amount to finding ways to make things happen in individual situations.

Scholars and practitioners frequently employ the term "dilemma" to describe painful decision making; but "quandary" would be more apt.[27] A dilemma involves two or more alternative courses of action with unintended but unavoidable and equally undesirable consequences. If consequences are equally unpalatable, then remaining inactive on the sidelines is an option rather than entering the scrum on the field. A quandary, on the other hand, entails tough choices among unattractive options with better or worse possible outcomes. While humanitarians are perplexed, they are not and should not be immobilized. The solution is not indifference or withdrawal but rather appropriate engagement. The key lies in making a good faith effort to analyze the advantages and disadvantages of different alloys of politics and humanitarianism, and then to choose what often amounts to the lesser of evils.

Thoughtful humanitarianism is more appropriate than rigid ideological responses, for four reasons: goals of humanitarian action often conflict; good intentions can have catastrophic consequences; there are alternative ways to achieve ends; and even if none of the choices is ideal, victims still require decisions about outside help. What Myron Wiener has called "instrumental humanitarianism" would resemble just war doctrine because contextual analyses and not formulas are required.[28] Rather than resorting to knee-jerk reactions to help, it is necessary to weigh options and make decisions about choices that are far from optimal.

Many humanitarian decisions in northern Iraq, Somalia, Bosnia, and Rwanda—and especially those involving economic or military sanctions—required selecting least-bad options. Thomas Nagle advises that "given the limitations on human action, it is naive to suppose that there is a solution to every moral problem."[29] Action-oriented institutions and staff are required in order to contextualize their work rather than apply preconceived notions of what is right or wrong. Nonetheless, classicists continue to insist on Pictet's "indivisible whole" because humanitarian principles "are interlocking, overlapping and mutually supportive. . . . It is hard to accept the logic of one without also accepting the others."[30]

The process of making decisions in war zones could be compared to that pursued by "clinical ethical review teams" whose members are on call to make painful decisions about life-and-death matters in hospitals.[31] The sanctity of life is complicated by new technologies, but urgent decisions cannot be finessed. It is impermissible to long for another era or to pretend that the bases for decisions are unchanged. However emotionally wrenching, finding solutions is an operational imperative that is challenging but intellectually doable. Humanitarians who cannot stand the heat generated by situational ethics should stay out of the post–Cold War humanitarian kitchen.

Why are humanitarians in such a state of moral and operational disrepair? In many ways Western liberal values over the last few centuries have been moving toward interpreting moral obligations as going beyond a family and intimate networks, beyond a tribe, and beyond a nation. The impalpable moral ideal is concern about the fate of other people, no matter how far away.[32] The evaporation of distance with advances in technology and media coverage, along with a willingness to intervene in a variety of post–Cold War crises, however, has produced situations in which humanitarians are damned if they do and if they don't. Engagement by outsiders does not necessarily make things better, and it may even create a "*moral* hazard by altering the payoffs to combatants in such a way as to encourage *more* intensive fighting."[33]

This new terrain requires analysts and practitioners to admit ignorance and question orthodoxies. There is no comfortable theoretical framework or world vision to function as a compass to steer between integration and fragmentation, globalization and insularity. Michael Ignatieff observes, "The world is not becoming more chaotic or violent, although our failure to understand and act makes it seem so."[34] Gwyn Prins has pointed to the "scary humility of admitting one's ignorance" because "the new vogue for 'complex emergencies' is too often a means of concealing from oneself that one does not know what is going on."[35] To make matters more frustrating, never before has there been such a bombardment of data and instant analysis; the challenge of distilling such jumbled and seemingly contradictory information adds to the frustration of trying to do something appropriate *fast*.

International discourse is not condemned to follow North American fashions and adapt sound bites and slogans. It is essential to struggle with and even embrace the ambiguities that permeate international responses to wars, but without the illusion of a one-size-fits-all solution. The trick is to grapple with complexities, to tease out the general without ignoring the particular, and still to be inspired enough to engage actively in trying to make a difference.

Because more and more staff of aid agencies, their governing boards, and their financial backers have come to value reflection, an earlier policy prescription by Larry Minear and me no longer appears bizarre: "Don't just do something, stand there!"[36] This advice represented our conviction about the payoffs from thoughtful analyses and our growing distaste for the stereotypical, yet often accurate, image of a bevy of humanitarian actors flitting from one emergency to the next.

Searing experiences have led to such a voluminous literature that analysts are now categorizing the types of criticism.[37] Countless conferences and internal agency debates indicate a cultural change under way in institutional behavior as practitioners grapple to comprehend the ugly terrains where they operate, to put what they are doing into a political context rather than react viscerally with the hope that good intentions alone will suffice. Even the most critical of critics, Alex de Waal, observes that "as critiques of humanitarianism become more common and more accepted, some thoughtful agency staff are becoming more questioning."[38]

"Humanitarianism" means helping and protecting victims irrespective of who and where they are and why they are in need. The three main types of "politics" are: the competition among states for survival and supremacy and for maximizing national interests in an anarchical world (realpolitik); the struggle for power and influence within donor and crisis states (partisan or factional politics depending on the existence of democratic rules or the law of the jungle); and efforts to agree upon desirable international public policies within governmental, intergovernmental, and nongovernmental arenas. Humanitarians have a stake in political outcomes at every level, and their actions influence and are influenced by such outcomes.

The intersection of politics and humanitarianism—obvious to elected officials, pundits, and political scientists but not to classicists—alters considerably the usual procedure of seeking consent from belligerents and respecting neutrality and impartiality.[39] Much contemporary humanitarian action occurs in countries torn by civil war (that is, in countries of origin and not of asylum) where civilians are targets and outside military forces are sometimes deployed despite objections from sovereign authorities. Outside resources—usually favoring one side (or so perceived)—are actively fought over by local factions, and have unintended and unanticipated negative consequences. Because civilians are now prime targets instead of accidental victims, humanitarians often are obliged to confront those responsible for massive abuses of fundamental rights. In 1992 Jarat Chopra and I wrote in this journal, "Sovereignty is no longer sacrosanct."[40] A fitting corollary in 1999 is "Humanitarian principles are no longer sacrosanct."

The sanctity of human life is the first principle of all humanitarians and overrides other considerations; but neutrality, impartiality, and consent are second-order principles that may or may not be accurate tactical guides. Traditional principles were developed as means to safeguard life, but they no longer provide unequivocal guidance and should be modified when necessary. Classicists disagree with this conclusion, but not with the painful reality suggested by such conference titles as "Principled Aid in an Unprincipled World," which was sponsored in April 1998 in London by the European Community Humanitarian Office (ECHO) and the Overseas Development Institute (ODI).

In a 1997 speech, ICRC president Sommaruga pointed to the need for dialogue among humanitarian and political players because they have "different roles but complementary responsibilities."[41] The argument here is different. Whether these players are dealing with the disproportionate burdens on vulnerable groups of economic sanctions, the complications from military enforcement, or the need to balance tensions between protection of human rights and access, they face not only intense interactions and complementary responsibilities but also clashes between political and humanitarian imperatives.

It is crucial to flush out differences and not airbrush them away. The assumption that politics and humanitarianism can be entirely separated, as if they were parts of two different and self-contained worlds, is a fiction. The "dark side" of humanitarian action would include: food and other aid usurped by belligerents to sustain a war economy (for example, in Liberia); assistance that has given legitimacy to illegitimate political authorities, particularly those with a guns economy (for example, in Somalia); aid distribution patterns that have influenced the movement of refugees (for example, first in eastern Zaire and then in the renamed Democratic Republic of the Congo); resource allocations that have promoted the proliferation of aid agencies and created a wasteful aid market that encourages parties to play organizations against one another (for example, in Afghanistan); elites that have benefited from the relief economy (for example, in Bosnia); and resources that have affected strategic equilibriums (for example, in Sierra Leone).

There is also a subtle and oft-ignored "bright side" of humanitarian action in that humanitarians can exert a modest positive influence on peace building and conflict resolution. Humanitarians can play diplomatic roles by taking advantage of their local connections and knowledge to build bridges among warring parties. Rehabilitation and development undoubtedly can take place concurrently with relief, particularly in parts of a country where relative peace is present. Finally, and although it has been minimized in both analyses and budgetary allocations, enhanced protection of human rights also can result from the mere presence of outside humanitarians and military forces.

In brief, reflection is becoming a priority for the staff of most aid agencies, wherever they are on the spectrum of humanitarianism. The laudable action-oriented humanitarian ethos is being tempered with more consideration of missions, mandates, performance, operating styles, and results. Complexity is not an excuse for complacency or a pretext to abandon large numbers of people to their Hobbesian fate in civil wars, but it does introduce elements of confusion and frustration in the formerly more certain and straightforward worldview of humanitarians. Contemporary complex emergencies can and must be understood better, just as humanitarian agencies can and must train and equip their personnel to be more effective.

What are the pros and cons of impartial versus political humanitarianism, and what form do differences in approach take in designing assistance and protection activities? Although agencies frequently have performed well under arduous circumstances, the disastrous consequences of much contemporary humanitarian action constitute a serious enough indictment of past procedures to force a thorough reexamination of how all humanitarian agencies approach their work in war zones. Classicists, whose impulses and mores have compelled them to respond automatically to the plight of victims in the past, now face a painful quandary. If the objective of relieving suffering suffices, there is no reason to scrutinize the short- or longer-term impacts of assistance—responding with one's heart and guts is adequate. However, if impacts beyond the immediate intervention are as or more important than the immediate relief of suffering, then a painful process of questioning should begin. Classicists are obliged to take adequately into account the results of the realpolitik calculations by states, factional politics within war zones and partisan politics in donor countries, and outcomes of international public policy debates. Honest questions should be asked about engagement *and* disengagement. Rushing immediately to the scene of a disaster is not preordained. Doing nothing is an option.

Reflections and not reflexes are required because, in David Rieff's words, "despite the best intentions of aid workers, and at times because of them, they become logisticians in the war efforts of warlords, fundamentalists, gangsters, and ethnic cleansers."[42] The 1998 background document for the second off-the-record Wolfsberg Humanitarian Forum organized by the ICRC was less poignant but similar in its conclusion: "Aid in complex emergencies is always determined by a highly politicized context and has political implications itself, whether as a direct consequence of its provision or by way of intentional or unintentional side-effects."[43]

The "good Samaritan" figures prominently in ICRC documentation, and many humanitarians agree implicitly or explicitly with Sommaruga's biblical interpretation and his perennial praise for apolitical humanitarianism as an "act of charity."[44] Paul's First Letter to the Corinthians praises charity as the greatest of virtues, but John Hutchinson has criticized the "champions of charity" on the grounds that they helped make war more palatable.[45]

In light of substantial evidence of the counterproductive effects of well-intentioned humanitarian action, there are still other reasons to question visceral charity. Altruism should infuse debate but not constitute policy. It is impermissible to cede to virtue if it hinders rather than helps a political solution, leads to more violence and conflict, supports unduly the growth of a war economy, or undermines local coping capacities. Classical humanitarianism may seem unequivocally noble, but counterproductive efforts are uncharitable. Benign motivations are insufficient if the results are dreadful—just as selfish motivations are sufficient if the results are beneficial. Alain Destexhe, former secretary-general of the international office of MSF and now president of the International Crisis Group and member of the Belgian Senate, argues: "Humanitarian action is noble when coupled with political action and justice. Without them, it is doomed to failure and . . . a conscience-salving gimmick."[46]

Although politics and humanitarianism are inextricably linked, senior ICRC officials continue publicly to defend the apolitical fiction.[47] Anything added to or subtracted from the traditional mandate of saving lives allegedly diminishes the humanitarian mission. There is no need to denigrate unselfish acts or compassion and courage. Analysts should be clear, however, that classicists do not engage in the task of—indeed they remain agnostic about—linking emergency help to the longer-term requirements of bringing a society back to some type of equilibrium. Their claims are limited to saving lives and reducing suffering today, to a discrete incrementalism that can be praised or lambasted as the "one more blanket" theory.[48] This reality creates serious problems for classicists in coming to grips with minimalist and maximalist objectives of a more conscious political humanitarianism, and it continues to compel classicists to reject out-of-hand the approach of solidarists.

The minimalist approach, associated especially with the work of Mary Anderson,[49] allows the ICRC and other classicists to engage in a conversation in order to determine the conditions under which it is possible, in two recent formulations, "to do good without doing harm" or "to do the least harm."[50] Both classicists and minimalists acknowledge that poorly designed humanitarian action can promote or nourish violence. Thus, project design and implementation should take into account, for instance, such matters as the location and lighting of women's latrines, which can reduce dramatically instances of rape. Moreover, they should ensure, to the extent possible, that projects take advantage of development possibilities that could be sustainable once expatriates and external resources evaporate. Public relations and speeches emanating from Geneva notwithstanding, the most savvy field staff of the ICRC already act on such insights. In many ways, this is common sense for reflective humanitarians, although it may not be for reflexive ones.

This is not the place to examine criticisms of this modified Hippocratic oath, which include the lack of empirical evidence to warrant an emphasis on humanitarian institutions instead of states; the difficulties in disaggregating the effects of humanitarian shortcomings from the effects of local war economies; the inappropriateness of applying concepts from natural disasters to manmade ones; the anecdotal nature of successful cases of peace building; and the questionable sustainability of most projects once outsiders and their funds disappear. There is no pejorative connotation to the term "minimalist" which is intended to indicate a location left of center on the spectrum. Indeed, given the nature of contemporary tragedies, accomplishing the minimalist agenda is ambitious.

If humanitarian agencies are persuaded by the evidence that they are not exacerbating conflict or causing more harm than good, they are pursuing a defensible strategy. Whether or not they maintain the fiction of separating humanitarianism from politics, they can choose to respect the humanitarian imperative and alleviate life-threatening suffering as a stop-gap until political actors catch up. They can take advantage of opportunities, however limited, to pursue "developmentalist relief" that helps build sustainable local capacities for peace.[51]

Humanitarian angst results because doing nothing or withdrawing under some circumstances may be necessary, and such eventualities go against the impulse to help. Thus, even the commonsensical notion that relief should do more good than harm is not without controversy. In Britain some observers are so determined to counteract pessimism and halt any erosion in public funds devoted to relief and development that they have attacked the do-no-harm notion with a vehemence ordinarily reserved for the political opposition.[52] This short-sighted stance, which verges on humanitarian know-nothingness, is hard to fathom because counterproductive efforts are more of a threat to public support over the long haul than is the minimalist position.

The partial entente between classicists and minimalists does not extend much farther along the spectrum of political humanitarianism. The long-standing feud by classicists with solidarists, especially Doctors Without Borders, is well known. But maximalists also pursue a brand of political humanitarianism that is anathema to apolitical classicists. A serious conversation between maximalists and classicists is virtually unthinkable because overt and self-conscious political considerations supposedly corrode the pure humanitarian imperative.

Maximalists go beyond compassion and charity to argue that the relief of life-threatening suffering can no longer be the sole justification for outside assistance. They are determined to tackle the underlying causes of violence and to reform humanitarianism to prevent, mitigate, and resolve conflicts. Sommaruga described the maximalist agenda as "dangerous" because it amounts to "subordinating humanitarian action to political considerations, for instance, or bringing humanitarian issues into broader negotiations where diplomatic or military bargains can sometimes be struck at the expense of humanitarian concerns."[53]

At this juncture, maximalists are arguing on behalf of a largely untested proposition—indeed, their harshest critics would argue that results thus far have demonstrated that politicized aid has made matters worse, not better. Careful empirical research is required to verify the hypothesis, but it is plausible that placing humanitarian activities within a conflict resolution framework could ultimately work in favor of humanitarian interests, to bring substantially more benefits to victims than myopic or misplaced humanitarian action.

Properly conceived politically motivated assistance would use carrots and sticks, with conditionalities to reward or punish behavior. The notion is that such maximalist projects can reduce violence—effectively turning on its head the argument that aid can be manipulated by belligerents and exacerbate armed conflict. The calculation would be that the greatest good for the greatest number over the longer term would be better served by successful conflict management than by successful relief. In spite of billions of dollars of aid, the "well-fed dead" in Bosnia and the African Great Lakes suggest why emergency aid may not maximize relief of suffering even in the medium term.

The Dutch, Canadian, British, and Swedish governments have reorganized to foster better programmatic connections between humanitarian assistance and conflict resolution, and the World Bank has become a major actor in post-conflict peace building in such places as Bosnia, thereby reviving the "R" in their original IBRD acronym (International Bank for *Reconstruction* and Development). A recent report financed by the government of Norway, with guidance from former UN under-secretary-general Marrack Goulding, recommends "close cooperation between the political and humanitarian parts of the UN, which implies that in certain circumstances the purely humanitarian mandate may have to be adjusted temporarily to take account of political requirements."[54] Recent donor practice in Afghanistan and Sierra Leone suggests that political humanitarianism has gained ground and that relief appeals must increasingly aim to do more than save lives in order to sustain financing. Mark Duffield has characterized these institutional changes as a "shift in aid policy away from humanitarian assistance towards attempting to support development in conflict situations."[55] There are clear implications of this shift in mainstream policy toward developmental relief for both UN agencies and NGOs that have, in the market-driven aid economy, come to depend on government funding or intergovernmental subcontracts.[56]

Instead of the neutral and impartial provision of aid, humanitarian action as a tool of conflict management implies choice, and choices involve political decisions. In describing aid conditionality for peace processes, two observers note: "In an inversion of the children's fable, the unmentionable truth is that the emperor does indeed wear clothes, tailored to the political fashion of the day. . . . The real issue is not whether political effects will result, but what these will be."[57] The difficulty of outsiders making decisions about the legitimacy and desirability of different national institutions should not be underestimated. An in-depth familiarity with local values and institutions is required to begin to act effectively. Even in Western societies themselves, social engineering experiments have hardly been unalloyed successes. Moreover, well-intentioned and well-informed outsiders without a long-term stake in the local economy and political outcomes have no right to influence decisions. At the same time, it is inevitable that the leverage from resources necessarily entails judgments by outsiders about what is just and right, about whose capacities are built, about which local groups are favored. Power imbalances provide at least a cautionary note for political humanitarians.

Moreover, there are risks for political humanitarians. Aid can be held hostage to politics or withheld without commensurate payoffs. Politicians can seize upon the expanded objectives in order to justify isolationism and a reduction in resources devoted to emergency succor. The primacy of humanitarian values can be further eroded. And the overselling of humanitarian action could lead to additional disenchantment by politicians and the public if the more ambitious efforts to link emergency aid and conflict resolution fail. Thus, the maximalist experiment could lead to the worst of many worlds just as the minimalist one can be tritely inadequate.

Nonetheless, growing programmatic emphasis on doing no harm and linking relief with conflict resolution means that major donors increasingly are asking humanitarians to save lives in acute emergencies while simultaneously finding better ways to address underlying vulnerabilities. It is worth considering dispassionately that political humanitarianism may not necessarily be a threat to classicists. Under the right circumstances, the maximalist approach could be viewed as an opportunity to address the roots of violence rather than place emergency Band-Aids, however well funded and effective, on wounds. Nonetheless, some of the more grandiose claims of maximalists should lead to extreme skepticism: there literally is no space for conflict resolution or development activities when deep insecurity prevails. In the darkest moments of civil war, only emergency relief efforts are plausible, and even these often are under siege.

Minimalists, maximalists, and solidarists contribute to today's international tool kit in spite of protests by classicists. Keeping politics and humanitarian action separate appears increasingly problematic. Oxfam, for example, is calling upon humanitarian agencies to conduct "conflict impact assessments" before undertaking what previously would have been apolitical and knee-jerk reactions to come to the rescue.[58]

Conceptions of both "humanitarianism" and "politics" are changing, but stereotypes persist. The ideal is a humanitarianism that is unaffected by political factors in the countries that receive or provide assistance or by the bureaucratic politics of aid agencies themselves. Humanitarianism, after all, means helping and protecting innocent victims. Rooted in morality and principle, such undertakings are unequivocally noble.

There is a mirror image of this stereotype: if humanitarianism claims the moral high ground, politics occupies the nether terrain because it refers to jockeying for power, prestige, and a piece of the pie. Whether one cites Machiavelli or Henry Kissinger, international politics is the self-interested struggle among states over *raisons d'état*. Within borders, partisan or factional politics occur where deals or throats are cut and where integrity is in short supply. At the level of international public policy, politics refers to the competition and struggle to pursue one's own definition of a desirable outcome, and this too can seem ignoble.

The experience of the post–Cold War era suggests that the reality in Bosnias, Rwandas, and Somalias is more complicated than these stereotypes. Humanitarian organizations have attenuated human suffering and saved lives; but they have not been apolitical. Although humanitarian agencies go to great lengths to present themselves as nonpartisan and their motives as pure, they are deeply enmeshed in politics. Budget allocations and turf protection require vigilance. Humanitarians also negotiate with local authorities for visas, transport, and access, which all require compromises. They feel the pain of helping ethnic cleansers, feeding war criminals, and rewarding military strategies that herd civilians into camps. They decide whether or not to publicize human rights abuses. They look aside when bribes occur and food aid is diverted for military purposes. They provide foreign exchange and contribute to the growth of war economies that redistribute assets from the weak to the strong.

Humanitarians not only need to understand the prevailing political environment to secure resources and protect organizational mandates, they also deal with and accommodate host governments and a variety of opposition or insurgent political authorities. Local economic, political, and power dynamics are altered whenever outsiders enter a resource-scarce environment. To pretend that pragmatic political calculations are not taken into account as part of legitimate compromises in choosing among several unpalatable options obfuscates the actual nature of humanitarian decision-making in complex emergencies. At a minimum, the vast majority of humanitarians now acknowledge the need to minimize their impact on the relative power of warring parties or to affect them as equally as possible. And they certainly influence and are influenced by the outcomes of realpolitik and partisan politics in donor countries as well as by debates on international public policy.

At the same time, political and military responses have demonstrated on occasion the centrality of humanitarian values to governments and policy debates. In the post–Cold War era, governmental interpretations of vital national interests and of international conventions have been present along with notions of human solidarity. There is no exit strategy for humanitarians if states do not take their humanitarian responsibilities seriously and use coercion to halt genocide and other massive abuses of civilians. Involvement in politics by humanitarians is necessary in war zones and elsewhere. In the words of Jeffrey Herbst:

> It is naive, at best, to believe that peace will break out in some countries without a change in the balance of power given that political influence often flows from the barrel of the gun. Such a reversal of political fortunes can only be achieved through the use of force.[59]

A more subdued version of this idea comes from UN secretary-general Kofi Annan in a 1997 Economic and Social Council (ECOSOC) document: "Humanitarian activities take place in a political environment and thus are affected by and affect that environment."[60]

It is hard to square this view with the ICRC's official stance, shared by other classicists, that "humanitarian work must be disassociated from military operations aimed at ensuring security and restoring law and order in regions affected by conflict."[61] In more and more wars, efficacious remedial efforts have little to do with consent and traditional peacekeeping. Rather, effective action often requires such robust coercion as seizing airports in the midst of a Rwandan genocide, creating truly safe areas in Bosnia, disarming thugs in Somalia, and eliminating war criminals from the management of camps in eastern Congo or Tanzania. These actions are, by definition, coercive and partial. They are political *and* humanitarian; they certainly are not neutral, impartial, or consensual.

Humanitarians cannot deny political realities. Or if they do, which has been the practice for decades, they do so increasingly at their own peril and to the detriment of victims. They cannot set themselves above the political fray, because they are part of it, in both the countries where they work and the countries where they are incorporated. They should realize that humane values are best served by understanding and minimizing the manipulation inherent in civil wars. They should make use of political momentum and advocate political involvement to halt violence and ensure respect for human rights. They should determine the ultimate impact of emergency assistance on the conflict arena and adapt or even withhold aid if it increases violence, fuels conflict dynamics, legitimizes armed factions, or supports the growth of a war economy. And they should employ their leverage, whenever and wherever possible, to foster conflict transformation.

The fact that humanitarian space cannot be opened or maintained by humanitarians themselves suggests clear benefits from thinking politically and collaborating with diplomatic and military institutions. This political vision transforms humanitarianism. At the same time, the political sphere needs to be widened to ensure that the international arena is as hospitable as possible for both emergency aid and the protection of rights. Politics at its best embraces a vision of human solidarity and works to operationalize a strategy for making that solidarity real rather than rhetorical.

Political actors have a newfound interest in principles, while humanitarians of all stripes are increasingly aware of the importance of politics. Yet, there remain two distinct approaches—politics and humanitarianism as self-contained and antithetical realities or alternatively as overlapping spheres.

Nostalgia for aspects of the Cold War or other bygone eras is perhaps understandable, but there never was a "golden age" when humanitarianism was insulated from politics. Much aid was an extension of the foreign policies of major donors, especially the superpowers. Nonetheless, it was easier, conceptually and practically, to compartmentalize humanitarianism and politics before the 1990s. Then, a better guide to action was provided by an unflinching respect for traditional principles, although they never were absolute ends but only intermediate means.

In today's world, humanitarians must ask themselves how to weigh the political consequences of their action or inaction; and politicians must ask themselves how to gauge the humanitarian costs of their action or inaction. The calculations are tortuous, and the mathematics far from exact. However, there is no longer any need to ask *whether* politics and humanitarian action intersect. The real question is how this intersection can be managed to ensure more humanized politics and more effective humanitarian action. To this end, humanitarians should be neither blindly principled nor blindly pragmatic.

Notes

1 Neutrality and impartiality are important because they are central to the humanitarian ethos and give rise to much controversy. Consent is emphasized here because nonintervention in domestic affairs is the glue of international relations, and consent guides virtually all UN actions with the exception of Chapter VII coercion. See Marion Harroff-Tavel, "Neutrality and Impartiality: The Importance of These Principles for the International Red Cross and Red Crescent Movement and the Difficulties Involved in Applying Them," *International Review of the Red Cross*, no. 273 (November-December 1989), 536–52. See also Yves Sandoz, "The International Committee of the Red Cross and the Law of Armed Conflict Today," *International Peacekeeping* 4 (Winter 1997): 86–99.

2 Jean Pictet, "The Fundamental Principles of the Red Cross," *International Review of the Red Cross*, no. 210 (May-June 1979): 135, and *Development and Principles of International Humanitarian Law* (Dordrecht: Martinus Nijhoff, 1985). Humanity, impartiality, neutrality, independence, universality, voluntary service, and unity are principles of "humanitarian action" (guiding relief and protection of rights) as distinct from principles of "international humanitarian law" (for example, the distinctions between combatant and noncombatant), which are not the subject of this inquiry.

3 Mark Duffield, "The Political Economy of Internal War: Asset Transfer and the Internationalisation of Public Welfare in the Horn of Africa," in *War and Hunger: Rethinking International Responses to Complex Emergencies*, ed. Joanna Macrae and Anthony Zwi (London: Zed Books, 1994), 50–69. For a discussion of humanitarian tragedies as growth opportunities see, for example, Michael Maren, *The Road to Hell: The Ravaging Effects of Foreign Aid and International Charity* (New York: Free Press, 1997). See also David Keen, *The Economic Functions of Violence in Civil Wars* (Oxford: Oxford University Press, 1998), Adelphi Paper 320; and François Jean and Christophe Rufin, eds., *Economies des Guerres Civiles* (Paris: Hachette, 1996).

4 The debate was initiated by Alex de Waal and Rakiya Omaar, *Humanitarianism Unbound? Current Dilemmas Facing Multi-Mandate Relief Operations in Political Emergencies* (London: African Rights, 1994), Discussion Paper No. 5.

5 Steering Committee, "Background Paper: Humanitarian and Political Action: Key Issues and Priorities for a Concerted Strategy," Report on the Second Wolfsberg Humanitarian Forum, 5–7 June 1998 (Geneva: ICRC, 1998), 1, hereafter Second Wolfsberg report.

6 Cornelio Sommaruga, "Concluding Remarks," Second Wolfsberg report, 3.

7 Pierre Perrin, "The Impact of Humanitarian Aid on Conflict Development," *International Review of the Red Cross*, no. 323 (June 1998): 332.

8 Jonathan Moore, ed., *Hard Choices: Moral Dilemmas in Humanitarian Intervention* (Lanham, Md.: Rowman & Littlefield, 1998).

9 David Forsythe, *Humanitarian Politics: The International Committee of the Red Cross* (Baltimore, Md.: Johns Hopkins University Press, 1977), 3.

10 Sadako Ogata, "Keynote Address," Second Wolfsberg report, 1.

11 Andrew Natsios, "Commentary," *Ethics & International Affairs* 11 (1997): 133.

12 Steering Committee, "Background Paper," 4.

13 See Jarat Chopra, *Peace-Maintenance: The Evolution of International Political Authority* (London: Routledge, 1999); and Jarat Chopra, ed., *The Politics of Peace-Maintenance* (Boulder, Colo.: Lynne Rienner, 1998).

14 See Michael J. Smith, "Humanitarian Intervention: An Overview of the Ethical Issues," *Ethics & International Affairs* 12 (1998): 63–80.

15 Adam Roberts, "Threats to Humanitarian Action: Remedies," Report on the Wolfsberg Humanitarian Forum, 8–10 June 1997 (Geneva: ICRC, 1997), 1, hereafter First Wolfsberg report.

16 David Rieff, "The Humanitarian Illusion," *New Republic*, 16 March 1998, 29.

17 Eric Hobsbawm, *The Age of Extremes: A History of the World, 1914–1991* (New York: Vintage, 1996), 13.

18 These are: relieving life-threatening suffering, proportionality to need, nonpartisanship, independence, accountability, appropriateness, subsidiarity of suffering, and contextualization. See Larry Minear and Thomas G. Weiss, *Humanitarian Action in Times of War: A Handbook for Practitioners* (Boulder, Colo.: Lynne Rienner, 1993), 7–41.

19 Forsythe, *Humanitarian Politics*, 28. See also Jean-Luc Blondel, "The Fundamental Principles of the Red Cross and the Red Crescent: Their Origin and Development," *International Review of the Red Cross*, no. 283 (July-August 1991): 349–57.

20 Michael Ignatieff, *The Warrior's Honor: Ethnic War and the Modern Conscience* (New York: Henry Holt and Company, 1997), 5.

21 Charles William Maynes, "Principled Hegemony," *World Policy Journal* 14 (Fall 1997): 36.

22 Mark Duffield, "The Symphony of the Damned: Racial Discourse, Complex Political Emergencies and Humanitarian Aid," *Disasters* 20 (September 1996): 191.

23 Joanna Macrae, "The Death of Humanitarianism? An Anatomy of the Attack," *Disasters* 22 (December 1998): 316. This is part of a special issue entitled "The Emperor's New Clothes: Charting the Erosion of Humanitarian Principles."

24 Chr. Michelsen Institute, *Humanitarian Assistance and Conflict* (Bergen, Norway: Chr. Michelsen Institute, 1997), 3. This publication contains a good review of the literature of the 1990s.

25 See Donald C. F. Daniel and Bradd C. Hayes, "Securing Observance of UN Mandates through the Employment of Military Force," *International Peacekeeping* 3 (Winter 1996): 105–25; and Kofi Annan, "Challenges of the New Peacekeeping," in *Peacemaking and Peacekeeping for the New Century*, ed. Olara A. Otunnu and Michael W. Doyle (Lanham, Md.: Rowman & Littlefield, 1998), 169–87.

26 Hugo Slim, "International Humanitarianism's Engagement with Civil War in the 1990s: A Glance at Evolving Practice and Theory," a briefing paper for ActionAid UK, document dated 19 December 1997, 16.

27 See Thomas G. Weiss and Cindy Collins, *Humanitarian Challenges and Intervention: World Politics and the Dilemmas of Help* (Boulder, Colo.: Westview, 1996), 97–134.

28 Myron Wiener, "The Clash of Norms: Dilemmas in Refugee Policies," *Journal of Refugee Studies* 11 (1998): 1–21. See also Dan Smith, "Interventionist Dilemmas and Justice," in *Humanitarian Force*, ed. Anthony McDermott (Oslo: International Peace Research Institute, 1997), 13–39, especially 29–31.

29 Thomas Nagle, *Moral Questions* (New York: Cambridge University Press, 1991), 74.

30 Pictet, "The Fundamental Principles," 136; and Nicholas Leader, "Proliferating Principles or How to Sup with the Devil Without Getting Eaten," *Disasters* 22 (December 1998): 305.

31 The author is grateful to Charles Keely for this thought.

32 ICRC founder Henry Dunant's efforts could be contrasted with the more circumscribed assessment of his Swiss compatriot Jean-Jacques Rousseau, who earlier had emphasized the importance of kin, kith, and ken: "It appears that the feeling of humanity evaporates and grows feeble in embracing all mankind, and that we cannot be affected by the calamities of Tartary or Japan, in the same manner as we are by those of European nations." Jean-Jacques Rousseau, "A Discourse on Political Economy," *The Social Contract and Discourses* (New York: Dutton, 1950), 301. See also Nancy Sherman, "Empathy, Respect, and Humanitarian Intervention," *Ethics & International Affairs* 12 (1998): 103–19.

33 Dave Rowlands and David Carment, "Moral Hazard and Conflict Intervention," in *The Political Economy of War and Peace*, ed. Murray Wolfson (The Hague: Kluwer, 1998), 2, emphasis in original.

34 Ignatieff, *The Warrior's Honor*, 8.

35 Gwyn Prins, "Modern Warfare and Humanitarian Action," keynote lecture to an ECHO-ICRC conference entitled "Humanitarian Action: Perception and Security," Lisbon, 27–28 March 1998, 6.

36 Minear and Weiss, *Humanitarian Action in Times of War*, 37.

37 See, for example, Macrae, "The Death of Humanitarianism? An Anatomy of the Attack"; and Cindy Collins, "Critiques of Humanitarianism and Humanitarian Action," in *Humanitarian Coordination: Lessons Learned* (New York: Office for the Coordination of Humanitarian Affairs, 1998), 12–26.

38 Alex de Waal, *Famine Crimes: Politics and the Disaster Relief Industry in Africa* (Oxford: James Currey, 1997), 145.

39 See, for example, Taylor B. Seybolt, "The Myth of Neutrality," *Peace Review* 8 (1996): 521–7; and Richard Betts, "The Delusion of Impartial Intervention," *Foreign Affairs* 73 (1994): 20–33.

40 Jarat Chopra and Thomas G. Weiss, "Sovereignty Is No Longer Sacrosanct: Codifying Humanitarian Intervention," *Ethics & International Affairs* 6 (1992): 95–118.

41 "Objectives and Agenda of the Forum," First Wolfsberg report, 1.

42 Rieff, "The Humanitarian Illusion," 30.

43 Steering Committee, "Background Paper," 4.

44 "Introductory Address by Dr. Cornelio Sommaruga," First Wolfsberg report, 3.

45 John F. Hutchinson, *Champions of Charity: War and the Rise of the Red Cross* (Boulder, Colo.: Westview, 1996).

46 Alain Destexhe, "Foreword," in *Populations in Danger 1995*, ed. François Jean (London: Médecins Sans Frontières, 1995), 13–14.

47 Eric Roethlisberger, "Faced with Today's and Tomorrow's Challenges, Should the International Red Cross and Red Crescent Movement Rethink Its Code of Ethics?" speech of 20 March 1998, 2; and "Guiding Principles on the Right to Humanitarian Assistance," *International Review of the Red Cross*, no. 297 (November–December 1993): 519–25.

48 Forsythe, *Humanitarian Politics*, 234.

49 Mary B. Anderson, *Do No Harm: Supporting Local Capacities for Peace Through Aid* (Cambridge, Mass.: Collaborative for Development Action, 1996).

50 Astri Surhke and Kathleen Newland, "Humanitarian Assistance in the Midst of Armed Conflict," paper presented for a conference on "The Evolution of International Humanitarian Response in the 1990s," Carnegie Endowment and the Gilman Foundation, Yulee, Florida, 23–26 April 1998, 2; and Michael Bryans, Bruce D. Jones, and Janice Gross Stein, *Mean Times: Humanitarian Action in Complex Political Emergencies— Stark Choices, Cruel Dilemmas* (Toronto: Program on Conflict Management and Negotiation, 1999), vi.

51 See Mary B. Anderson and Peter J. Woodrow, *Rising from the Ashes: Development Strategies in Times of Disaster* (Boulder, Colo.: Westview, 1989); and Ian McAllister, *Sustaining Relief with Development* (Dordrecht: Nijhoff, 1993).

52 See Dylan Hendrickson, "Humanitarian Action in Protracted Crises: The New Relief 'Agenda' and Its Limits," RRN Network Paper 25 (London: ODI, April 1998).

53 "Concluding remarks by Dr. Cornelio Sommaruga," First Wolfsberg report, 2.

54 Development Assistance as a Means of Conflict Prevention (Oslo: Norwegian Institute of International Affairs, February 1998), 14.

55 Mark Duffield, *Aid Policy and Post-Modern Conflict: A Critical Review* (Birmingham, UK: School of Public Policy, 1998), Occasional Paper 19, 3.

56 See Development Assistance Committee, *Policy Statement on Conflict, Peace and Development Co-operation on the Threshold of the 21st Century* (Paris: Organisation for Economic Co-operation and Development, 1997).

57 James K. Boyce and Manuel Pastor, Jr., "Aid for Peace: Can International Financial Institutions Help Prevent Conflict?" *World Policy Journal* 15 (Summer 1998): 42.

58 Edmund Cairns, *A Safer Future: Reducing the Human Cost of War* (Oxford: Oxfam Publications, 1997), 94.

59 Jeffrey Herbst, *Securing Peace in Africa* (Cambridge, Mass.: World Peace Foundation, 1998), WPF Reports no. 17, 10.

60 "Review of the Capacity of the United Nations System for Humanitarian Assistance: Report of the Secretary-General," UN document E/1997/98, 10 July 1997, para. 6.
61 Jean de Courten, "ICRC Statement on Security Environment," Geneva, draft presented at the Humanitarian Liaison Working Group, 24 April 1997, 2. For a discussion against the use of force from the classicist perspective, see *Symposium on Humanitarian Action and Peacekeeping Operations*, ed. Umesh Palwankar (Geneva: ICRC, 1994).

17

A RESEARCH NOTE ABOUT MILITARY-CIVILIAN HUMANITARIANISM

More questions than answers

Groping by decision makers and humanitarians in November 1996 to respond appropriately in east Africa demonstrated again that experimentation with humanitarian delivery and protection continues as a dominant characteristic of world politics. Numerous variables including the end of East-West tensions, the erosion of sovereignty, the development of norms, genuine altruism, domestic politics, media coverage, the desire to contain refugee flows—explain why the West is sometimes willing to intervene. The most striking one, however, is unleashing the humanitarian impulse often with outside military forces in the forefront of the charge. Whether or not we actually are in Raimo Väyrenen's "age of humanitarian emergencies,"[1] ensuring better access to and treatment of victims clearly preoccupies policymakers, pundits, parliamentarians, and the public. One out of every 115 citizens worldwide is displaced by war, and probably an equal number remain behind whose lives are totally disrupted.[2] These tragic human consequences are an obvious motivation for analysts seeking to improve third-party military responses in war zones.

However, pessimism has supplanted bullishness after the initial flurry of new peacekeeping operations in the late 1980s and the first enforcement action since the early 1950s in Korea, which rolled back Iraqi aggression against Kuwait in 1991. There remain inveterate optimists and visionaries[3] in spite of well-publicized, if not always accurate, depictions of UN shortcomings or outright failures in Bosnia, Croatia, Somalia, Haiti, and Rwanda, along with less-visible ones in Angola, Afghanistan, and Sudan. Much of the criticism confuses the "two United Nations" —the first, where governments meet and make decisions, and the second, comprising the various secretariats, officials, and soldiers who implement these decisions.[4] Although both have been at fault, the old adage should be repeated here that the latter mainly can do what the former permit.

Whatever the apportionment of blame, a new reality emerged in 1993 with the label of the "Somalia syndrome."[5] Facile notions about intervening militarily to help sustain civilians trapped in war zones have been replaced by more realistic estimates about the limits of such undertakings. Former US assistant secretary of state Richard Holbrooke, who is generally credited with engineering the Dayton agreements to curtail the war in the former Yugoslavia, suggests that "The damage that Bosnia did to the UN was incalculable."[6] Whichever of the two United Nations is most at fault and whichever debacle wins first prize, the conventional wisdom in policy circles is now to refrain from robust involvement by the military in complex humanitarian emergencies. Former secretary-general Boutros Boutros-Ghali codified the rhetorical retreat from his bullish 1992 *An Agenda for Peace* in his far more cautious 1995 *Supplement to "An Agenda for Peace."*[7]

In spite of a widespread tendency among both analysts and practitioners to lump them into a single category, "military-civilian humanitarianism" (or the coming together of military forces and civilian aid agencies to deal with the human suffering from complex emergencies) has actually taken numerous forms.[8] Whatever the variations, however, disenchantment has definitely resulted from what the editor of *Foreign Affairs* had described prematurely as the "springtime for interventionism."[9] There has been a backlash—among civilians and humanitarians and the military, with parliaments and editorial boards—in spite of success in northern Iraq and Haiti as well as, arguably, valuable contributions in Rwanda and, more arguably still, in Somalia and Bosnia. The growing conventional wisdom is that humanitarian intervention is not feasible or sustainable.[10] Moreover, many civilian humanitarians argue that military force complicates their work because, in the short run, it works against the impartiality and neutrality that have traditionally underpinned their work; while in the long run, it solves none of the structural problems that led to the eruption of grisly violence.

Benevolence is never adequate, but the provision of military support seems to have caused more problems than it has solved. Or has it? Leslie Gelb's "wars of national debilitation,"[11] in which former neighbors resort to daily war crimes against one another, can thwart rational thought by both analysts and practitioners and indeed induce nihilism. But they can also push us to ask: is it not possible to harness better military operations in conjunction with humanitarian action in order to thwart violence and mitigate suffering? There is little political will for them at present, and they may become less prevalent than in the last five years. However, the contention here is that there is sufficient evidence from the first half decade of the post–Cold War era to suggest how multilateral military operations could expand or contract in the years ahead to the benefit or peril of war victims. In short, the emphasis should be on the direct provision of security.

This piece forms a part of my own intellectual journey for a project on "The Political Economy of Humanitarian Emergencies" sponsored by UN University's World Institute for Development Economics Research (WIDER) in Helsinki. The dialogue that I hope to begin here among scholars and practitioners about the costs and benefits of using the armed forces in humanitarian emergencies should go beyond participants' respective ideological predispositions toward the use or non-use of military coercion. This essay is in part a literature review, but more importantly a framework for reading and interpreting recent publications. It is hoped that debate may move beyond the "*dialogue de sourds*" of exchanging assertions about sovereignty, morality, and practicality from realist, Marxist, pacifist, and liberal perspectives.

The recent literature in context

I begin with a contextualization of the recent literature before proceeding to define military-civilian humanitarianism and its historical development and discussing the range of possible military contributions to humanitarian action. There follows a framework to assess the effectiveness of military-civilian humanitarianism and a preliminary analysis of experience from five crucial cases of multilateral military operations and humanitarian action in war zones after the end of the Cold War (northern Iraq, Somalia, Bosnia, Rwanda, and Haiti). I conclude with some tentative and preliminary generalizations as well as issues for further research. *Caveat lector*: at this moment, there are still "more questions than answers."

The dramatic acceleration in the number and variety of UN military missions has been widely noted—the Security Council approved over twice as many operations between 1989 and 1997 as in the previous four decades. There has also been a proliferation of analyses about multilateral military operations, of which an exhaustive literature review will be available in a *Review of the Peacekeeping Literature, 1990–1996.*[12] It would be useful to summarize briefly impressions about the literature, as a prelude to our consideration of using armed forces in support of humanitarian action.

There has been an avalanche of peace operations literature produced from a variety of perspectives since 1990, mostly in journal rather than book form. Judith Stiehm, an adjunct professor at the US Army Peacekeeping Institute, and Alan James, a professor of politics at Keele University, remarked in interviews that this trend is reminiscent of the early 1960s when the women-in-politics and strategic studies literatures exploded, and for many of the same reasons. A new field meant opportunities for scholars and other interested parties to capture what amounted to an open market for the publication of ideas, analyses, and reflections about gender and East-West nuclear issues. Government and philanthropic funding provided an additional incentive to establish oneself quickly as an "expert" or risk being "recycled." The field of peacekeeping has witnessed a similar pattern. The increasing demand for analyses of peace operations partially explains the recent supply in the literature. This is not a judgement about the quality of analyses; it is simply an explanation for the quantity produced in a relatively short time.

The sheer volume of publications since 1990 is unsettling—our preliminary in-house database holds 1,800 entries, and is incomplete even for the English-language works from numerous countries on which we have concentrated. It has become increasingly arduous for newcomers to select publications that are grounded equally in logic and hard data and provide the necessary description, analysis, and assessment to understand past and present peace operations and their potential future role in international conflict management. Nowhere do these generalizations apply more than to the growth industry within the growth industry: the interface between humanitarian action in war zones and the use of outside military forces. If we count the citations that are specifically focused on this issue (especially the five cases analyzed here), approximately one-quarter are relevant for our consideration of the costs and benefits of multilateral military involvement in humanitarian action in war zones.

The literature overflows with claims to knowledge about the nature of changing world politics, theories and recommendations for institutional reform and conflict resolution, and first-hand accounts from the field. The volume and accelerated pace of literature generation rivals that of the peace operations themselves. As Tharoor remarked: we "too often find ourselves steering a rattling vehicle that is moving at breakneck speed, without an up-to-date roadmap, while trying to fix the engine at the same time."[13]

So much has changed in such a brief period that even William Durch's well-received comparative work of 1993, *The Evolution of UN Peacekeeping: Case Studies and Comparative Analysis*, will soon have a lengthy companion volume, *UN Peacekeeping, American Policy, and the Uncivil Wars of the 1990s*.[14] It is of some interest to note that because of lead times, the earlier volume makes virtually no reference to humanitarian actors (either UN or nongovernmental [NGO]) and their impact on peace making, peacekeeping, or peace enforcement. One of Durch's fears at that time was that the UN would proceed down the slippery slope into humanitarian intervention. Shortly thereafter, and as the second volume was being conceived, we were trying to understand where we were on the slope and when to apply the brakes to slow the speed at which we were slipping. As the second volume appeared, the conventional wisdom has it that "never again" will there be humanitarian interventions and that even traditional peacekeeping is unlikely to be used with any frequency.

We are now at the point in the evolution of the literature to take stock of the insights gained by the community of writers, institutions, policymakers and practitioners as well as what lessons have been learned—keeping in mind, however, a clear distinction between the two activities of gaining insights and actually learning lessons.[15] If indeed the latter is applicable to the policymaking and planning realms, those who profess such knowledge should address directly who has learned the lessons and which procedural and institutional changes have actually been implemented. Otherwise, one is vaguely speaking only of insights compiled about patterns of behavior that either support or undermine the effectiveness of multilateral security efforts. "The art of learning from experience begins with understanding linkages and the conditions under which events took place" and requires the institutional integrity to expose rather than paper over mistakes.[16] In short, more is required than merely establishing "lessons-learned" units as have the UN's departments of peacekeeping operations, political affairs, and humanitarian affairs.

Defining military-civilian humanitarianism

The military performs two sets of functions in the humanitarian arena: logistics (relief activities and support for civilian relief agencies) and security. In spite of the emphasis on physical succor to victims, the armed forces also protect the human rights of victims. Increasingly, observers of war zones point to the difficulties in distinguishing between the two components of humanitarian "action"—that is, delivery and protection—because they are linked so intimately.[17] Nonetheless, it still is easier to quantify the former than the latter, which is why so much attention is normally paid to the volume and value of goods and personnel devoted to the delivery of food, medicines, and shelter in war zones. "Protection" amounts to more than the total number of human rights monitors or legal protection officers in the employ of the UN High Commissioner for Refugees (UNHCR), but is hard to measure.

The unwillingness of governments to interpret the mandate of the Implementation Force led by the North Atlantic Treaty Organization to include pursuing indicted war criminals in the former Yugoslavia was properly criticized, but the military's mere presence there and elsewhere can sometimes halt or slow down abuses. Protecting human rights entails safeguarding the well-being of victims by ensuring that they have access to sufficient material assistance. Protection minimizes the damaging impact of violence and can also facilitate respect for international norms by belligerents and political authorities. Operationally, protection can result from the insertion of soldiers or aid personnel between victims and combatants. These same points should be kept in mind while examining the contribution of third-party military forces in Iraq, Somalia, Bosnia, Rwanda, and Haiti. Although almost always such forces could have done more—which is the criticism made by Human Rights Watch of regular UN peacekeeping operations—their mere presence almost certainly reduced abuses.[18]

Regular third-party military involvement in humanitarian efforts in war zones is a phenomenon of the post–Cold War era, but the use of military forces for such purposes is not new.[19] In fact, often there is an almost automatic association in the Western public's mind between the military and disaster relief, with the expectation that the armed forces will assist civilian populations after emergency strikes. The earliest recorded instances predate Alexander the Great. They continued in Europe through the Napoleonic wars and into the twentieth century. Sometimes assistance was seen as a humane gesture to the vanquished, usually mixed with the desire to help secure loyalty from newly subject populations. Variations on this theme were played by colonial armies who orchestrated assistance to the civil authority. A quantum expansion of the military into the humanitarian arena took place after World War II. The task of occupying Germany and Japan, as well as reconstructing as quickly as possible Europe's economic base, required new types of personnel within the armed forces: administrators, planners, developmentalists, and logisticians. At that time, there were relatively few international NGOs, and the UN's humanitarian delivery mechanisms were just beginning to function.

In the last half century, military assistance during natural disasters has become a routine extension of civil defense. Armed forces often possess an abundance of precisely those resources that are in the shortest supply when disaster strikes: transport, fuel, communications, commodities, building equipment, medicines, and large stockpiles of provisions. In addition, the military's much-vaunted "can-do" mentality, self-supporting character, and rapid-response capabilities as well as its hierarchical discipline are useful within the turmoil of acute tragedies. The same capacities that are relevant for help in a domestic disaster can also be applied to international tragedies.

The end of the Cold War meant the evaporation of the raison d'être for the bulk of military spending. But this development coincided with a renaissance of sorts in UN conflict management.[20] The statistics about the expansion of third-party military forces tell an important story about the dramatic increase in demand for UN troops. After stable levels of about 10,000 troops and with budgets of a few hundred million dollars (US) in the early post–Cold War period, numbers jumped rapidly. In the mid-1990s, 70,000 to 80,000 blue-helmets were authorized by the UN's annual peacekeeping budget that approached $4 billion in 1995. Accumulated total arrears in these years hovered around $3.5 billion—that is, almost equal this budget and approaching three times the regular UN budget. The roller-coaster ride continued until 1996 when both the numbers of soldiers and the budget dropped precipitously, by two-thirds, at least partially reflecting the world organization's overextension and professional inadequacies. Arrears remained at the same critical level, with Washington leading an undistinguished group of some 50 deadbeat governments that continue to ignore their international treaty obligations to finance the UN's activities.

Western public opinion at first demanded downsizing of military establishments. When the much-vaunted "peace dividend" failed to materialize, the availability of military help for humanitarian tasks seemed to be a "dividend" of sorts. The successful allied mobilization for the Gulf War and the subsequent use of the armed forces in support of humanitarianism in northern Iraq—along with substantial if sometimes less popular versions in Somalia, Bosnia, Rwanda, and Haiti—have provided a means for militaries to fend-off pressures to reduce their infrastructure and personnel. For example, an extensive shopping-list has been formulated by the United States for "Possible Uses of Military Force for Humanitarian Missions in Complex Emergencies."[21] Proposals and conferences sponsored by the Canadian, Dutch, and Danish militaries provide evidence that "operations other than war" are not simply a concern for the largest powers,[22] although the United States may present a special case.[23] One observer's characterization of the American military has more general applicability: "For the near future our military is more likely to participate in humanitarian interventions and in peacekeeping than it is to participate in war or in peace enforcement."[24]

Although too infrequently distinguished in both eulogies and critiques, the advantages, or disadvantages depending on one's point of view, of using the armed forces in war zones are twofold. The first benefit is the logistics cornucopia—some cynics argue that such aid frequently amounts to military surplus disposal—through the provision of direct assistance to people in need and also to support the work of civilian organizations. Military engagements of this type have taken place with a rapidity and regularity as well as on a scale unknown until recently—including burying bodies, digging latrines, purifying water, and conducting large-scale inoculations.

The second benefit, or shortcoming, results from the military's direct exercise of security capacities, related to its primary function of waging war and using force to overwhelm an enemy. They can gain access to suffering civilians, when insecurity makes it impossible or highly dangerous, and foster a secure enough environment to permit succor and protection for civilians. The security function has come under severe commentary from sympathizers and critics alike, with "humanitarian intervention" and "humanitarian war" more and more often viewed as oxymorons.[25] Moreover, in the absence of leadership by major powers, the political costs of body bags or of getting mired down in a protracted conflict have led to something akin to a zero-casualty foreign policy, an obvious constraint on the exercise of this second capacity.

Logistics and security tasks should be kept analytically separate. They provide the framework for assessing the effectiveness of military-civilian humanitarianism within the context of five case studies.

Assessing the effectiveness of military-civilian humanitarianism: criteria used and issues confronted

There are three problems growing from this literature that have a direct bearing on an attempt to establish costs and benefits of multilateral military operations and humanitarian action in war zones. As well as the host of usual problems for analysts seeking to compare incomparable cases, there are additional peculiarities in trying to let the data speak for themselves.

First, both the armed forces and humanitarian agencies are not any more forthcoming about data nor do they employ more comparable accounting methods than when, as part of a team, I first began studying this problem in Sudan in 1989. We then recommended international expert discussions to suggest standards to harmonize reporting,[26] but almost nothing has happened in the interim. Reliable data about the actual costs of delivery (of goods and alternative modes) is sketchy and usually not comparable among sources. Hence, digging for data and compiling them are not the only problem for social scientists. There is still no standard methodology for reporting, even among the members of the Development Assistance Committee of the Organisation for Economic Co-operation and Development.

Second, the emphasis on costs and benefits necessarily entails a number of ambiguities. The first is that it biases analyses in favor of delivery over protection even though both are essential and mutually reinforcing components of humanitarian action. Effective action in war relieves life-threatening suffering by providing emergency assistance and protecting fundamental human rights. It is, however, difficult to measure the latter except by its absence or presence whereas relief is easier to quantify. It is also difficult to gauge with any precision how much better or worse the human rights situation would have been in the absence of soldiers because of the usual problems with counterfactual analyses not to mention the ethics of even proposing to pull out troops in order to test the hypothesis. Consequently, more attention customarily is paid to delivery than protection, which may favor accounting more accurately for short-term benefits than for longer-term shortcomings.

In this regard, it is unfair to condemn the military for not doing what is not their business and what they would never agree to do (for example, reconciliation or addressing the roots of a conflict). It is, however, fairer to criticize their unwillingness to undertake tasks that they could have agreed to do but did not (for example, demining or disarmament or arresting war criminals). It is unreasonable to judge the military in acute emergencies by standards—for example, empowerment of local communities, avoiding dependence, fostering reconciliation—against which both development and civilian humanitarian agencies measure up poorly.[27] This line of criticism would appear ridiculous in relation to military help in the face of a natural disaster because such assistance failed to address the "roots" of hurricanes or earthquakes; but somehow such arguments receive more credibility in war zones. Outside military intervention can improve access and help move relief supplies as well as contribute to an environment where human rights abuses become less frequent. It can provide time for belligerents to come to their senses and for outside mediators and negotiators to launch activities. But the presence of outside military forces in and of itself cannot be expected to end an armed conflict. Without a coherent political strategy, the decision to use military forces should be seen as a temporary respite, not a solution.

There also is a fundamental ambiguity in trying to qualify any of the five cases as a "success" or a "failure" in terms of their external and internal impact. Perceptions in a troop-contributing country about a particular humanitarian intervention determine the willingness of a state to mount other diplomatic and military efforts and for the public and parliament to support subsequent humanitarian undertakings. In historical perspective, we would probably have the clearest contrast in the United States between the action in northern Iraq that led to bullish presidential discourse from both Republican and Democratic administrations about a "new world order" and "assertive multilateralism," on the one hand, and the pessimism and withdrawal as a result of the "Somalia syndrome," on the other.[28] Attempting to measure impact within affected areas necessitates attaching a value to human life, which poses uncomfortable philosophical and moral challenges.

Even if we sidestep this problem and move directly to a comparison of country cases, there are inescapable value judgments and differing time frames and objectives held by various actors along with the hidden agendas that are the essence of UN politics and deliberations, as is obvious from trying to formulate answers to such questions as the following: Were military efforts in northern Iraq a success because 1.5 million Kurds were saved, or a failure because there is still no political solution with Saddam Hussein ensconced in Baghdad? Were military operations in Somalia successful because death rates dropped in 1993, or a long-term failure because billions were spent to stop the clock temporarily? Were military efforts in Bosnia successful because they saved lives and avoided a wider conflict in Europe, or a failure because the international community has not stood up to aggression, war crimes, and the forced movement of peoples? Were military and police operations to restore President Aristide in Haiti a success because a precedent against a seizure of power by a junta was set and peaceful elections for his successor held, or a failure because fundamentally skewed economic structures remain in place to exploit the vast majority of the population? Were military efforts in Rwanda a success because the carnage was stopped and lives saved, or a failure because the genocide took place?

Third, the five examples are not the only historical cases of military operations and humanitarian action. They are, however, the most prominent ones of the post–Cold War era, which have undoubtedly affected the calculations of the ministries of defense of the major powers—for example, these five operations provide the basis for the conclusions drawn by the Independent Task Force at the Council on Foreign Relations chaired by George Soros.[29] Moreover, and what is essential for the selection of the sample for the cases here, all were subject to scrutiny by the UN Security Council before the outside military forces intervened. All took place without consent from local political authorities and with Chapter VII authorization for coercion so that both the logistics and security functions of the military were in evidence in war-like situations. We are not concerned here with the humanitarian work often accomplished by traditional UN peacekeepers in their noncoercive capacities.[30]

We thus are examining humanitarian action without the pretence of neutrality —the outmoded notion that somehow saving lives and reducing suffering does not advance anyone's political agenda. This notion, long championed by the International Committee of the Red Cross (ICRC) and many other humanitarian organizations, is increasingly viewed by critics as both naive and wrong. The crises of the post–Cold War era are inspiring a growing literature about the politics of humanitarian rescue,[31] although humanitarian efforts have never really been neutral. Richard Betts has recommended recognizing "the delusion of impartial intervention"[32] because there is no such thing as "pure" humanitarianism. All decisions about aid have distributional effects with political ramifications, as former US secretary of state for African affairs Chester A. Crocker reminded us when commenting upon the November 1996 crisis in Zaire: "[I]ntervention (just like nonintervention) is an inherently political action with inescapable political consequences."[33]

Even without military forces, humanitarian efforts are profoundly political; and unless they are carefully designed, they can actually exacerbate conflicts.[34] If done properly, civilian humanitarian efforts, and certainly ones supported by the use of military force, should alter the balance of power in favor of victims. Decisions to remain on the sidelines can be considered a form of intervention in that by failing to help the oppressed, humanitarians are in complicity with the oppressors. This latter view, championed especially by Médecins Sans Frontières, has been gaining ground in the debate with the more traditional view espoused by the ICRC.

There are varying circumstances and purposes for the use of force and myriad differences in UN involvement among our five case studies, and even within various phases of the same case.[35] However, the working assumption here is in line with Hoffmann's contention that a significant change in the 1990s is that "the emphasis has shifted from unilateral interventions." Multilateral military intervention will, and should, be used in the future rather than the more unilateral forms of the past. Even if military coordination is problematic, it is politically and economically more suitable.

Nonetheless, Liberia and Georgia are not included because information about them is very sketchy; the UN Security Council began to focus on them long after the beginning of outside intervention thereby making international accountability even less significant than for the five chosen cases.[36] Moreover, comparative cost data about outside military forces from such natural disasters as volcanic eruptions in the Philippines or monsoons in Bangladesh are also not included because they would take us too far from the terrain of war zones and be even less comparable for purposes of hazarding some policy generalizations. In fact, for purposes of comparison, it would probably be more useful to examine transport and logistics in a war zone without outside military forces, for example, Sudan.[37]

Notwithstanding these difficulties, there are in-depth case studies by other analysts of northern Iraq from 1991 to 1996;[38] Somalia from 1992 to 1995;[39] Bosnia from 1992 to 1995;[40] Rwanda from 1994 to 1995;[41] and Haiti from 1995 to 1996.[42] The data in them are comparable and readily available, even if less than ideal. This information could provide the groundwork for some hesitant generalizations about whether the role of the military should expand or contract in order to respond better in future complex humanitarian emergencies, which I would define in the following manner: "war-induced and sudden catastrophes involving substantial increases in involuntary displacements and in suffering (especially as measured by famine, disease, and human rights abuses) of noncombatants accompanied by a crisis, and oftentimes a collapse, of state authority."

The five cases thus were all complex humanitarian emergencies at the moment when the UN Security Council authorized Chapter VII coercion. They can illustrate both the logistics and security capacities of the armed forces acting in a post–Cold War world in which multilateral support for humanitarian intervention is preferable to more unilateral procedures of the past. There is no need to rehearse the details of these operations for the readers of these pages. Although the analysis is incomplete at this juncture, Table 17.1 sets out the elements of a possible framework to interpret the existing case materials and compare costs and benefits of multilateral military operations and humanitarian action in war zones.

In an effort to paint as accurate a picture as possible for each case, the first thing to establish is military costs. These should be broken down into the following three components.

TABLE 17.1 Estimating military costs and civilian benefits

1. Military costs of the intervention	$ value	Casualties/ fatalities	Political impact
	A	B	C
2. Humanitarian challenge before the intervention	Displacement	Suffering	State of the state
	D	E	E
3. Civilian benefits after the intervention	Displacement	Suffering	State of the state
	D′	E′	F′

Box A: There should be three indicators of costs, two military and one civilian. The dollar values of the military presence for security purposes should be those officially reported by troop contributors as well as any well-regarded estimates that differ (usually multiples higher). When possible, the value of purely military security should be distinguished from military humanitarian aid, and net figures (or incremental costs) should be given to indicate the "true" cost over and above what finances would have been spent by troop-contributing countries to support troops at home bases. UN budgetary figures should be reported although these understate the costs for industrialized troop contributors. There should be an indication of the value of civilian humanitarian aid, the assumption being that the volume is facilitated by the military's presence. These figures should no doubt be calculated as a ratio, however crude, measured against the total population of an affected area because everyone within it, not simply people officially at risk, benefit or are penalized by the military's presence.

Box B: Accidental and battle casualties and fatalities should be reported. The size, scope, and duration of an operation should be taken into account, but an absolute number is probably the most relevant statistic in light of the low tolerance for casualties in troop-contributing countries.

Box C: There should be an appreciation of conventional wisdom regarding the overall weight of political and parliamentary reactions to a particular effort that influence the willingness to support subsequent international efforts in the multi-lateral arena.

The nature of the humanitarian challenge (or crisis for civilians) on the eve of the military intervention should be reflected for three criteria. These same criteria should be reflected for the period immediately after the outside humanitarian intervention as a way to suggest the benefits to civilians.

Box D: In spite of the well-known controversies about accuracy,[43] involuntary migration is probably the best reflection of the magnitude of a complex humanitarian emergency and should be shown in UNHCR figures about refugees and internally displaced people. In some cases, the latter category of "internal refugees" should also be accompanied by numbers of war victims who have not moved but are living in "refugee-like situations." A rapid improvement in this number

(Box D′) closely following an outside intervention would provide an important gauge of enhanced security, protection, and confidence in the future.

Box E: Suffering should be measured by hunger, disease, and human rights abuse. The first measurement reflects those whose lives are at risk from a lack of calories, a variable number that comes from many agencies. The second measurement should indicate through the statistics of the World Health Organization or the UN Children's Fund the status of women and children, the most vulnerable members of a society who are also the most numerous (usually 80 percent) among those involuntarily displaced. Finally, human rights abuses are probably the most contested and unreliable of statistics within and across cases; and even essential measurements can change from case to case (for example, rape is much more of a factor, however contested the figures, in some conflicts than others). Nonetheless, a reflection of human rights is essential to capture accurately the nature of some suffering in war zones. Again, rapid improvements in these three criteria (Box E′) after an intervention would capture important pay-offs from intervention.

Box F: There should be a reflection of widespread judgments regarding the ability of the governmental authorities in the country in crisis to have effective control over territory, exercise effective administrative authority over its inhabitants, and provide security for them. The extent to which these three attributes of sovereignty are present or absent should provide an indication, however subjective, of the extent to which there is a crisis or even a collapse of state sovereignty. The improvement in local governmental authority (Box F′) would be another indicator of possible benefits from intervention.

Preliminary analysis from the five case studies

The preceding discussion of variables indicates a lack of clarity, specificity, and objectivity that statistics sometimes indicate. No such quantitative depiction could possibly be presented for even one of the five cases; so my goal here is to suggest a comparison across them. Hence, it is more feasible and useful at this stage to suggest visually and qualitatively the value-laden judgments that emanate from a comparison of suggestive data across cases. In this way, readers can identify immediately whether and why their bottom-line differs from mine. As such, Table 17.2 is a first attempt to capture my interpretation of comparative data. The legend indicates that the more darkened circles, the more successful a particular case is in comparison with others in this sample; and the more whitened circles, the less successful. The assumption is that the more successful operations are characterized by a relatively graver humanitarian challenge before the intervention and relatively more substantial improvements in the humanitarian situation after the intervention.

In addition to the earlier words of caution regarding the non-comparability of data and cases, the biases and ambiguities emanating from costs and benefits, and the rationale for case selection, there are four other salient issues that should be kept in mind as part of this attempt at an overall evaluation. First, earlier military action in all cases undoubtedly would have saved lives and resources. However pleasant

TABLE 17.2 Depicting military costs and benefits across cases

		Northern Iraq (1991–96)	Somalia (1992–95)	Bosnia (1992–95)	Rwanda (1994–95)	Haiti (1993–96)
● Least costly ◐ Costly ○ Most costly	1. Miltary costs *($ value)* • Military security • Military • Civilian humanitarian aid • Casualities/fatalities • Political impact	 ● ● ◐ ● ●	 ○ ○ ◐ ○ ○	 ○ ◐ ◐ ○ ○	 ○ ○ ◐ ◐ ◐	 ● ● ● ● ◐
● Most critical ◐ Critical ○ Least critical	2. Civilian crisis *(before intervention)* Displacement Suffering • Hunger • Health • Human rights • State of the state	 ◐ ● ◐ ◐ ○	 ◐ ◐ ● ○ ●	 ● ◐ ◐ ● ◐	 ● ● ● ● ●	 ○ ○ ○ ◐ ◐
● Most beneficial ◐ Beneficial ○ Least beneficial	3. Civilian benefits *(after intervention)* Displacement Suffering • Hunger • Health • Human rights • State of the state	 ● ● ◐ ◐ ○	 ◐ ● ◐ ○ ○	 ○ ◐ ◐ ○ ◐	 ○ ◐ ◐ ● ◐	 ● ● ◐ ● ●

the ring to multilateral ears of "a stitch in time" and the increase in rhetoric about its necessity,[44] preventive deployment is a highly implausible policy for the foreseeable future—leading one analyst to caricature it as a contemporary version of "alchemy."[45] Second, the media played a distinct role in drawing attention to each of the crises. But the positive and negative influences vary from case to case, a subject that is in dire need of more quantitative analysis than it has received to date.[46]

Third, the focus on the potential for third-party military forces in complex humanitarian emergencies is necessarily short-term. Among the least disputed of "The Mohonk Criteria for Humanitarian Assistance in Complex Emergencies" is the sensible view that "military forces should be used only as a last resort."[47] It is not germane to ask whether military action, even when deemed successful, slows down work on longer-term issues as rehabilitation, reconstruction, and conflict management. Adam Roberts, for one, has criticized the incomplete nature of intervention: "what is deplorable, though, is the pretense that, in the absence of a serious long-term purpose, it suffices to call an action 'humanitarian.'"[48] According to this line of argument, for example, five years of protecting the Kurds has saved lives but left them prisoners in their own land—targets of Baghdad and unwelcome in neighboring countries—and divided among themselves.

Nonetheless, nation building has hardly been a success anywhere and certainly not in other traditional peacekeeping operations. For example, the usual criticism of the UN's peacekeeping operation in Cyprus—that after three decades there is no incentive for the belligerents to negotiate or invest in the future—thus is also relevant for military-civilian humanitarianism. The use of traditional Chapter VI UN peacekeepers or Chapter VII enforcers ideally should be part of a comprehensive political strategy to resolve conflict. The existence of a political vacuum about conflict resolution, however, is not the fault of soldiers but of the governments that send them.

The problem with Roberts' criticism is that it sets up a straw man. It goes without saying that the military is no substitute for longer-term nation-building efforts or a sensible means to address the oxymoron of a "protracted" emergency; but it can be an ally at the outset of a crisis. By criticizing the military for a failure to consult more with local authorities and to address the socioeconomic roots of the conflict and begin reconciliation is to set up criteria that will never be met. As mentioned earlier, this type of criticism would appear ludicrous and be dismissed in relationship to natural disasters, and it should be accorded similar treatment here.

There may even be an additional irony in the growing conceptual consensus about moving away from emergency delivery and toward the continuum of relief to development.[49] The continued decrease in development assistance and the crisis in development thinking are now givens in the contemporary humanitarian equation. The new relief-to-development orthodoxy calls upon donors and aid organizations to move more quickly toward the kinds of projects and activities that have patently failed in the past and even to make greater commitments of the kind that are diminishing everywhere.[50] With development aid in crisis[51] and with massive humanitarian needs, emergency help is precisely what is required from outsiders. In fact, some observers are calling into question analytical efforts to distinguish emergency from development assistance in war-torn societies.[52]

Fourth, an evaluation should reflect an adequate appreciation of the challenge on the ground at the time of an intervention. As with Olympic diving, the degree of difficulty in the assignment should be combined with the degree of execution to reach a composite overall assessment.[53] This concept needs to be refined for three variables:

- how dangerous and chaotic is a particular humanitarian situation;
- how physically challenging is a specific terrain; and
- how ambitious is the operation's mandate.

The Multinational Force in Haiti, for example, would undoubtedly receive high marks for execution on the first two but with a relatively low degree of difficulty in comparison with far more dangerous and challenging operations in the other four cases. At the same time, even the partial pursuit of a mandate to enhance local police, judiciary, and penal systems was considerably more ambitious than for the other cases, and this too has to be factored into a composite judgement.

In light of all the previous uncertainties, some would perhaps question the wisdom of any effort to draw conclusions. Nonetheless and with a desire to advance the debate, I would place Iraq and Haiti at one end of an analytical spectrum with humanitarian benefits (in terms of lives saved, improved access to alleviate famine and disease, and fewer human rights violations) worth the military costs. Bosnia (prior to Dayton, which is the focus here) would be at the opposite end as a case when the high economic and political costs and low effectiveness of military forces were not commensurate with humanitarian benefits. In between, Rwanda would be closer to the successful end of the spectrum (at least after July 1994), and Somalia the failure (particularly in terms of the political backlash against multilateralism in the United States). At the same time, a shift in subjective appreciation or even in emphasis toward or away from particular data or priorities could push Rwanda and Somalia closer to one end of the spectrum or the other. The lowest three on this scale coincide with Hoffmann's judgement of the UN's "perceived failures: Somalia (where the record is complex); Rwanda (where indeed the UN did not cover itself with glory); and above all Yugoslavia." The impact of multilateral military operations on humanitarian action in war zones is neither as harmful as many detractors think nor as helpful as proponents often argue.

After all is said and done, moving toward a bottom-line for either of the two basic humanitarian functions—logistics or security—requires value-laden and subjective judgements. The down side to military logistics consists largely of looking at a particular military operation and asking: what is it worth? Every case demonstrates that the military is the most costly option—the best data, from Rwanda, indicate that military aircraft are four to eight times more expensive than commercial ones, and the latter is already 20 to 40 times as expensive as normal road transport, which in turn is more expensive than bulk shipments by rail.[54] But in certain situations, military options may be the only ones available. Certainly northern Iraq in spring 1991 was such a case. And even the unilateral and multilateral efforts in Goma in mid-1994 demonstrated that an effective humanitarian response can sometimes require the human resources, logistics, and rapid deployment capacity available only to the military.

Moreover, defense departments sometimes foot the bill, and then high costs are not directly deducted from civilian efforts but are genuine add-ons. It would be naive to apply blindly the notion of opportunity costs. Assuming that a sum approaching the resources disbursed by or attributed to the military somehow could be handed over to civilian humanitarians would be simplistic. It is impossible to determine the extent to which civilian emergency relief let alone military humanitarianism is being deducted from development resources, although this is the usual implication when noting the steady side-by-side decreases in official development assistance and increases in emergency aid. In fact, this judgement is in many ways beside the point because in today's world we must take conflict for granted. As Dutch minister for development co-operation Jan Pronk has remarked, emergency and development assistance are difficult to distinguish when "ever more countries linger in prolonged states of half peace/half war."[55] Another serious criticism, although even more difficult to substantiate, is that outside military helping hands ultimately "increase the nonmilitary operations of local armies . . . [and] undermine the process of democratization."[56]

Evaluating alternatives for military logistics depends essentially on their existence and, if there is none, on the value attached to individual human lives by the contributors of such logistical assistance and by domestic pressure groups who make themselves heard. Civilian humanitarian organizations are learning to live with this and adopting procedures with stand-by arrangements for staff, equipment, and supplies in order better to engage and collaborate with the armed forces.

Although not calculable nor evident from the figures, interviews over the years suggest that a potential disadvantage of relying extensively upon the military for its logistics and support roles may possibly discourage the acceptance of tougher, security-related tasks. In light of the pressures on governments "to do something," there is a seductive appeal of sending the military to supply emergency goods and logistics rather than security. In fact, the preoccupation with having a clear "exit strategy" and avoiding "mission creep" in Washington and elsewhere, makes it appear easier and more attractive to provide clean water than to challenge genocide or even to embark on de-mining. In the absence of the logistics function and the presence of the Somalia and Bosnia syndromes, politicians would not necessarily be more willing to commit soldiers to improving security, the function for which they are uniquely qualified.

Rather than new methods and training to permit more effective and less expensive humanitarian delivery, there emerges a central and stark finding from the successes in northern Iraq and Haiti, the successful elements of the French presence in Rwanda, and even from the least successful moments in Somalia and Bosnia. The emphasis should be on the direct provision of security by armed forces in war zones. Guaranteeing access or supporting the work of civilians by means of armed convoys or air cover are directly related to the military's ability to wage wars— even if such a capacity is only a threat and not fully employed.

Calculating the costs and benefits of using the military when belligerents deny access is considerably more problematic and controversial than evaluating logistics. Uncertainty abounds. The West lacks leadership and a willingness to stay the course when fickle voters tolerate only a zero-casualty foreign policy. Knowing where to deploy in a civil war is not easy. Impartiality and neutrality are destroyed when enforcement begins. Costs for providing military security are not fungible. Yet there is simply no substitute for the armed forces in order to foster a secure environment. Whether this capacity will be used with any frequency in the future is an open question.

The notion of costs may be pertinent in attempting to pin-point longer-term effects on a targeted country resulting from the application of outside military force. These costs, both direct and indirect, are like those of humanitarian aid in general; they are incalculable with any degree of precision and without subjective criteria. Yet it is useful to pose some thorny questions that emanate from trying to take such a perspective. In the same way that we are discovering how outside aid influences the dynamics of conflicts, and even exacerbates them, it also is important to contextualize the limitations of multilateral military operations. Will the application of military might enhance the role of violence in determining local leadership? Will any foreign power be willing and able to commit its soldiers for anything except the short term? Will the abandonment of the norms of nonintervention lead to further instability and the weakening of the nascent institutions of civil society? Will the use of outside military force postpone not only a reckoning among local parties but also addressing the root causes of conflict?

This last question is particularly critical. What if the use of military force in complex emergencies resembles counterproductive development aid and actually leads to more war? Are there questions about the use of multilateral military operations and humanitarian action similar to one from a study that argues that "the acceleration or the attempt to accelerate economic, social, and political change often intensifies the historic tensions among different groups in society"?[57] What if humanitarian interventions resemble structural adjustment programs, so that even when they attain their objectives they often contribute to more armed conflicts? What if, as another study argues, securing lasting peace in ethnic conflicts is often best pursued by placing opposing groups into demographically separate and defensible enclaves?[58] Under these circumstances and in spite of the widespread humanitarian "impulse"—some like the ICRC would say "imperative"—perhaps outsiders should simply wait for battle fatigue, or for the weaker belligerents to be subjugated or eliminated?

Perhaps most unsettling here is the morally repugnant notion of triage.[59] In this regard, humanitarian practitioners estimate that 10 to 20 times more could be accomplished with the same limited resources by attacking what UNICEF's late executive director Jim Grant first called poverty's "silent" emergencies, rather than the "loud" emergencies caused by warfare,[60] a theme that has been picked up by many including the last UN secretary-general.[61] Each day, for example, 35,000–40,000 children worldwide perish from poverty and preventable diseases. What claim should they have on the resources that now go to soldiers and civilians who intervene in civil wars? What is the meaning of "tough love" in this context?

We clearly require more satisfactory answers. But until we have them, should we refrain from humanitarian intervention? If both practitioners and scholars are so unsure about whether military or civilian medicine is going to help or hurt patients in the longer run, is it sensible to forge ahead with alacrity? This line of argument adds still more fuel to the fire ignited by scathing criticisms of emergency relief in Somalia, Bosnia, and Rwanda—namely that it has contributed, albeit inadvertently and unwittingly, to the continuation of civil war. It also requires responding to the ICRC's contention that outside military intervention justified exclusively in terms of protecting humanitarian assistance is unviable and their interpretation of the Geneva Conventions and Additional Protocols as "not permit[ting] the imposition of humanitarian assistance by the use of force."[62]

Finally, the logic of these questions leads us to pursue more fundamental research about the complexities faced in international responses to sustain humane values in times of war. Whether the sum of the total experience in the five cases falls on the plus or minus side of the ledger is ambiguous at this stage of knowledge and analysis. If we were to add the terrible toll of Liberia or the continuation of the war in Chechnya or the plight of East Africa, for example, a broader trend shatters any pretence of omniscient humanitarianism by the outside world. The absence of consistent and hearty diplomacy and military action suggests a possible return to the "bad old days," akin to those of the Cold War, when abusive treatment by political authorities of "their" populations was largely beyond effective international challenge.

As we think about a future research agenda, analysts should be wary of dramatic pronouncements that are too closely tied to contemporary events, a lesson that many of us are learning. For instance, in April 1991, the dominant mood in policy and analytical circles after the Gulf War and Operation Provide Comfort was "we can do anything." A bare three years later, almost to the day in April 1994, these same groups had a different mood, "we can do nothing" to halt the genocide in Rwanda.

We thus should take extreme care not to extrapolate from the most recent experiences. At present, the mood about multilateral military operations is somewhat akin to the early and mid-1980s when the subject of UN military operations was exotic and of interest to only a small group of *cognescenti*. This had followed other periods of enthusiasm about peacekeeping (after 1956 and again in the mid-1970s following efforts in the Middle East) as well as of despair (in the mid-1960s after the Congo). Alan James, whose earlier work on peacekeeping is still widely cited,[63] restated recently a theme from his historical work: "Peacekeeping is *ad hoc* in every way, including its frequency and popularity."

There are bound to be instances when traditional peacekeeping, peace enforcement, and everything messy in between will be relevant policy options in the next decade for humanitarians. Mary Anderson recommends that analysts should identify the range and variety of ways in which outside assistance worsens rather than relieves violence. She proposes her own bottom-line for any emergency help: "do no harm," as part of a new "Hippocratic Oath of Aid."[64] Similar modesty and humility, both analytical and political, should also guide our pursuit of multilateral military operations and humanitarian action. Understanding better the limitations of military coercion and of charity is a wise point of departure when formulating international responses to the complex emergencies of the post–post–Cold War era.

Notes

1 Raimo Väyrenen, *The Age of Humanitarian Emergencies* (Helsinki: World Institute for Development Economics Research, 1996).

2 Office of the United Nations High Commissioner for Refugees, *The State of the World's Refugees 1995: In Search of Solutions* (New York: Oxford University Press, 1995); US Committee for Refugees, *1996 World Refugee Report* (Washington, DC: US Committee for Refugees, 1996); International Federation of Red Cross and Red Crescent Societies, *World Disasters Report 1996* (Oxford: Oxford University Press, 1996); and Bread for the World Institute, *Countries in Conflict* (Silver Glen, Md.: Bread for the World, 1995).

3 Commission on Global Governance, *Our Global Neighbourhood* (Oxford: Oxford University Press, 1995); South Centre, *For a Strong and Democratic United Nations: A South Perspective on UN Reform* (Geneva: South Centre, 1996); Independent Working Group on the Future of the United Nations, *The United Nations in Its Second Half-Century* (New York: Ford Foundation, 1995); and Gareth Evans, *Cooperating for Peace: The Global Agenda for the 1990s and Beyond* (St. Leonard's, Australia: Allen and Unwin, 1993).

4 Inis L. Claude, Jr., "Peace and Security: Prospective Roles for the Two United Nations," *Global Governance* 2, no. 3 (1996): 289–98; and Thomas G. Weiss, "Triage: Humanitarian Interventions in a New Era," *World Policy Journal* 21, no. 1 (1994): 1–10.

5 Tom J. Farer, "Intervention in Unnatural Humanitarian Emergencies: Lessons of the First Phase," *Human Rights Quarterly* 18, no. 1 (1996): 1–22; and Thomas G. Weiss, "Overcoming the Somalia Syndrome: Operation Rekindle Hope?" *Global Governance* 1, no. 2 (1995): 171–87.

6 Alison Mitchell, "Clinton's About-Face," *New York Times*, 24 September 1996.

7 Boutros Boutros-Ghali, *An Agenda for Peace 1995* (New York: United Nations, 1995).

8 Thomas G. Weiss, "Military-Civilian Humanitarianism: The 'Age of Innocence' is Over," *International Peacekeeping* 2, no. 2 (1995): 157–74; Thomas G. Weiss and Kurt M. Campbell, "Military Humanitarianism," *Survival* 33, no. 5 (1991): 451–65; and Robert H. Jackson, "Armed Humanitarianism," *International Journal* 68, no. 4 (1993): 579–606.

9 James F. Hoge, "Editor's Note," *Foreign Affairs* 73, no. 6 (1994): v.

10 Stephen J. Stedman, "The New Interventionists," *Foreign Affairs* 72, no. 1 (1993): 1–16; Oliver Ramsbotham and Tom Woodhouse, *Humanitarian Intervention in Contemporary Conflict* (Cambridge: Polity Press, 1996); John Harriss, ed., *The Politics of Humanitarian Intervention* (London: Pinter, 1995); James Mayall, ed., *The New Interventionism: United Nations Experience in Cambodia, Former Yugoslavia, and Somalia* (New York: Cambridge University Press, 1996); and Jan N. Pieterse, ed., *World Orders in the Making: Humanitarian Intervention and Beyond* (London: Macmillan, 1998).

11 Leslie H. Gelb, "Quelling the Teacup Wars," *Foreign Affairs* 73, no. 6 (1994): 5.

12 Cindy Collins and Thomas G. Weiss, "Review of the Peacekeeping Literature, 1990–96," Occasional Paper No. 28 (Providence, RI: Watson Institute, 1997).

13 Shashi Tharoor, "Foreword," in *Beyond Traditional Peacekeeping*, ed. Donald C. Daniel and Bradd C. Hayes (London: Macmillan, 1995): xviii.

14 William J. Durch, ed., *The Evolution of UN Peacekeeping: Case Studies and Comparative Analysis* (New York: St. Martin's Press, 1993), and *UN Peacekeeping, American Policy, and the Uncivil Wars of the 1990s* (New York: St. Martin's Press, 1996).

15 Jay Luvaas, "Lessons and Lessons Learned: A Historical Perspective," in *The Lessons of Recent Wars in the Third World: Approaches and Case Studies*, Vol. 1, ed. Robert E. Harkavy and Stephanie G. Neuman (Lexington, Mass.: Heath, 1985), 68.

16 Joseph J. Collins, "Desert Storm and the Lessons of Learning," *Parameters* 22, no. 3 (1992): 94.

17 Larry Minear and Thomas G. Weiss, *Humanitarian Politics* (New York: Foreign Policy Association, 1995); Larry Minear and Thomas G. Weiss, *Mercy Under Fire: War and the Global Humanitarian Community* (Boulder, Colo.: Westview, 1995); Thomas G. Weiss and Cindy Collins, *Humanitarian Challenges and Intervention: World Politics and the Dilemmas*

of Help (Boulder, Colo.: Westview, 1996); and Jonathan Moore, *The UN and Complex Emergencies* (Geneva: UN Research Institute for Social Development, 1996).

18 Human Rights Watch, *The Lost Agenda: Human Rights and U.N. Field Operations* (New York: Human Rights Watch, 1993); Human Rights Watch, *Human Rights Watch World Report 1995* (New York: Human Rights Watch, 1994); Paul LaRose-Edwards, *Human Rights Principles and Practice in United Nations Field Operations* (Ottawa: Department of Foreign Affairs, 1995); Roberta Cohen, and Jacques Cuénod, *Improving Institutional Arrangements for the Internally Displaced* (Washington, DC: Brookings Institution and Refugee Policy Group, 1995); and Alice H. Henkin, ed., *Honoring Human Rights and Keeping the Peace: Lessons from El Salvador, Cambodia, and Haiti* (Washington, DC: Aspen Institute, 1995).

19 Frederick C. Cuny, "Dilemmas of Military Involvement in Humanitarian Relief," in *Soldiers, Peacekeepers and Disasters*, ed. Leon Gordenker and Thomas G. Weiss (London: Macmillan, 1991), 52–81.

20 Thomas G. Weiss and Meryl A. Kessler, eds., *Third World Security in the Post-Cold War Era* (Boulder, Colo.: Lynne Rienner, 1991); and Mohammed Ayoob, *The Third World Security Predicament: State Making, Regional Conflict, and the International System* (Boulder, Colo.: Lynne Rienner, 1995).

21 US Mission to the United Nations, *Global Humanitarian Emergencies* (New York: US Mission to the United Nations, 1995).

22 See *Improving the UN's Rapid Reaction Capability: A Canadian Study* (February 1995); *A UN Rapid Deployment Brigade: The Netherlands Non-paper* (January 1995); and *A Multifunctional UN Stand-by Forces High-Readiness Brigade: Chief of Defence, Denmark* (25 January 1995). Most defense ministries are now arranging special training, or establishing dedicated facilities, following those established earlier by the Nordic countries. The International Association of Peacekeeping Training Centres held an inaugural meeting in mid-1995 at the Lester B. Pearson Canadian International Peacekeeping Training Centre in Cornwallis, Nova Scotia, and a second session in Pisa in April 1996.

23 Robert D. Kaplan, "Fort Leavenworth and the Eclipse of Nationhood," *The Atlantic Monthly* 278, no. 3 (1996): 74–90.

24 Chris Seiple, *The U.S. Military/NGO Relationship in Humanitarian Interventions* (Carlisle, Penn.: US Army War College, 1996), v–vi.

25 Adam Roberts, "Humanitarian War: Military Intervention and Human Rights," *International Affairs* 69 (1993): 429–49.

26 Tabyiegen Agnes Aboum, Eshetu Chole, Koste Manibe, Larry Minear, Abdul Mohammed, Jennefer Sebstan, and Thomas G. Weiss, *A Critical Review of Operation Lifeline Sudan: A Report to the Aid Agencies* (Washington, DC: Refugee Policy Group, 1991), 55.

27 Peter Uvin, *Development, Aid and Conflict: Reflections from the Case of Rwanda* (Helsinki: World Institute for Development Economics Research, 1996).

28 Warren Christopher, "America's Leadership, America's Opportunity," *Foreign Policy* 98 (1995): 6–27; Robert Dole, "Shaping America's Global Future," *Foreign Policy* 98 (1995): 29–43; and Jesse Helms, "Saving the U.N.: A Challenge to the Next Secretary-General," *Foreign Affairs* 75, no. 5 (1996): 2–7.

29 Independent Task Force chaired by George Soros, *American National Interest and the United Nations* (New York: Council on Foreign Relations, 1996).

30 Michael Pugh, "Humanitarianism and Peacekeeping," *Global Society* 10, no. 3 (1996): 205–24; and F.T. Liu, "Peacekeeping and Humanitarian Assistance," in *Soldiers, Peacekeepers and Disasters*, ed. Leon Gordenker and Thomas G. Weiss (London: Macmillan, 1991): 33–51.

31 Rakiya Omaar and Alex de Waal, "Humanitarianism Unbound? Current Dilemmas Facing Multi-Mandate Relief Operations in Political Emergencies," African Rights Discussion Paper No. 5 (London: African Rights, 1994); Alex De Waal and Rakiya Omaar, "The Genocide in Rwanda and the International Response," *Current History* 94 (1995): 156–61; Michael Walzer, "The Politics of Rescue," *Social Research* 62, no. 1 (1995): 53–66; David

Rieff, "The Humanitarian Trap," *World Policy Journal* 12, no. 4 (1994–95): 1–11; and Amir Pasic and Thomas G. Weiss, "The Politics of Rescue: Yugoslavia's Wars and the Humanitarian Impulse 1991–95," *Ethics & International Affairs* 11 (1997): 105–31.

32 Richard K. Betts, "The Delusion of Impartial Intervention," *Foreign Affairs* 73, no. 6 (1994): 20–33.

33 Chester A. Crocker, "All Aid is Political," *New York Times*, 21 November 1996.

34 John Prendergast, *Frontline Diplomacy: Humanitarian Aid and Conflict in Africa* (Boulder, Colo.: Lynne Rienner, 1996); and Michael Maren, *The Road To Hell: The Ravaging Effects of Foreign Aid and International Charity* (New York: Free Press, 1997).

35 Marrack Goulding, "The Use of Force by the United Nations," *International Peacekeeping* 3, no. 1 (1996): 1–18.

36 Larry Minear, Colin Scott, and Thomas G. Weiss, *Humanitarian Action and Security in Liberia 1989–1994*, Occasional Paper No. 20 (Providence, RI: Watson Institute, 1995); and S. Neil MacFarlane, Larry Minear, and Stephen D. Shenfield, *Armed Conflict in Georgia: A Case Study in Humanitarian Action and Peacekeeping*, Occasional Paper No. 21 (Providence, RI: Watson Institute, 1996).

37 Ataul Karim and Mark Duffield, *OLS, Operation Lifeline Sudan, A Review* (Geneva: UN Department of Humanitarian Affairs, 1996).

38 Larry Minear, U. B. P. Chelliah, Jeff Crisp, John MacKinlay, and Thomas G. Weiss, *United Nations Coordination of the International Humanitarian Response to the Gulf Crisis 1990–1992*, Occasional Paper No. 13 (Providence, RI: Watson Institute, 1992); Seiple, *The U.S. Military/NGO Relationship in Humanitarian Interventions*; Michael M. Gunter, *The Kurds of Iraq: Tragedy and Hope* (New York: St. Martin's Press, 1992); Carl Builder, Robert Lempert, Kevin Lewis, Eric Larson, and Milton Weiner, *Report of a Workshop on Expanding U.S. Air Force Noncombat Mission Capabilities* (Santa Monica, Calif.: Rand Corporation, 1992); and Franca Brilliant, Frederick C. Cuny, Pat Reed, and Victor Tanner, eds., *Humanitarian Assistance Lessons of Operation Provide Comfort* (Dallas: Intertect, 1992).

39 John Sommer, *Hope Restored? Humanitarian Aid in Somalia 1990–1994* (Washington, DC: Refugee Policy Group, 1994); Jarat Chopra, Åge Eknes, and Toralv Nordbø, "Fighting for Hope in Somalia," Peacekeeping and Multinational Operations No. 6 (Norwegian Institute for International Affairs, 1995); Debarati G. Sapir and Hedwig Deconnick, "The Paradox of Humanitarian Assistance and Military Intervention in Somalia," in *The United Nations and Civil Wars*, ed. Thomas G. Weiss (Boulder, Colo.: Lynne Rienner, 1995), 151–72; Refugee Policy Group, *Lives Lost, Lives Saved: Excess Mortality and the Impact of Health Interventions in the Somalia Emergency* (Washington, DC: Refugee Policy Group, 1994); Robert G. Patman, "The UN Operation in Somalia," in *A Crisis of Expectations: UN Peacekeeping in the 1990s*, ed. Ramesh Thakur and Carlyle A. Thayer (Boulder, Colo.: Westview, 1995), 85–104; Samuel Makinda, *Seeking Peace from Chaos: Humanitarian Intervention in Somalia* (Boulder, Colo.: Lynne Rienner, 1993); Joshua Sinai, "United Nations Operation in Somalia I. and II (UNOSOM I and II)/United Task Force (UNITAF)," in *United Nations Peace Operations: Case Studies*, ed. Joshua Sinai, Peter Blood, Serge Demidenko, Ramon Miro, and Eric Solsten (Washington, DC: Library of Congress, 1995), 257–81; Andrew Natsios, "Food Through Force: Humanitarian Intervention and U.S. Policy," *Washington Quarterly* 17, no. 1 (1994): 129–44; and Walter S. Clarke, *Humanitarian Intervention in Somalia: Bibliography* (Carlisle, Penn.: US Army War College, 1995).

40 Larry Minear, Jeffrey Clark, Roberta Cohen, Dennis Gallagher, Iain Guest, and Thomas G. Weiss, *Humanitarian Action in the Former Yugoslavia: The U.N.'s Role 1991–1993*, Occasional Paper No. 18 (Providence, RI: Watson Institute, 1994); Joshua Sinai, "United Nations Protection Force," in *United Nations Peace Operations: Case Studies*, ed. Sinai, Blood, Serge, Miro, and Solsten, 49–69; Susan R. Lamb, "The UN Protection Force in Former Yugoslavia," in *A Crisis in Expectations: UN Peacekeeping in the 1990s*, ed. Ramesh Thakur and Carlyle A. Thayer (Boulder, Colo.: Westview, 1995): 65–84; Richard Caplan, "Post-Mortem on UNPROFOR," *Centre for Defence Studies*, no. 33

(London: Brassey's, 1996); and William J. Durch and James A. Schear, "Faultlines: UN Operations in the Former Yugoslavia," in *UN Peacekeeping, American Policy, and the Uncivil Wars of the 1990s*, ed. William J. Durch (New York: St. Martin's Press, 1996), 193–274.

41 Larry Minear and Philippe Guillot, *Soldiers to the Rescue: Humanitarian Lessons from Rwanda* (Paris: OECD, 1996); Gérard Prunier, *The Rwanda Crisis: History of a Genocide* (New York: Columbia University Press, 1995); John Eriksson, "The International Response to Conflict and Genocide: Lessons from the Rwandan Experience," Steering Committee of the Joint Evaluation of Emergency Assistance to Rwanda (Copenhagen/London: Danida/ODI, 1996); Joshua Sinai, "United Nations Observer Mission Uganda/Rwanda (UNOMUR)/ United Nations Assistance Mission for Rwanda (UNAMIR)," in *United Nations Peace Operations: Case Studies*, ed. Sinai, Blood, Serge, Miro, and Solsten, 327–64; and Nan Borton, "Rwanda-Civil Strife/Displaced Persons," Situation Report no. 6, Fiscal Year 1995 (Washington, DC: Office of Foreign Disaster Assistance, 1995).

42 Robert Maguire, Edwige Balutansky, Jacques Fomerand, Larry Minear, William O'Neill, and Thomas G. Weiss, *Haiti Held Hostage: International Responses to the Quest for Nationhood 1986–1996*, Occasional Paper No. 23 (Providence, RI: Watson Institute, 1996); Yvonne Daudet, ed., *La crise d'Haïti (1991–1996)* (Paris: Editions Montchrestien, 1995); Roland I. Perusse, *Haitian Democracy Restored, 1991–1995* (New York: University Press of America for the Inter-American Institute, 1995); and Ramon Miro and Joshua Sinai, "United Nations Observer Mission in Haiti (UNMIH)/ Multinational Force-Haiti," in *United Nations Peace Operations: Case Studies*, ed. Sinai, Blood, Demidenko, Miro, and Solsten, 430–48. A word is perhaps in order about including Haiti, which has not really endured a civil war. However, it is included as part of the analysis for several reasons. Haiti has all the attributes—in particular, massive migration and human rights abuse—of countries that have suffered from violent armed conflict. It has also been the target of international coercive actions—that is, economic and military sanctions under Chapter VII of the UN Charter—that are like those in the other war-torn countries analyzed earlier. Moreover, the basis for outside intervention was the restoration of a democratically elected government; this precedent has crucial humanitarian implications because of its potentially widespread relevance for international application elsewhere.

43 UNHCR, *The State of the World's Refugees 1995: In Search of Solutions*, 244–6.

44 Thomas G. Weiss, "The UN's Prevention Pipe-dream," *Berkeley Journal of International Law* 14, no. 2 (1997): 501–15.

45 Stephen J. Stedman, "Alchemy for a New World Order: Overselling 'Preventive Diplomacy,'" *Foreign Affairs* 74, no. 3 (1995): 14–20.

46 Robert I. Rotberg and Thomas G. Weiss, eds., *From Massacres to Genocide: The Media, Public Policy, and Humanitarian Crises* (Washington, DC: Brookings Institution, 1996); Larry Minear, Colin Scott, and Thomas G. Weiss, *The News Media, Civil War, and Humanitarian Action* (Boulder, Colo.: Lynne Rienner, 1996); Charles Moskos and Thomas E. Ricks, *Reporting War When There Is No War* (Chicago: McCormick Tribune Foundation, 1996); Edward R. Girardet, ed., "Somalia, Rwanda, and Beyond: The Role of the International Media in Wars and Humanitarian Crises," Crosslines Special Report no. 1 (Dublin: Crosslines Communications, 1995); Johanna Neuman, *Lights, Camera, War* (New York: St. Martin's Press, 1996); and Nik Gowing, *Real-Time Television Coverage of Armed Conflicts and Diplomatic Crises* (Cambridge, Mass.: Harvard University Shorenstein Center, 1994).

47 Task Force on Ethical and Legal Issues in Humanitarian Assistance, "The Mohonk Criteria for Humanitarian Assistance in Complex Emergencies," Program on Humanitarian Assistance, World Conference on Religion and Peace (New York: World Conference on Religion and Peace, 1994), 6.

48 Adam Roberts, "The Road to Hell . . . A Critique of Humanitarian Intervention," *Harvard International Review* 16, no. 1 (1993): 13.

49 Mary B. Anderson and Peter J. Woodrow, *Rising from the Ashes: Development Strategies at Times of Disaster* (Boulder, Colo.: Westview, 1989).

50 Judith Randel and Tony German, eds., *The Reality of Aid 1996* (London: Earthscan, 1996).

51 Mark Duffield, "Complex Emergencies and the Crisis in Developmentalism," *IDS Bulletin* 25, no. 4 (1994): 37–45.

52 Joe Macrae and John Borton, "Aid Trends: The State of the Humanitarian System," in *World Disasters Report 1996*, International Federation of Red Cross and Red Crescent Societies (Oxford: Oxford University Press, 1996), 54–63.

53 This task is part of the continuing agenda of the Humanitarianism and War Project at Brown University and at Tufts University.

54 Eriksson, "The International Response to Conflict and Genocide," 103.

55 Jan Pronk, "Statement in the General Debate in the Second Committee," Permanent Mission of the Kingdom of the Netherlands to the United Nations, New York, 14 October 1996, 3.

56 Joy Olson with Preston Pentony, *U.S. Military Humanitarian and Civic Assistance Programs and Their Application in Central America* (Albuquerque, NM: Interhemispheric Resource Center, 1995), 8.

57 Robert Miller, *Aid As Peacemaker: Canadian Development Assistance and Third World Conflict* (Ottawa: Carleton University Press, 1992), 5.

58 Chaim Kaufmann, "Possible and Impossible Solutions to Ethnic Wars," *International Security* 20, no. 4 (1996): 136–75; and John J. Mearsheimer and Stephen Van Evera, "Hateful Neighbors," *New York Times*, 24 September 1996.

59 Weiss, "Triage: Humanitarian Interventions in a New Era."

60 United Nations Children's Fund, *The State of the World's Children, 1993* (New York: Oxford University Press, 1993).

61 Boutros Boutros-Ghali, *An Agenda for Development 1995* (New York: United Nations, 1995).

62 Umesh Palwankar, ed., *Symposium on Humanitarian Action and Peace-keeping Operations— Report* (Geneva: International Committee of the Red Cross, 1994), 102.

63 Alan James, *The Politics of Peace-keeping* (London: Chatto and Windus, 1969), and *Peacekeeping in International Politics* (London: Macmillan, 1990).

64 Mary B. Anderson and Peter J. Woodrow, *Do No Harm: Supporting Local Capacities for Peace through Aid* (Cambridge: Collaborative for Development Action, 1996).

INDEX

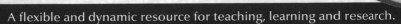